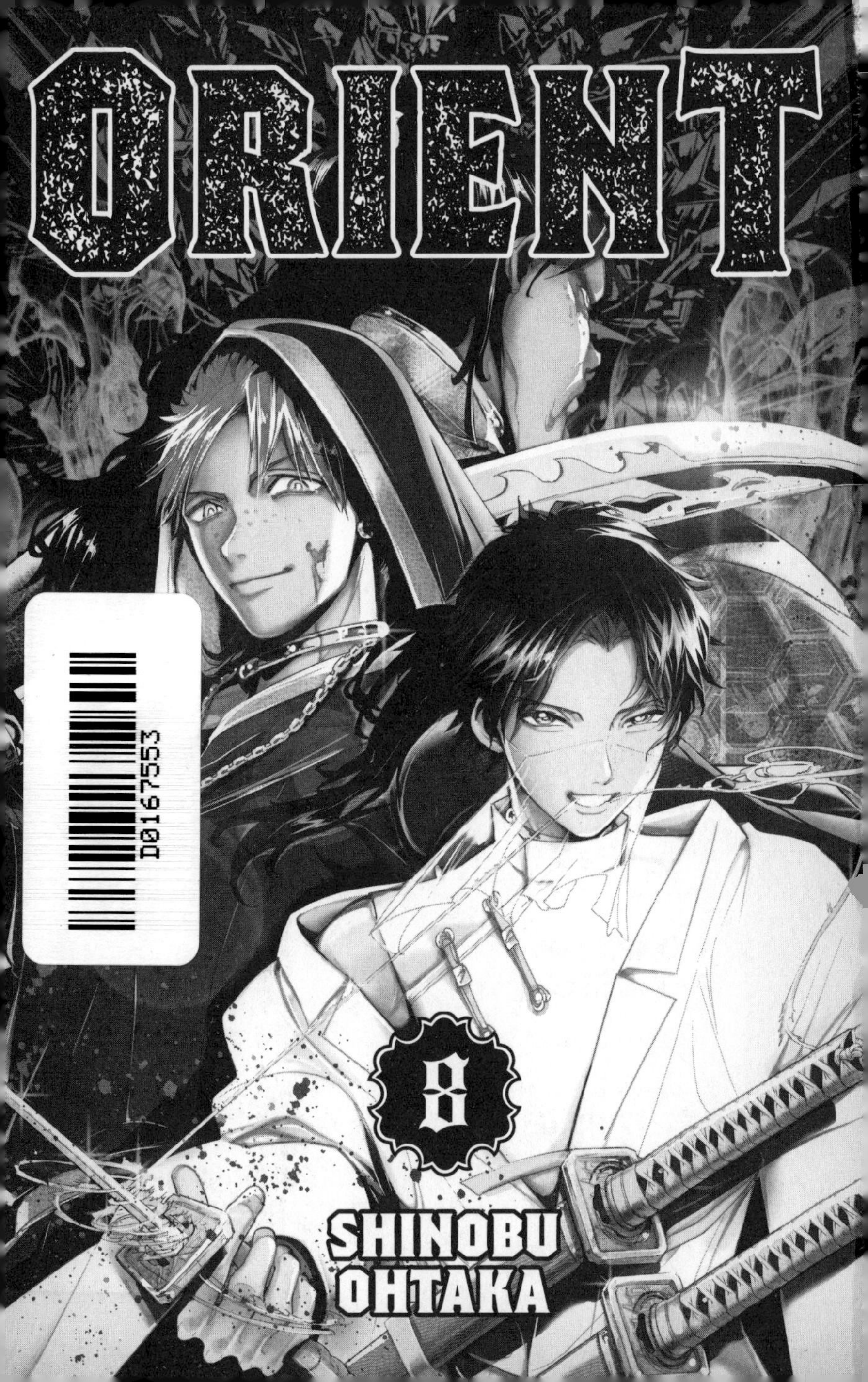
ORIENT
8
SHINOBU
OHTAKA

ORIENT

SHINOBU OHTAKA

CONTENTS

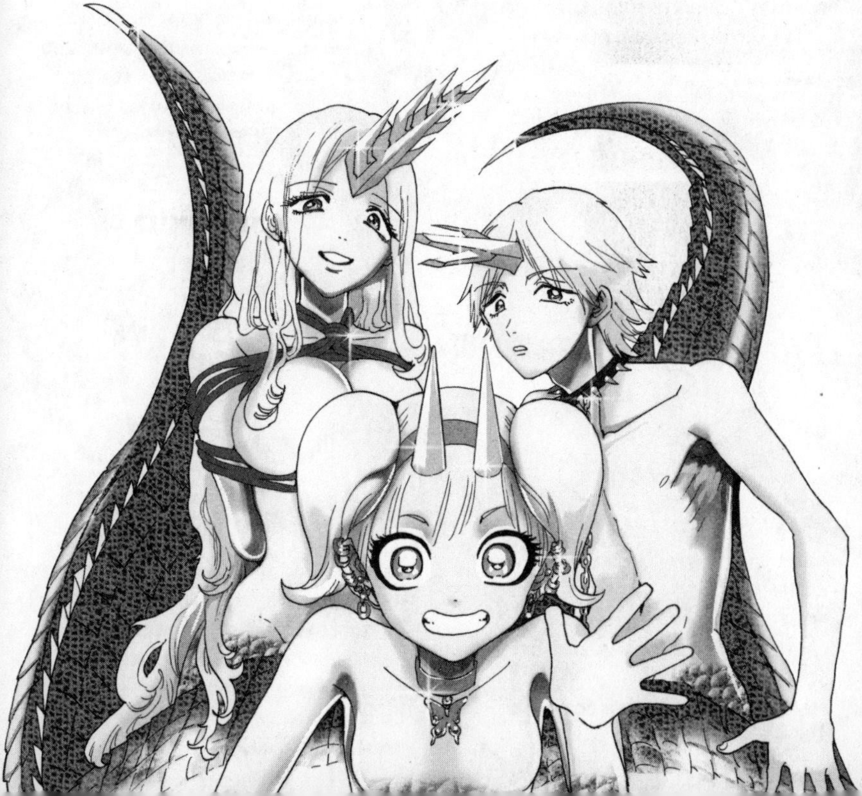

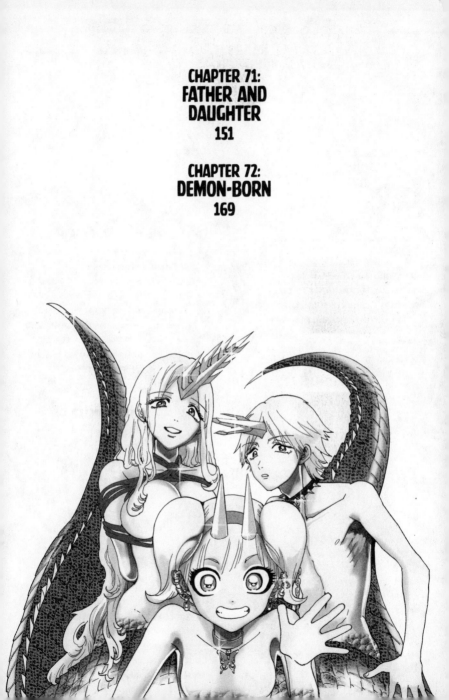

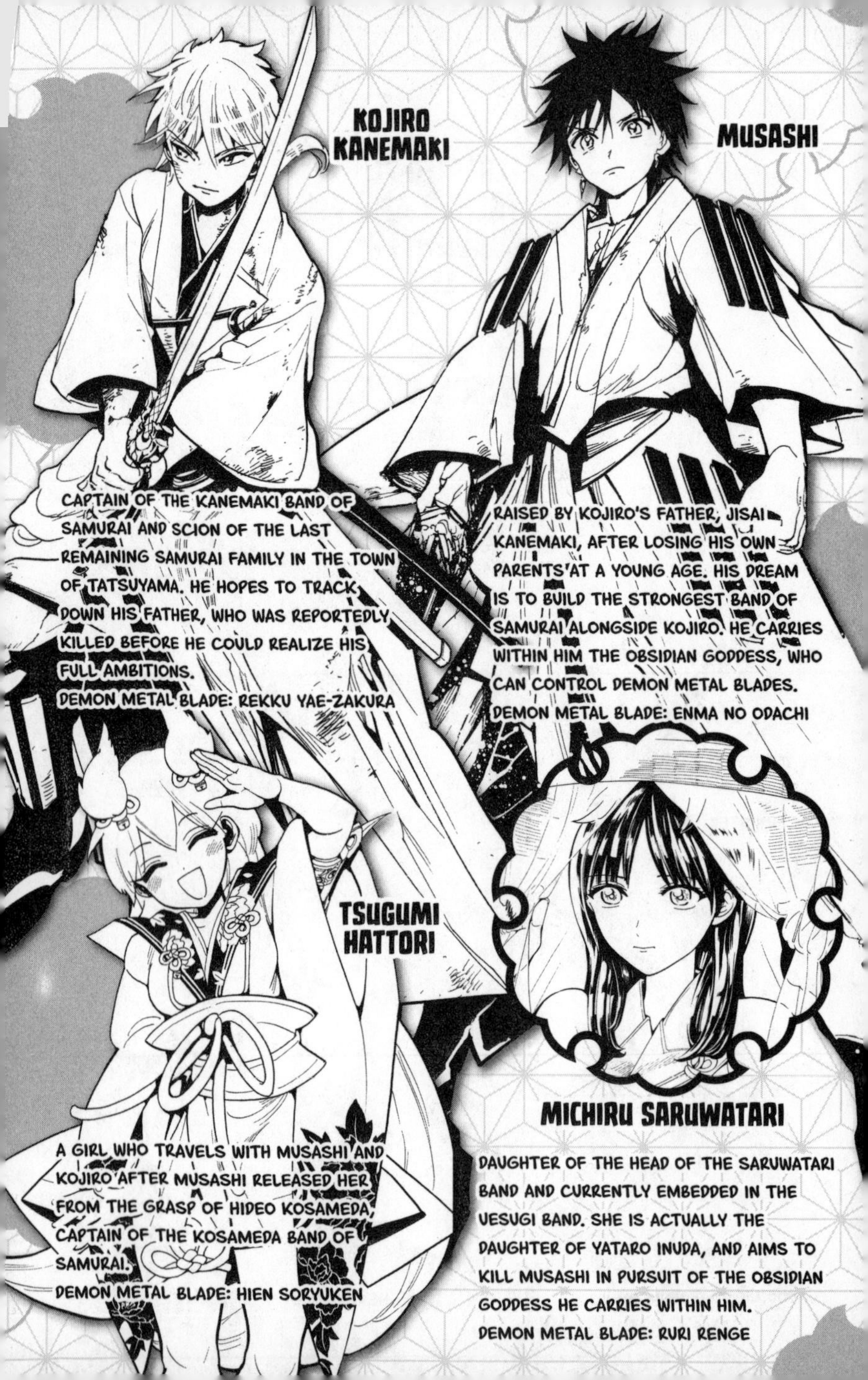
KOJIRO KANEMAKI
CAPTAIN OF THE KANEMAKI BAND OF SAMURAI AND SCION OF THE LAST REMAINING SAMURAI FAMILY IN THE TOWN OF TATSUYAMA. HE HOPES TO TRACK DOWN HIS FATHER, WHO WAS REPORTEDLY KILLED BEFORE HE COULD REALIZE HIS FULL AMBITIONS.
DEMON METAL BLADE: REKKU YAE-ZAKURA
MUSASHI
RAISED BY KOJIRO'S FATHER, JISAI KANEMAKI, AFTER LOSING HIS OWN PARENTS AT A YOUNG AGE. HIS DREAM IS TO BUILD THE STRONGEST BAND OF SAMURAI ALONGSIDE KOJIRO. HE CARRIES WITHIN HIM THE OBSIDIAN GODDESS, WHO CAN CONTROL DEMON METAL BLADES.
DEMON METAL BLADE: ENMA NO ODACHI
TSUGUMI HATTORI
A GIRL WHO TRAVELS WITH MUSASHI AND KOJIRO AFTER MUSASHI RELEASED HER FROM THE GRASP OF HIDEO KOSAMEDA, CAPTAIN OF THE KOSAMEDA BAND OF SAMURAI.
DEMON METAL BLADE: HIEN SORYUKEN
MICHIRU SARUWATARI
DAUGHTER OF THE HEAD OF THE SARUWATARI BAND AND CURRENTLY EMBEDDED IN THE UESUGI BAND. SHE IS ACTUALLY THE DAUGHTER OF YATARO INUDA, AND AIMS TO KILL MUSASHI IN PURSUIT OF THE OBSIDIAN GODDESS HE CARRIES WITHIN HIM.
DEMON METAL BLADE: RURI RENGE

CHARACTERS

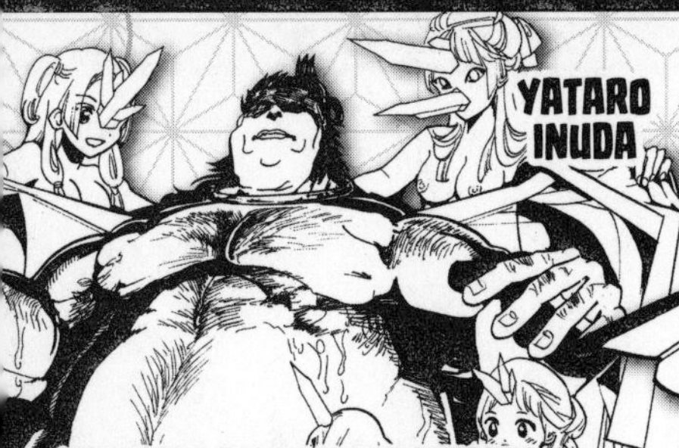

YATARO INUDA

MEMBER OF THE DEMON-WORSHIPPING OBSIDIAN EIGHT. HE AIMS TO DESTROY THE UESUGI BAND AND RETRIEVE THE OBSIDIAN GODDESS.

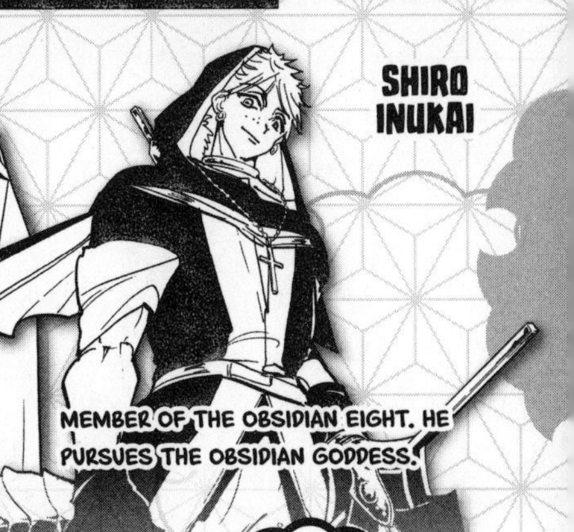

SHIRO INUKAI

MEMBER OF THE OBSIDIAN EIGHT. HE PURSUES THE OBSIDIAN GODDESS.

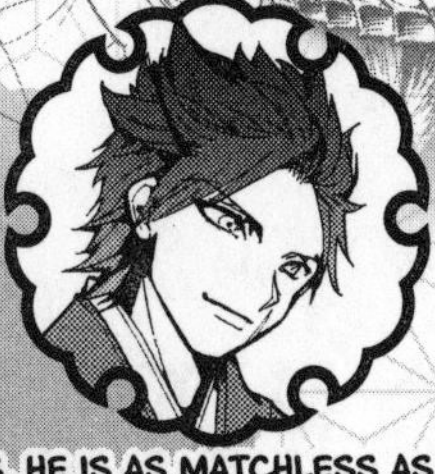

NAOTORA TAKEDA

CAPTAIN OF THE TAKEDA BAND OF SAMURAI AND ONE OF THE FIVE HEROIC GENERALS. HE IS AS MATCHLESS AS TATSUOMI UESUGI HIMSELF.

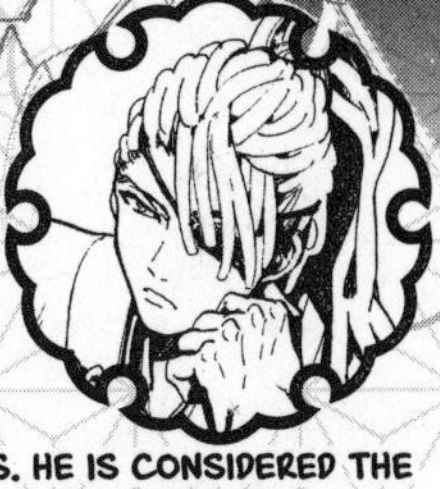

TATSUOMI UESUGI

CAPTAIN OF THE UESUGI BAND OF SAMURAI AND ONE OF THE FIVE HEROIC GENERALS. HE IS CONSIDERED THE MIGHTIEST IN THE LAND OF THE SETTING SUN.

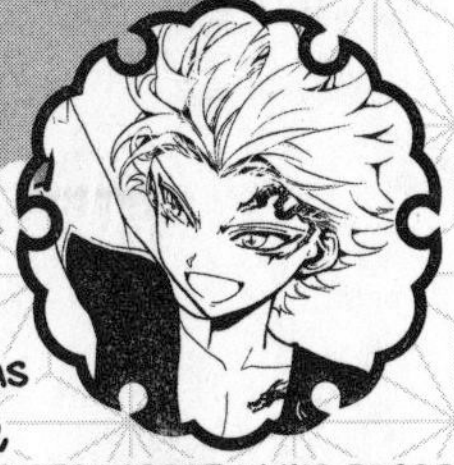

KANETATSU NAOE

A TOP MINISTER IN THE UESUGI BAND. REFERRED TO REVERENTLY AS THE DRAGON GOD, HE IS ONE OF THE STRONGEST IN HIS FORCE.

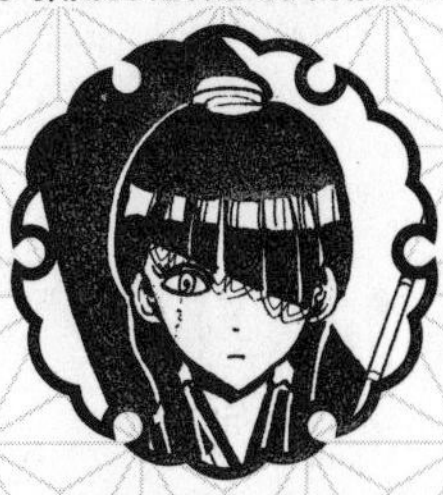

KUROKO USAMI

CHIEF TACTICIAN OF THE UESUGI BAND.

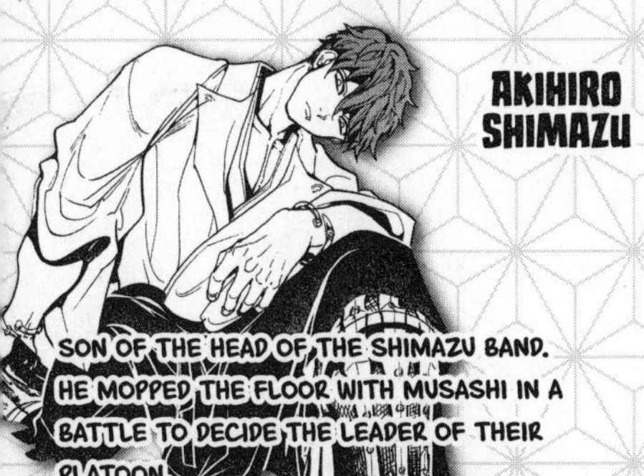

AKIHIRO SHIMAZU

SON OF THE HEAD OF THE SHIMAZU BAND. HE MOPPED THE FLOOR WITH MUSASHI IN A BATTLE TO DECIDE THE LEADER OF THEIR PLATOON.

DEMON METAL BLADE: TENRO TEKKYAKU

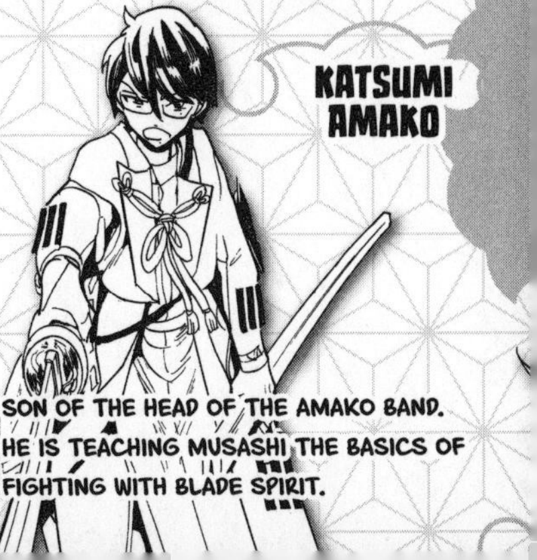

KATSUMI AMAKO

SON OF THE HEAD OF THE AMAKO BAND. HE IS TEACHING MUSASHI THE BASICS OF FIGHTING WITH BLADE SPIRIT.

ORIENT

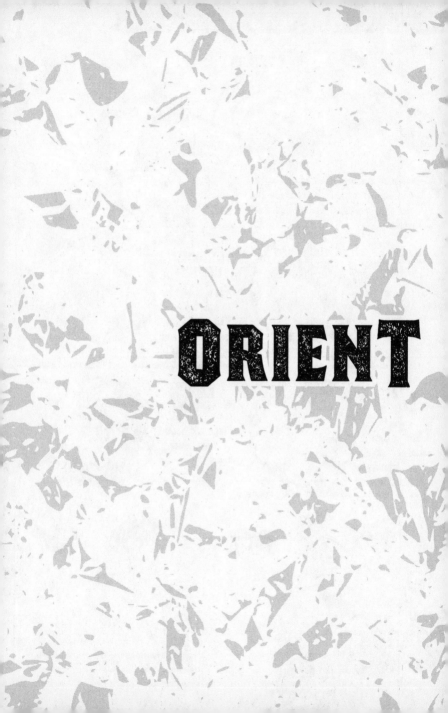

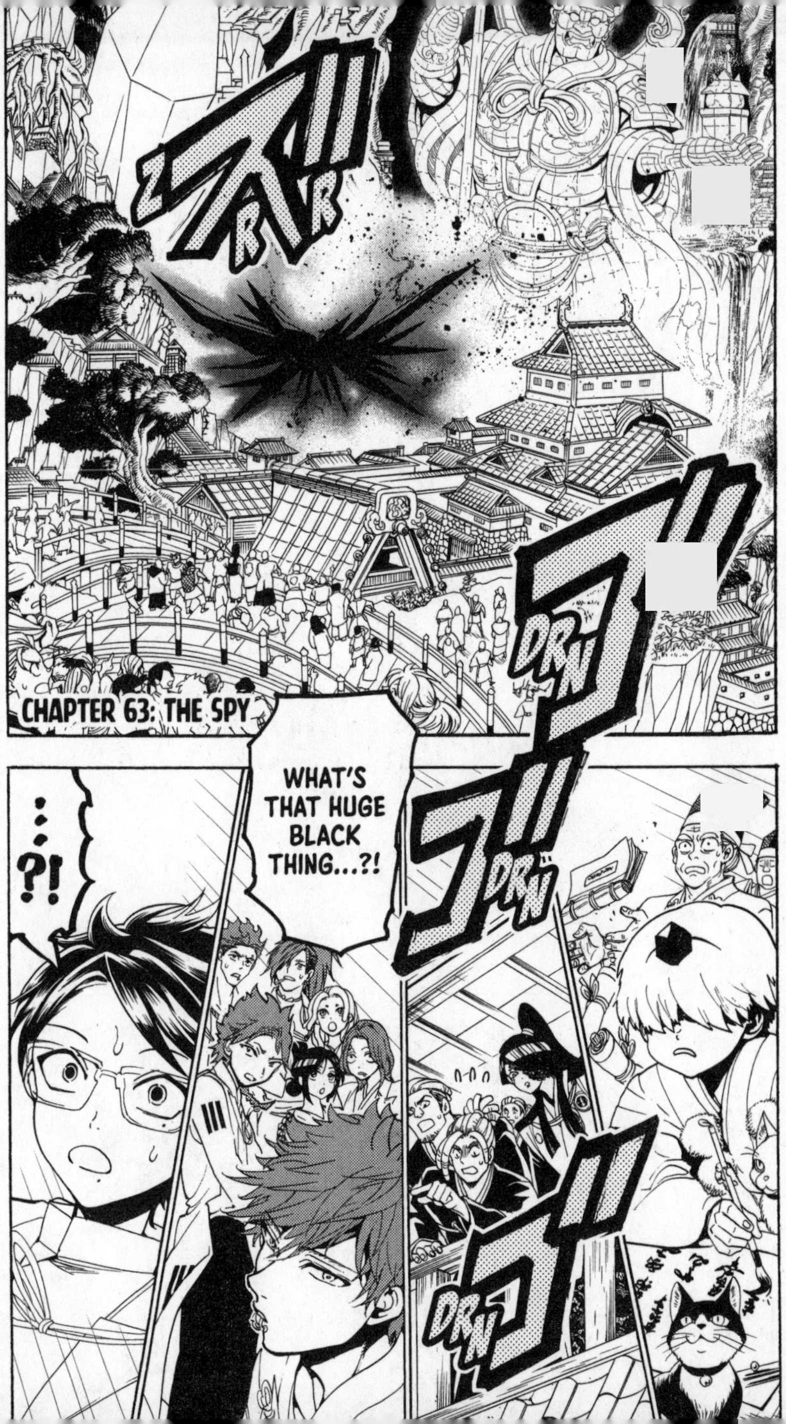
ZRRR
DRN
CHAPTER 63: THE SPY
DRN
DRN
WHAT'S THAT HUGE BLACK THING...?!
...?!

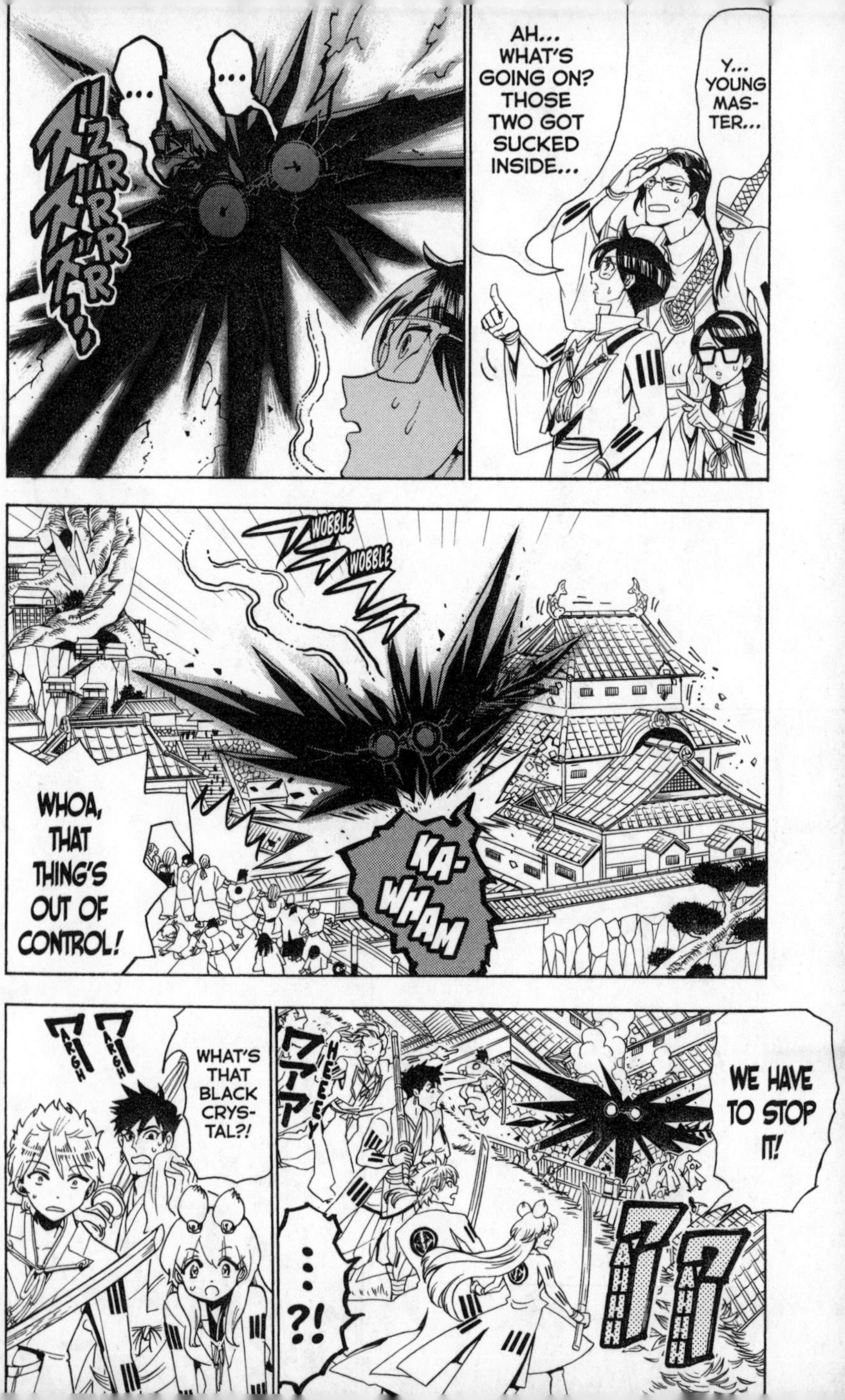
Y... YOUNG MASTER...
AH... WHAT'S GOING ON? THOSE TWO GOT SUCKED INSIDE...
...
...
ZRRRRR...
WOBBLE
WOBBLE
KA-WHAM
WHOA, THAT THING'S OUT OF CONTROL!
WE HAVE TO STOP IT!
AHHHH
AHHHH
HEEEEY
...
?!
WHAT'S THAT BLACK CRYSTAL?!
ARGH
ARGH

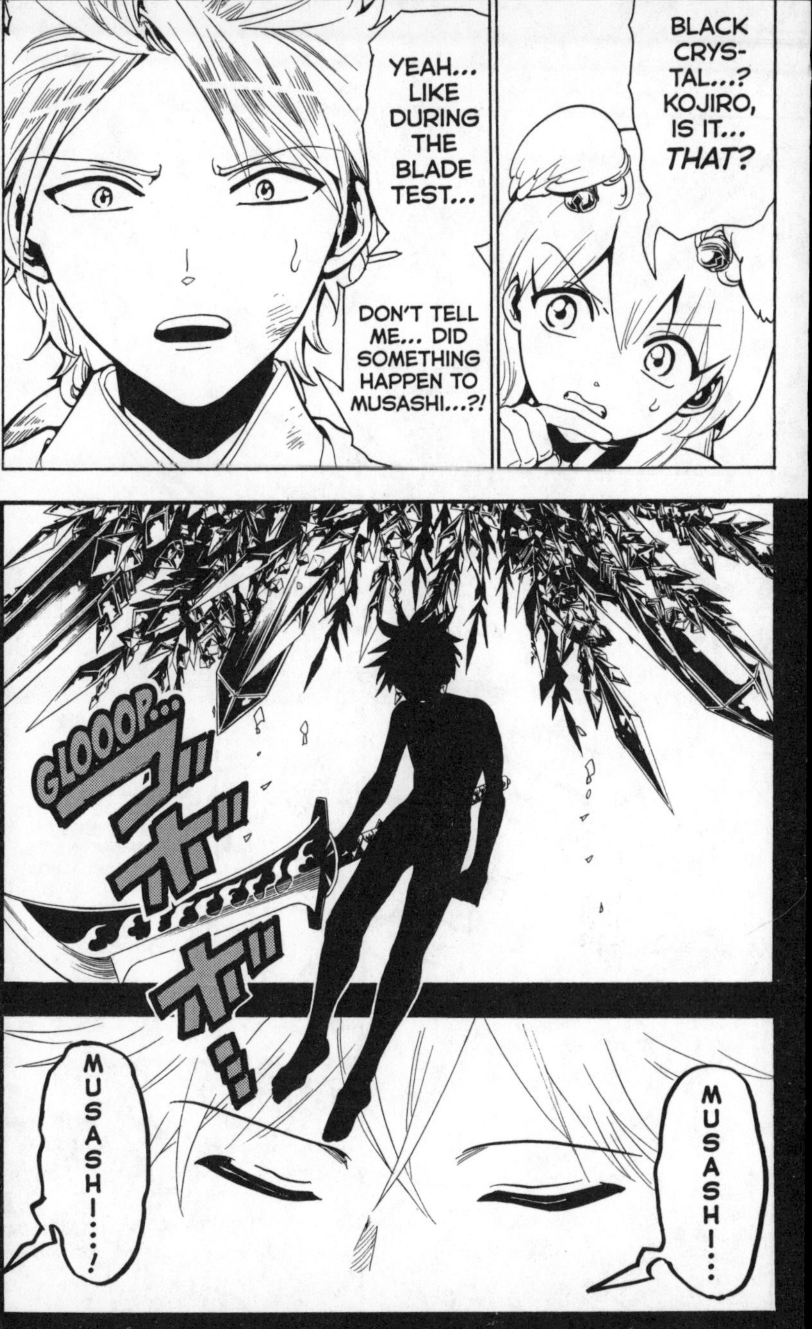
BLACK CRYS-TAL...? KOJIRO, IS IT... *THAT?*
YEAH... LIKE DURING THE BLADE TEST...
DON'T TELL ME... DID SOMETHING HAPPEN TO MUSASHI...?!
GLOOOP...
ゴボボ...
MUSASHI...
MUSASHI...!

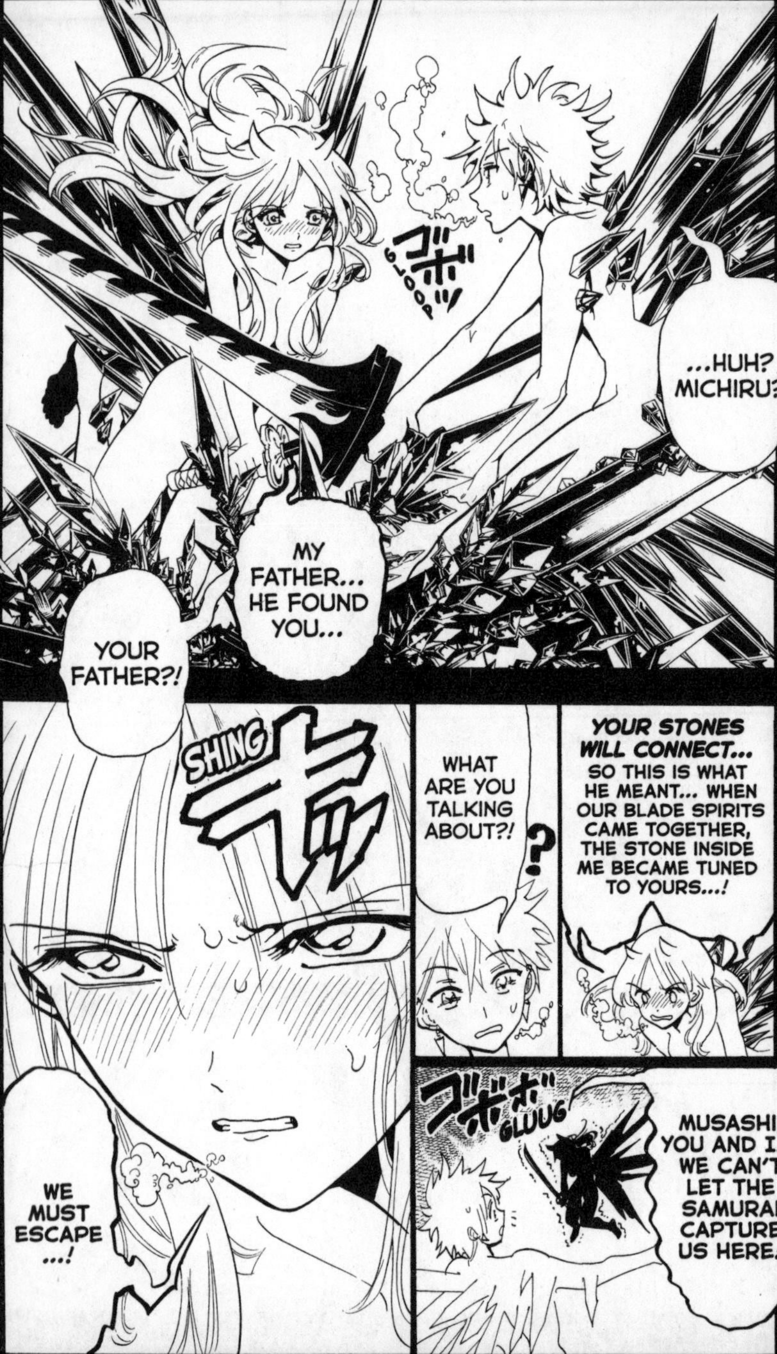

...HUH? MICHIRU?
ゴボッ
GLOOP
MY FATHER... HE FOUND YOU...
YOUR FATHER?!
YOUR STONES WILL CONNECT... SO THIS IS WHAT HE MEANT... WHEN OUR BLADE SPIRITS CAME TOGETHER, THE STONE INSIDE ME BECAME TUNED TO YOURS...!
WHAT ARE YOU TALKING ABOUT?!
?
ゴボボ
GLUUG
MUSASHI, YOU AND I... WE CAN'T LET THE SAMURAI CAPTURE US HERE!
SHING
WE MUST ESCAPE ...!

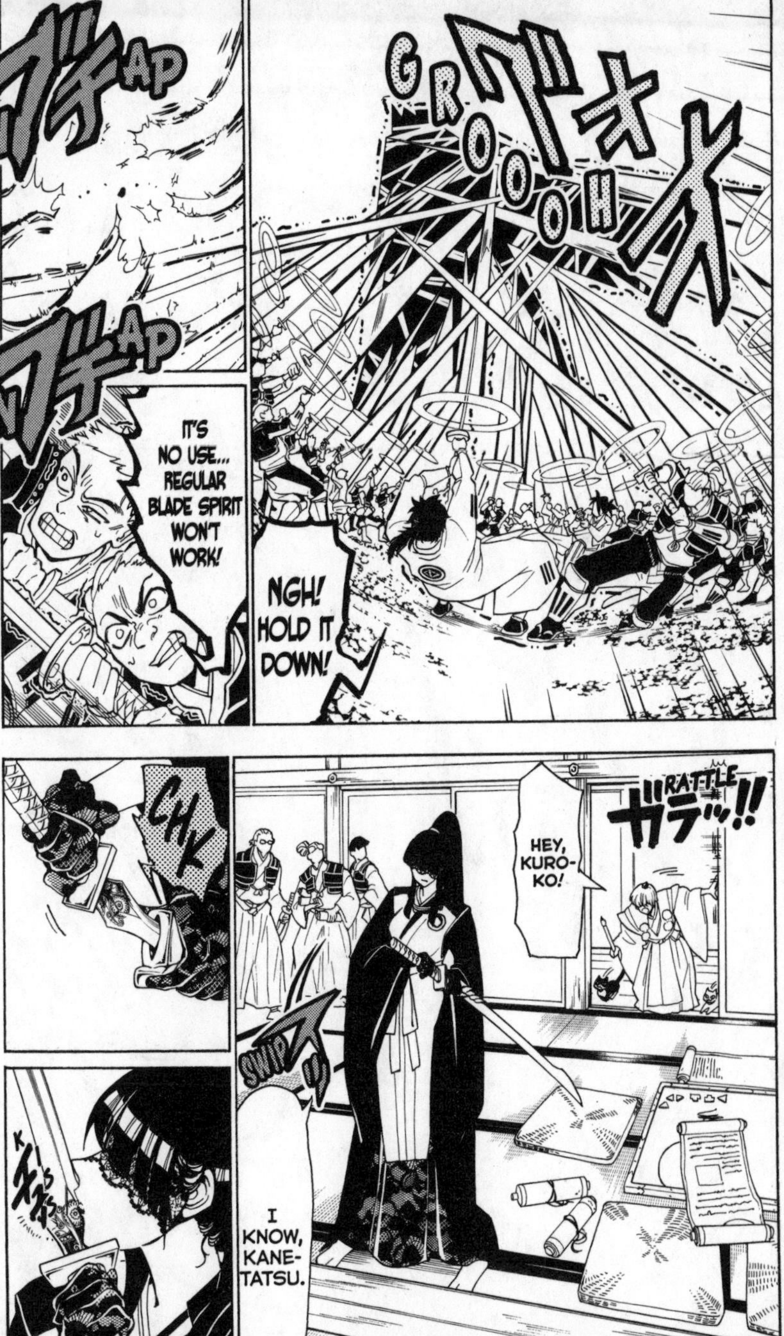
GROOOOH
NGH! HOLD IT DOWN!
SNAP
SNAP
IT'S NO USE... REGULAR BLADE SPIRIT WON'T WORK!
RATTLE
HEY, KURO-KO!
SWIP
I KNOW, KANE-TATSU.
CHK

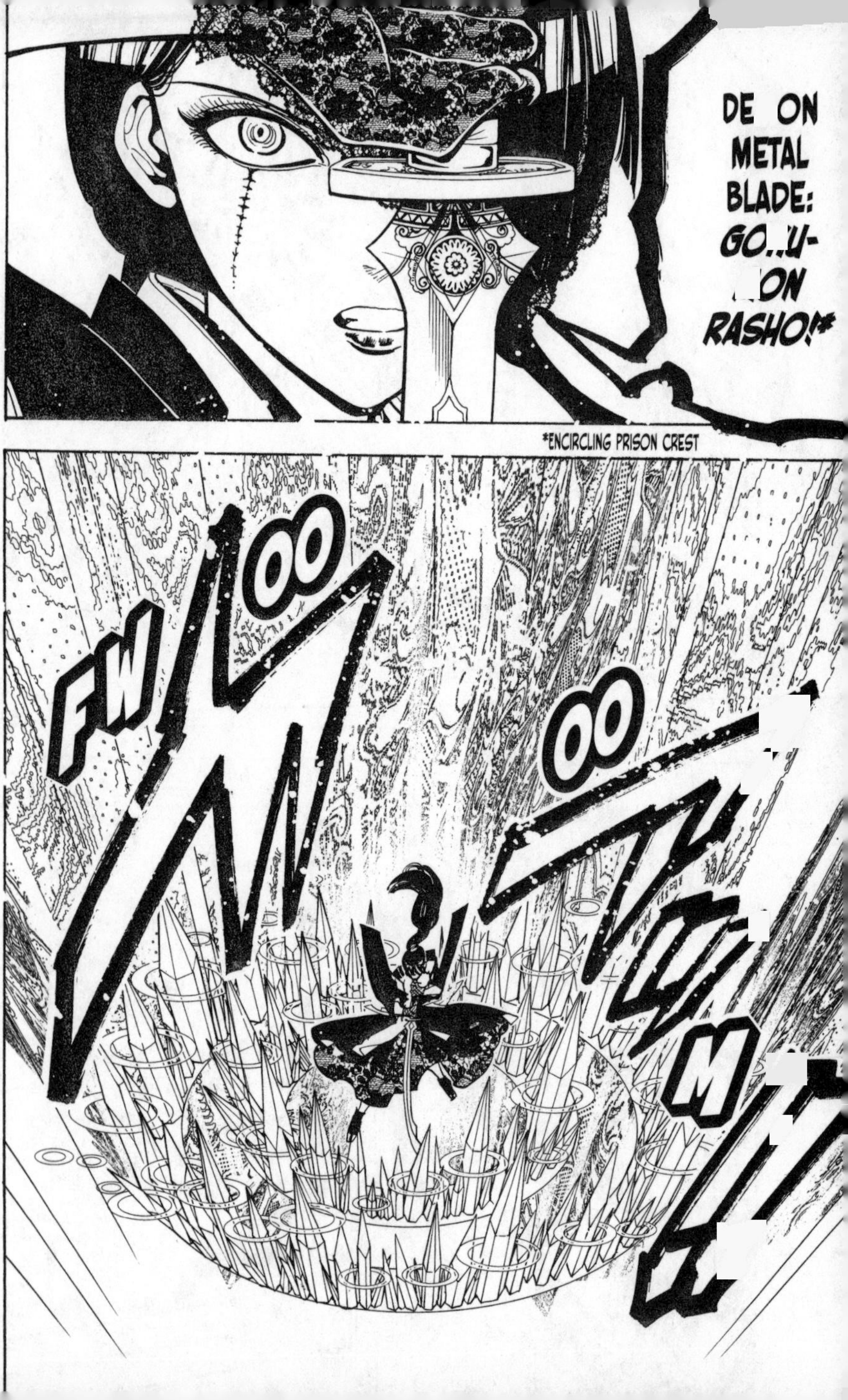
DE ON METAL BLADE: GO U- ON RASHO!*
*ENCIRCLING PRISON CREST
FWOOOOM

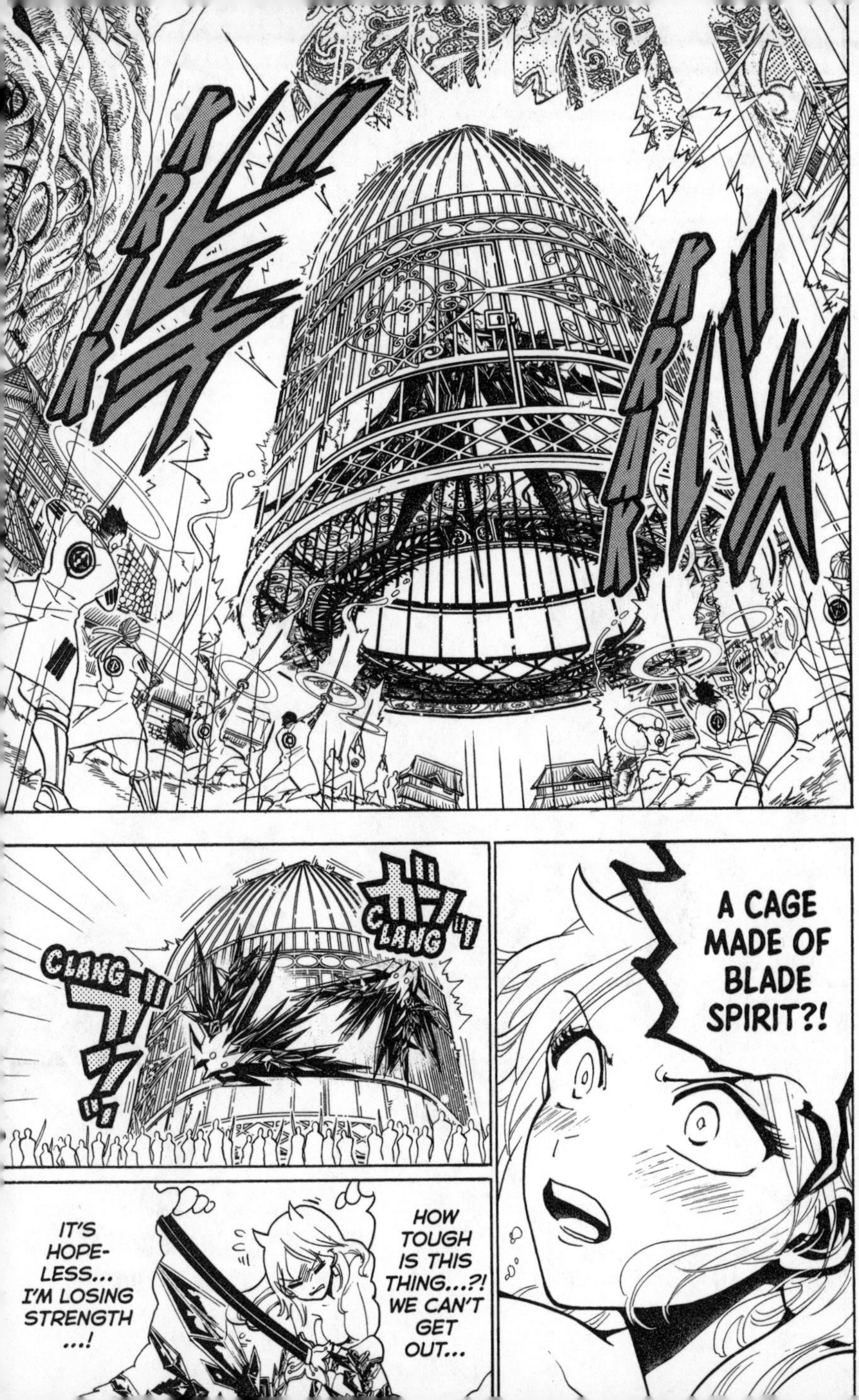
A CAGE MADE OF BLADE SPIRIT?!
CLANG!!
CLANG!!
HOW TOUGH IS THIS THING...?! WE CAN'T GET OUT...
IT'S HOPE-LESS... I'M LOSING STRENGTH ...!

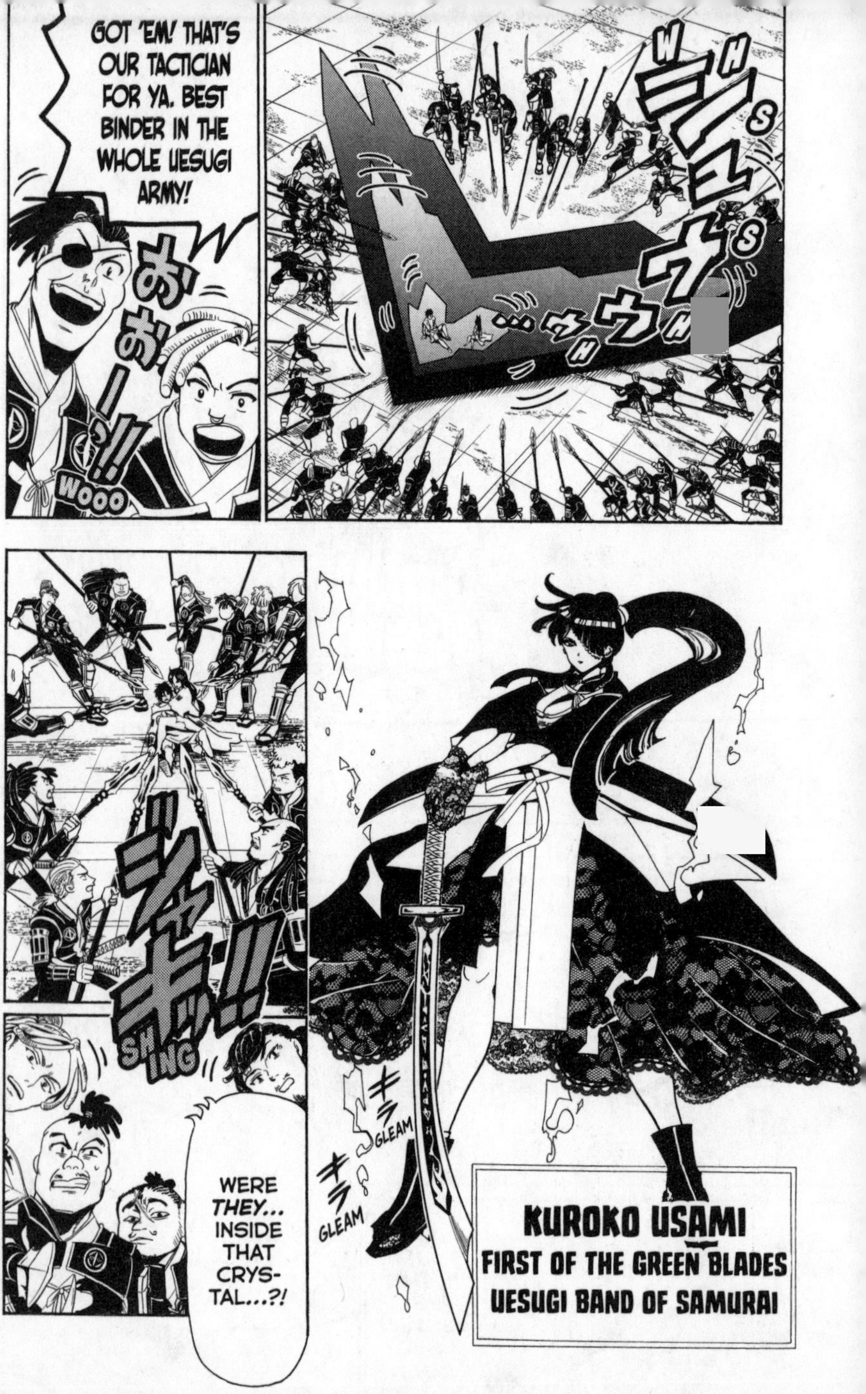
WHSSSH
GOT 'EM! THAT'S OUR TACTICIAN FOR YA. BEST BINDER IN THE WHOLE UESUGI ARMY!
WOOO
GLEAM
GLEAM
KUROKO USAMI
FIRST OF THE GREEN BLADES
UESUGI BAND OF SAMURAI
SHING
WERE THEY... INSIDE THAT CRYS-TAL...?!

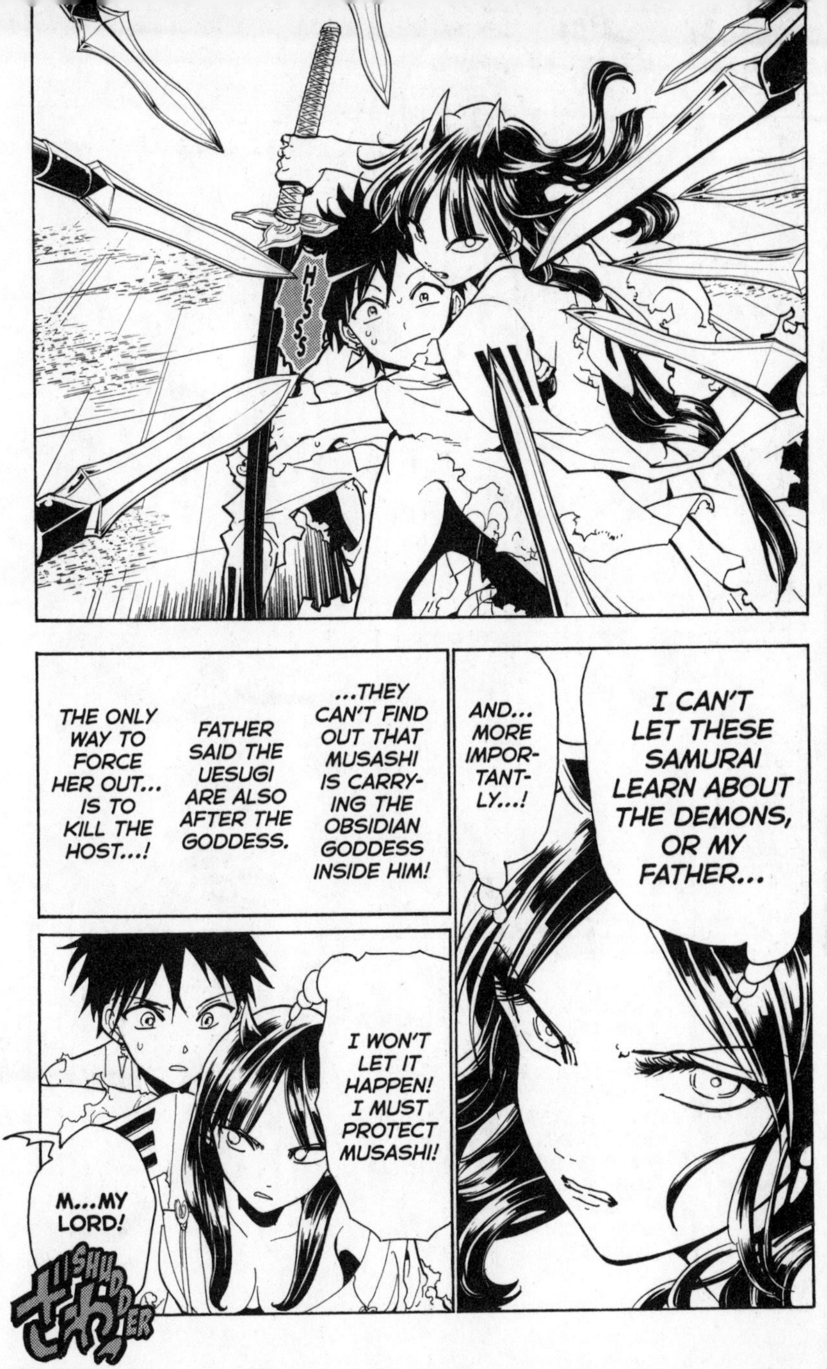
HISSS
AND... MORE IMPORTANTLY...!
I CAN'T LET THESE SAMURAI LEARN ABOUT THE DEMONS, OR MY FATHER...
...THEY CAN'T FIND OUT THAT MUSASHI IS CARRYING THE OBSIDIAN GODDESS INSIDE HIM!
FATHER SAID THE UESUGI ARE ALSO AFTER THE GODDESS.
THE ONLY WAY TO FORCE HER OUT... IS TO KILL THE HOST...!
I WON'T LET IT HAPPEN! I MUST PROTECT MUSASHI!
M...MY LORD!

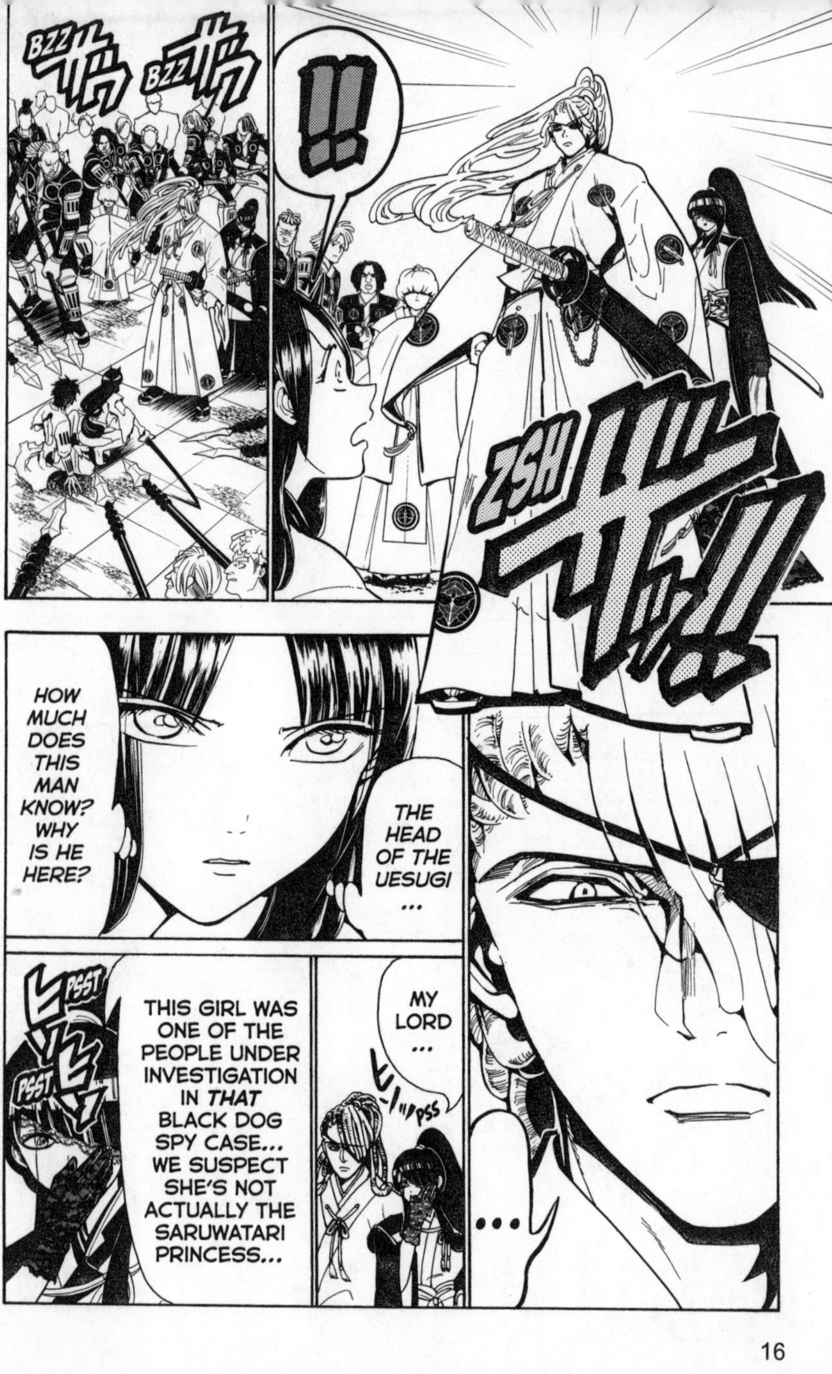

!!
ZSH
BZZ
BZZ
...
THE HEAD OF THE UESUGI ...
HOW MUCH DOES THIS MAN KNOW? WHY IS HE HERE?
MY LORD ...
PSS
PSST
PSST
THIS GIRL WAS ONE OF THE PEOPLE UNDER INVESTIGATION IN *THAT* BLACK DOG SPY CASE... WE SUSPECT SHE'S NOT ACTUALLY THE SARUWATARI PRINCESS...

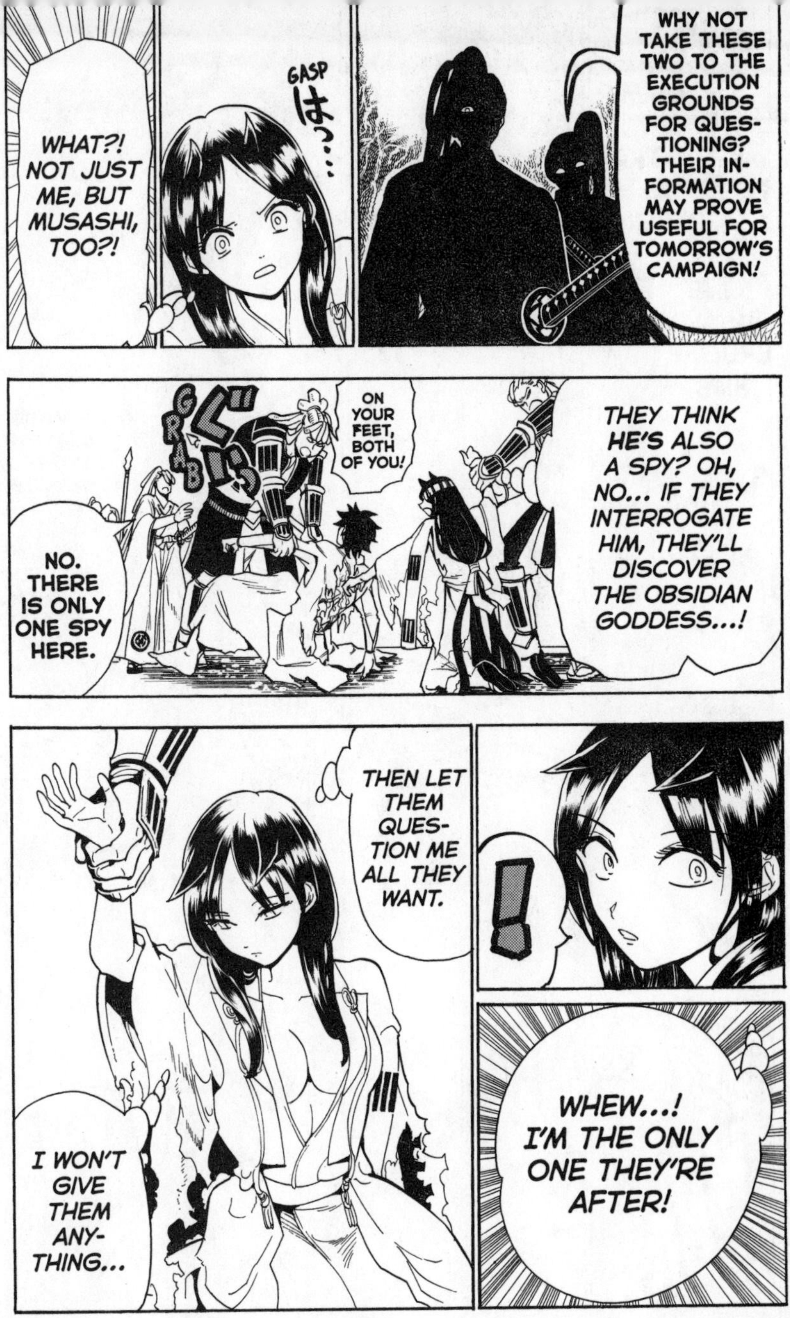
WHY NOT TAKE THESE TWO TO THE EXECUTION GROUNDS FOR QUES-TIONING? THEIR IN-FORMATION MAY PROVE USEFUL FOR TOMORROW'S CAMPAIGN!
GASP
はっ…
WHAT?! NOT JUST ME, BUT MUSASHI, TOO?!
THEY THINK HE'S ALSO A SPY? OH, NO... IF THEY INTERROGATE HIM, THEY'LL DISCOVER THE OBSIDIAN GODDESS...!
ON YOUR FEET, BOTH OF YOU!
GRAB
NO. THERE IS ONLY ONE SPY HERE.
!
WHEW...! I'M THE ONLY ONE THEY'RE AFTER!
THEN LET THEM QUES-TION ME ALL THEY WANT.
I WON'T GIVE THEM ANY-THING...

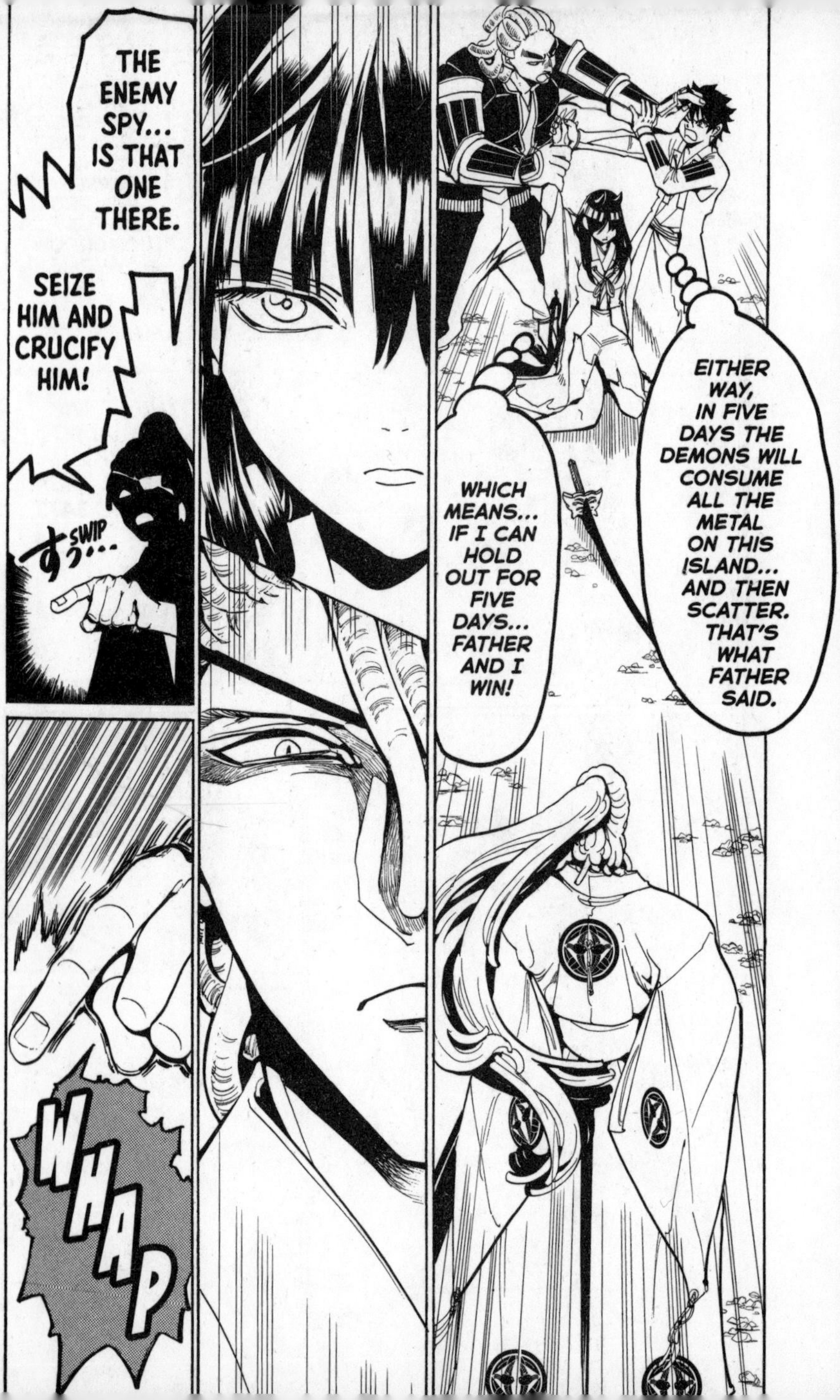
EITHER WAY, IN FIVE DAYS THE DEMONS WILL CONSUME ALL THE METAL ON THIS ISLAND... AND THEN SCATTER. THAT'S WHAT FATHER SAID.
WHICH MEANS... IF I CAN HOLD OUT FOR FIVE DAYS... FATHER AND I WIN!
THE ENEMY SPY... IS THAT ONE THERE.
SEIZE HIM AND CRUCIFY HIM!
すっ... SWIP
WHAP

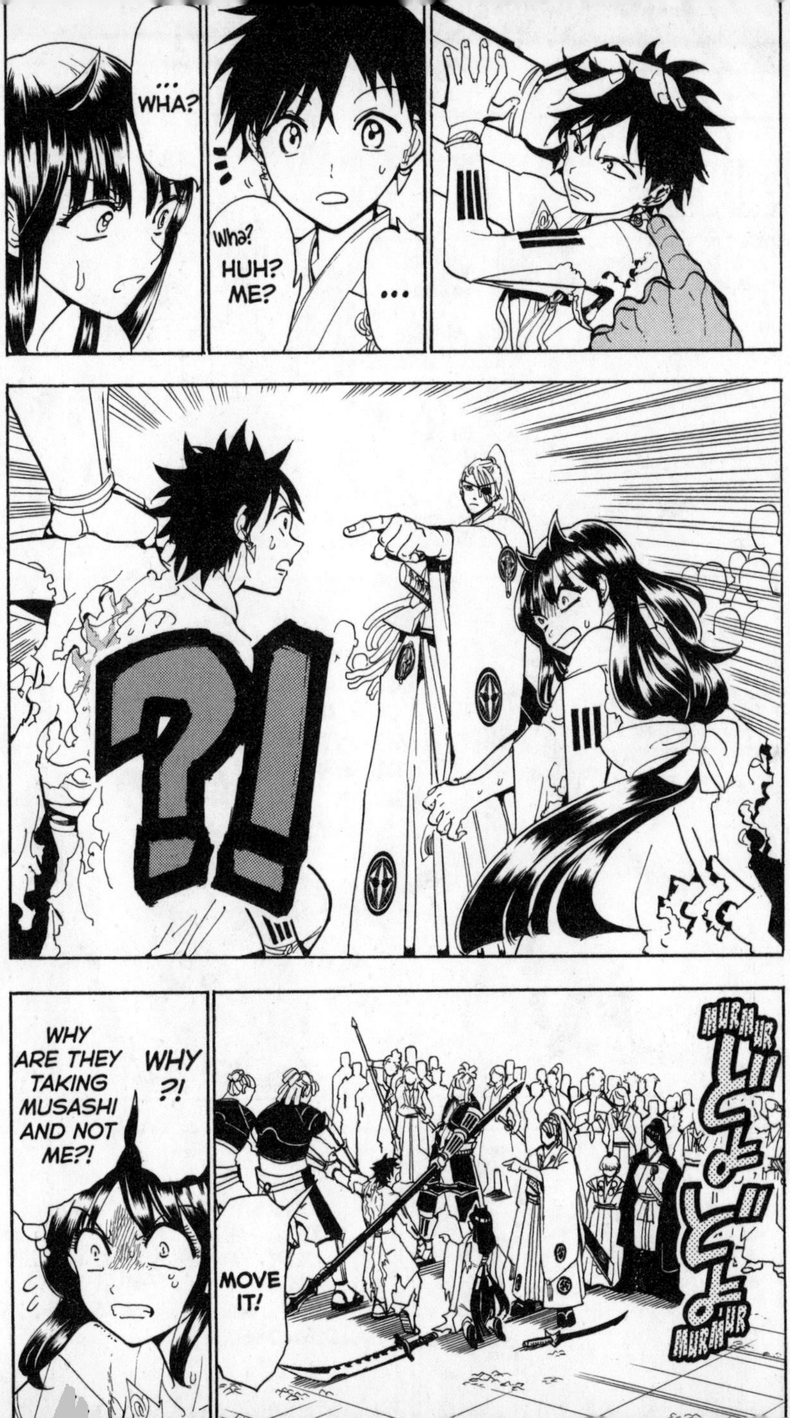

...
Wha?
HUH? ME?
... WHA?
?!
MURMUR
どよどよ
MURMUR
MOVE IT!
WHY ?!
WHY ARE THEY TAKING MUSASHI AND NOT ME?!

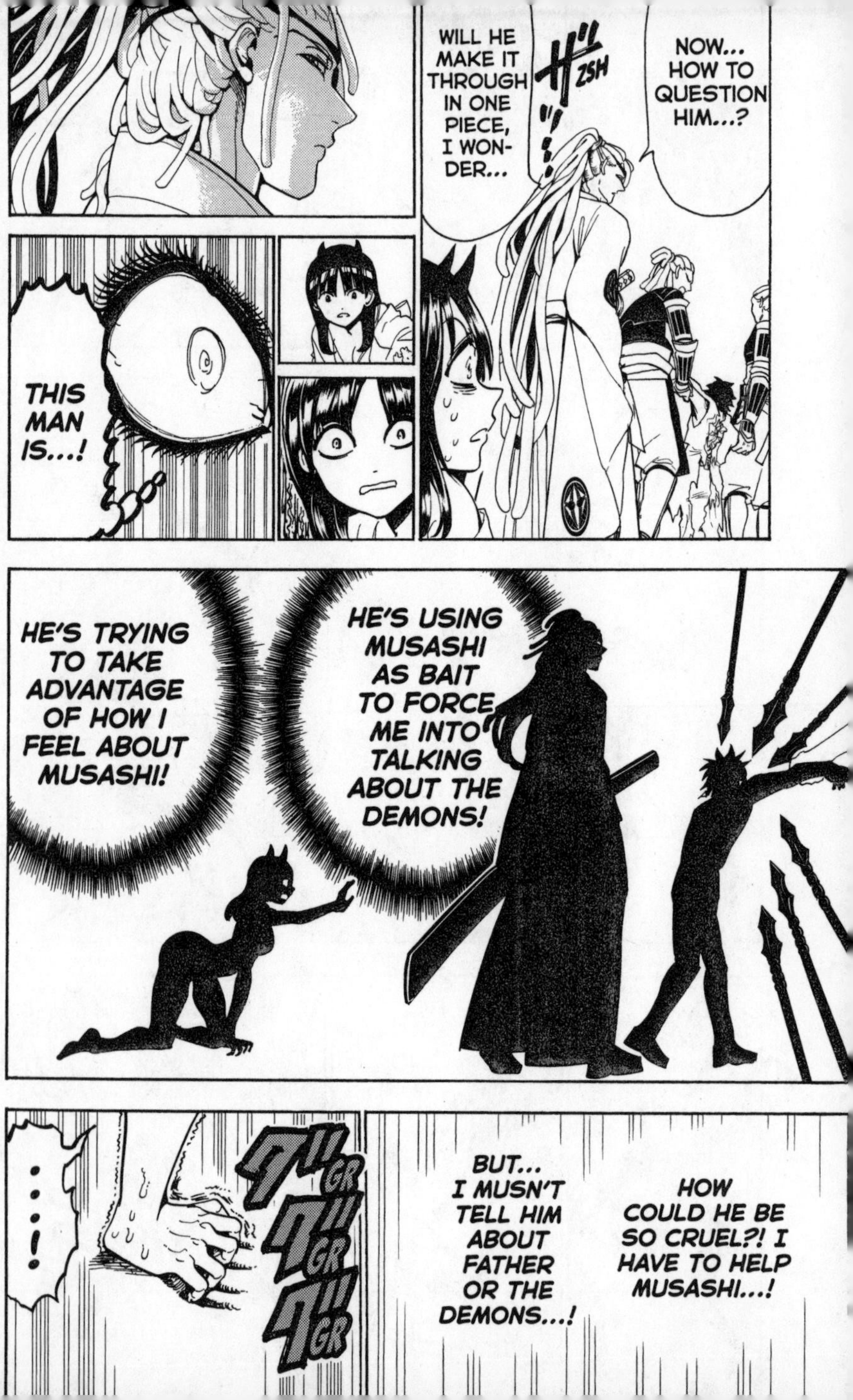
NOW... HOW TO QUESTION HIM...?
ZSH
WILL HE MAKE IT THROUGH IN ONE PIECE, I WONDER...
THIS MAN IS...!
HE'S USING MUSASHI AS BAIT TO FORCE ME INTO TALKING ABOUT THE DEMONS!
HE'S TRYING TO TAKE ADVANTAGE OF HOW I FEEL ABOUT MUSASHI!
HOW COULD HE BE SO CRUEL?! I HAVE TO HELP MUSASHI...!
BUT... I MUSN'T TELL HIM ABOUT FATHER OR THE DEMONS...!
GR GR GR
....!

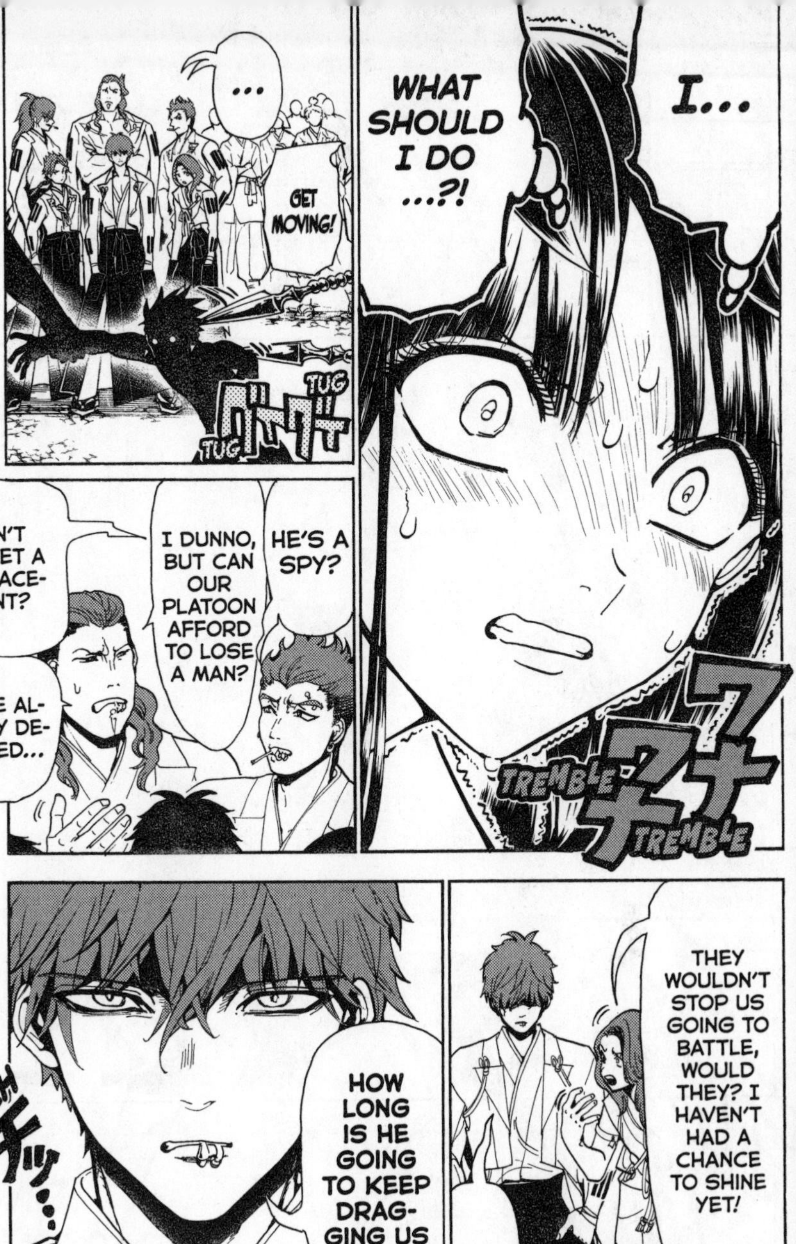

I...
WHAT SHOULD I DO ...?!
TREMBLE TREMBLE
...
GET MOVING!
TUG TUG
HE'S A SPY?
I DUNNO, BUT CAN OUR PLATOON AFFORD TO LOSE A MAN?
CAN'T WE GET A REPLACEMENT?
WE'RE ALREADY DEPLOYED...
THEY WOULDN'T STOP US GOING TO BATTLE, WOULD THEY? I HAVEN'T HAD A CHANCE TO SHINE YET!
...
HOW LONG IS HE GOING TO KEEP DRAGGING US DOWN?
TCH...

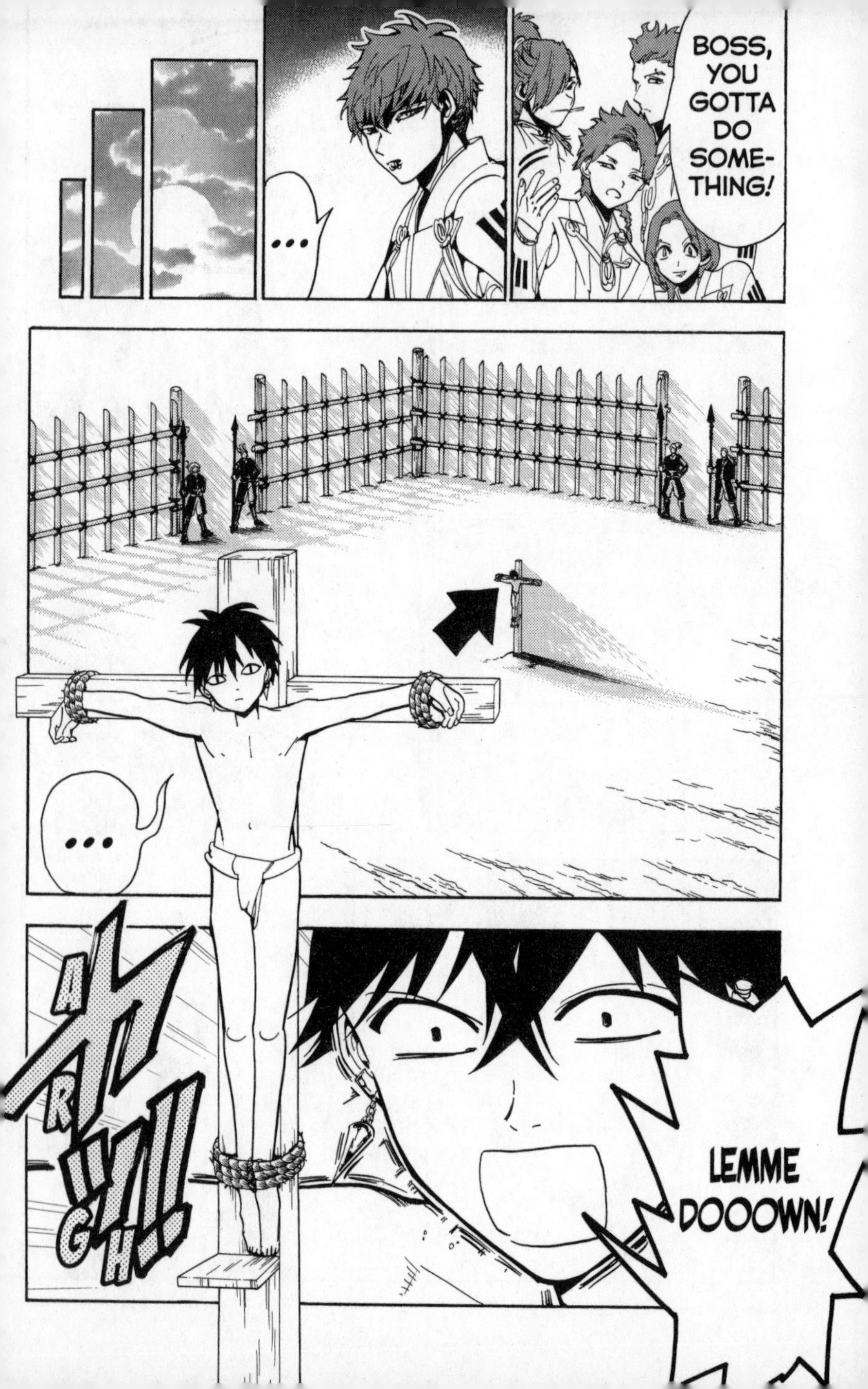
BOSS, YOU GOTTA DO SOME-THING!
...
...
LEMME DOOOWN!
ARRGH!!

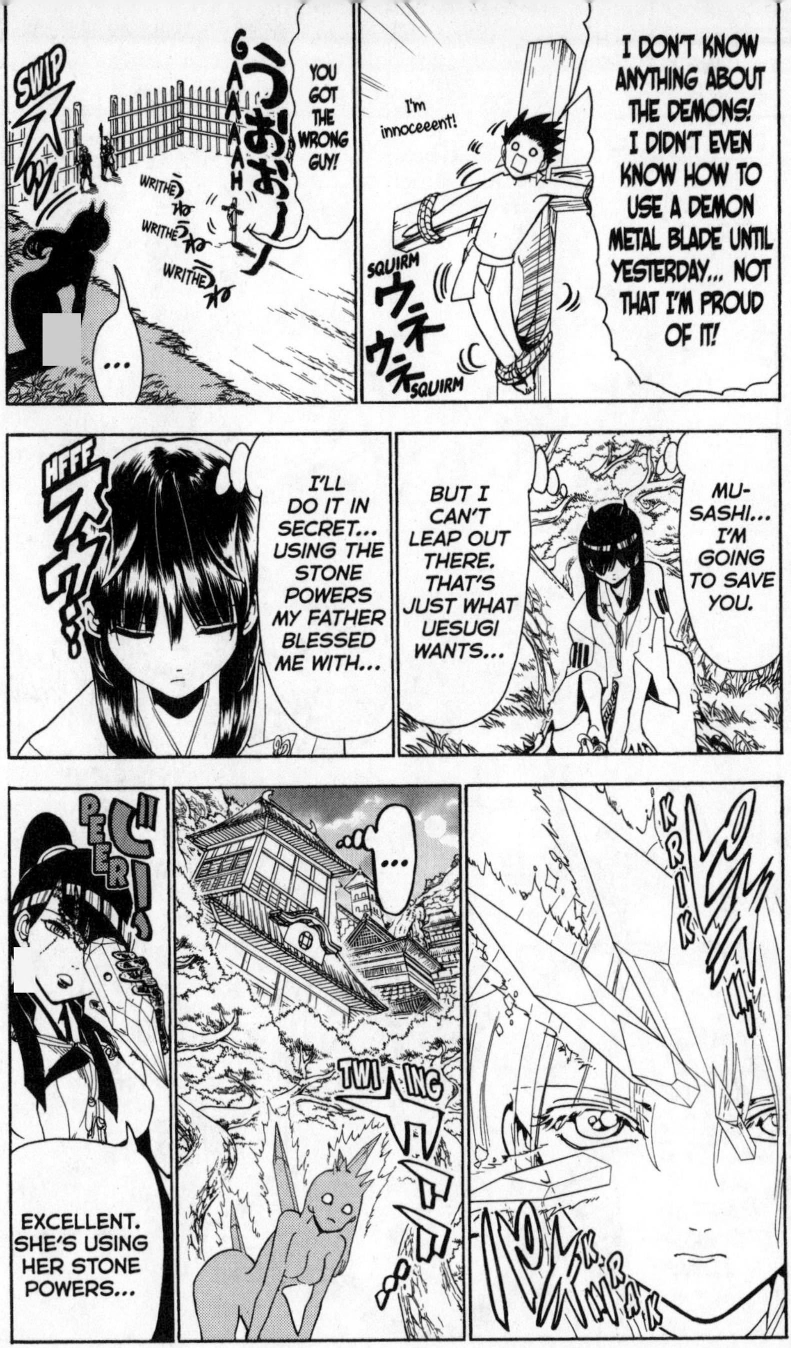

I DON'T KNOW ANYTHING ABOUT THE DEMONS! I DIDN'T EVEN KNOW HOW TO USE A DEMON METAL BLADE UNTIL YESTERDAY... NOT THAT I'M PROUD OF IT!
I'm innoceeent!
SQUIRM
ウネウネ
SQUIRM
YOU GOT THE WRONG GUY!
GAAAAAH
うおおー
WRITHE
WRITHE
WRITHE
SWIP
...
MU-SASHI... I'M GOING TO SAVE YOU.
BUT I CAN'T LEAP OUT THERE. THAT'S JUST WHAT UESUGI WANTS...
I'LL DO IT IN SECRET... USING THE STONE POWERS MY FATHER BLESSED ME WITH...
HFFF
KRIK
KRAK
...
TWI ING
PEER!
EXCELLENT. SHE'S USING HER STONE POWERS...

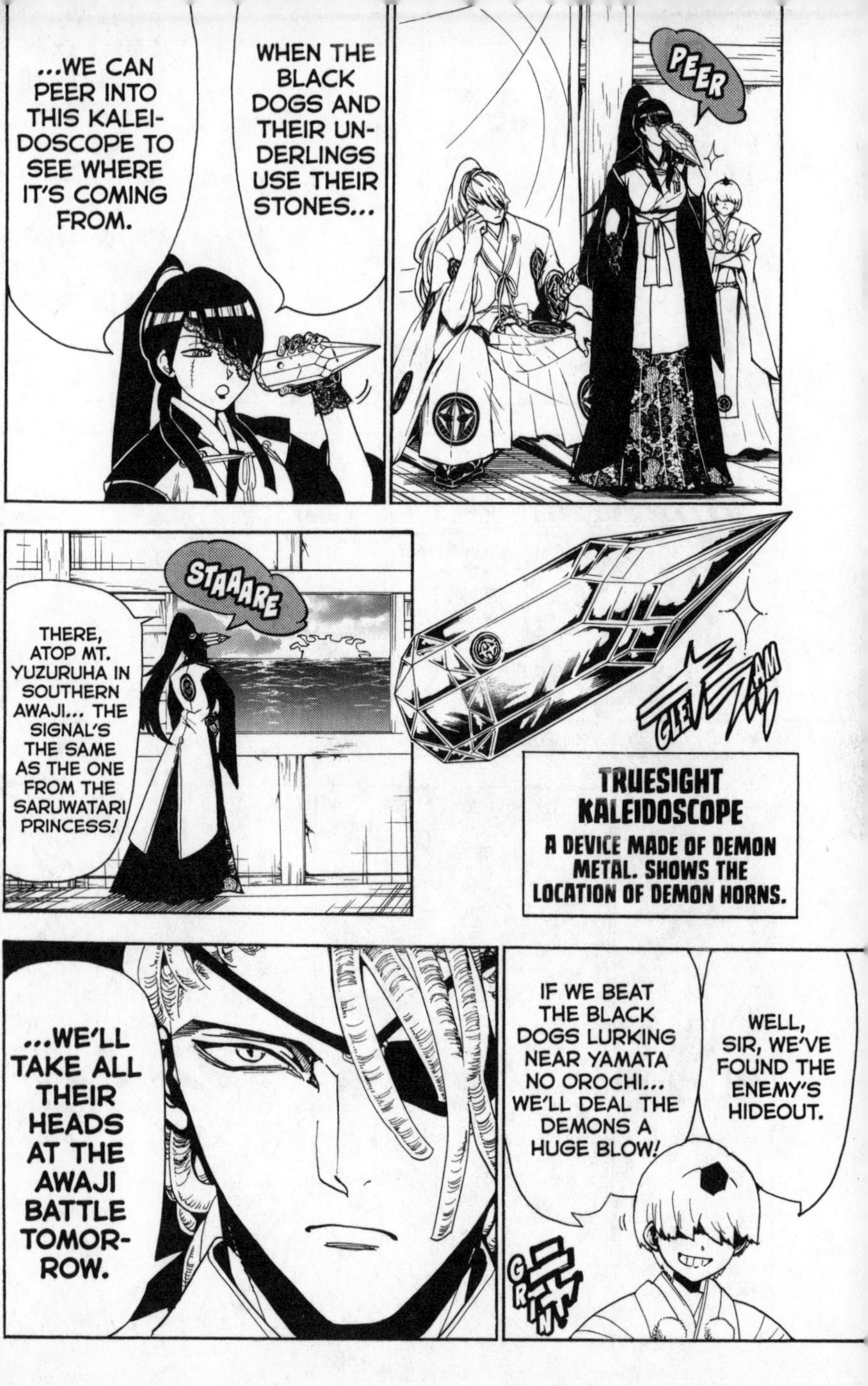
PEER
WHEN THE BLACK DOGS AND THEIR UNDERLINGS USE THEIR STONES...
...WE CAN PEER INTO THIS KALEIDOSCOPE TO SEE WHERE IT'S COMING FROM.
GLEAM
TRUESIGHT KALEIDOSCOPE
A DEVICE MADE OF DEMON METAL. SHOWS THE LOCATION OF DEMON HORNS.
STAAARE
THERE, ATOP MT. YUZURUHA IN SOUTHERN AWAJI... THE SIGNAL'S THE SAME AS THE ONE FROM THE SARUWATARI PRINCESS!
WELL, SIR, WE'VE FOUND THE ENEMY'S HIDEOUT.
IF WE BEAT THE BLACK DOGS LURKING NEAR YAMATA NO OROCHI... WE'LL DEAL THE DEMONS A HUGE BLOW!
GRIN
...WE'LL TAKE ALL THEIR HEADS AT THE AWAJI BATTLE TOMORROW.

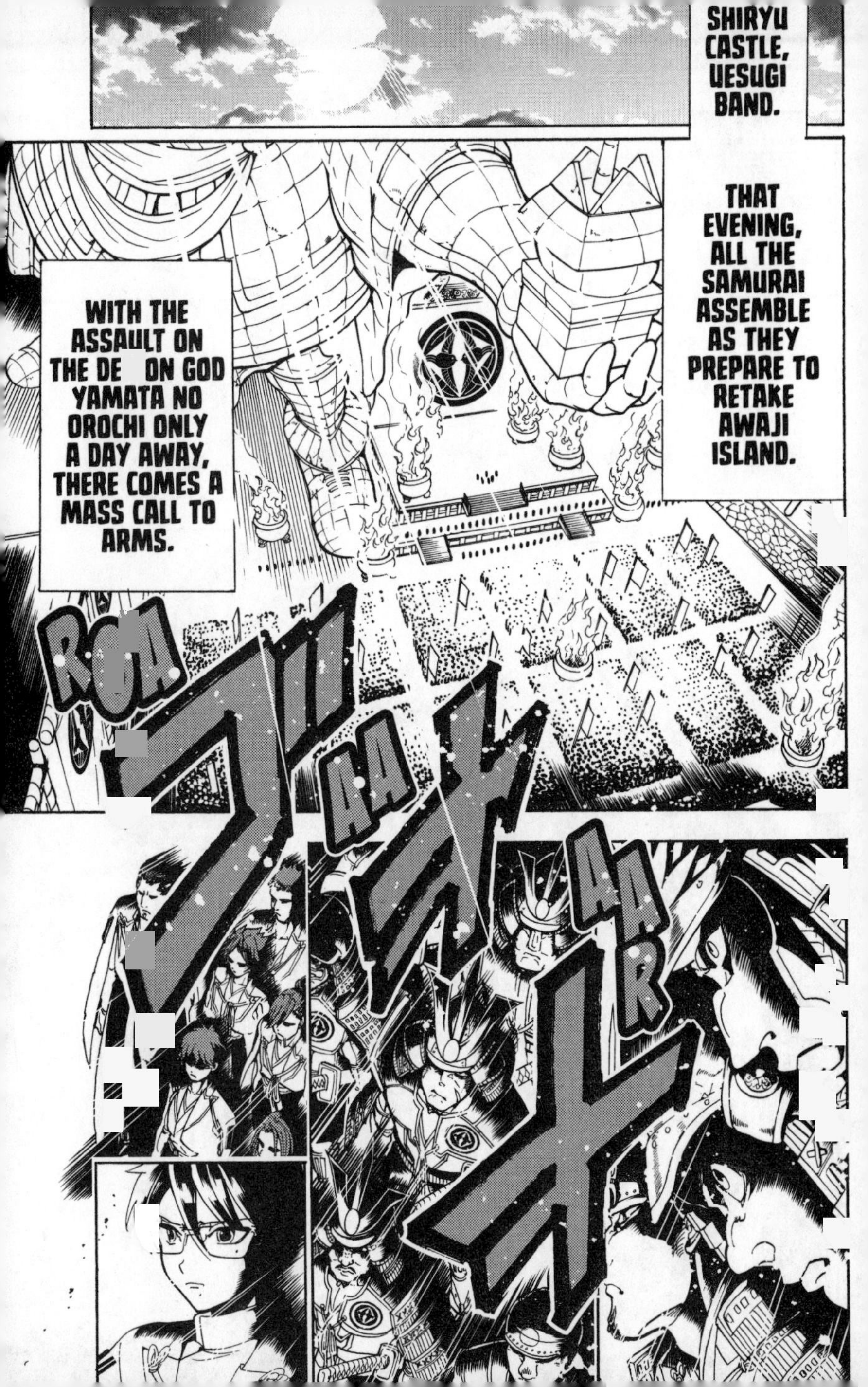
SHIRYU CASTLE, UESUGI BAND.
THAT EVENING, ALL THE SAMURAI ASSEMBLE AS THEY PREPARE TO RETAKE AWAJI ISLAND.
WITH THE ASSAULT ON THE DE ON GOD YAMATA NO OROCHI ONLY A DAY AWAY, THERE COMES A MASS CALL TO ARMS.
ROA
AA
AAR

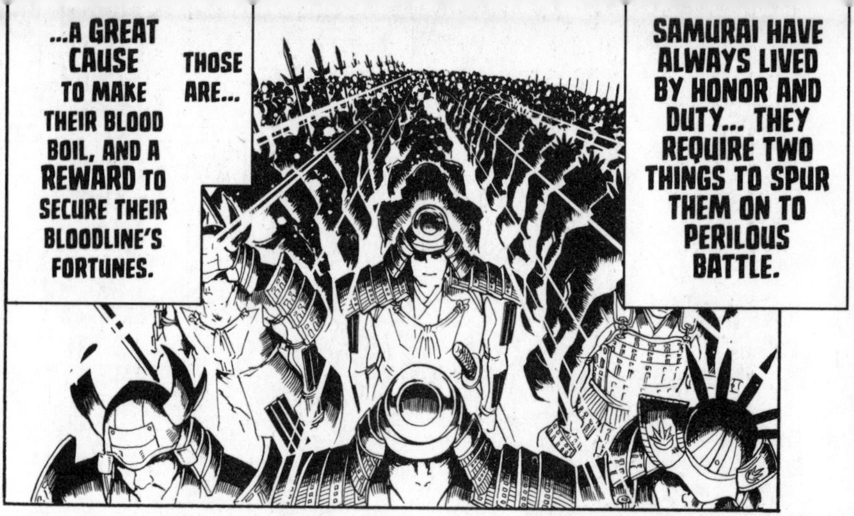
SAMURAI HAVE ALWAYS LIVED BY HONOR AND DUTY... THEY REQUIRE TWO THINGS TO SPUR THEM ON TO PERILOUS BATTLE.
THOSE ARE...
...A GREAT CAUSE TO MAKE THEIR BLOOD BOIL, AND A REWARD TO SECURE THEIR BLOODLINE'S FORTUNES.

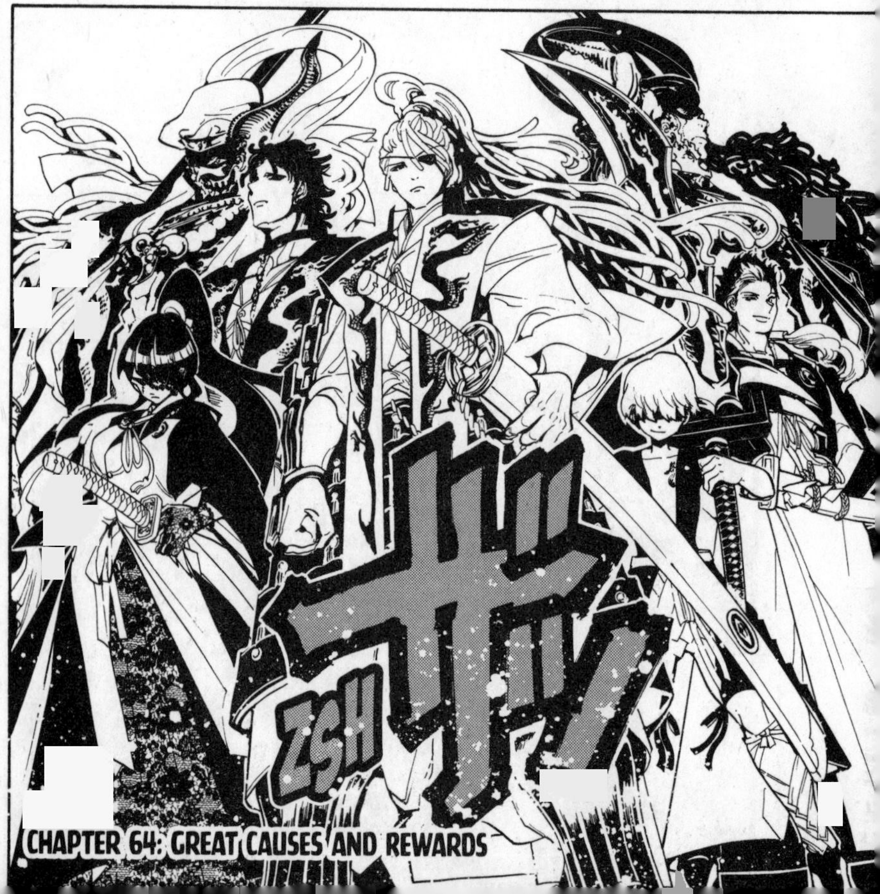
ZSH
CHAPTER 64: GREAT CAUSES AND REWARDS

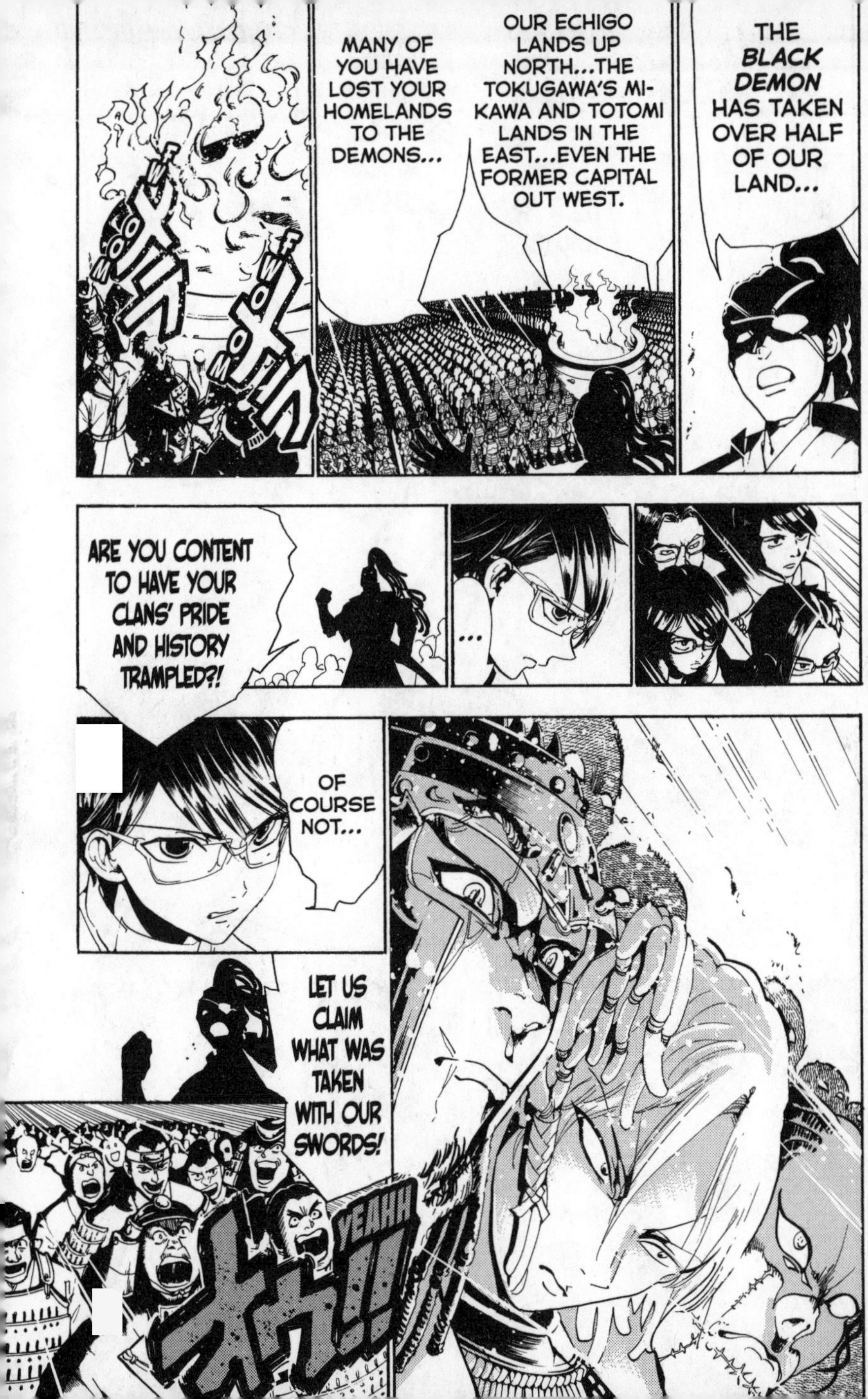
THE BLACK DEMON HAS TAKEN OVER HALF OF OUR LAND...
OUR ECHIGO LANDS UP NORTH...THE TOKUGAWA'S MI-KAWA AND TOTOMI LANDS IN THE EAST...EVEN THE FORMER CAPITAL OUT WEST.
MANY OF YOU HAVE LOST YOUR HOMELANDS TO THE DEMONS...
FWOOM
FWOOM
...
ARE YOU CONTENT TO HAVE YOUR CLANS' PRIDE AND HISTORY TRAMPLED?!
OF COURSE NOT...
LET US CLAIM WHAT WAS TAKEN WITH OUR SWORDS!
YEAHH

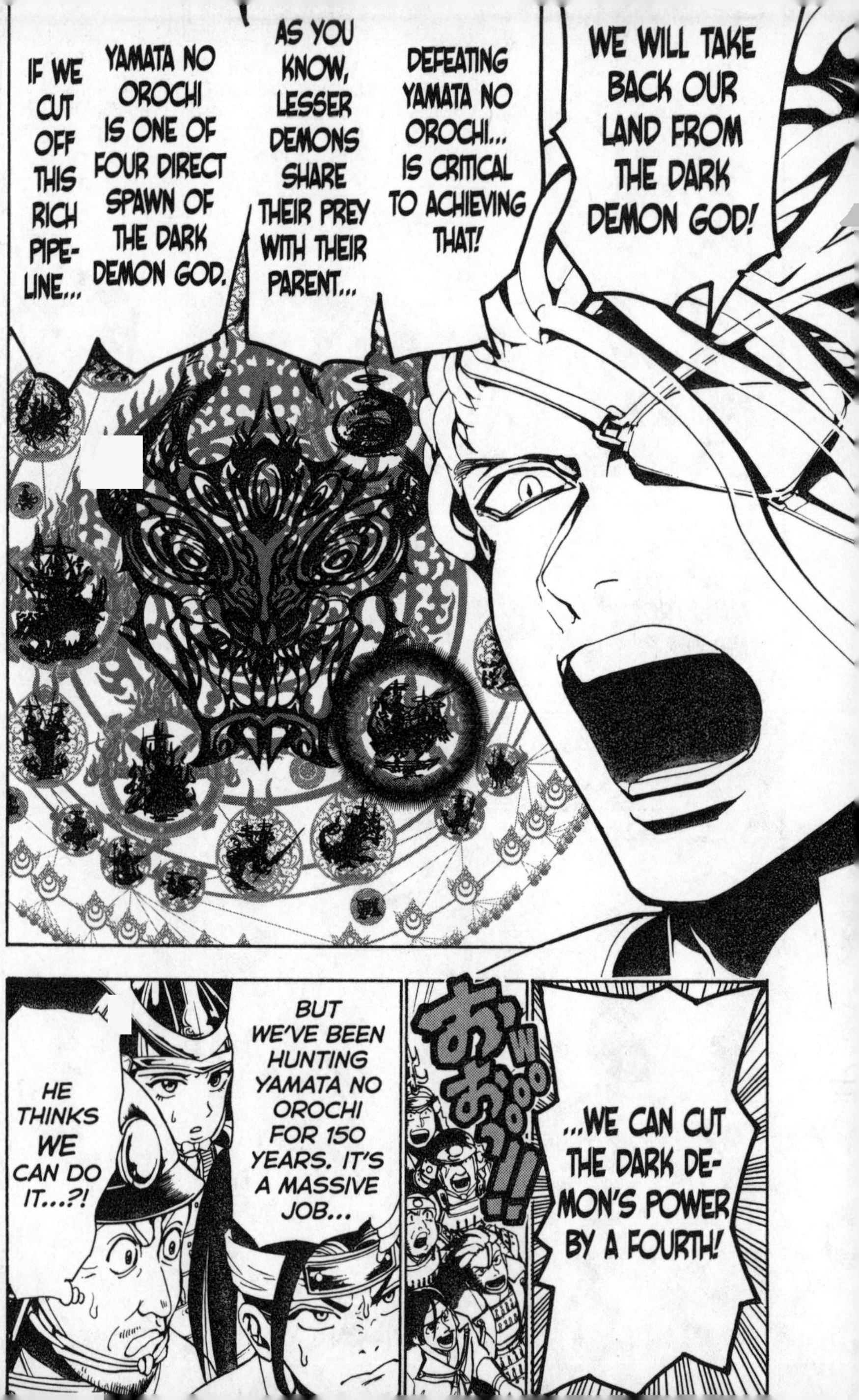

WE WILL TAKE BACK OUR LAND FROM THE DARK DEMON GOD!
DEFEATING YAMATA NO OROCHI... IS CRITICAL TO ACHIEVING THAT!
AS YOU KNOW, LESSER DEMONS SHARE THEIR PREY WITH THEIR PARENT...
YAMATA NO OROCHI IS ONE OF FOUR DIRECT SPAWN OF THE DARK DEMON GOD.
IF WE CUT OFF THIS RICH PIPELINE...
...WE CAN CUT THE DARK DEMON'S POWER BY A FOURTH!
おおっ!!
BUT WE'VE BEEN HUNTING YAMATA NO OROCHI FOR 150 YEARS. IT'S A MASSIVE JOB...
HE THINKS WE CAN DO IT...?!

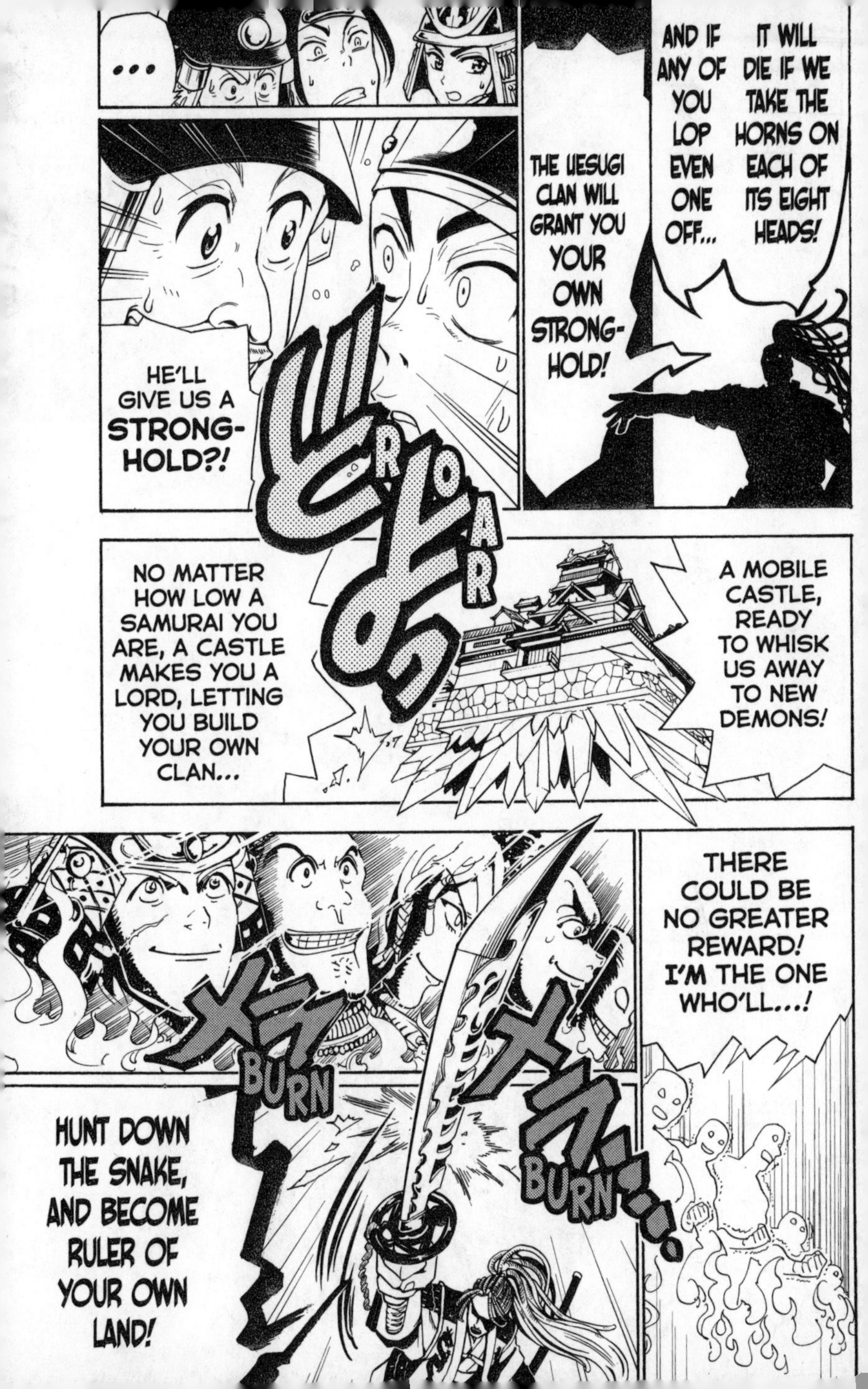
IT WILL DIE IF WE TAKE THE HORNS ON EACH OF ITS EIGHT HEADS!
AND IF ANY OF YOU LOP EVEN ONE OFF...
THE UESUGI CLAN WILL GRANT YOU YOUR OWN STRONGHOLD!
...
HE'LL GIVE US A STRONGHOLD?!
ROAR
A MOBILE CASTLE, READY TO WHISK US AWAY TO NEW DEMONS!
NO MATTER HOW LOW A SAMURAI YOU ARE, A CASTLE MAKES YOU A LORD, LETTING YOU BUILD YOUR OWN CLAN...
THERE COULD BE NO GREATER REWARD! I'M THE ONE WHO'LL...!
BURN
BURN...
HUNT DOWN THE SNAKE, AND BECOME RULER OF YOUR OWN LAND!

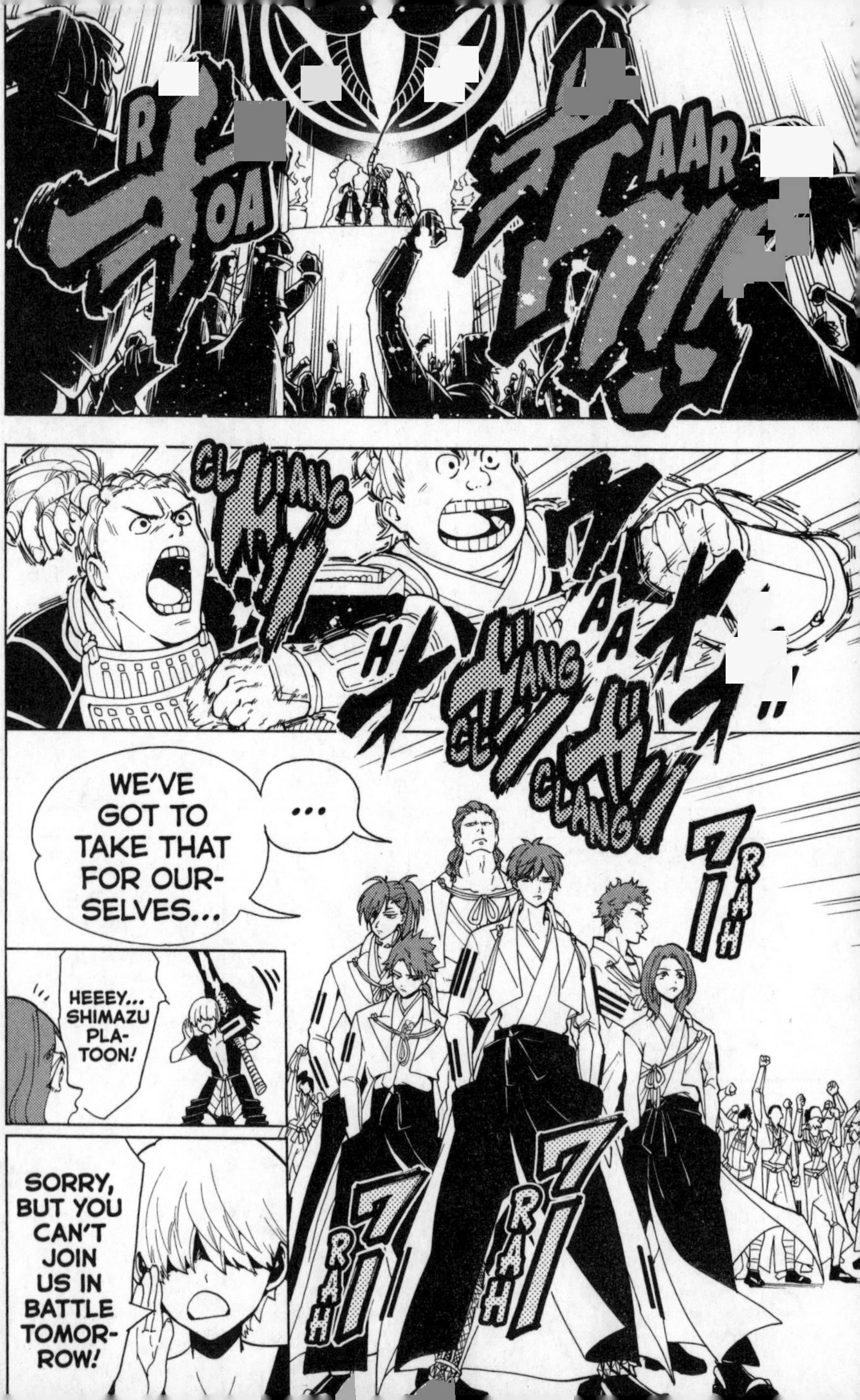
AAR
R
OA
CLANG
HAAA
CLANG
RAH
CLANG!
WE'VE GOT TO TAKE THAT FOR OURSELVES...
...
RAH
RAH
RAH
HEEEY... SHIMAZU PLATOON!
SORRY, BUT YOU CAN'T JOIN US IN BATTLE TOMORROW!

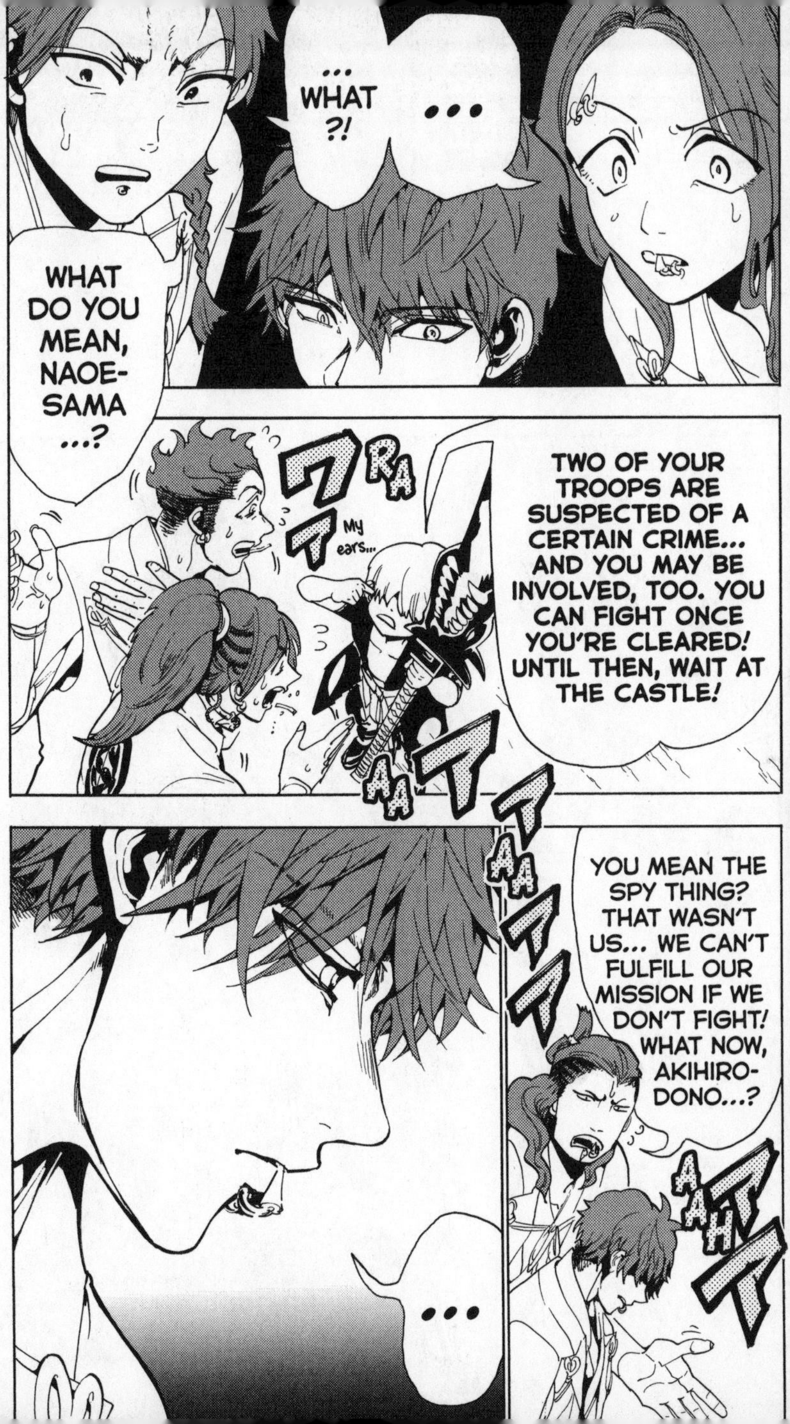
...
... WHAT ?!
WHAT DO YOU MEAN, NAOE-SAMA ...?
TWO OF YOUR TROOPS ARE SUSPECTED OF A CERTAIN CRIME... AND YOU MAY BE INVOLVED, TOO. YOU CAN FIGHT ONCE YOU'RE CLEARED! UNTIL THEN, WAIT AT THE CASTLE!
RA
AA
My ears...
AA
YOU MEAN THE SPY THING? THAT WASN'T US... WE CAN'T FULFILL OUR MISSION IF WE DON'T FIGHT! WHAT NOW, AKIHIRO-DONO...?
AAH
...

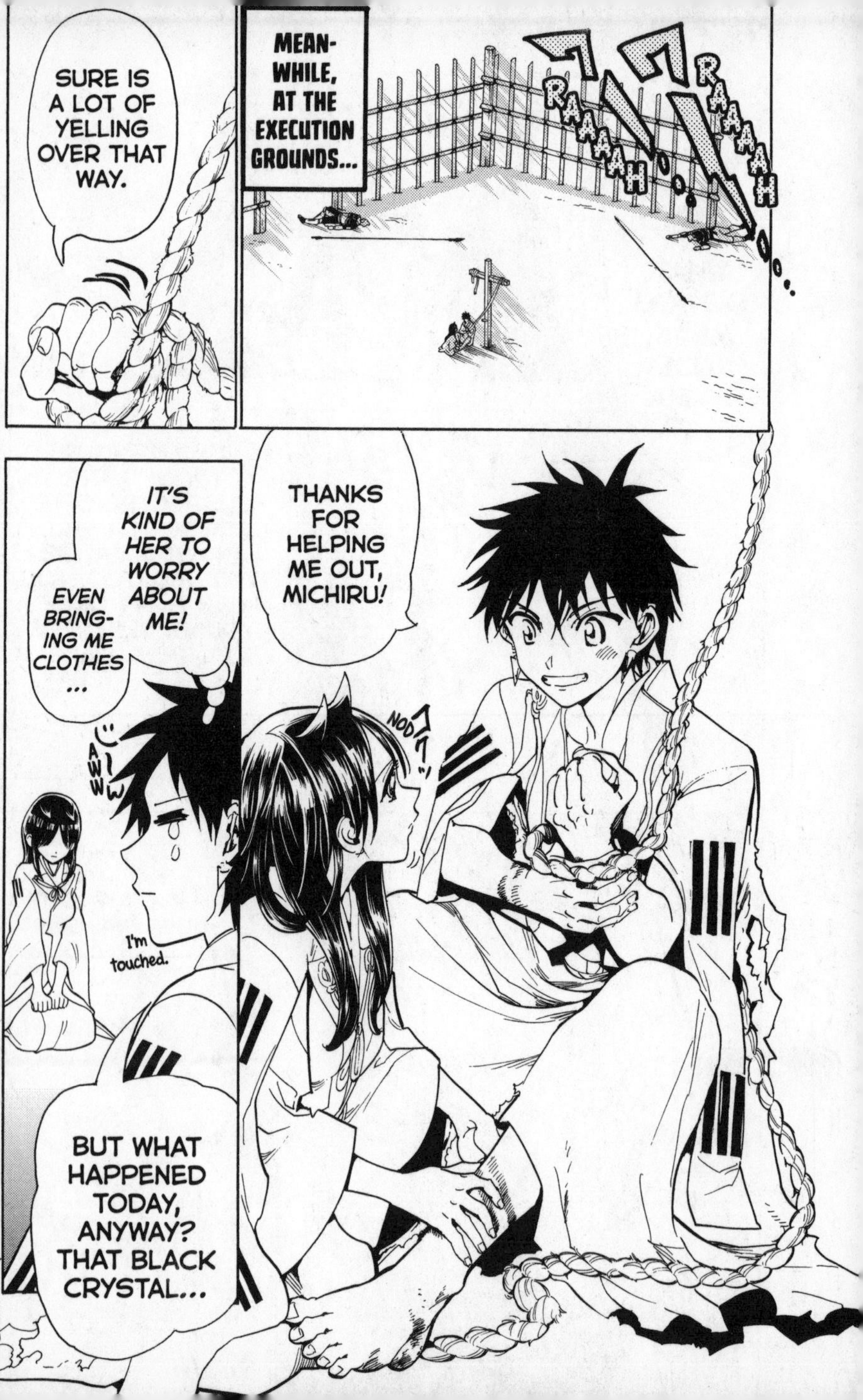
MEAN-WHILE, AT THE EXECUTION GROUNDS...
RAAAAH
RAAAAH
SURE IS A LOT OF YELLING OVER THAT WAY.
THANKS FOR HELPING ME OUT, MICHIRU!
NOD
IT'S KIND OF HER TO WORRY ABOUT ME!
EVEN BRINGING ME CLOTHES...
AWW
I'm touched.
BUT WHAT HAPPENED TODAY, ANYWAY? THAT BLACK CRYSTAL...

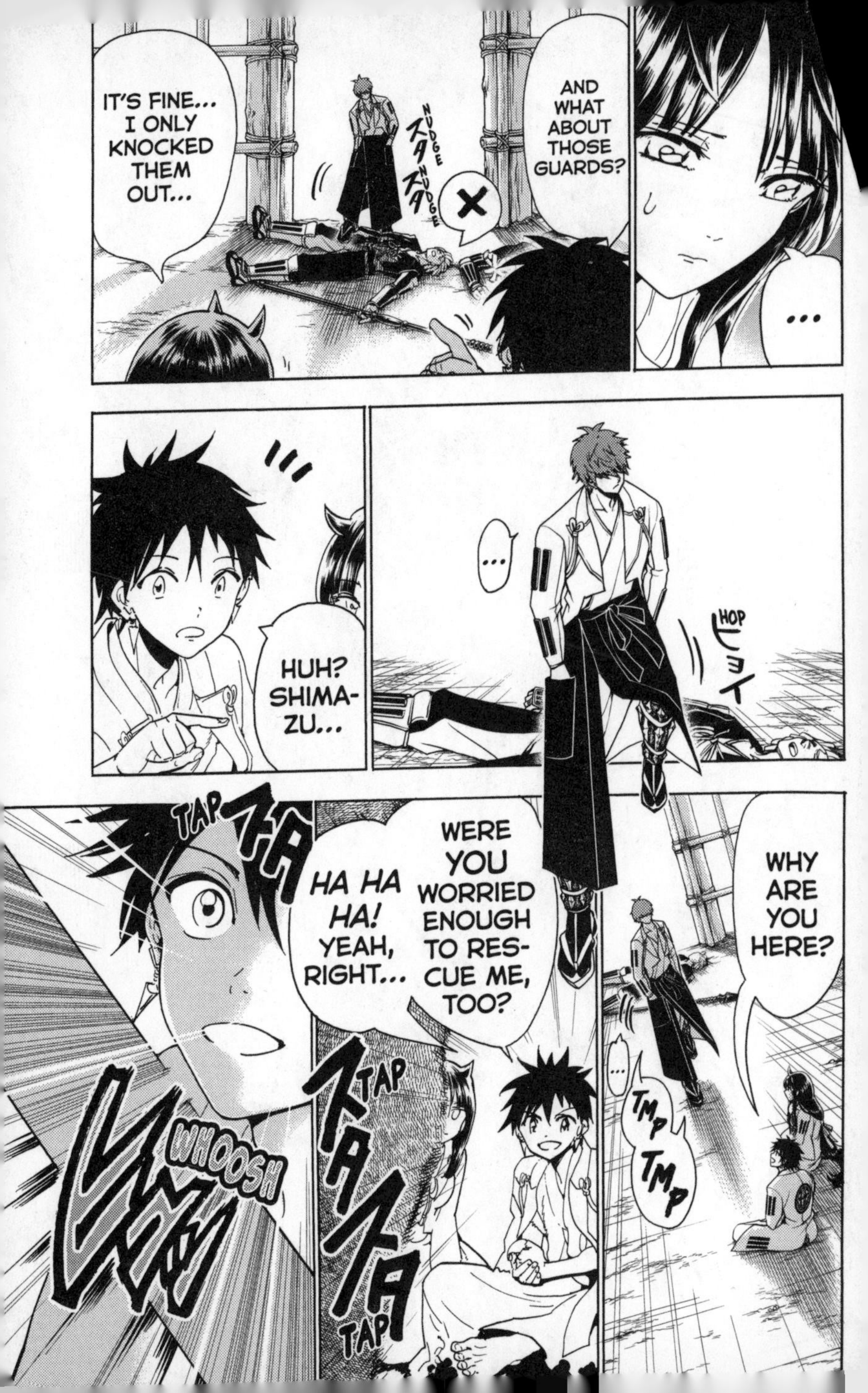
...
AND WHAT ABOUT THOSE GUARDS?
NUDGE NUDGE
×
IT'S FINE... I ONLY KNOCKED THEM OUT...
...
HOP
HUH? SHIMA-ZU...
WHY ARE YOU HERE?
...
TMP TMP
WERE YOU WORRIED ENOUGH TO RES-CUE ME, TOO?
HA HA HA! YEAH, RIGHT...
TAP TAP
TAP
WHOOSH

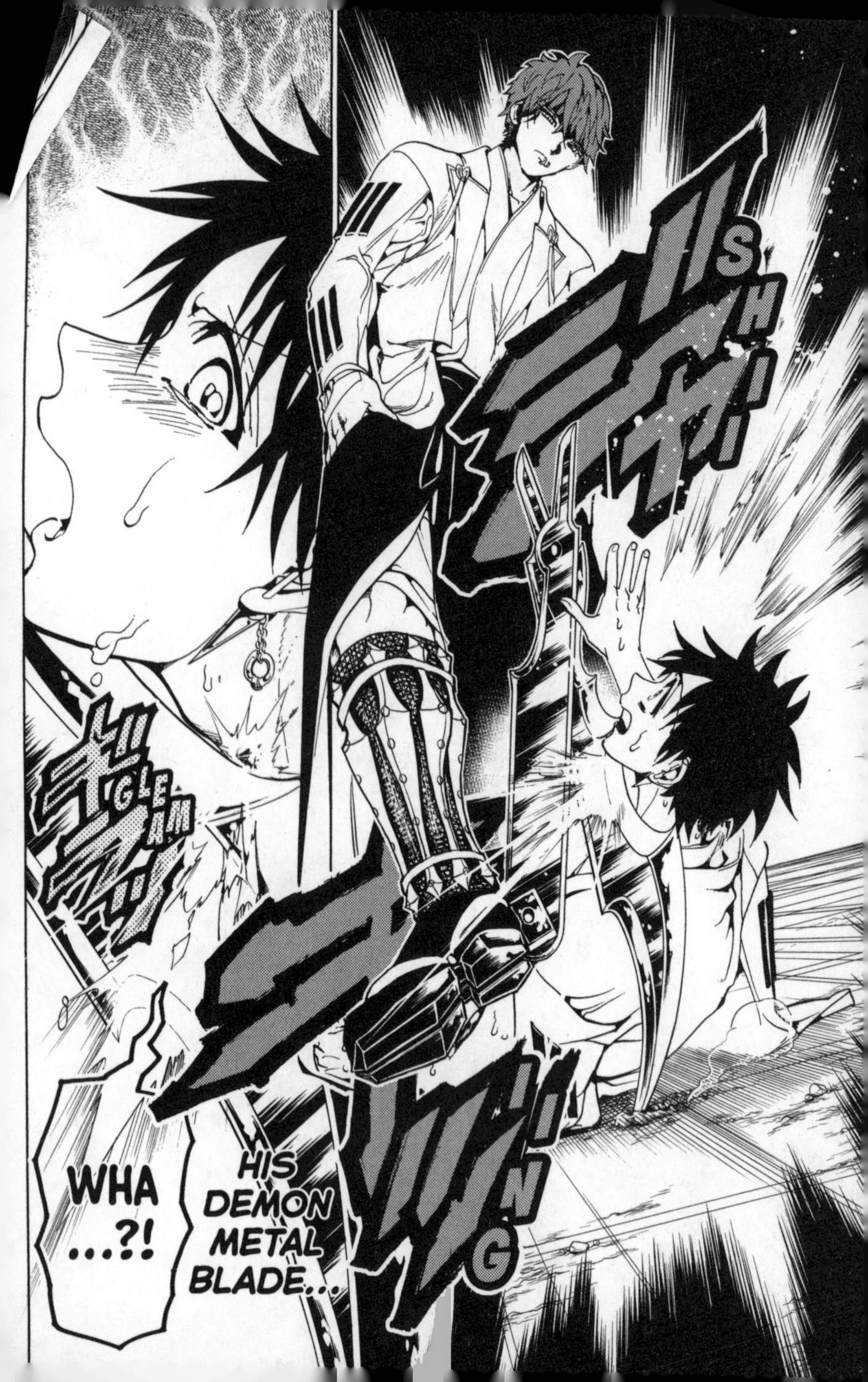
SHIIIN
GLEAM
HIS DEMON METAL BLADE...
WHA ...?!
NG

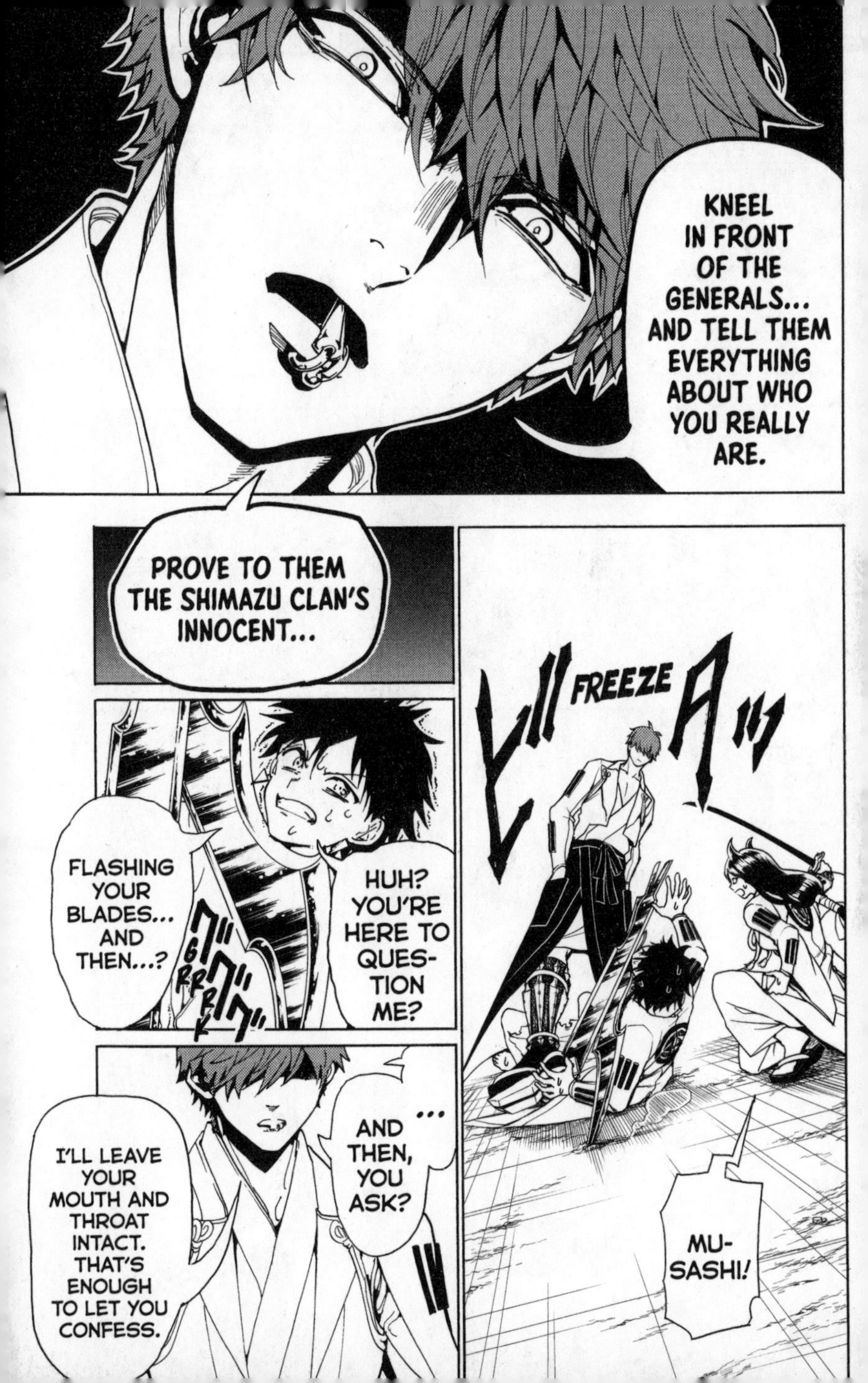
KNEEL IN FRONT OF THE GENERALS... AND TELL THEM EVERYTHING ABOUT WHO YOU REALLY ARE.
FREEZE
MU-SASHI!
PROVE TO THEM THE SHIMAZU CLAN'S INNOCENT...
HUH? YOU'RE HERE TO QUES-TION ME?
FLASHING YOUR BLADES... AND THEN...?
GRRRK
...
AND THEN, YOU ASK?
I'LL LEAVE YOUR MOUTH AND THROAT INTACT. THAT'S ENOUGH TO LET YOU CONFESS.

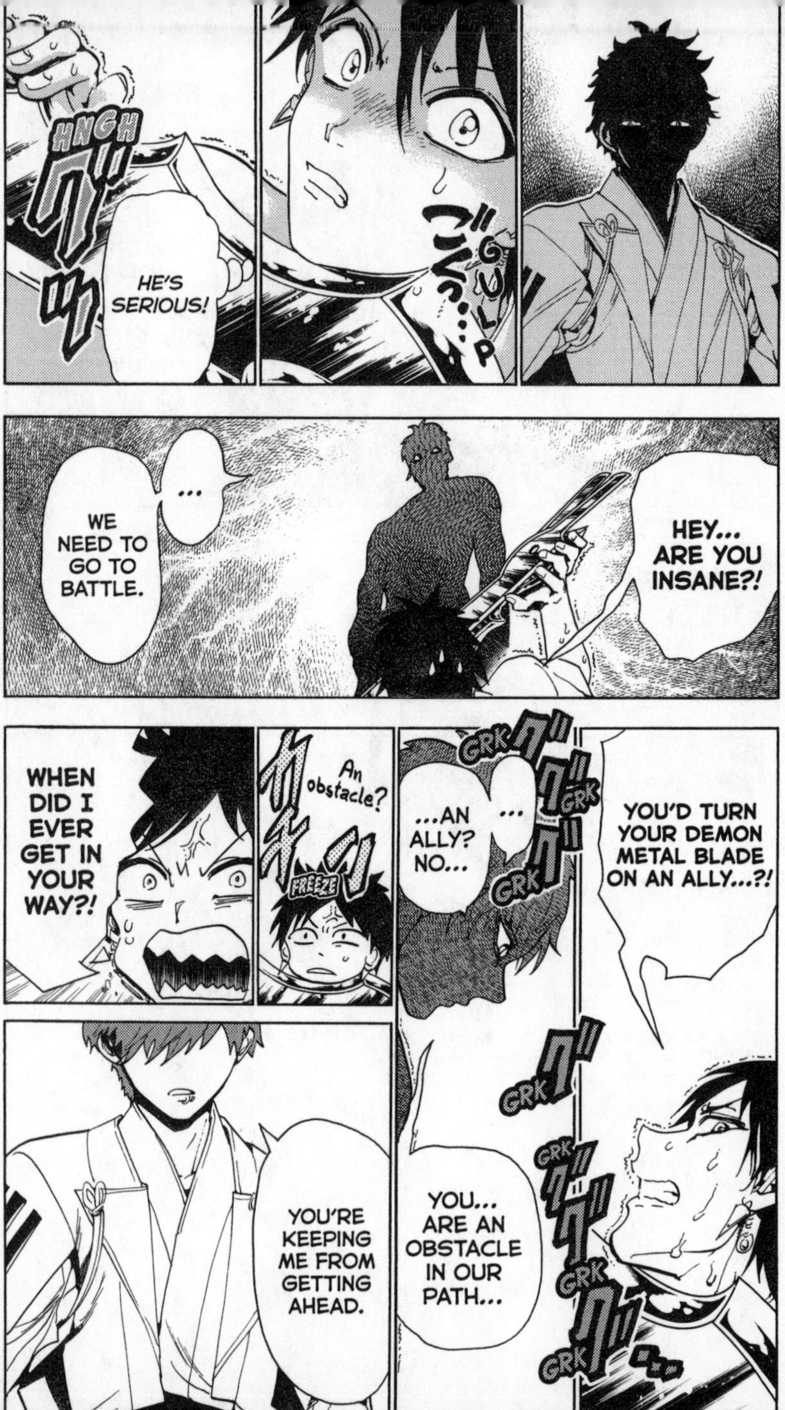
GULP
HNGH
HE'S SERIOUS!
HEY... ARE YOU INSANE?!
...
WE NEED TO GO TO BATTLE.
YOU'D TURN YOUR DEMON METAL BLADE ON AN ALLY...?!
GRK
GRK
GRK
...
...AN ALLY? NO...
An obstacle?
FREEZE
WHEN DID I EVER GET IN YOUR WAY?!
GRK
GRK
GRK
GRK
YOU... ARE AN OBSTACLE IN OUR PATH...
YOU'RE KEEPING ME FROM GETTING AHEAD.

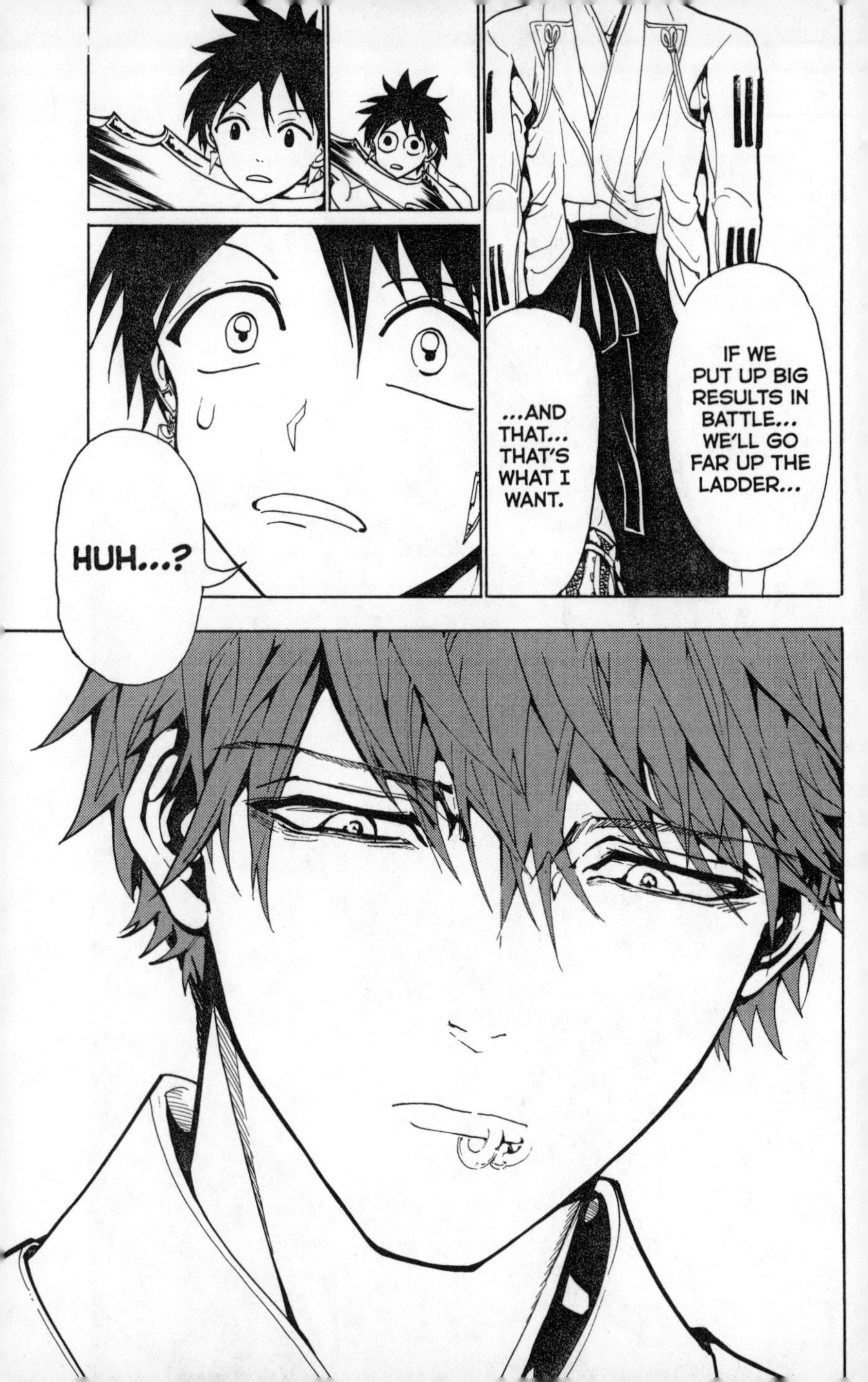
IF WE PUT UP BIG RESULTS IN BATTLE... WE'LL GO FAR UP THE LADDER...
...AND THAT... THAT'S WHAT I WANT.
HUH...?

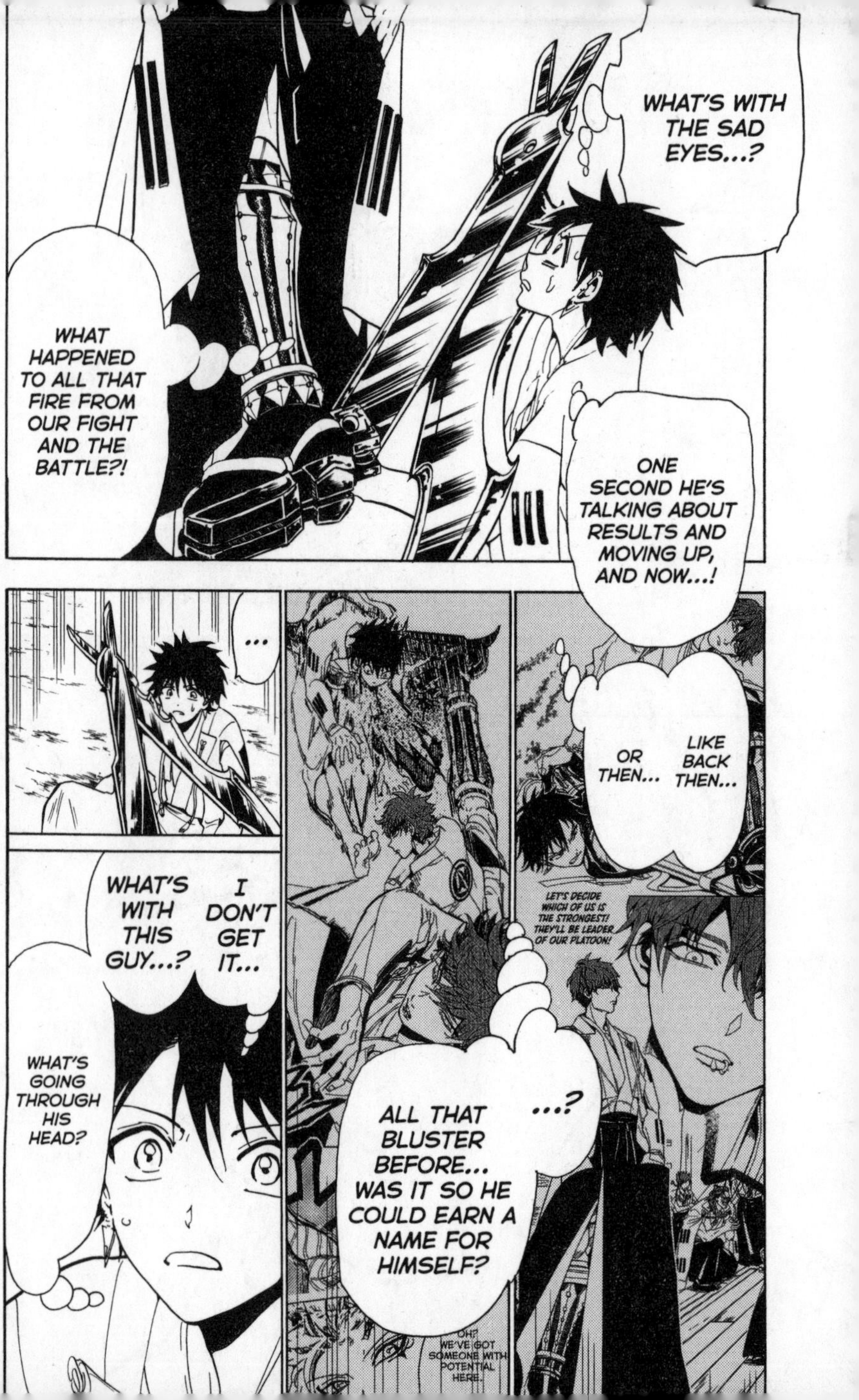
WHAT'S WITH THE SAD EYES...?
WHAT HAPPENED TO ALL THAT FIRE FROM OUR FIGHT AND THE BATTLE?!
ONE SECOND HE'S TALKING ABOUT RESULTS AND MOVING UP, AND NOW...!
LIKE BACK THEN...
OR THEN...
LET'S DECIDE WHICH OF US IS THE STRONGEST! THEY'LL BE LEADER OF OUR PLATOON!
OH? WE'VE GOT SOMEONE WITH POTENTIAL HERE.
...?
ALL THAT BLUSTER BEFORE... WAS IT SO HE COULD EARN A NAME FOR HIMSELF?
...
I DON'T GET IT...
WHAT'S WITH THIS GUY...?
WHAT'S GOING THROUGH HIS HEAD?

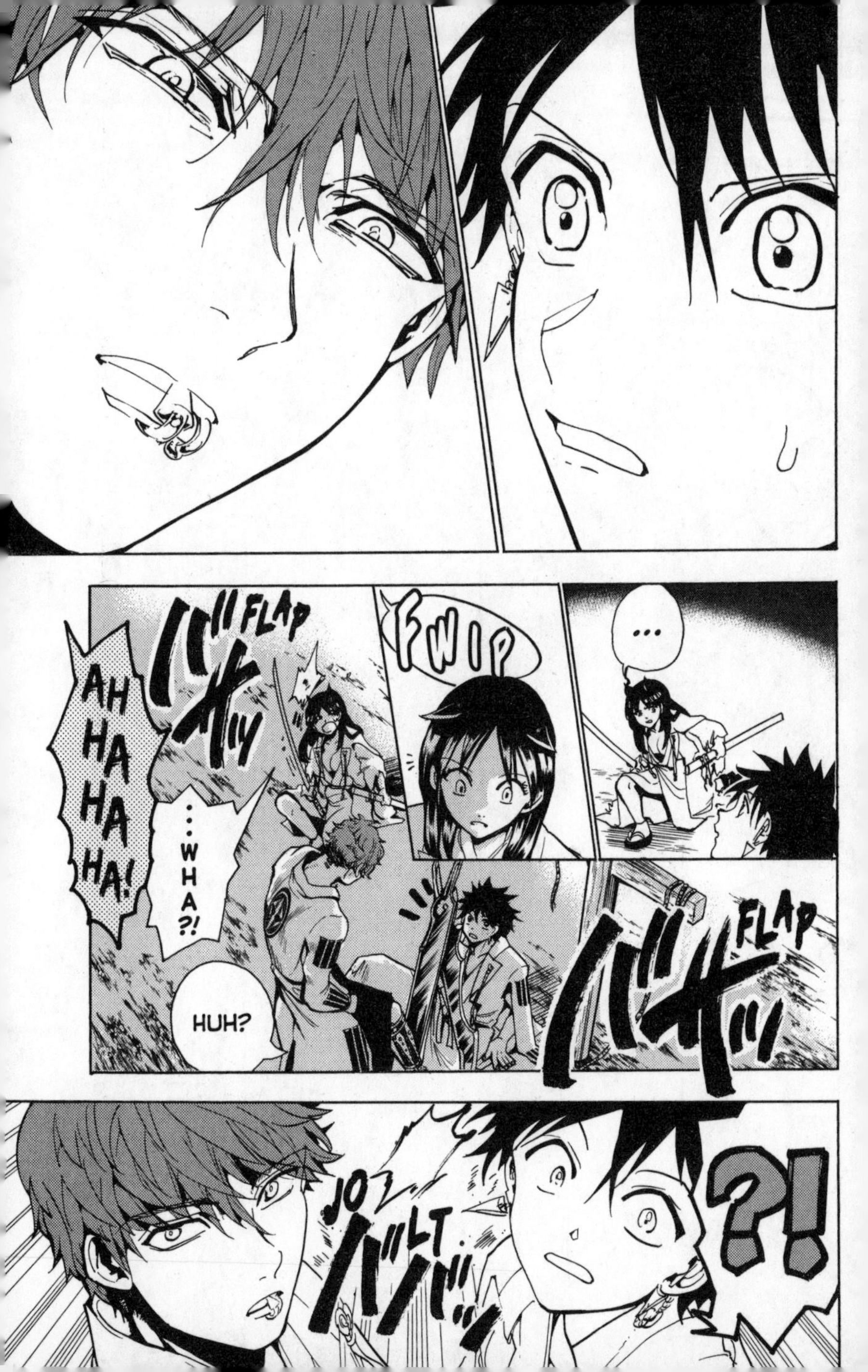
...
FWIP
FLAP
AH HA HA HA HA!
...WHA?!
FLAP
HUH?
?!
JOLT

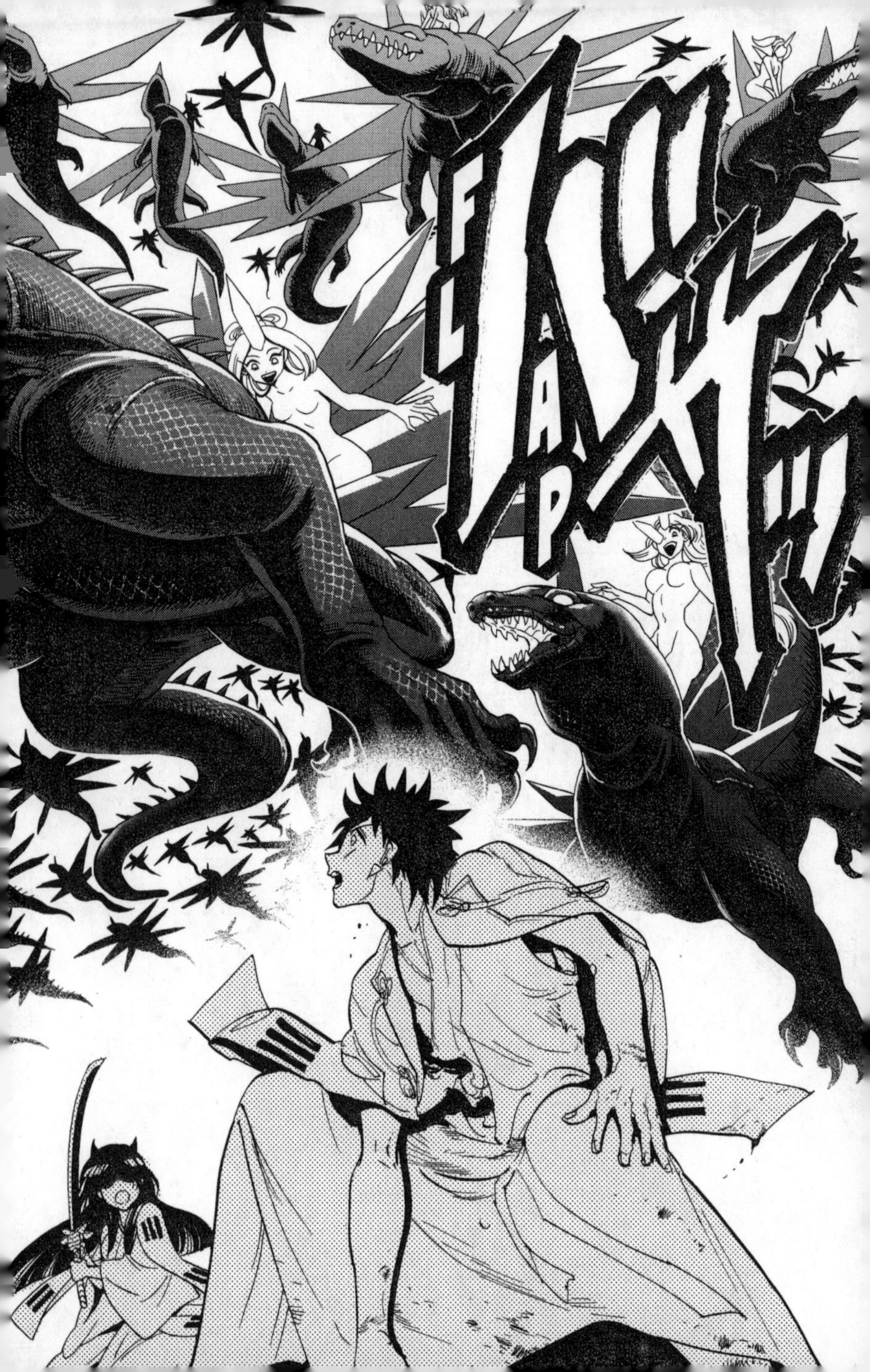
FLAP

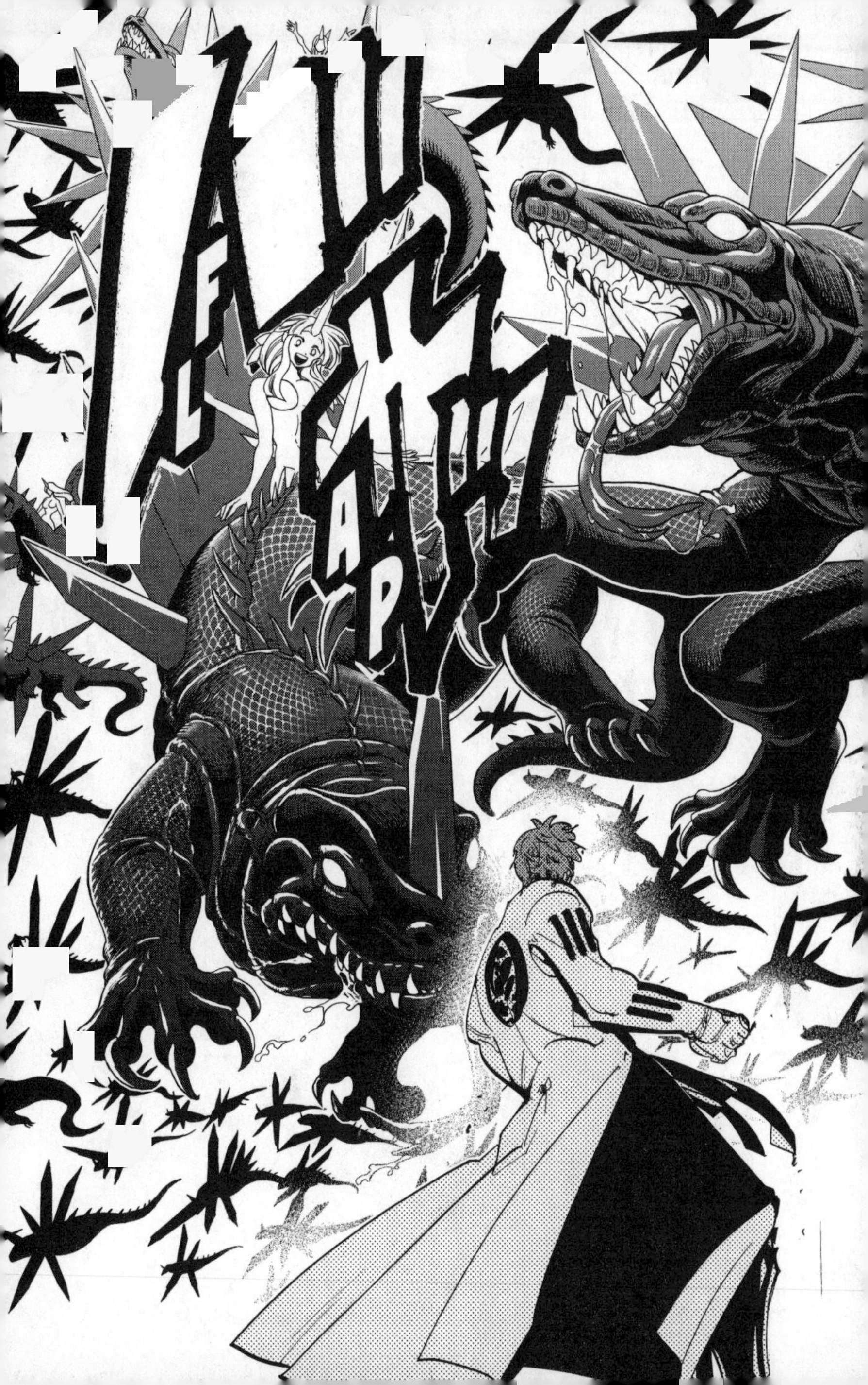

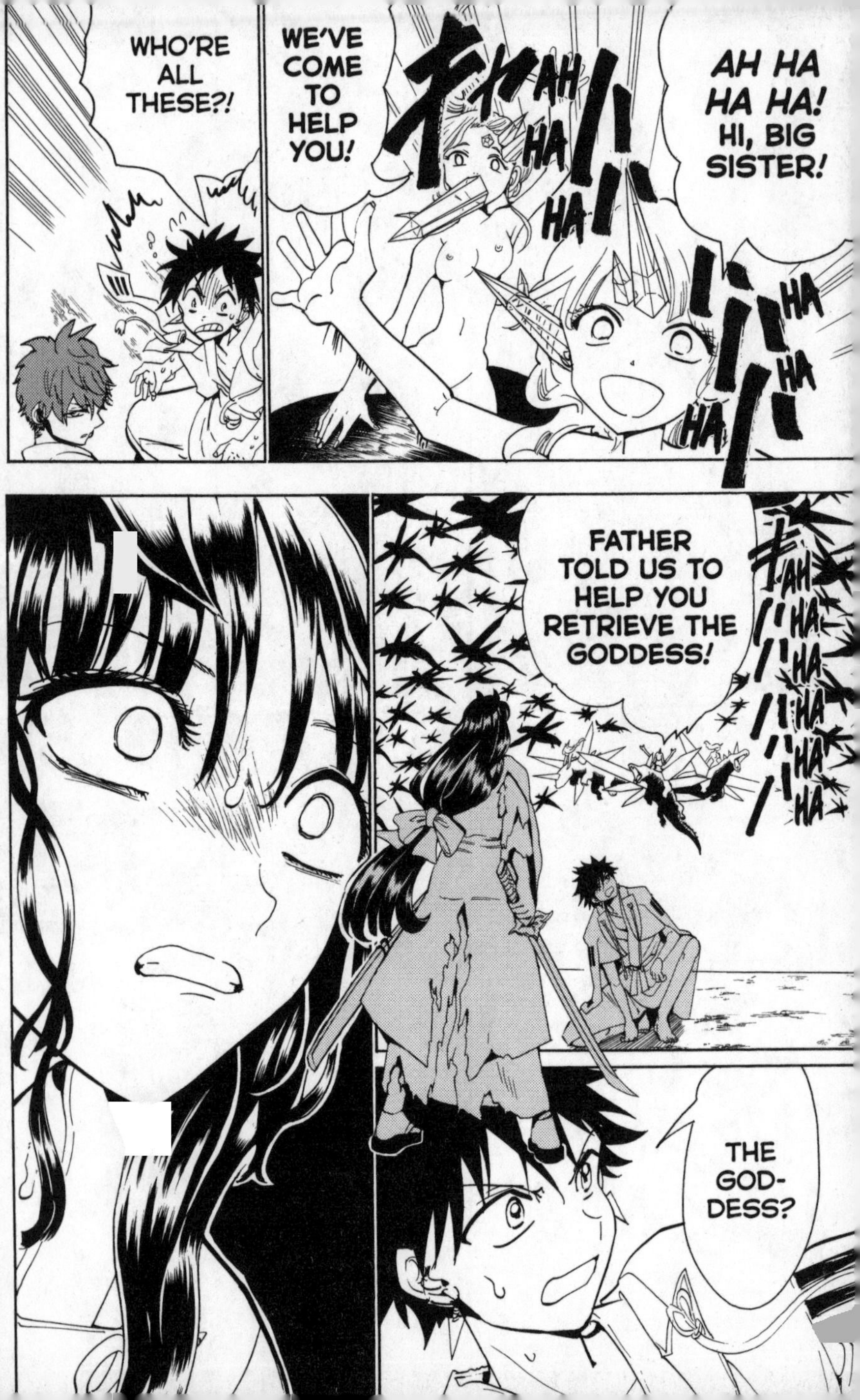
AH HA HA HA! HI, BIG SISTER!
HA HA HA
AH HA HA
WE'VE COME TO HELP YOU!
WHO'RE ALL THESE?!
FATHER TOLD US TO HELP YOU RETRIEVE THE GODDESS!
AH HA HA HA HA HA HA
THE GOD-DESS?

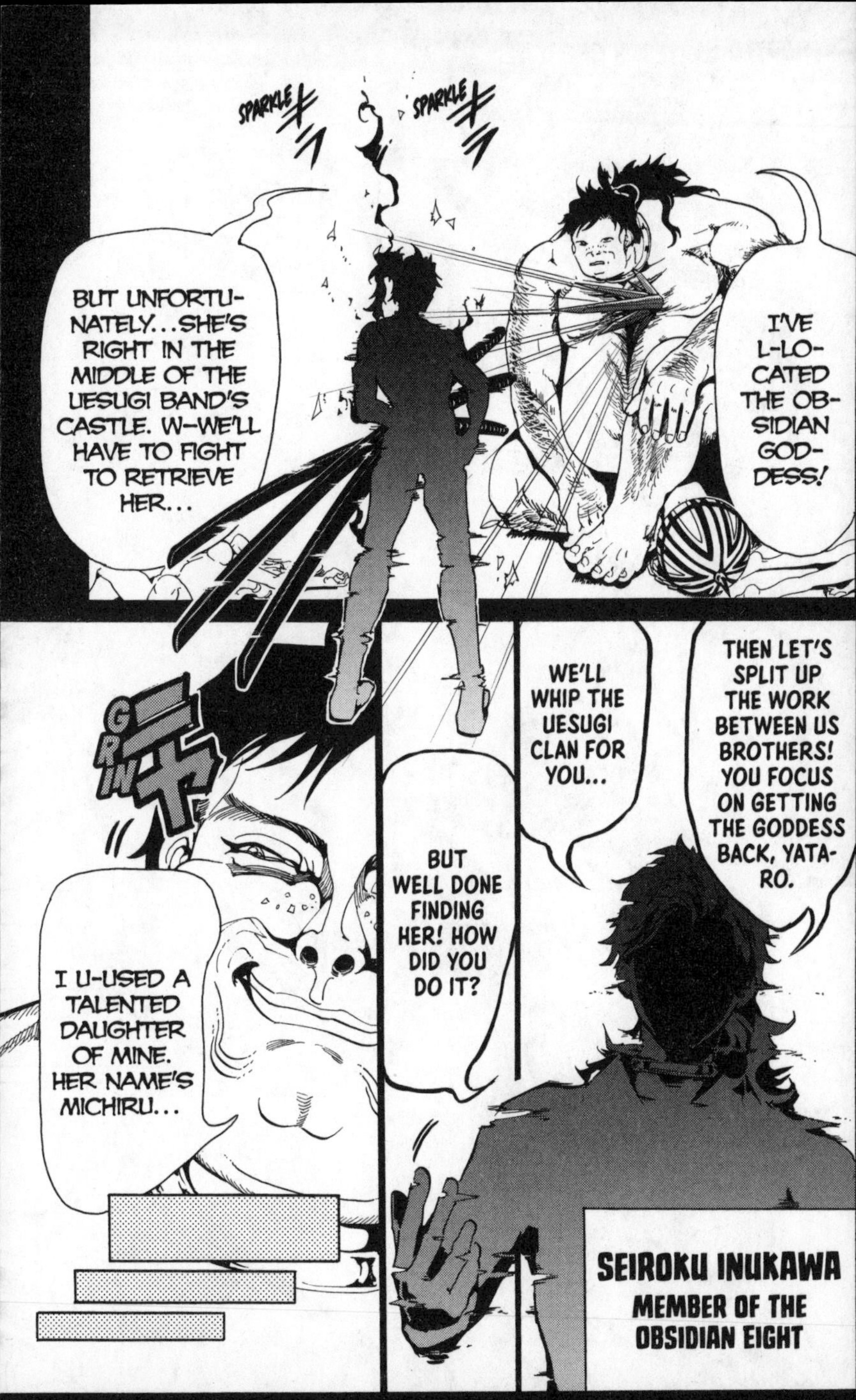
SPARKLE
SPARKLE
I'VE L-LO-CATED THE OB-SIDIAN GOD-DESS!
BUT UNFORTU-NATELY...SHE'S RIGHT IN THE MIDDLE OF THE UESUGI BAND'S CASTLE. W-WE'LL HAVE TO FIGHT TO RETRIEVE HER...
THEN LET'S SPLIT UP THE WORK BETWEEN US BROTHERS! YOU FOCUS ON GETTING THE GODDESS BACK, YATA-RO.
WE'LL WHIP THE UESUGI CLAN FOR YOU...
BUT WELL DONE FINDING HER! HOW DID YOU DO IT?
SEIROKU INUKAWA
MEMBER OF THE OBSIDIAN EIGHT
GRIN
I U-USED A TALENTED DAUGHTER OF MINE. HER NAME'S MICHIRU...

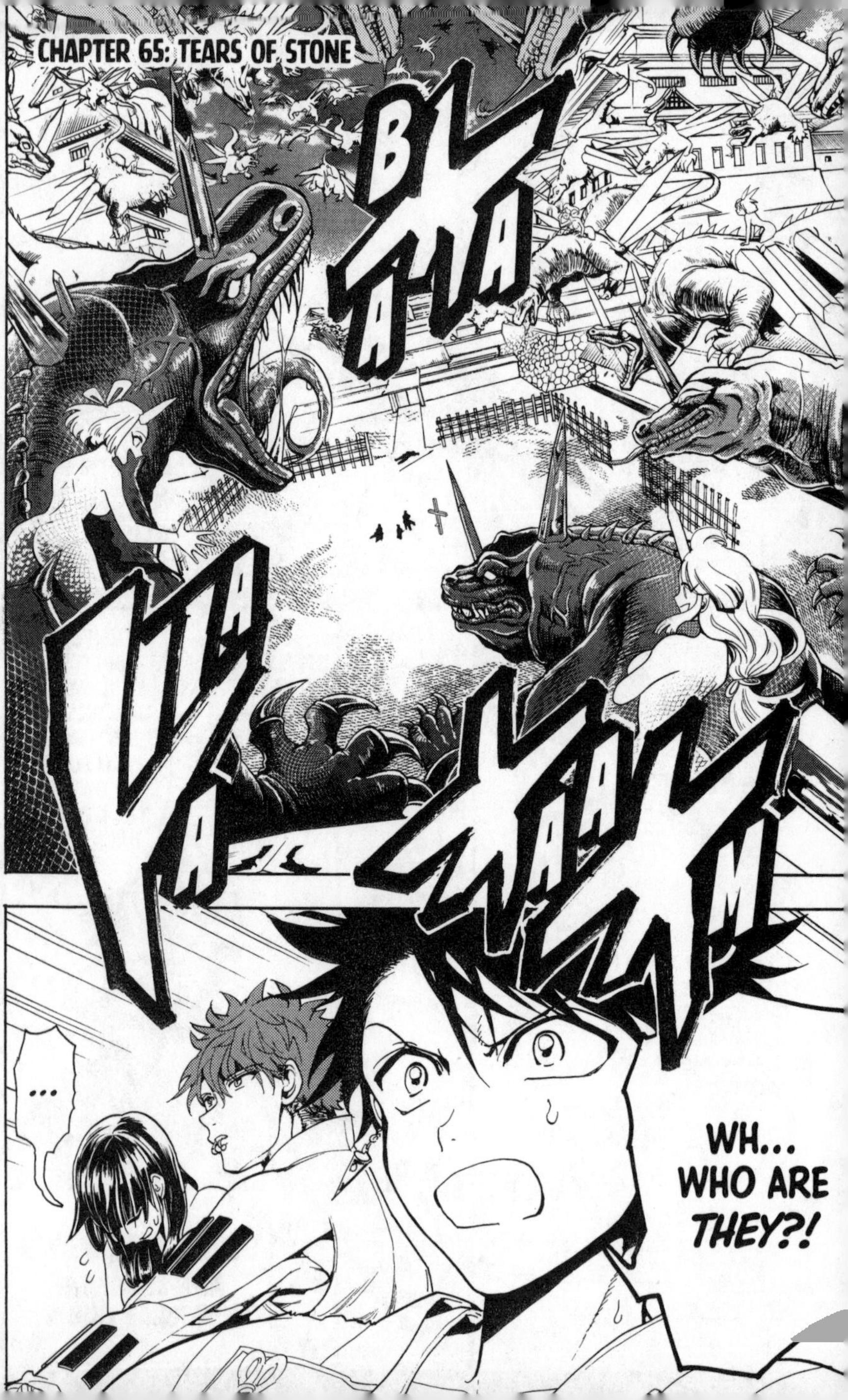
CHAPTER 65: TEARS OF STONE
BWAAA
WAAA
WAAAM
WH... WHO ARE THEY?!
...

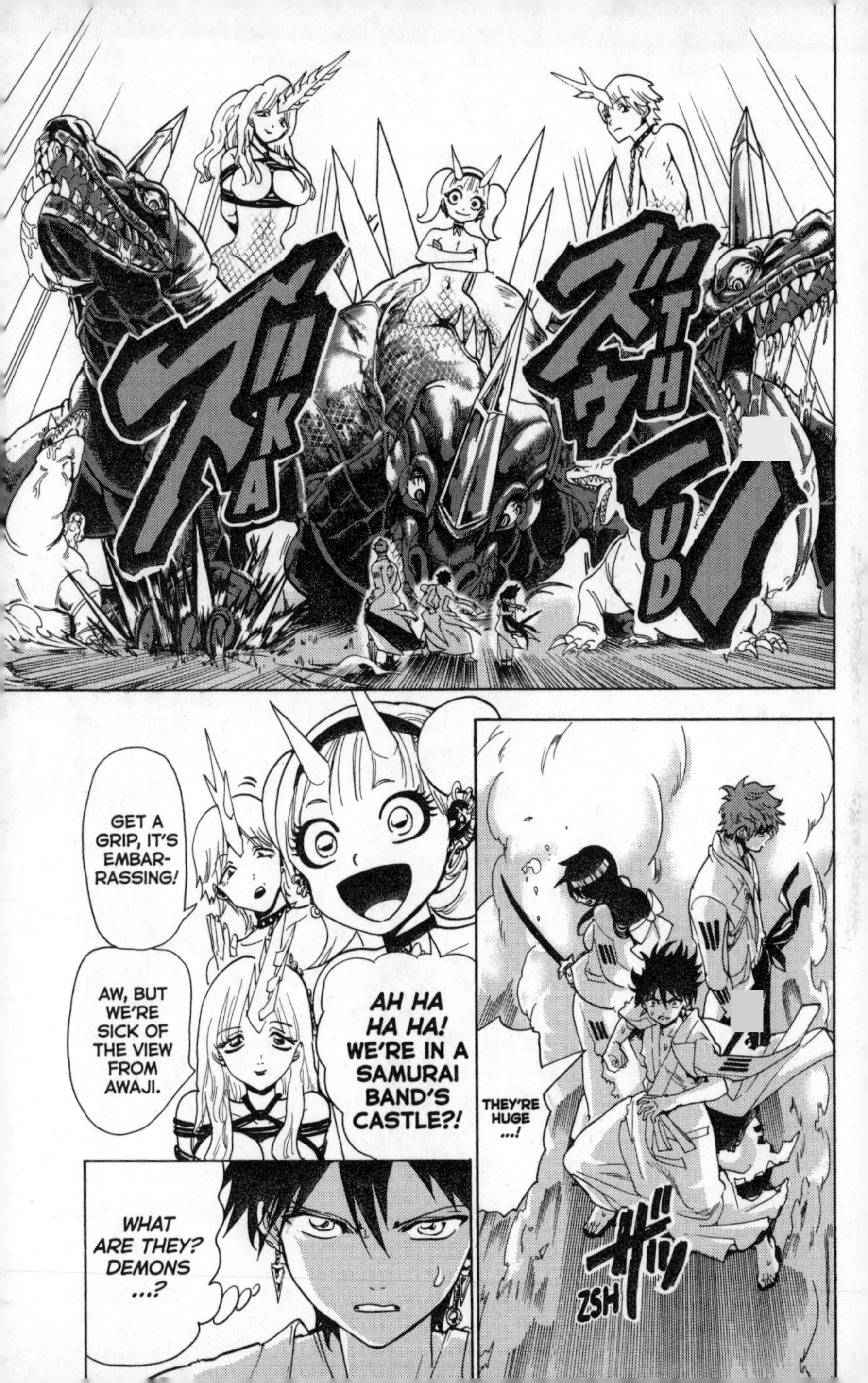
THUD
KA
THEY'RE HUGE ...!
ZSH
AH HA HA HA! WE'RE IN A SAMURAI BAND'S CASTLE?!
GET A GRIP, IT'S EMBAR-RASSING!
AW, BUT WE'RE SICK OF THE VIEW FROM AWAJI.
WHAT ARE THEY? DEMONS ...?

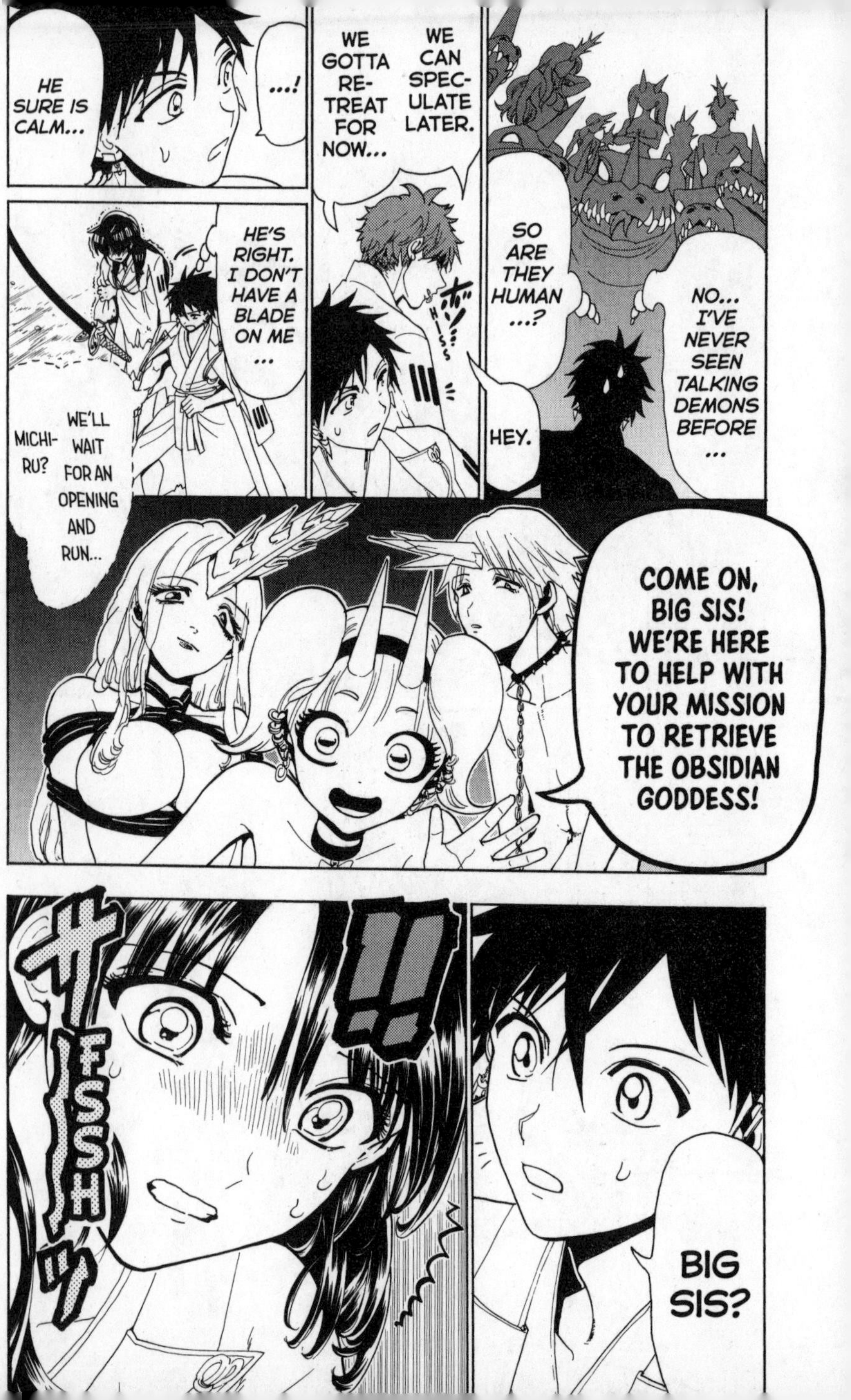
SO ARE THEY HUMAN ...?
NO... I'VE NEVER SEEN TALKING DEMONS BEFORE ...
HEY.
WE CAN SPECULATE LATER.
WE GOTTA RETREAT FOR NOW...
HISS
HE SURE IS CALM...
...!
HE'S RIGHT. I DON'T HAVE A BLADE ON ME ...
WE'LL WAIT FOR AN OPENING AND RUN...
MICHIRU?
COME ON, BIG SIS! WE'RE HERE TO HELP WITH YOUR MISSION TO RETRIEVE THE OBSIDIAN GODDESS!
BIG SIS?
FSSH
!!

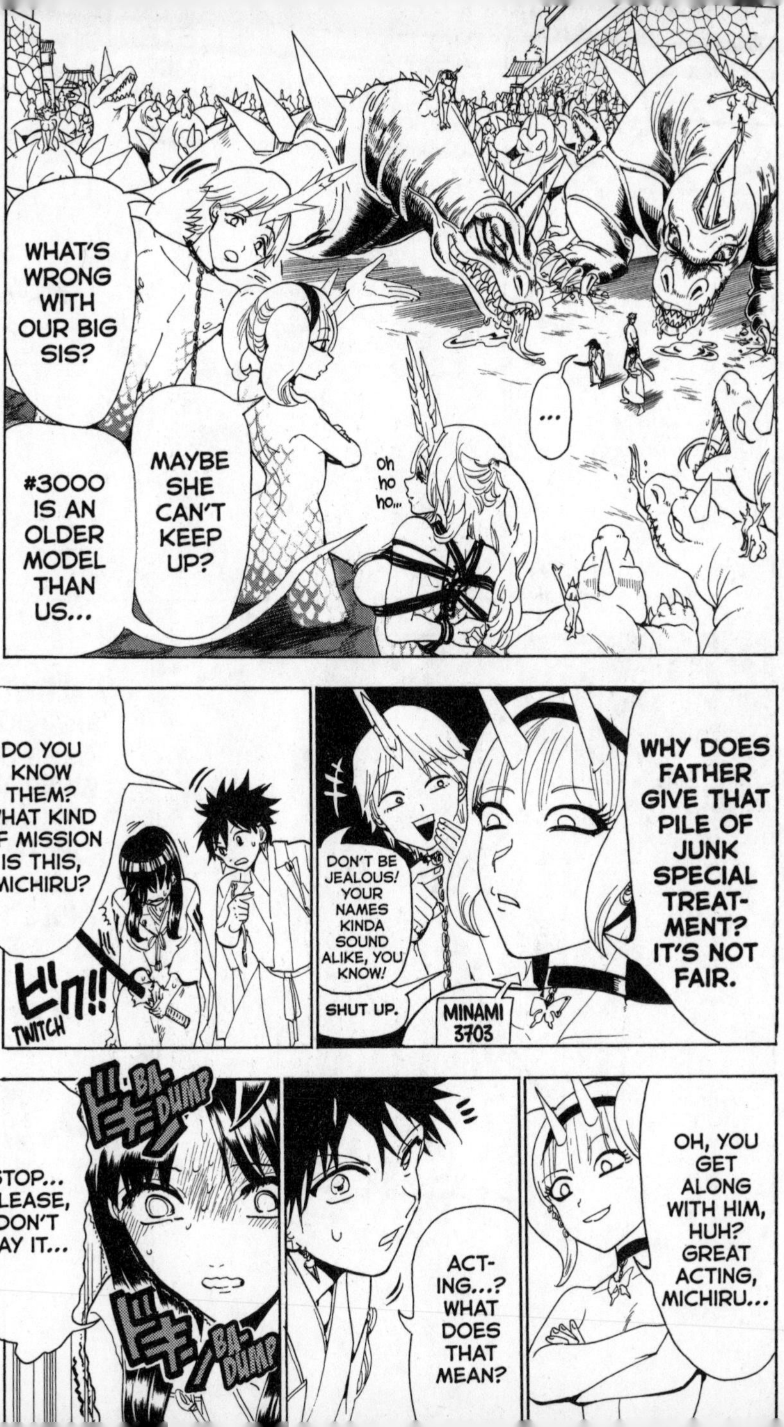
WHAT'S WRONG WITH OUR BIG SIS?
MAYBE SHE CAN'T KEEP UP?
#3000 IS AN OLDER MODEL THAN US...
oh ho ho...
...
WHY DOES FATHER GIVE THAT PILE OF JUNK SPECIAL TREATMENT? IT'S NOT FAIR.
DON'T BE JEALOUS! YOUR NAMES KINDA SOUND ALIKE, YOU KNOW!
SHUT UP.
MINAMI 3703
DO YOU KNOW THEM? WHAT KIND OF MISSION IS THIS, MICHIRU?
ビクッ!! TWITCH
OH, YOU GET ALONG WITH HIM, HUH? GREAT ACTING, MICHIRU...
ACT-ING...? WHAT DOES THAT MEAN?
ドキッ BA-DUMP
STOP... PLEASE, DON'T SAY IT...
ドキッ BA-DUMP

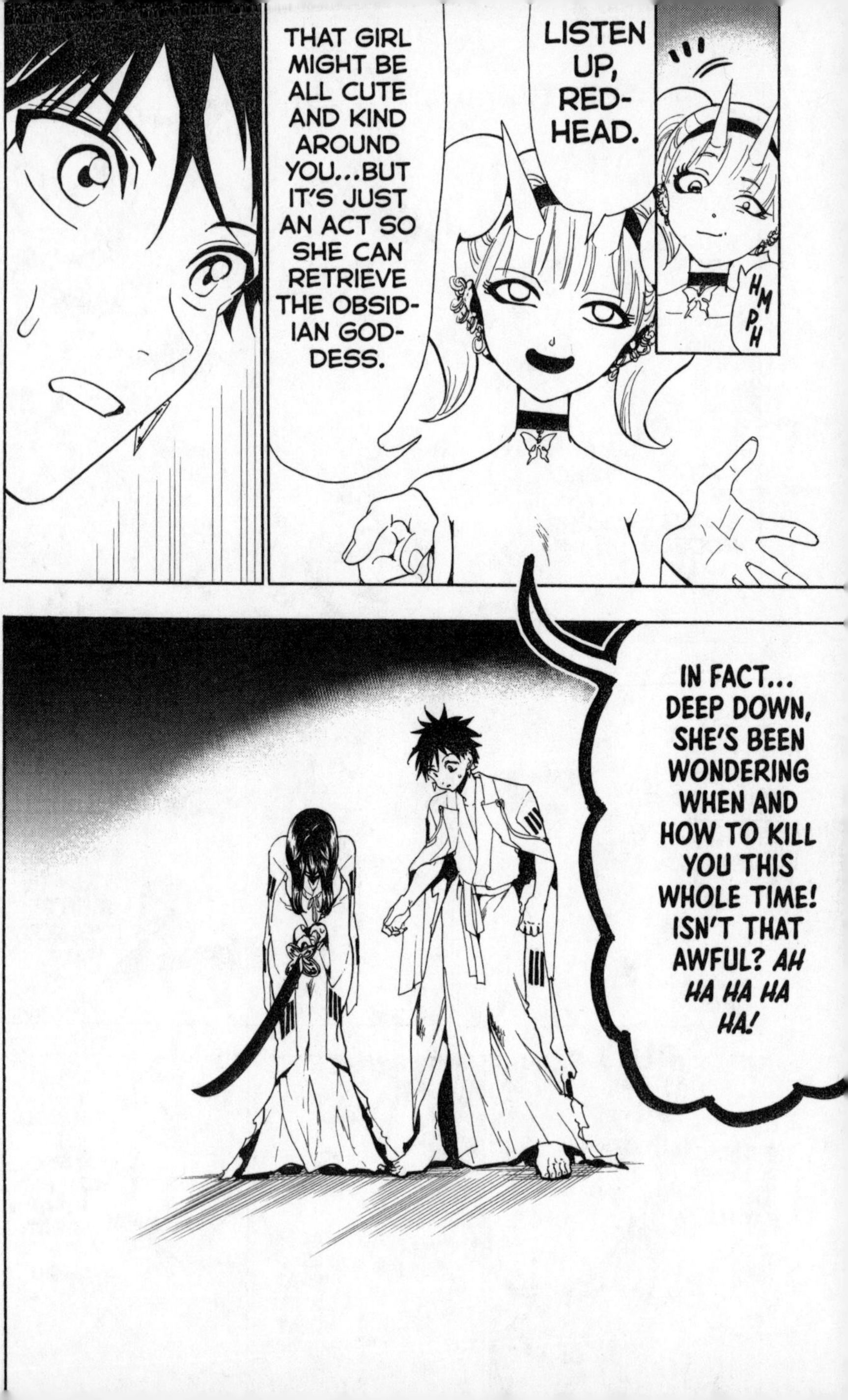
HMPH
LISTEN UP, RED-HEAD.
THAT GIRL MIGHT BE ALL CUTE AND KIND AROUND YOU...BUT IT'S JUST AN ACT SO SHE CAN RETRIEVE THE OBSIDIAN GODDESS.
IN FACT... DEEP DOWN, SHE'S BEEN WONDERING WHEN AND HOW TO KILL YOU THIS WHOLE TIME! ISN'T THAT AWFUL? AH HA HA HA HA!

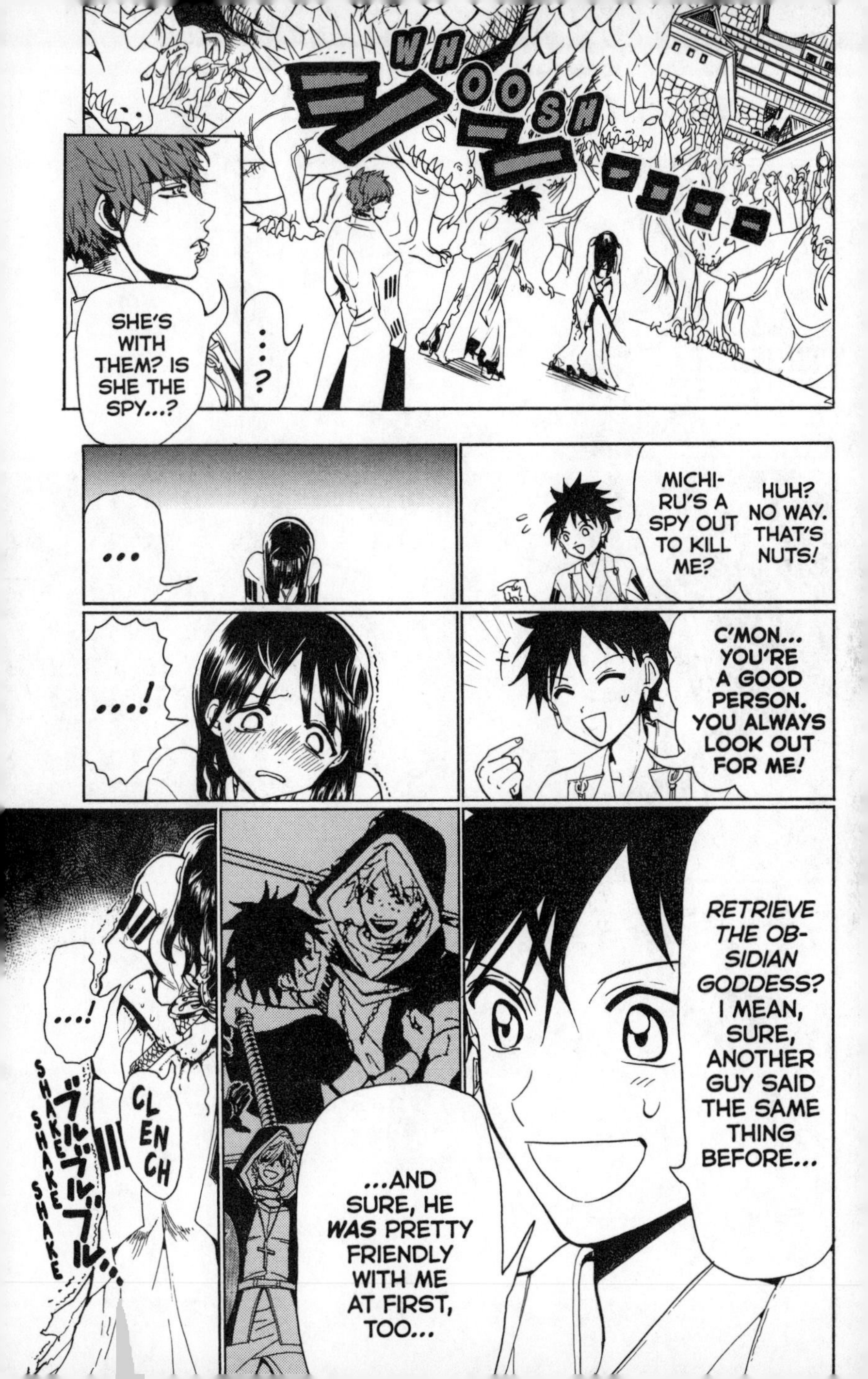
WHOOSH
...?
SHE'S WITH THEM? IS SHE THE SPY...?
HUH? NO WAY. THAT'S NUTS!
MICHI-RU'S A SPY OUT TO KILL ME?
...
C'MON... YOU'RE A GOOD PERSON. YOU ALWAYS LOOK OUT FOR ME!
...!
RETRIEVE THE OB-SIDIAN GODDESS? I MEAN, SURE, ANOTHER GUY SAID THE SAME THING BEFORE...
...AND SURE, HE *WAS* PRETTY FRIENDLY WITH ME AT FIRST, TOO...
...!
CLENCH
SHAKE SHAKE SHAKE
ブルブルブル...

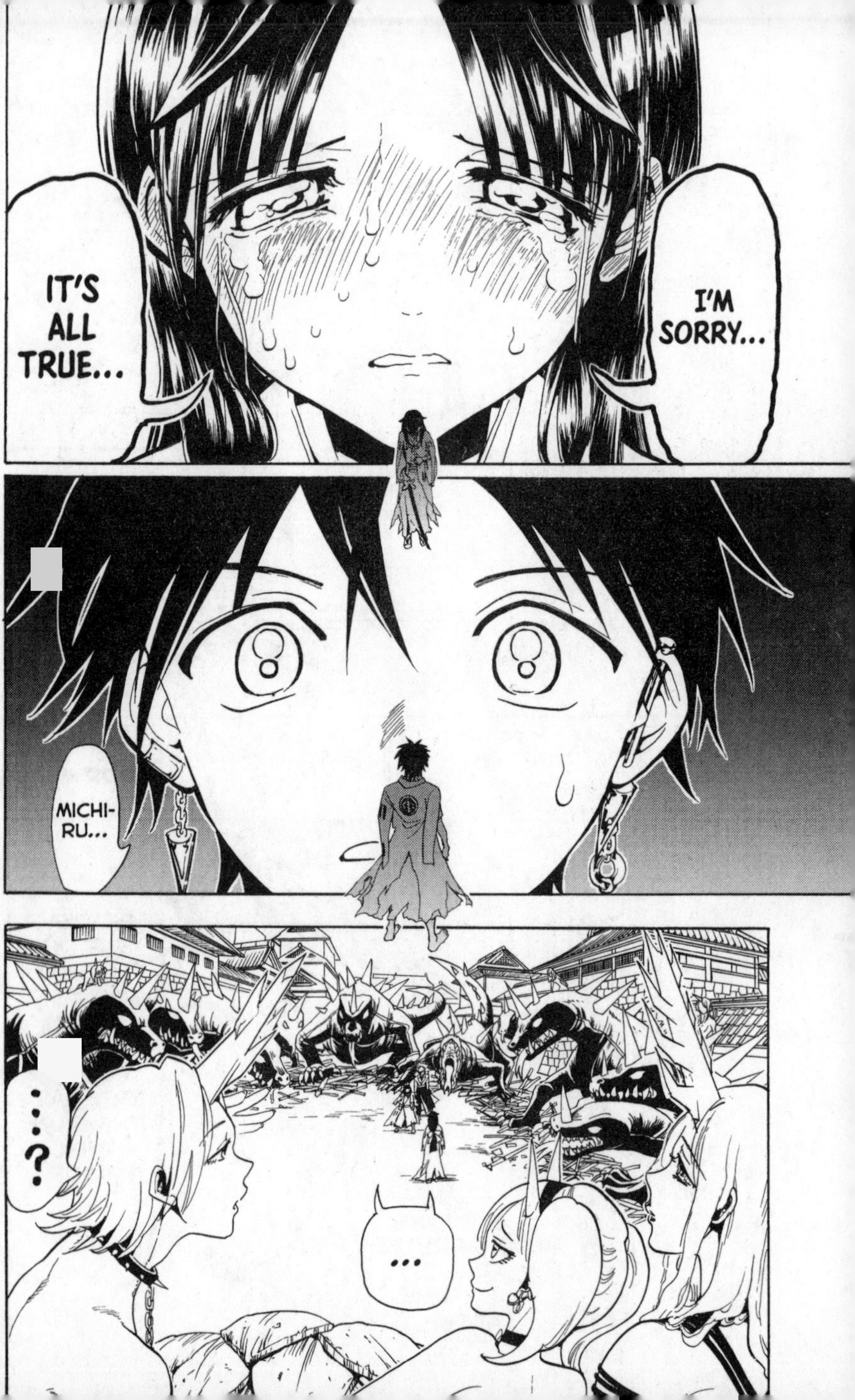
I'M SORRY...
IT'S ALL TRUE...
MICHI-RU...
...
...?

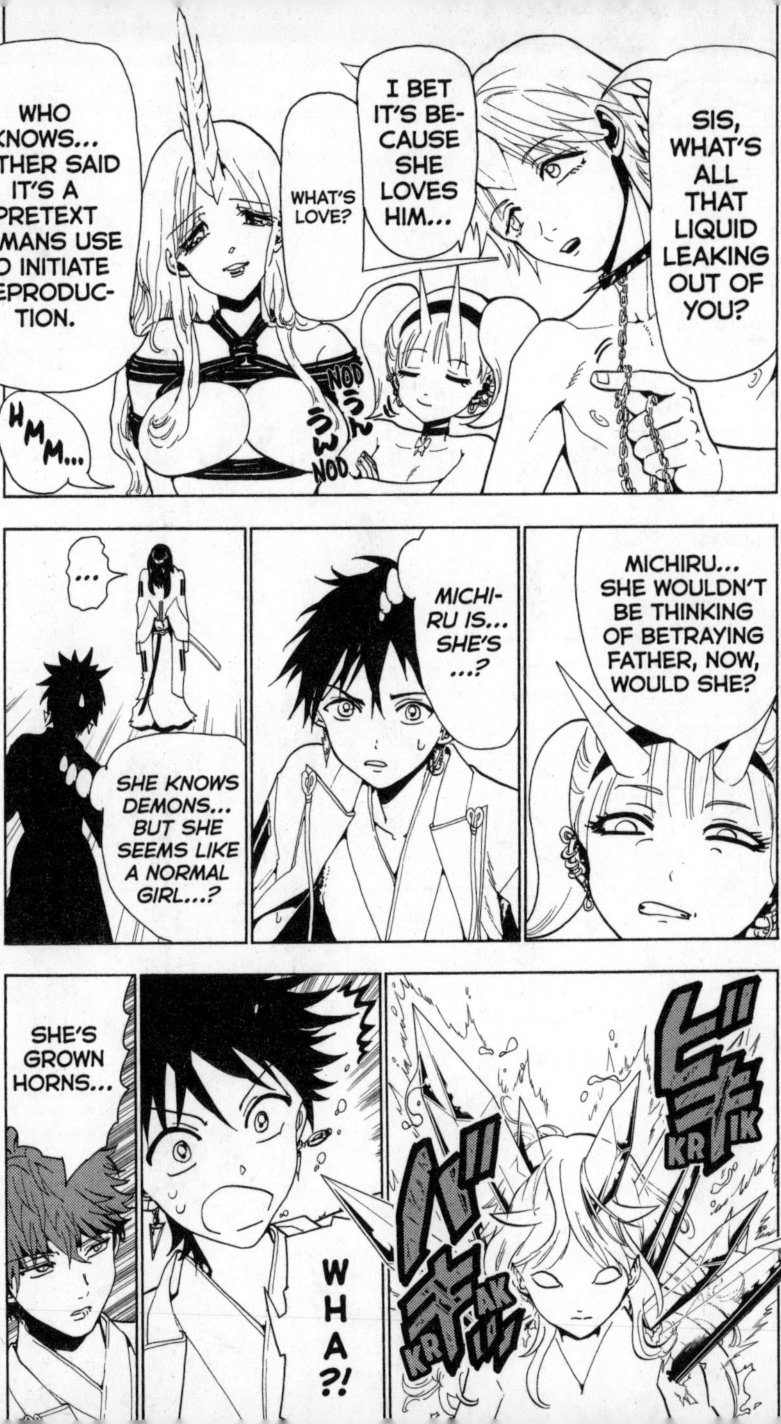
SIS, WHAT'S ALL THAT LIQUID LEAKING OUT OF YOU?
I BET IT'S BE-CAUSE SHE LOVES HIM...
WHAT'S LOVE?
WHO KNOWS... FATHER SAID IT'S A PRETEXT HUMANS USE TO INITIATE REPRODUC-TION.
うん NOD
うん NOD
HMM...
MICHIRU... SHE WOULDN'T BE THINKING OF BETRAYING FATHER, NOW, WOULD SHE?
MICHI-RU IS... SHE'S ...?
...
SHE KNOWS DEMONS... BUT SHE SEEMS LIKE A NORMAL GIRL...?
ビキ KRIK
バキ KRAK
WHA?!
SHE'S GROWN HORNS...

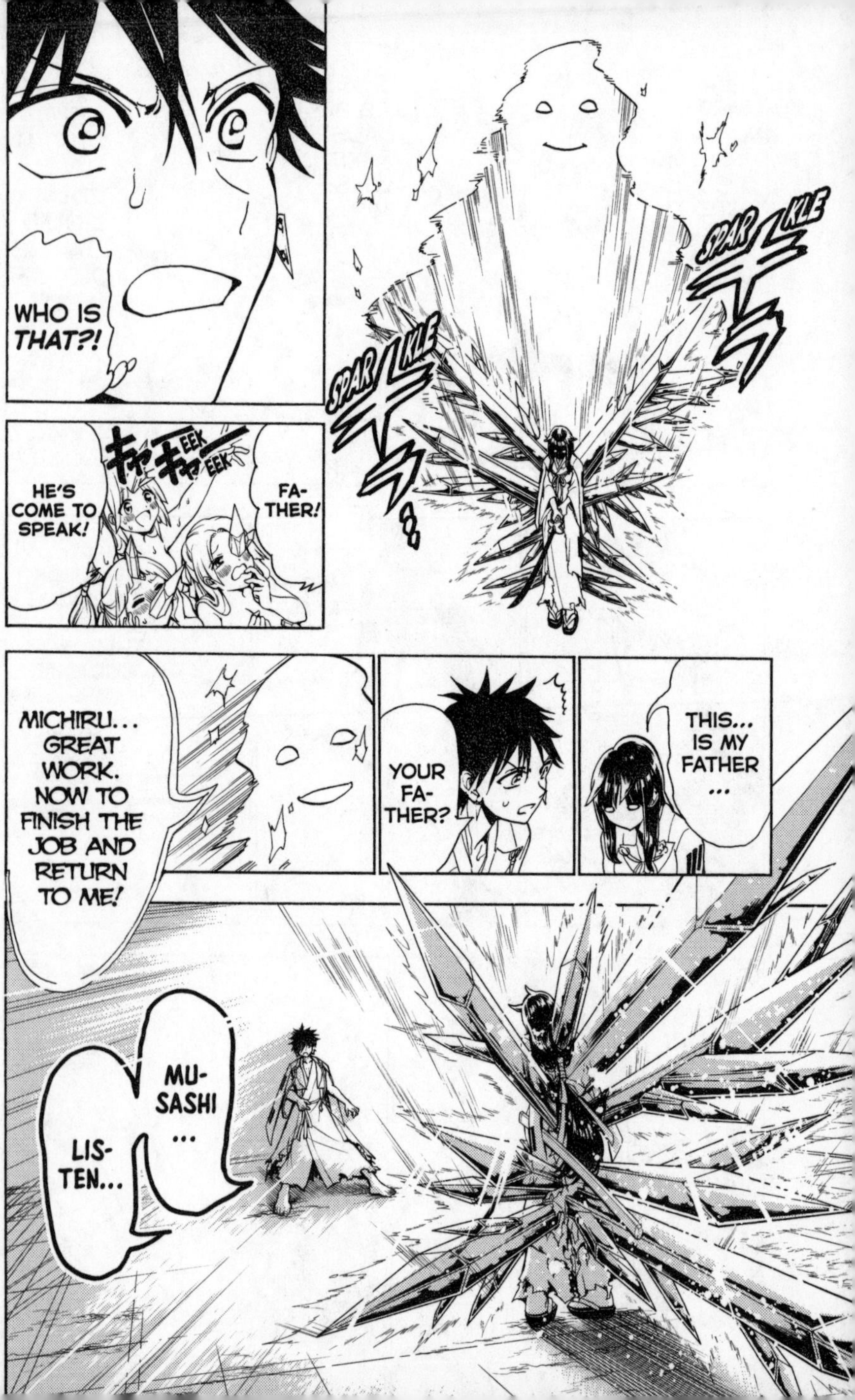
SPARKLE
SPARKLE
WHO IS THAT?!
FATHER!
EEK EEK
HE'S COME TO SPEAK!
THIS... IS MY FATHER...
YOUR FATHER?
MICHIRU... GREAT WORK. NOW TO FINISH THE JOB AND RETURN TO ME!
MUSASHI...
LISTEN...

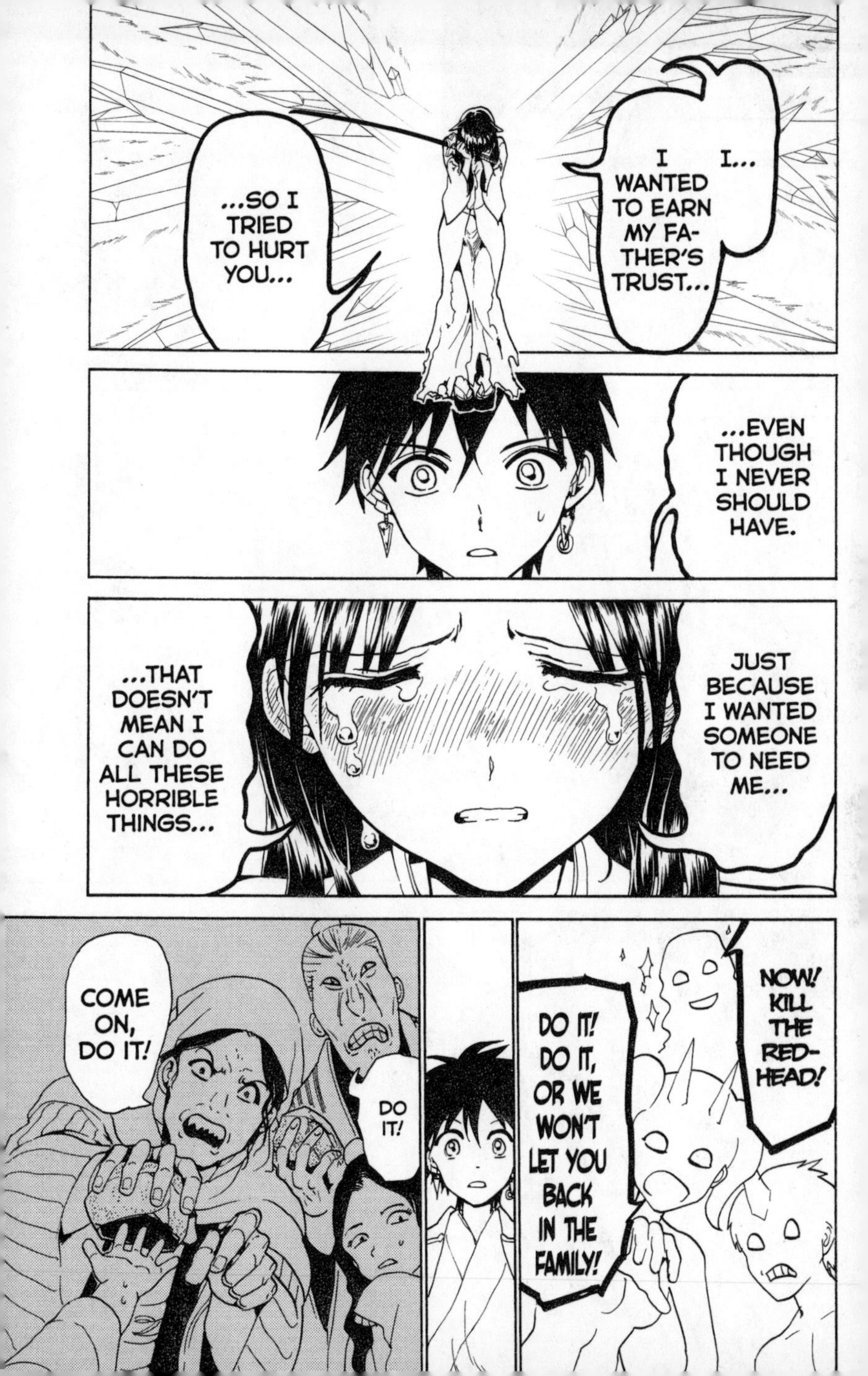
I... I WANTED TO EARN MY FA-THER'S TRUST...
...SO I TRIED TO HURT YOU...
...EVEN THOUGH I NEVER SHOULD HAVE.
JUST BECAUSE I WANTED SOMEONE TO NEED ME...
...THAT DOESN'T MEAN I CAN DO ALL THESE HORRIBLE THINGS...
NOW! KILL THE RED-HEAD!
DO IT! DO IT, OR WE WON'T LET YOU BACK IN THE FAMILY!
DO IT!
COME ON, DO IT!

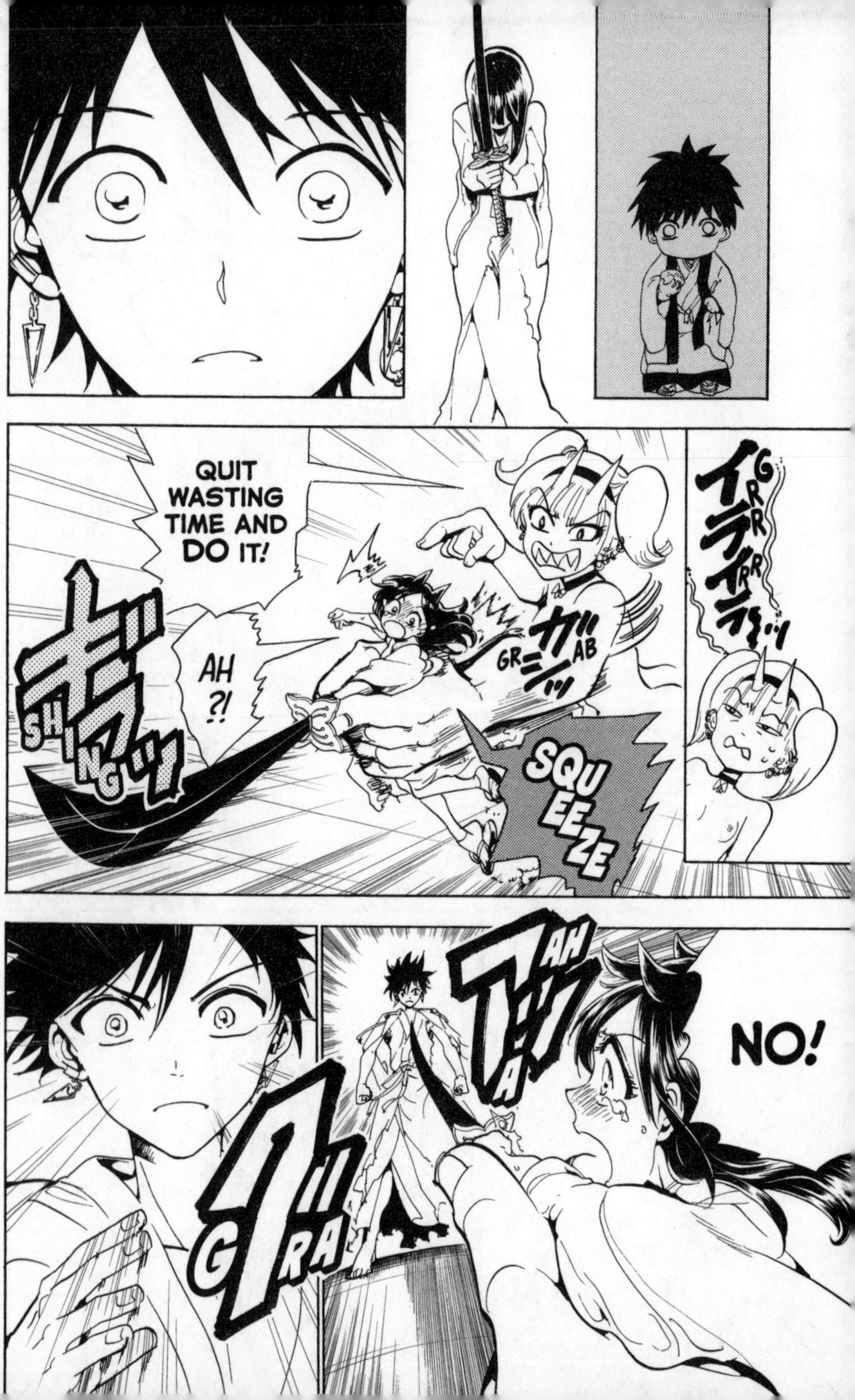
GRRRRR
QUIT WASTING TIME AND DO IT!
GRAB
AH ?!
SQUEEZE
SHING
NO!
AAH
GRA

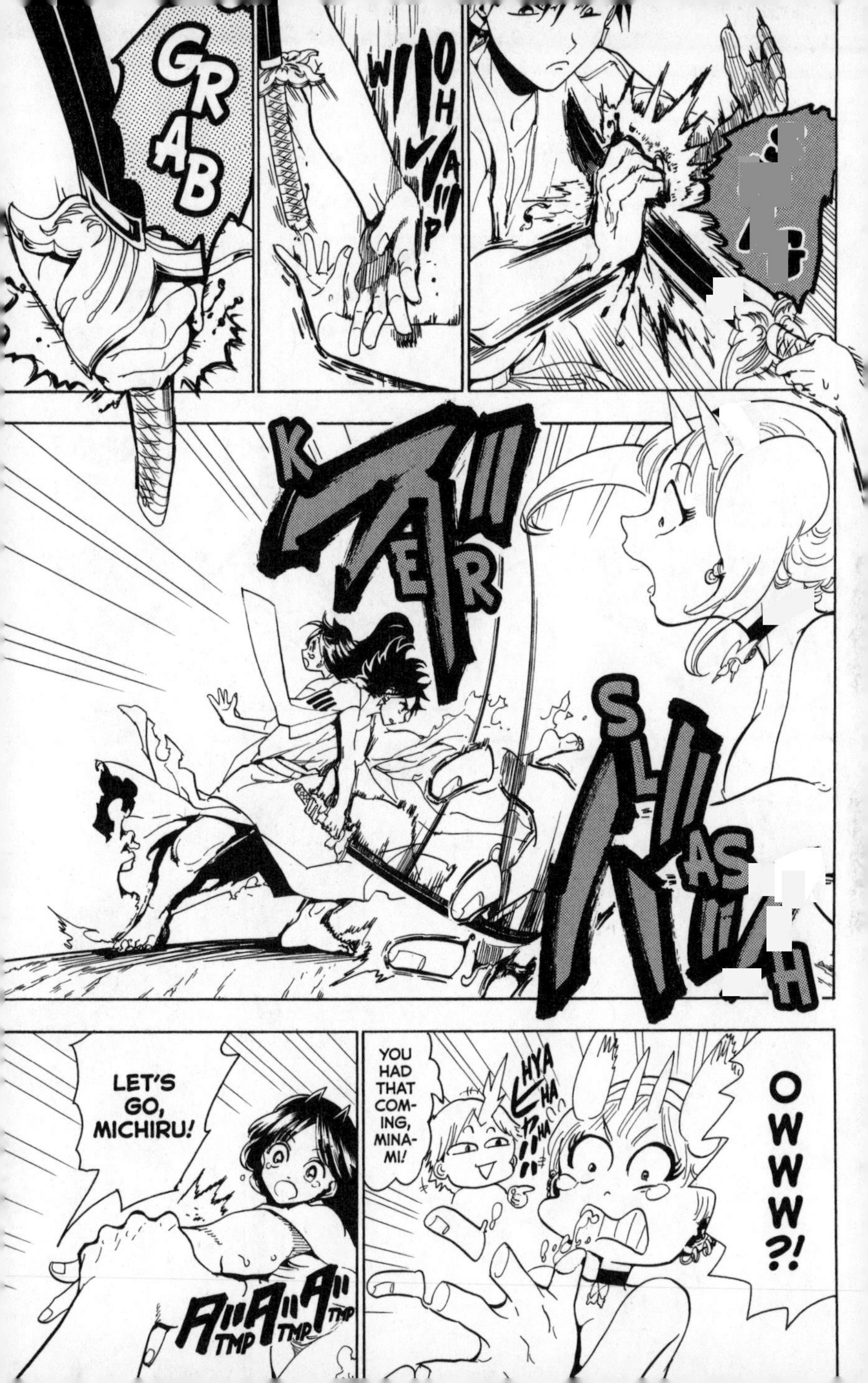
WHOAP
GRAB
SLASH
OWWW?!
HYA HA HA HA
YOU HAD THAT COMING, MINAMI!
LET'S GO, MICHIRU!
TMP TMP TMP

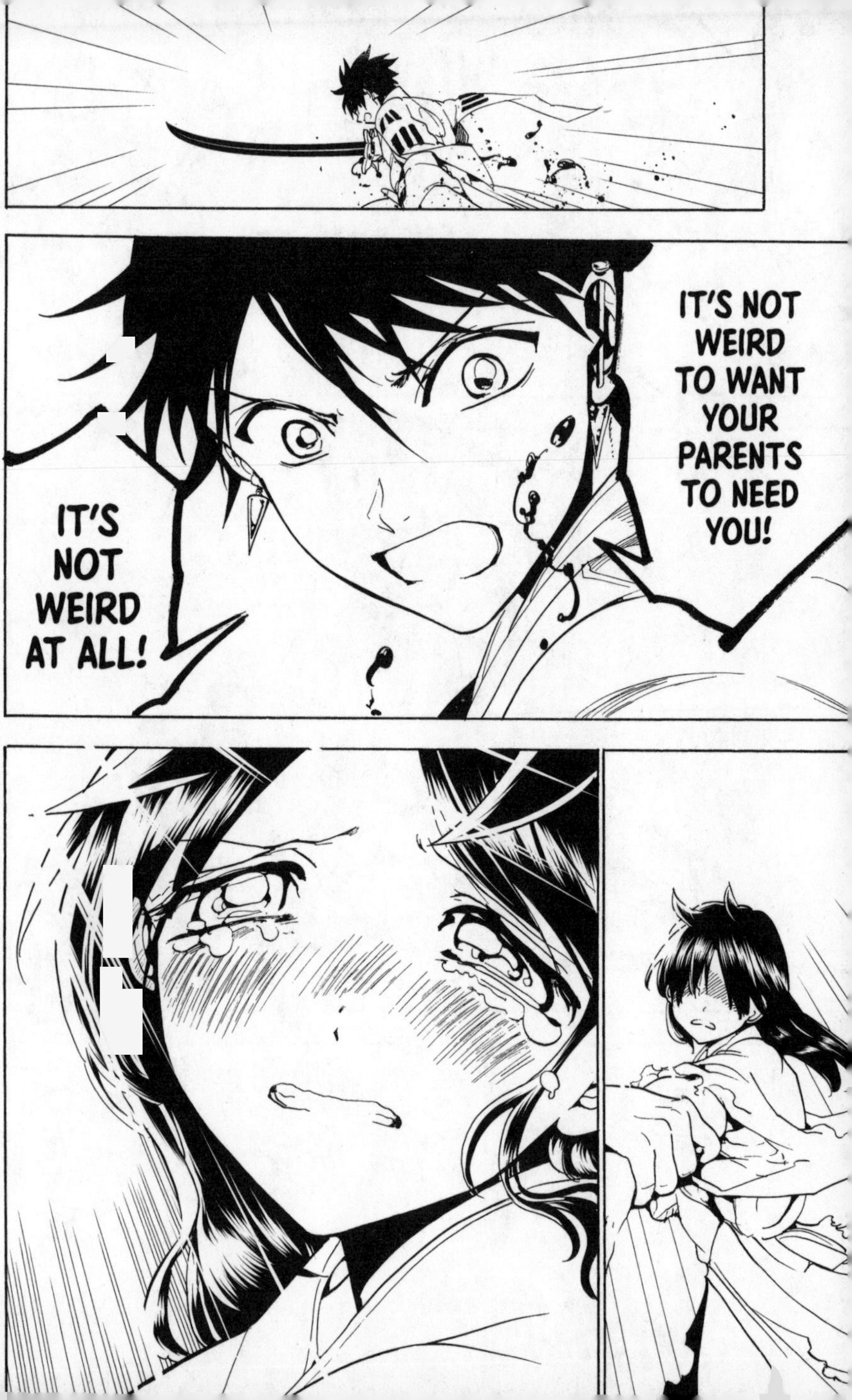
IT'S NOT WEIRD TO WANT YOUR PARENTS TO NEED YOU!
IT'S NOT WEIRD AT ALL!

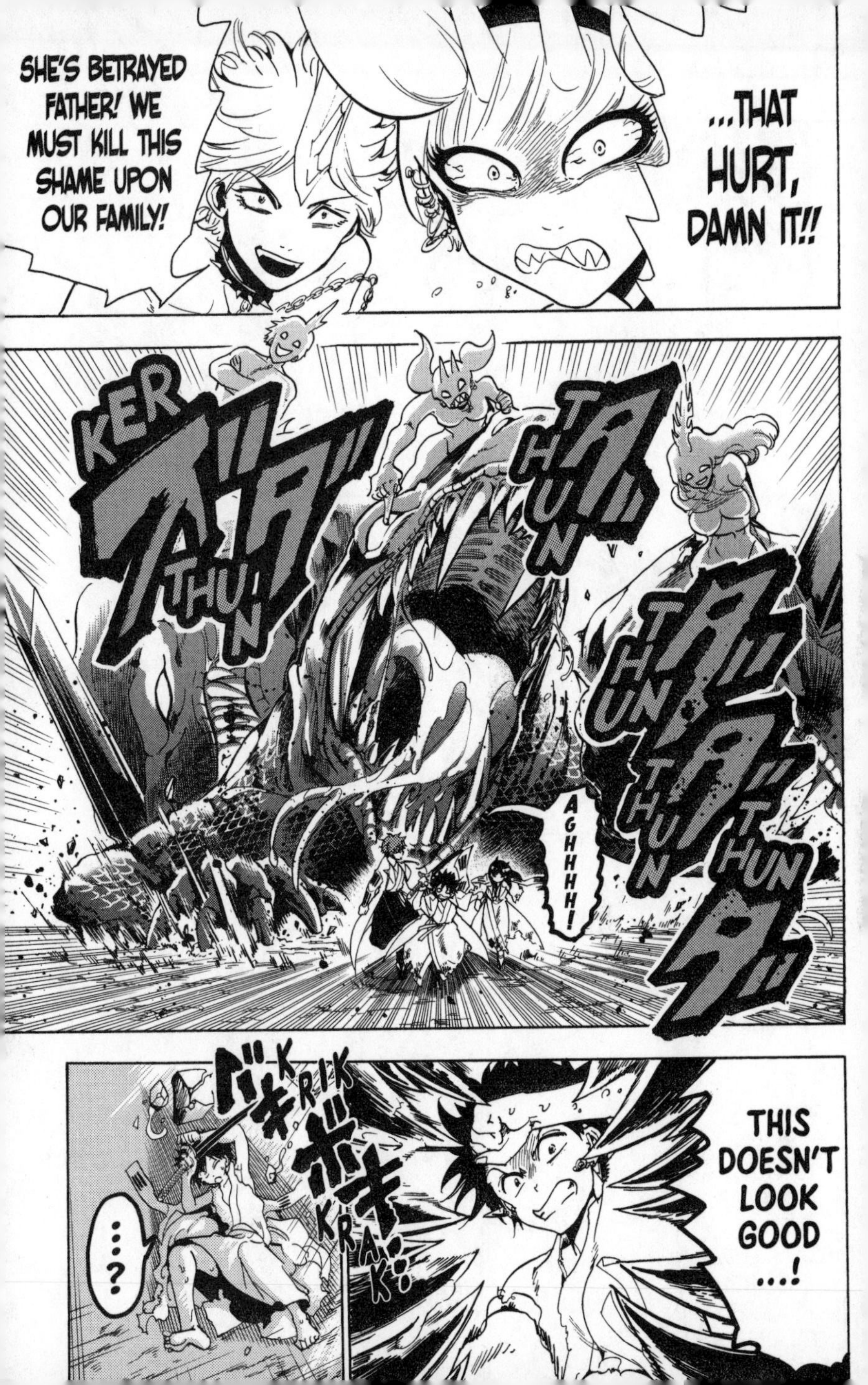
...THAT HURT, DAMN IT!!
SHE'S BETRAYED FATHER! WE MUST KILL THIS SHAME UPON OUR FAMILY!
THUNN
THUNN THUNN
THUNN
KER THUNN
AGHHHHH!
THIS DOESN'T LOOK GOOD ...!
バキ ボキ
KRIK KRAK
...?

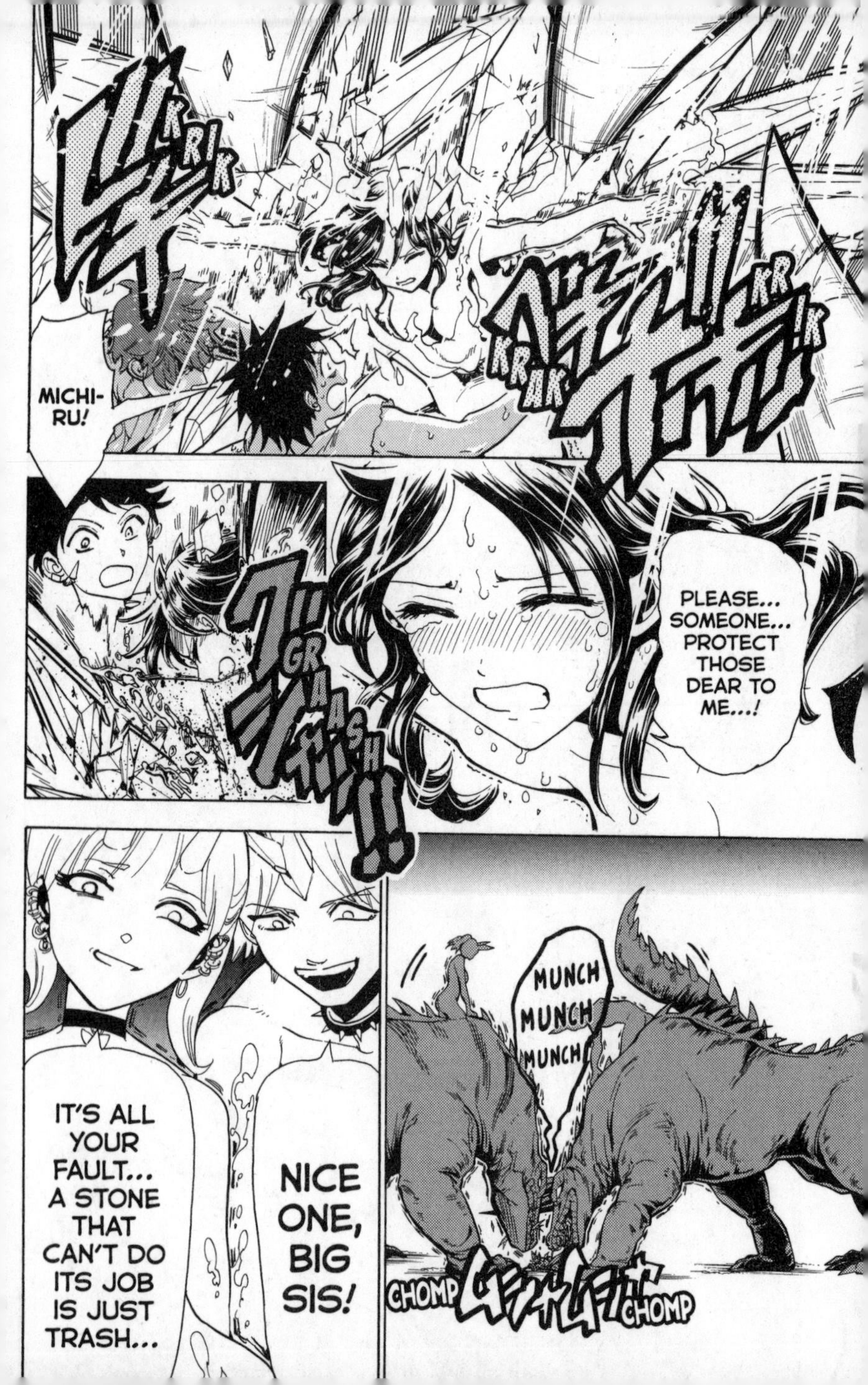
KRAK KRIK
KRIK
PLEASE... SOMEONE... PROTECT THOSE DEAR TO ME...!
GRAASH!!
MICHI-RU!
MUNCH MUNCH MUNCH
CHOMP CHOMP
NICE ONE, BIG SIS!
IT'S ALL YOUR FAULT... A STONE THAT CAN'T DO ITS JOB IS JUST TRASH...

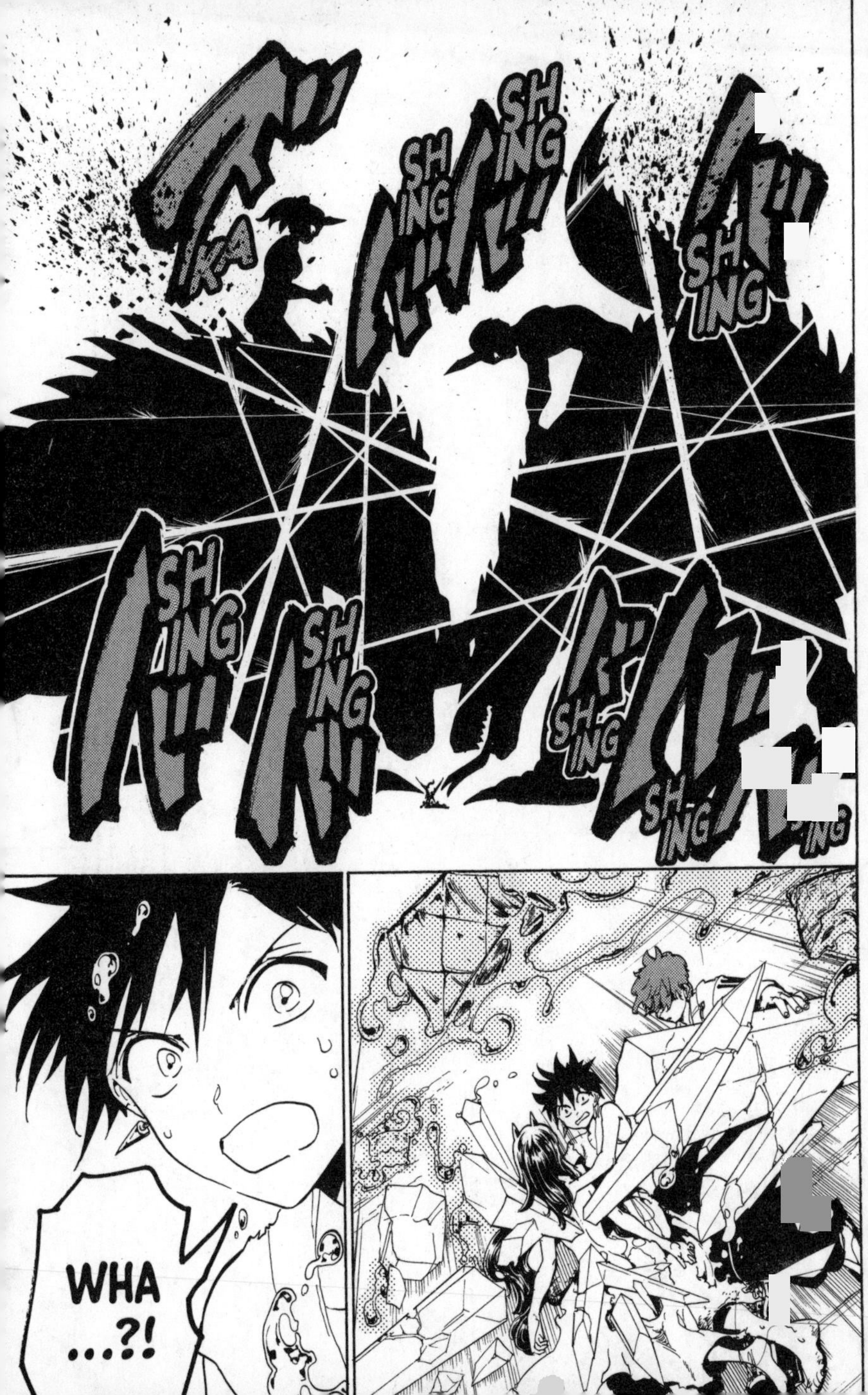
SHING
SHING
SHING
KA
SHING
SHING
SHING
SHING
WHA ...?!

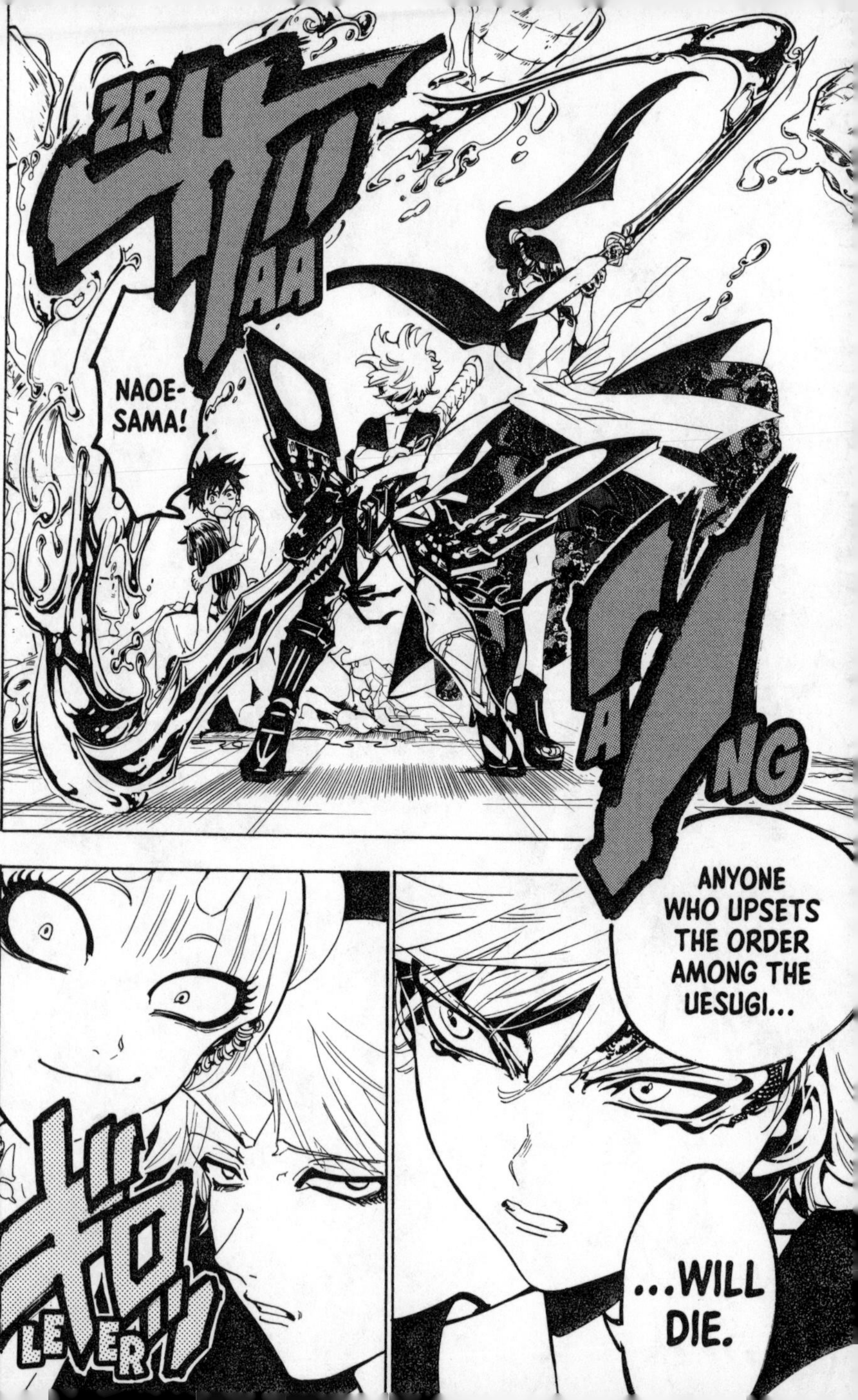
ZR AA
NAOE-SAMA!
A NG
ANYONE WHO UPSETS THE ORDER AMONG THE UESUGI...
...WILL DIE.
LE ER!!

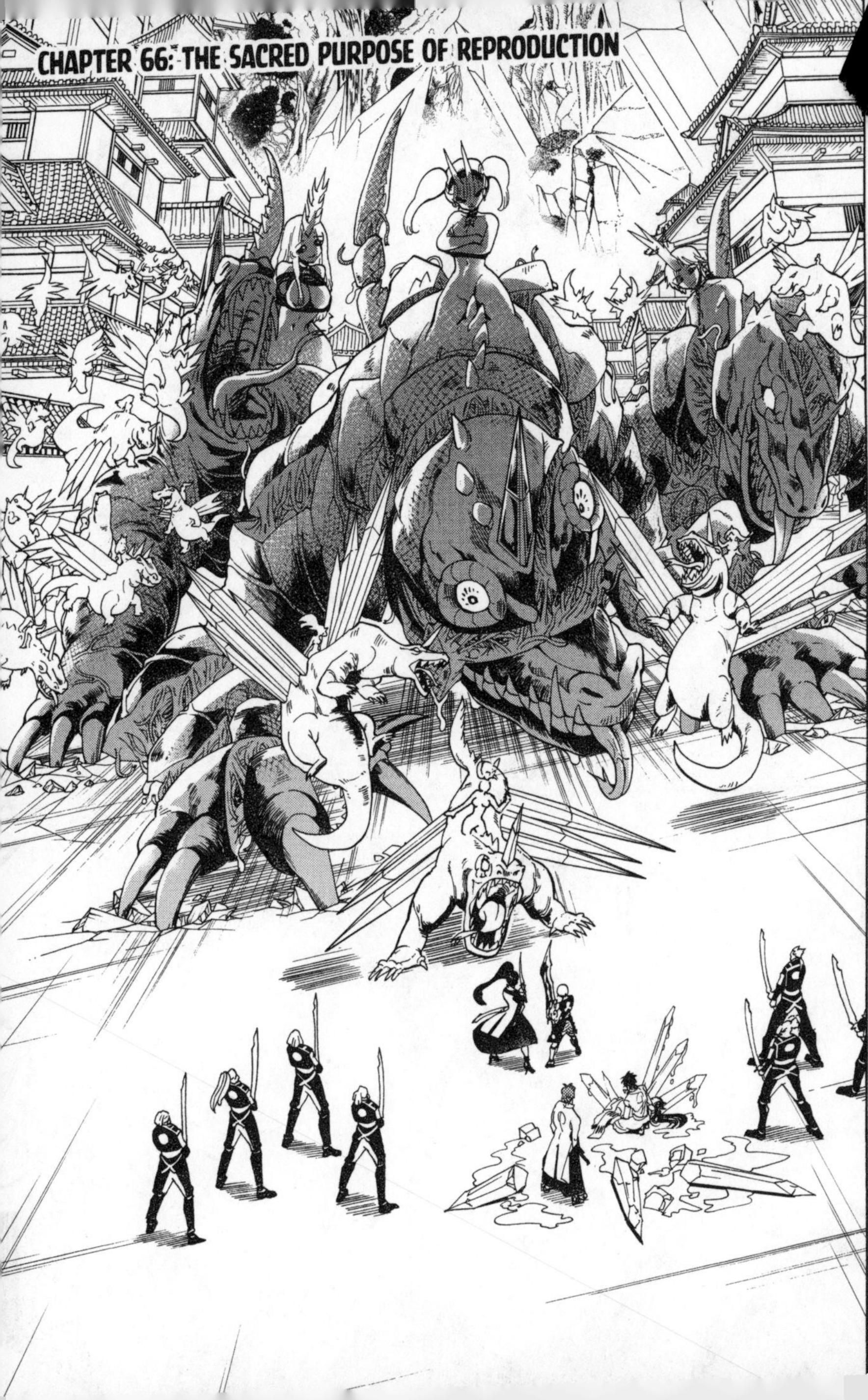
CHAPTER 66: THE SACRED PURPOSE OF REPRODUCTION

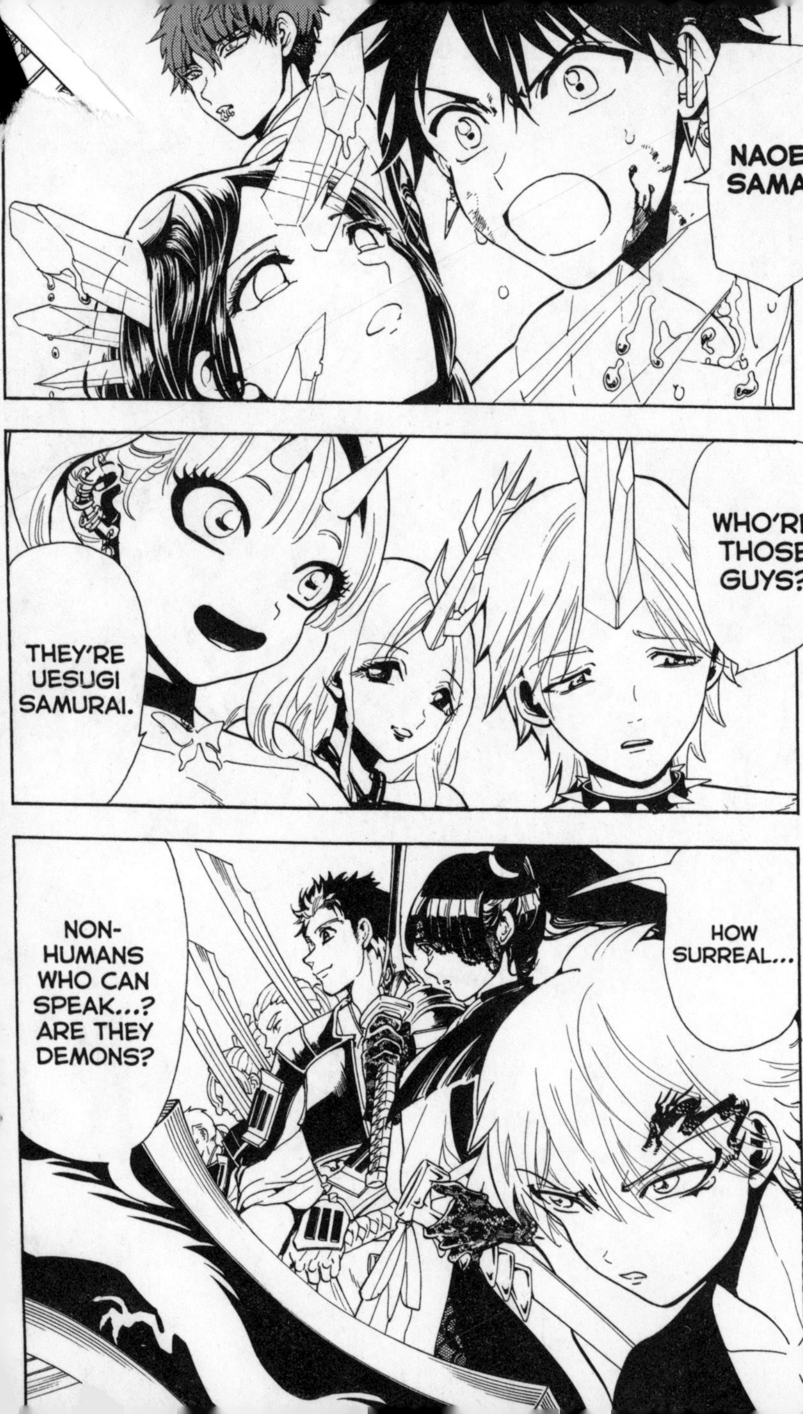
NAOE-SAMA!
WHO'RE THOSE GUYS?
THEY'RE UESUGI SAMURAI.
HOW SURREAL...
NON-HUMANS WHO CAN SPEAK...? ARE THEY DEMONS?

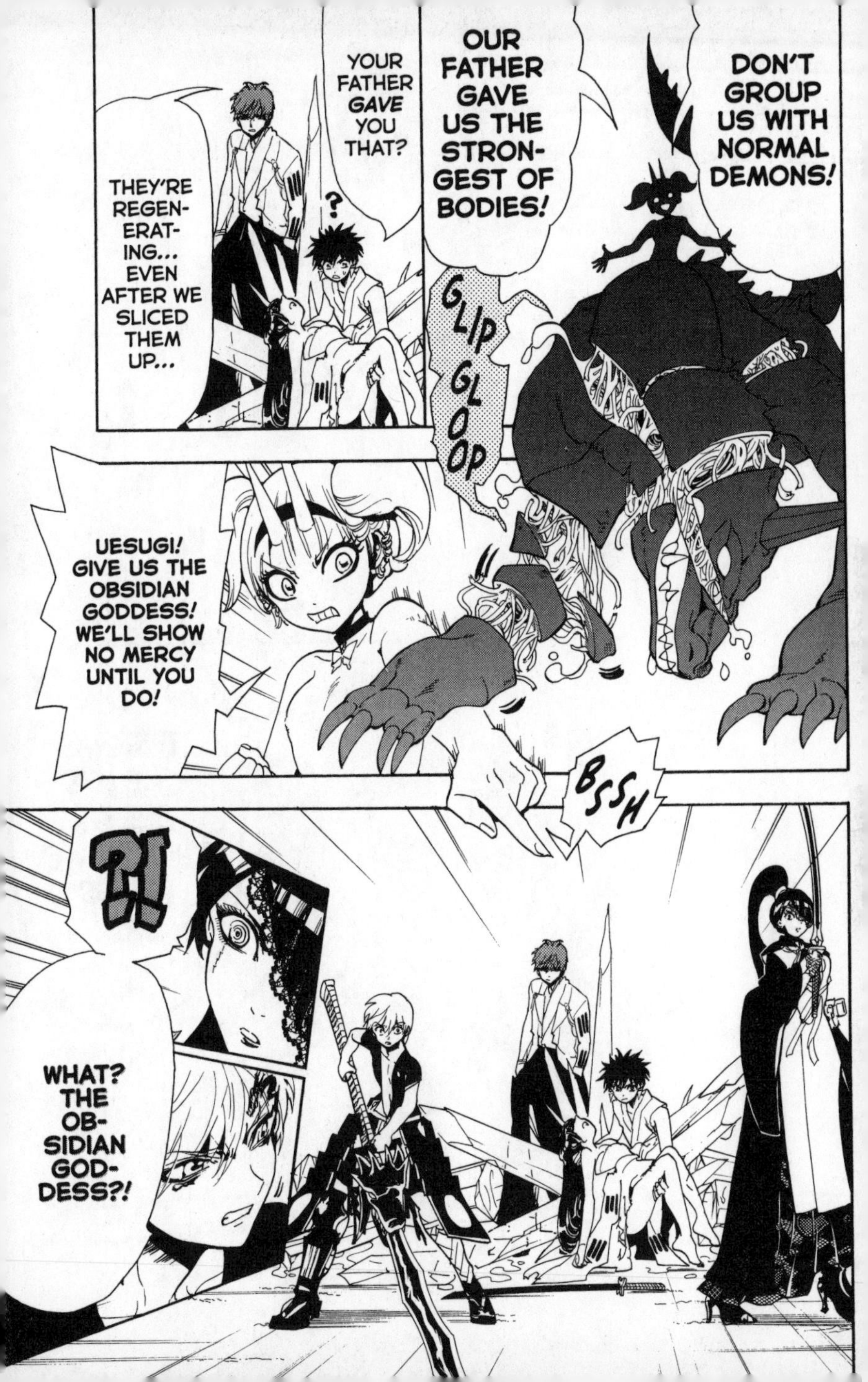
DON'T GROUP US WITH NORMAL DEMONS!
OUR FATHER GAVE US THE STRON-GEST OF BODIES!
GLIP GLOOP
YOUR FATHER GAVE YOU THAT?
?
THEY'RE REGEN-ERAT-ING... EVEN AFTER WE SLICED THEM UP...
UESUGI! GIVE US THE OBSIDIAN GODDESS! WE'LL SHOW NO MERCY UNTIL YOU DO!
BSSH
?!
WHAT? THE OB-SIDIAN GOD-DESS?!

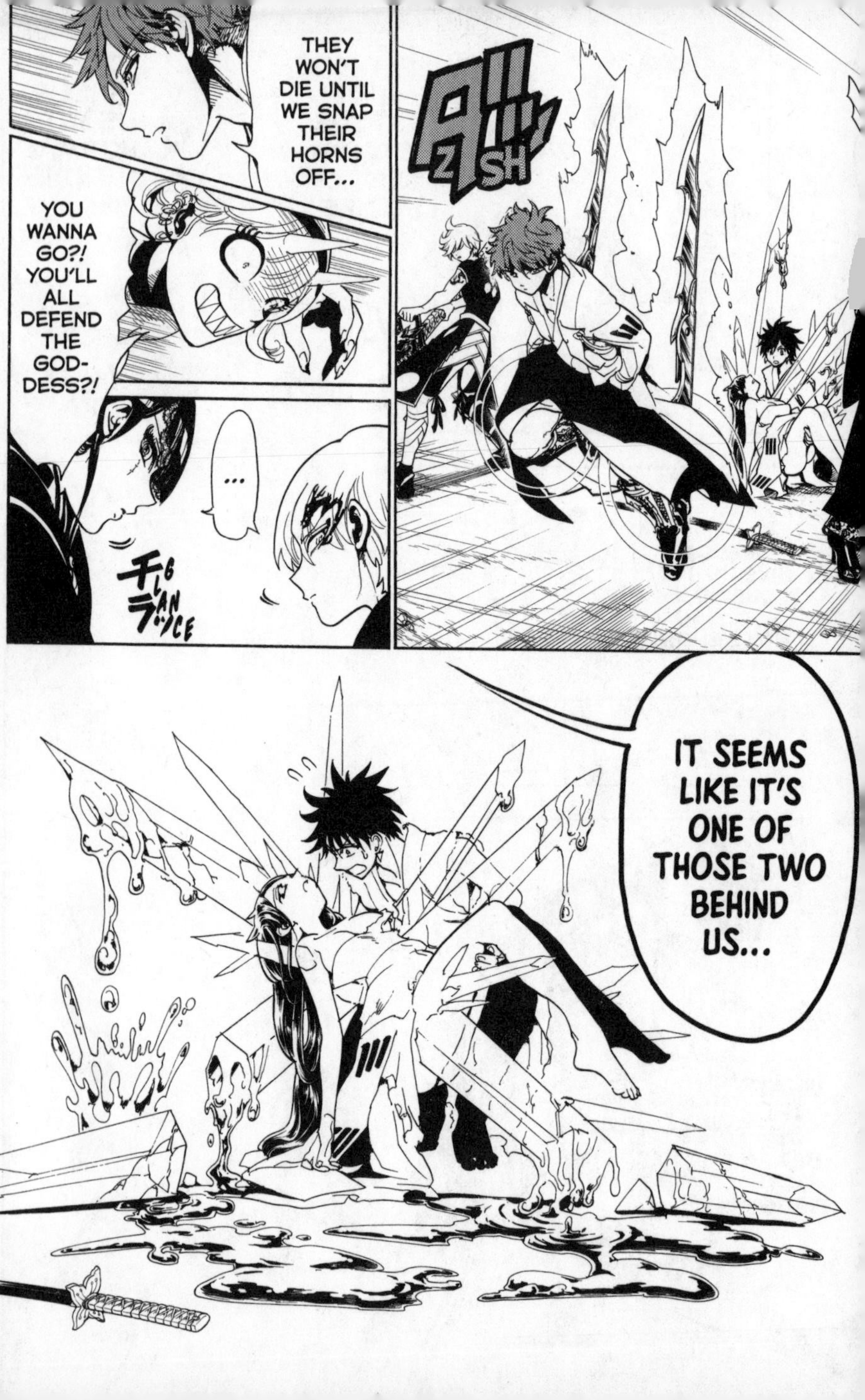
ZASH
THEY WON'T DIE UNTIL WE SNAP THEIR HORNS OFF...
YOU WANNA GO?! YOU'LL ALL DEFEND THE GOD-DESS?!
...
GLANCE
IT SEEMS LIKE IT'S ONE OF THOSE TWO BEHIND US...

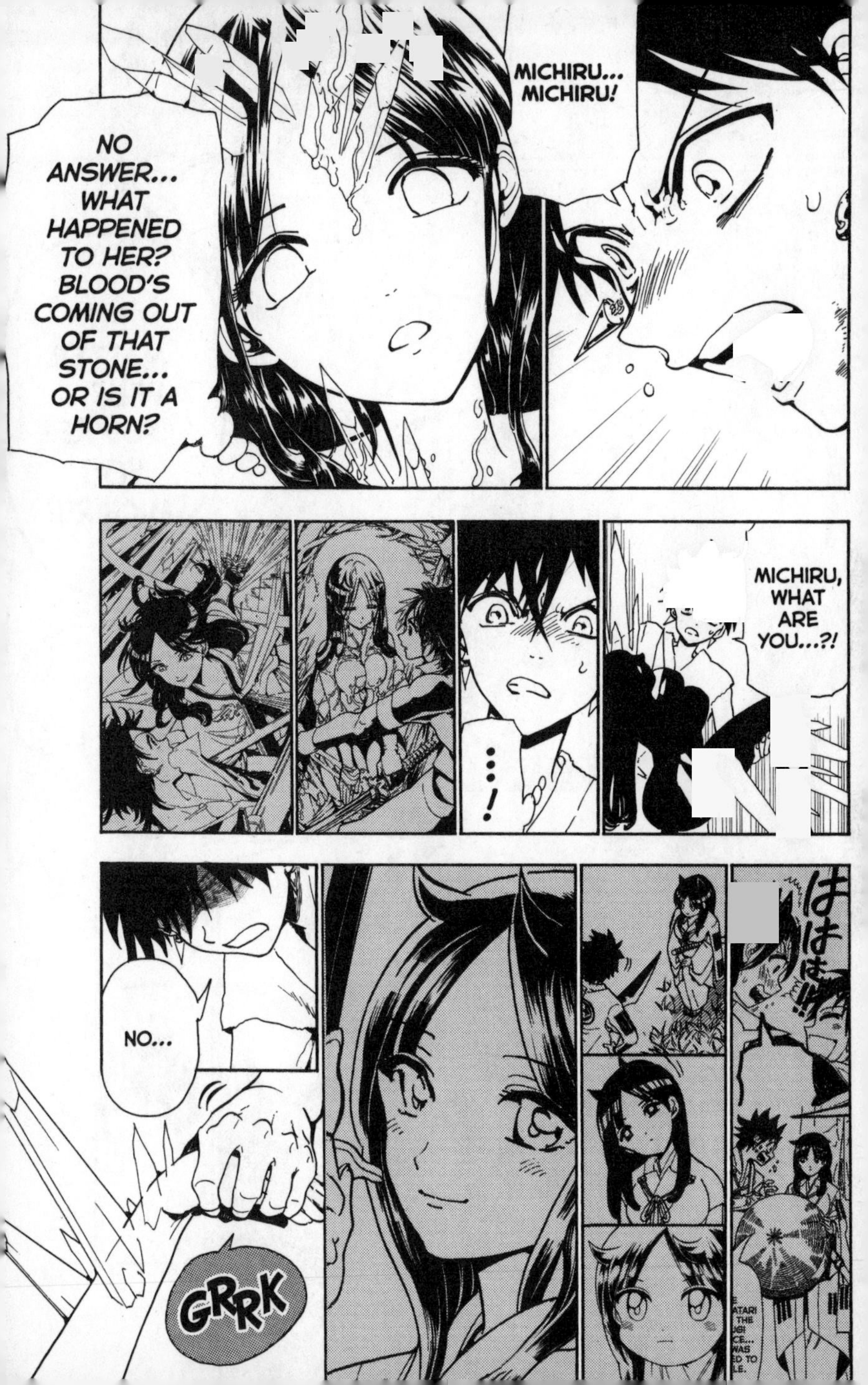
MICHIRU... MICHIRU!
NO ANSWER... WHAT HAPPENED TO HER? BLOOD'S COMING OUT OF THAT STONE... OR IS IT A HORN?
MICHIRU, WHAT ARE YOU...?!
...!
ははは!!
NO...
GRRK

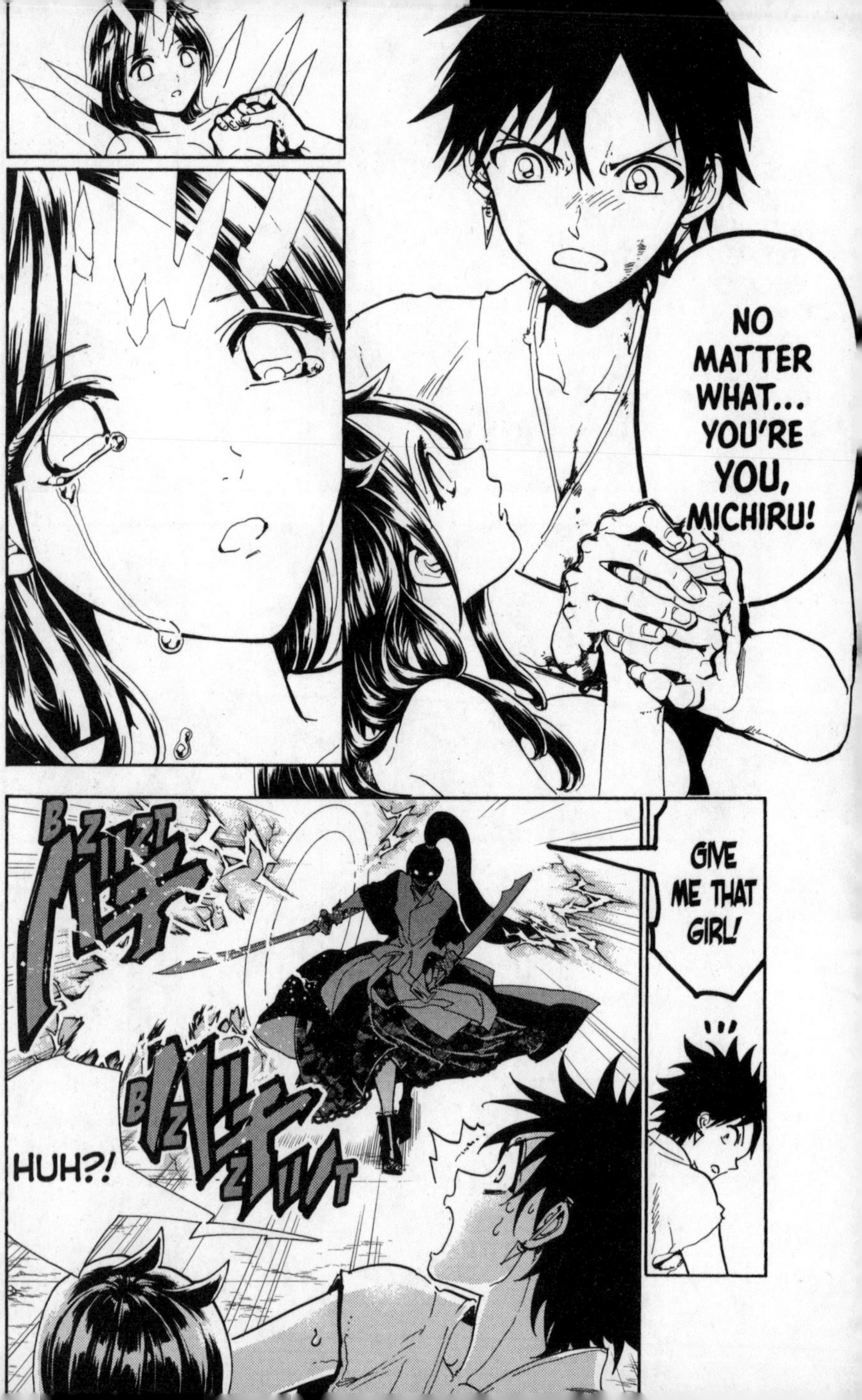
NO MATTER WHAT... YOU'RE YOU, MICHIRU!
GIVE ME THAT GIRL!
...
BZZZT
BZZZT
HUH?!

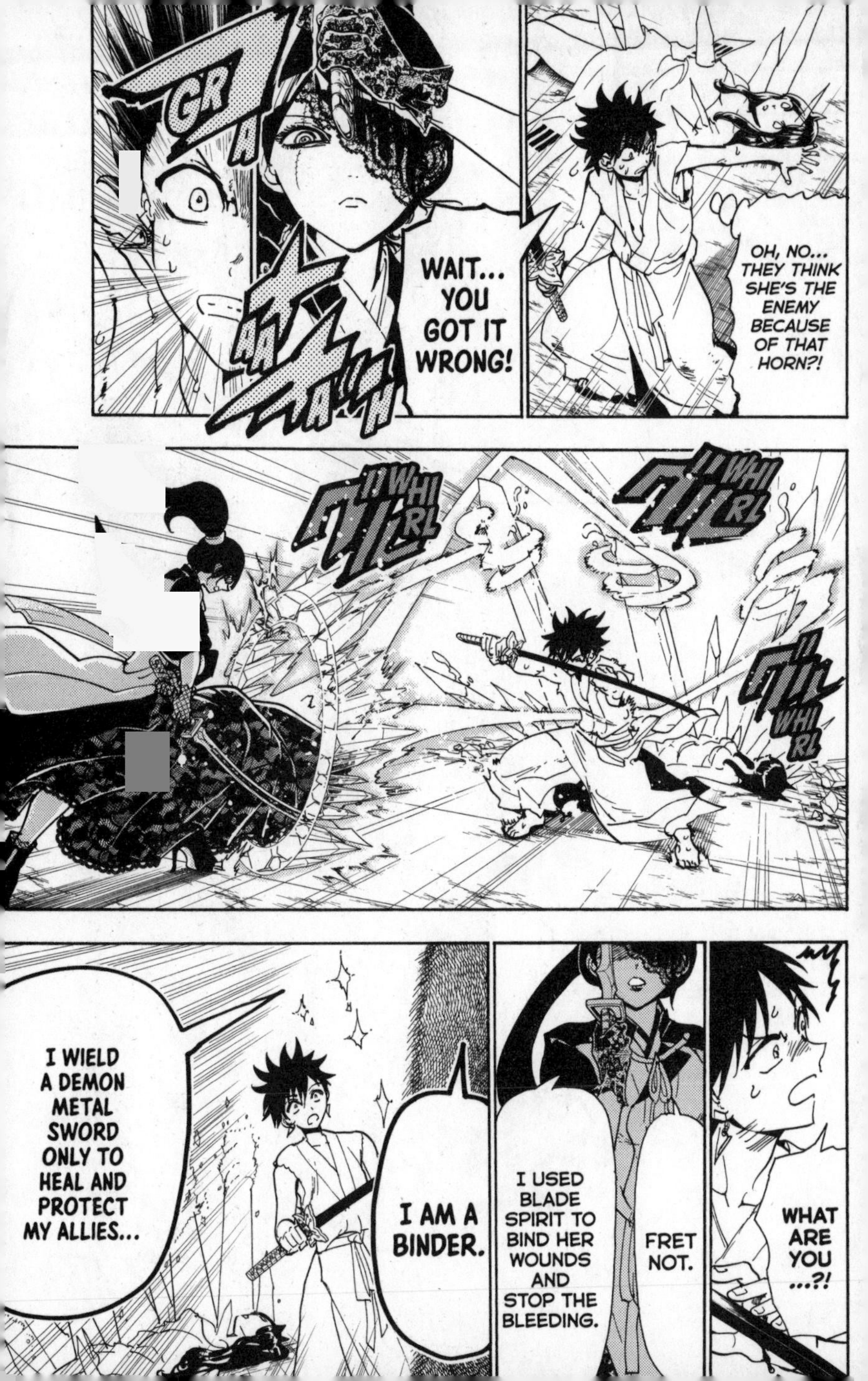
OH, NO... THEY THINK SHE'S THE ENEMY BECAUSE OF THAT HORN?!
WAIT... YOU GOT IT WRONG!
GR
WHIRL
WHIRL
WHIRL
WHAT ARE YOU ...?!
FRET NOT.
I USED BLADE SPIRIT TO BIND HER WOUNDS AND STOP THE BLEEDING.
I AM A BINDER.
I WIELD A DEMON METAL SWORD ONLY TO HEAL AND PROTECT MY ALLIES...

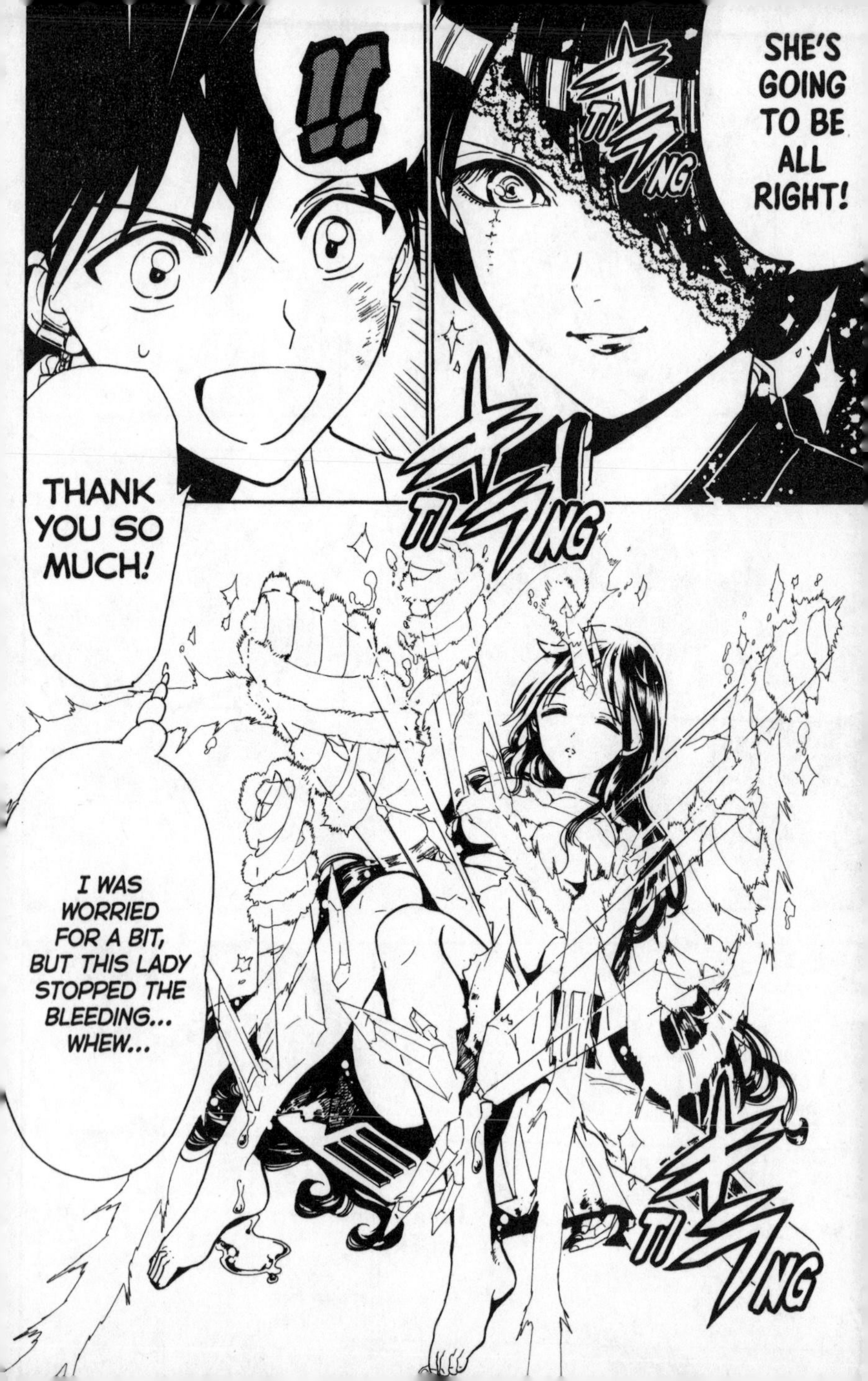
SHE'S GOING TO BE ALL RIGHT!
TING
TING
THANK YOU SO MUCH!
TING
I WAS WORRIED FOR A BIT, BUT THIS LADY STOPPED THE BLEEDING... WHEW...
TING

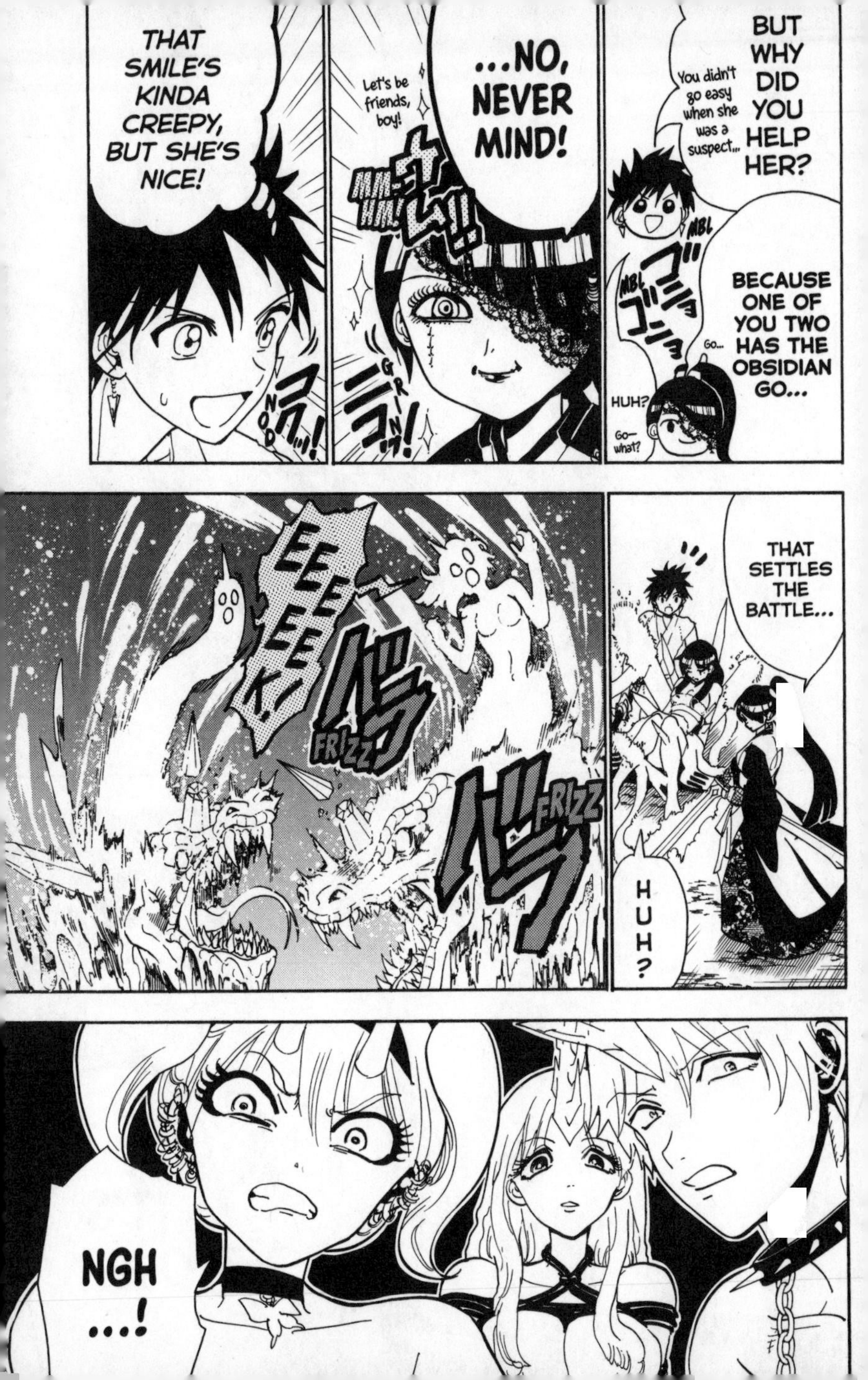
BUT WHY DID YOU HELP HER?
You didn't go easy when she was a suspect...
MBL
MBL
BECAUSE ONE OF YOU TWO HAS THE OBSIDIAN GO...
Go...
HUH?
Go—what?
...NO, NEVER MIND!
Let's be friends, boy!
MMM-HM!
GRIN
THAT SMILE'S KINDA CREEPY, BUT SHE'S NICE!
NOD
THAT SETTLES THE BATTLE...
HUH?
EEEEEEEK!
FRIZZ
FRIZZ
NGH ...!

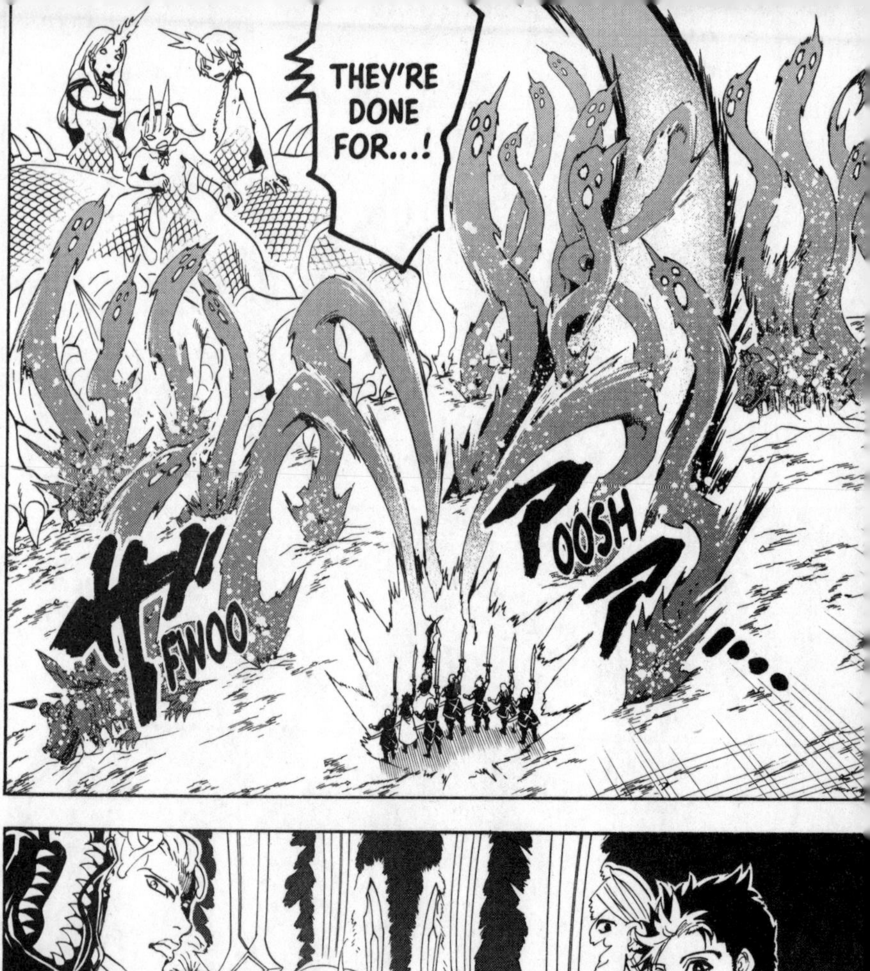
THEY'RE DONE FOR...!
OOSH
FWOO
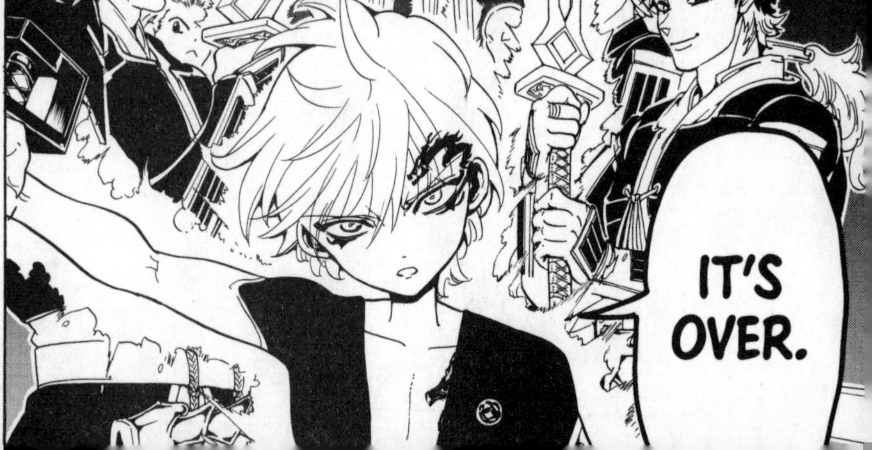
IT'S OVER.

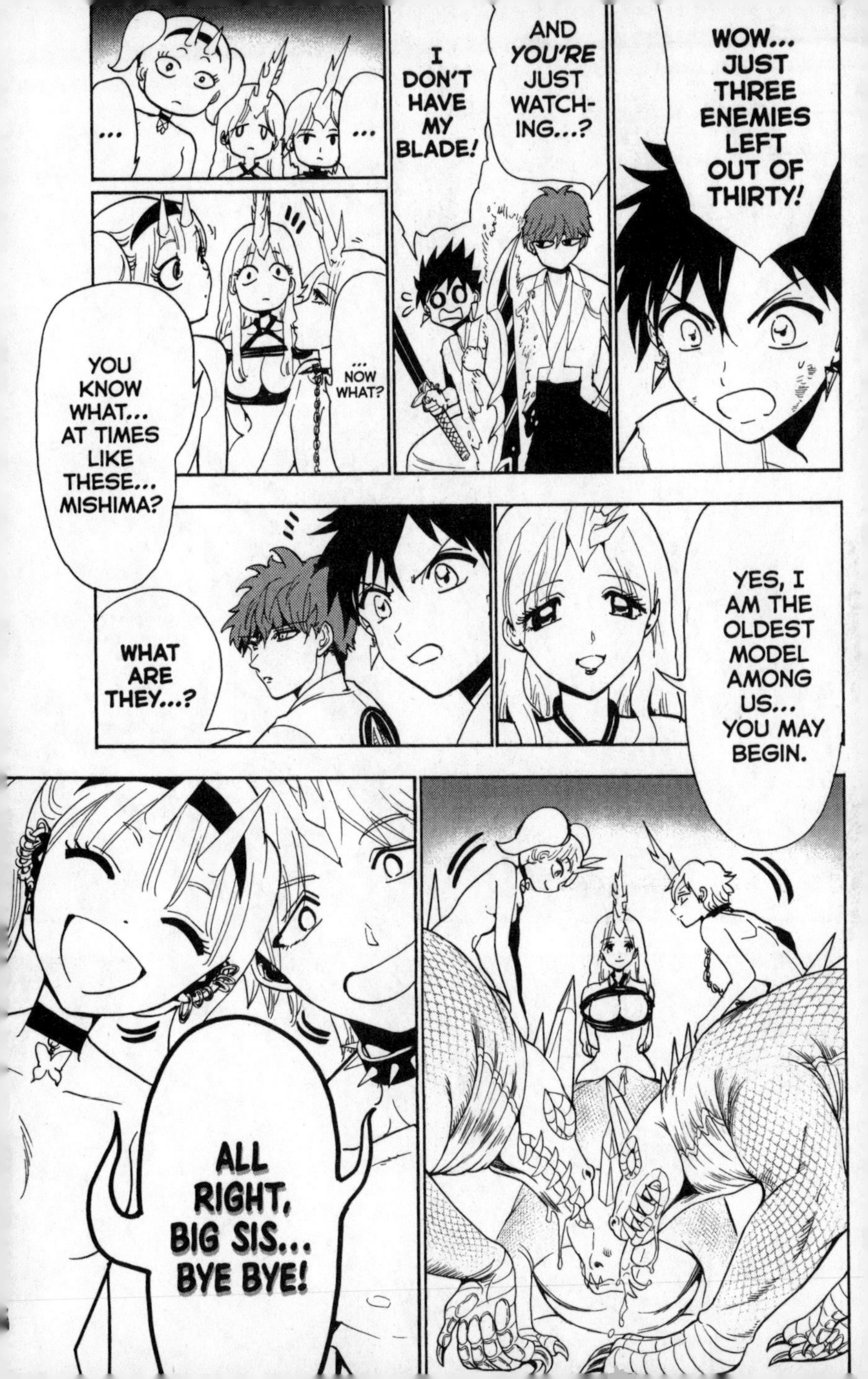
WOW... JUST THREE ENEMIES LEFT OUT OF THIRTY!
AND *YOU'RE* JUST WATCHING...?
I DON'T HAVE MY BLADE!
...
...
...NOW WHAT?
YOU KNOW WHAT... AT TIMES LIKE THESE... MISHIMA?
YES, I AM THE OLDEST MODEL AMONG US... YOU MAY BEGIN.
WHAT ARE THEY...?
ALL RIGHT, BIG SIS... BYE BYE!

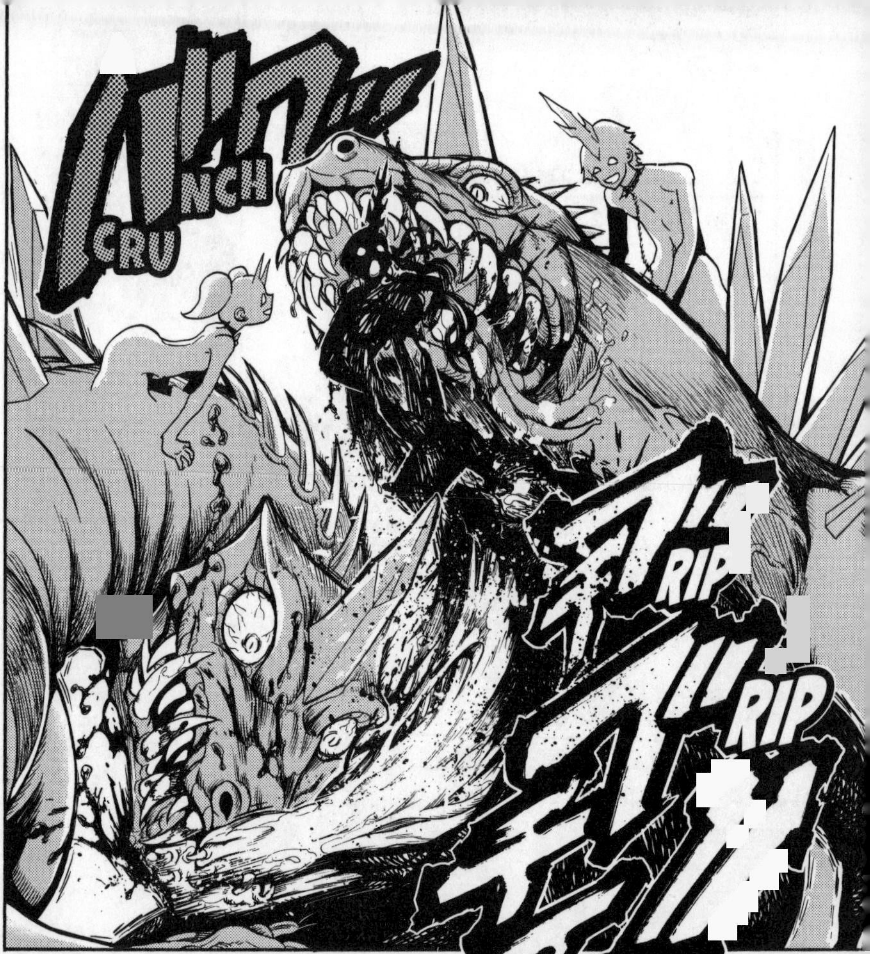
CRUNCH
RIP
RIP
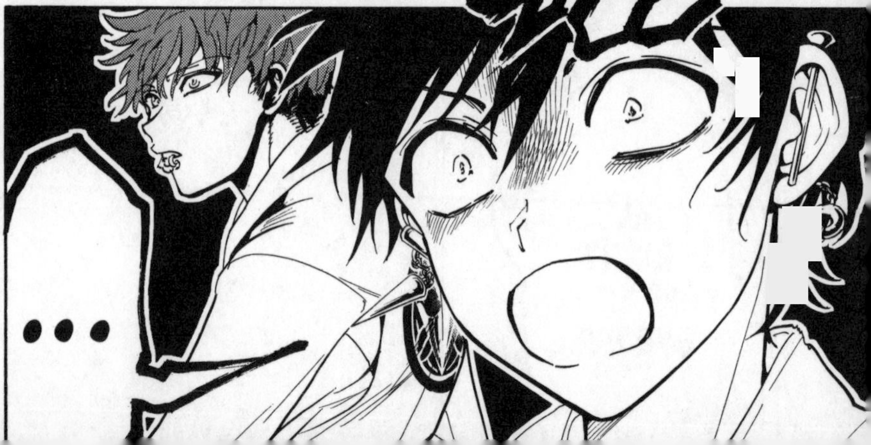
...

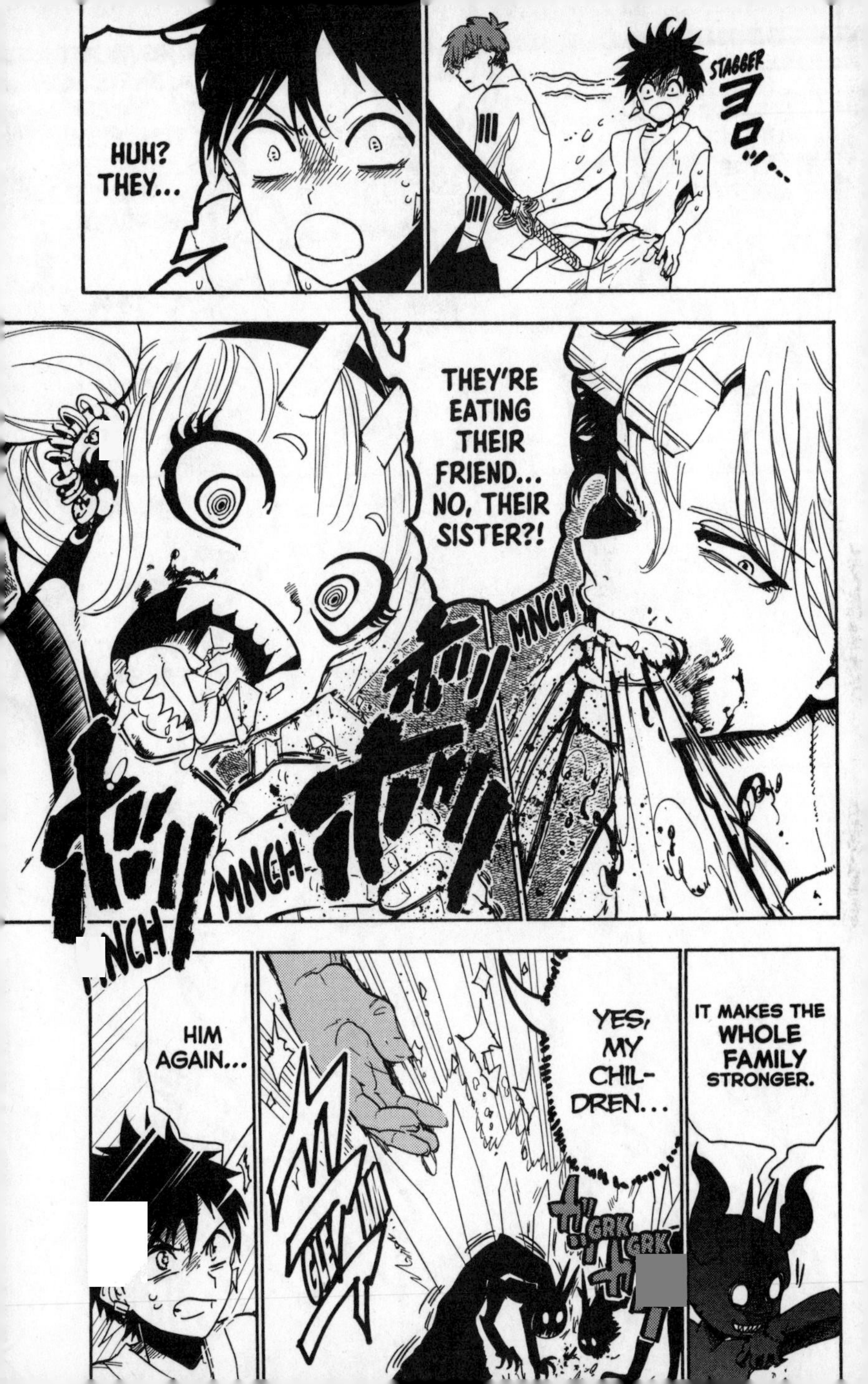
STAGGER
ヨロッ...
HUH? THEY...
THEY'RE EATING THEIR FRIEND... NO, THEIR SISTER?!
MNCH
MNCH
NCH
IT MAKES THE WHOLE FAMILY STRONGER.
YES, MY CHIL-DREN...
GRK
GRK
HIM AGAIN...

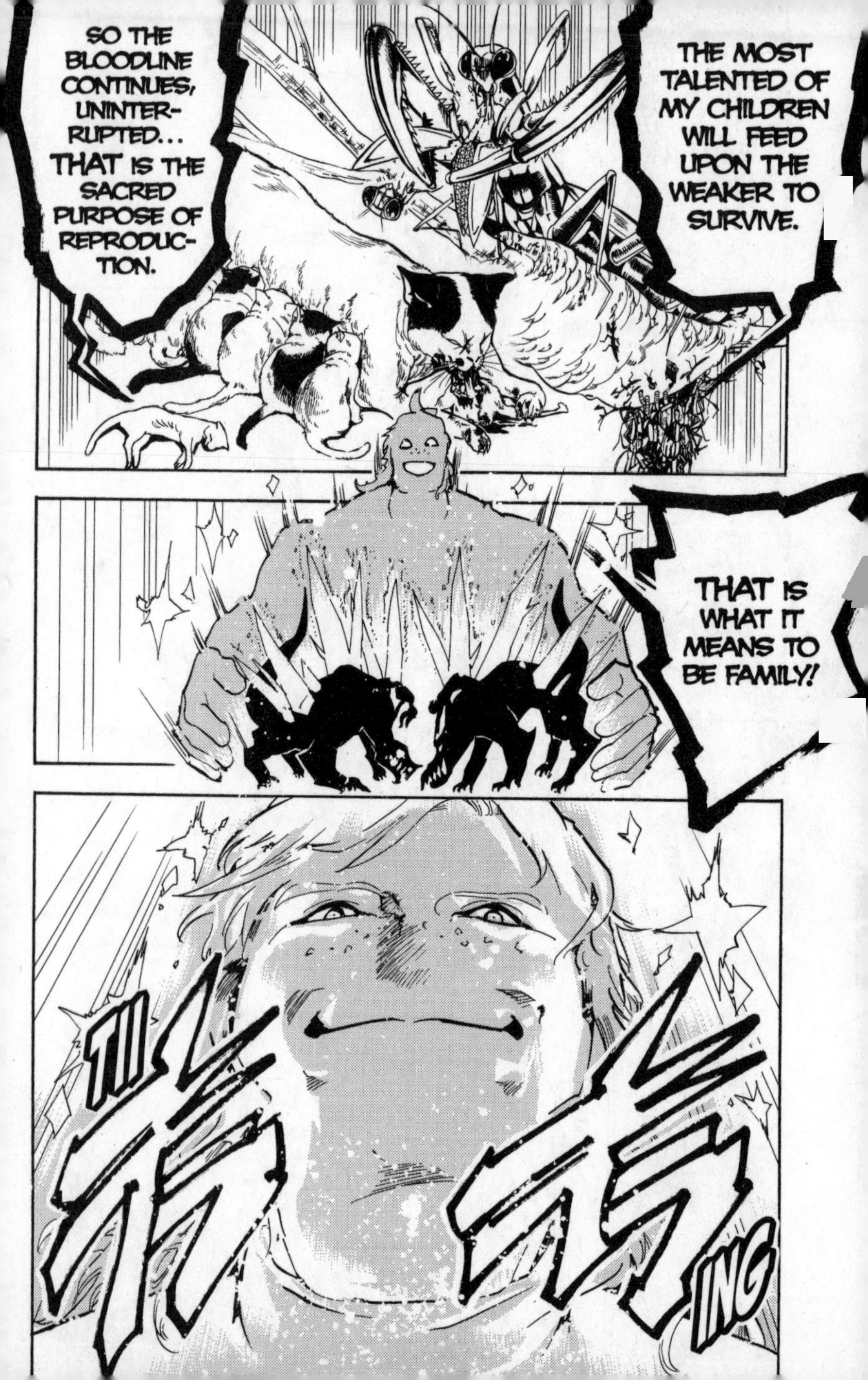
THE MOST TALENTED OF MY CHILDREN WILL FEED UPON THE WEAKER TO SURVIVE.
SO THE BLOODLINE CONTINUES, UNINTER-RUPTED... THAT IS THE SACRED PURPOSE OF REPRODUC-TION.
THAT IS WHAT IT MEANS TO BE FAMILY!

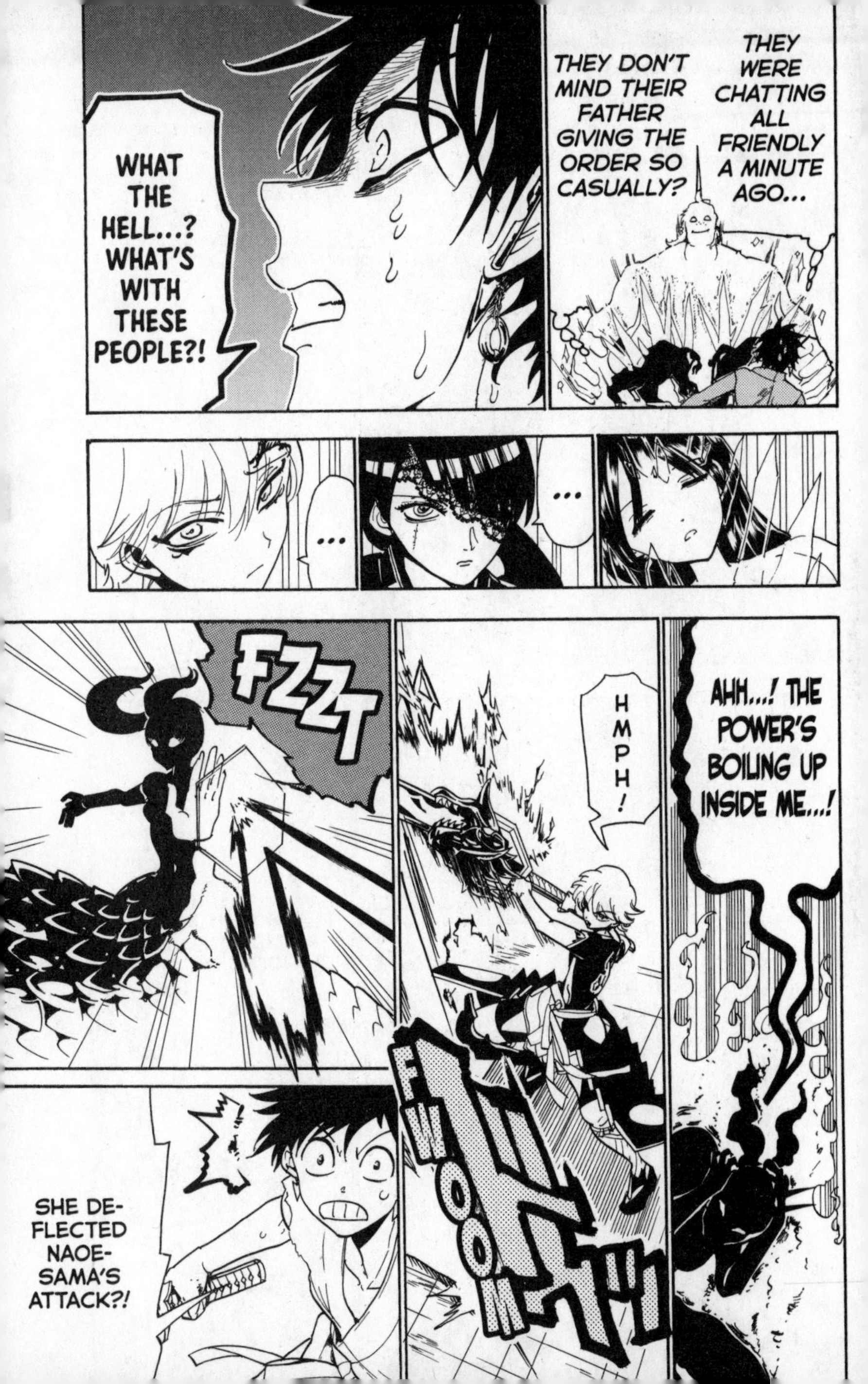
THEY WERE CHATTING ALL FRIENDLY A MINUTE AGO...
THEY DON'T MIND THEIR FATHER GIVING THE ORDER SO CASUALLY?
WHAT THE HELL...? WHAT'S WITH THESE PEOPLE?!
...
...
AHH...! THE POWER'S BOILING UP INSIDE ME...!
HMPH!
FZZZT
FWOOM
SHE DE-FLECTED NAOE-SAMA'S ATTACK?!

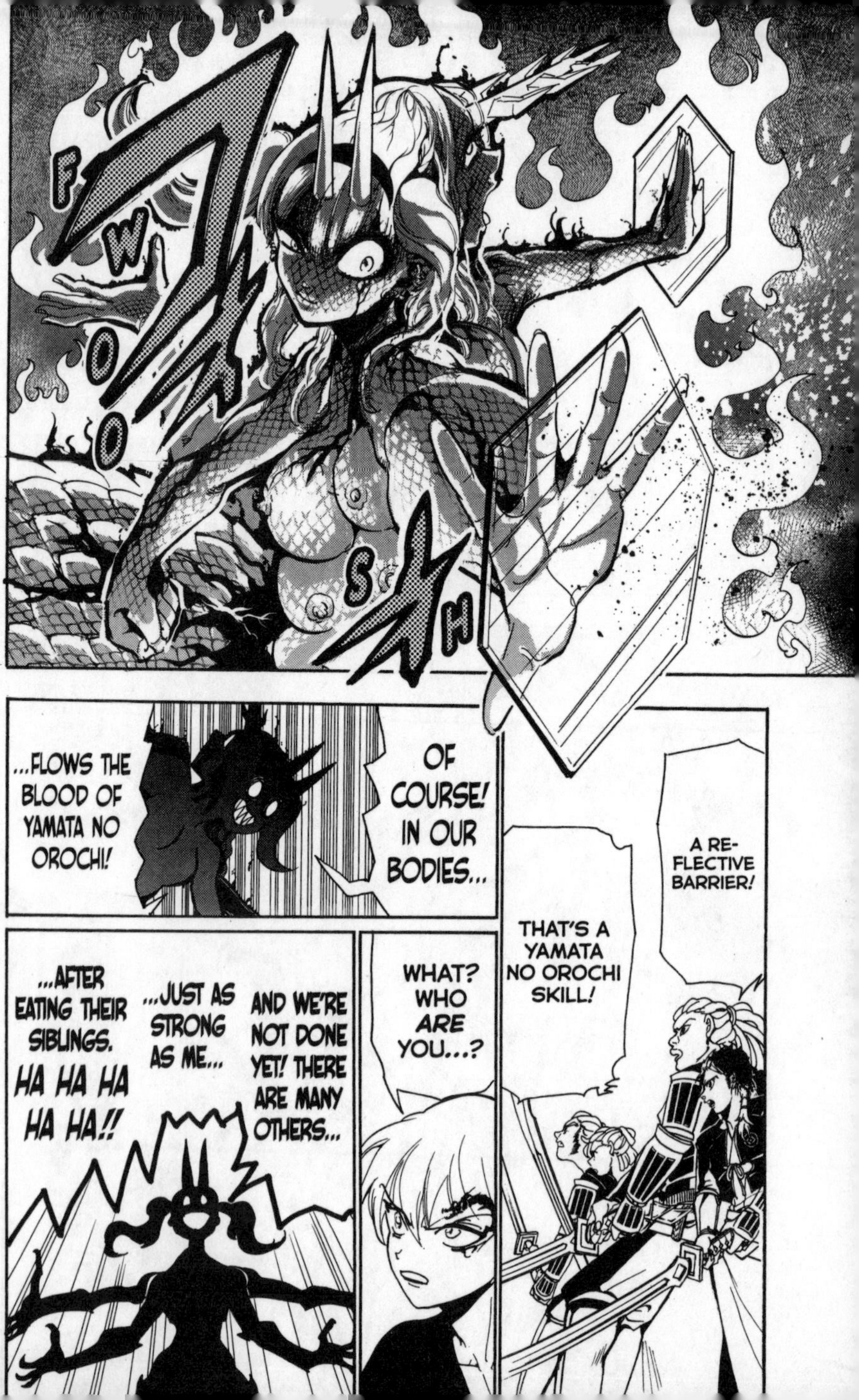
FWOOO
SHH
A RE-FLECTIVE BARRIER!
THAT'S A YAMATA NO OROCHI SKILL!
OF COURSE! IN OUR BODIES...
...FLOWS THE BLOOD OF YAMATA NO OROCHI!
WHAT? WHO ARE YOU...?
AND WE'RE NOT DONE YET! THERE ARE MANY OTHERS...
...JUST AS STRONG AS ME...
...AFTER EATING THEIR SIBLINGS. HA HA HA HA HA!!

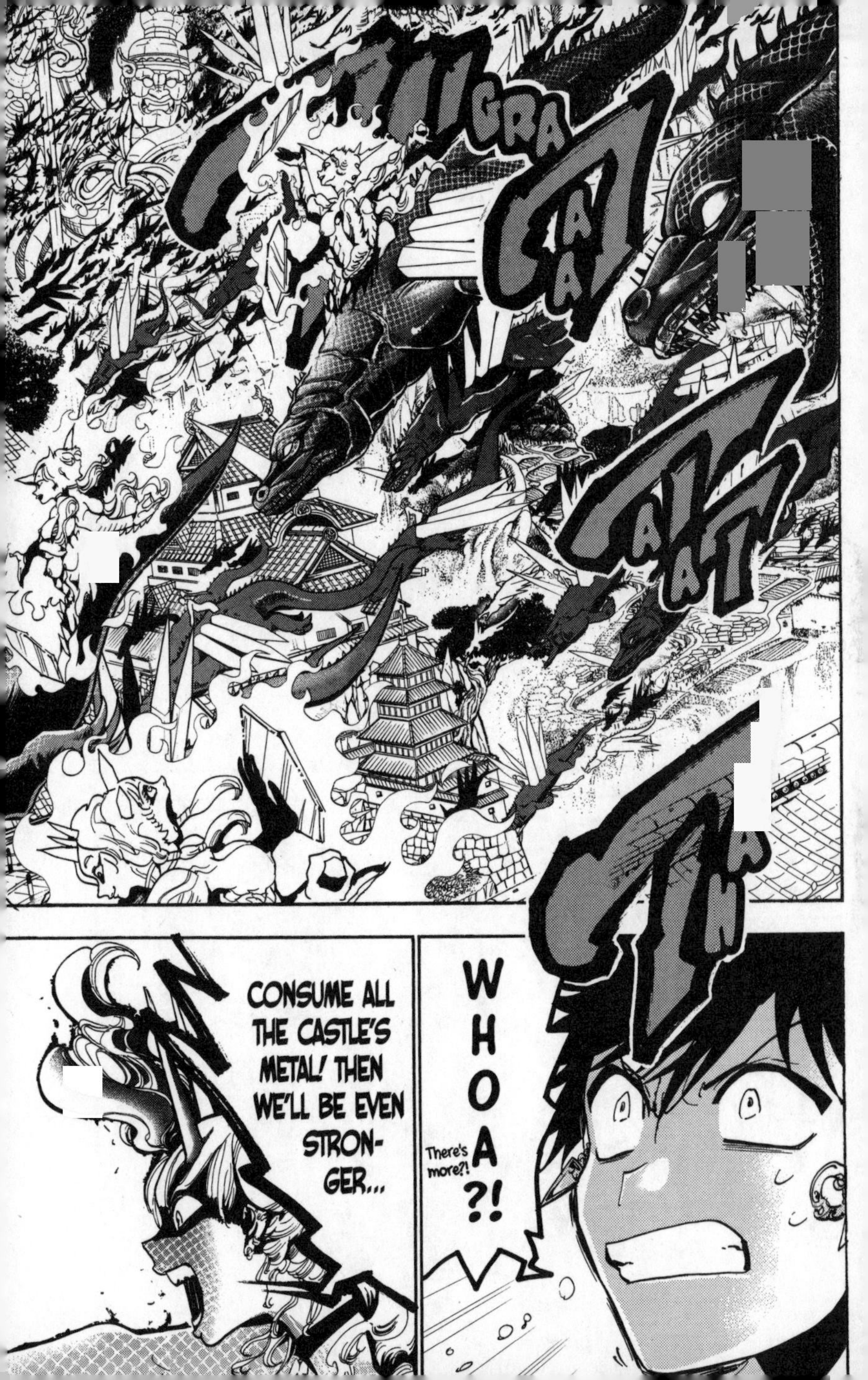
GRA
WHOA?!
There's more?!
CONSUME ALL THE CASTLE'S METAL! THEN WE'LL BE EVEN STRONGER...

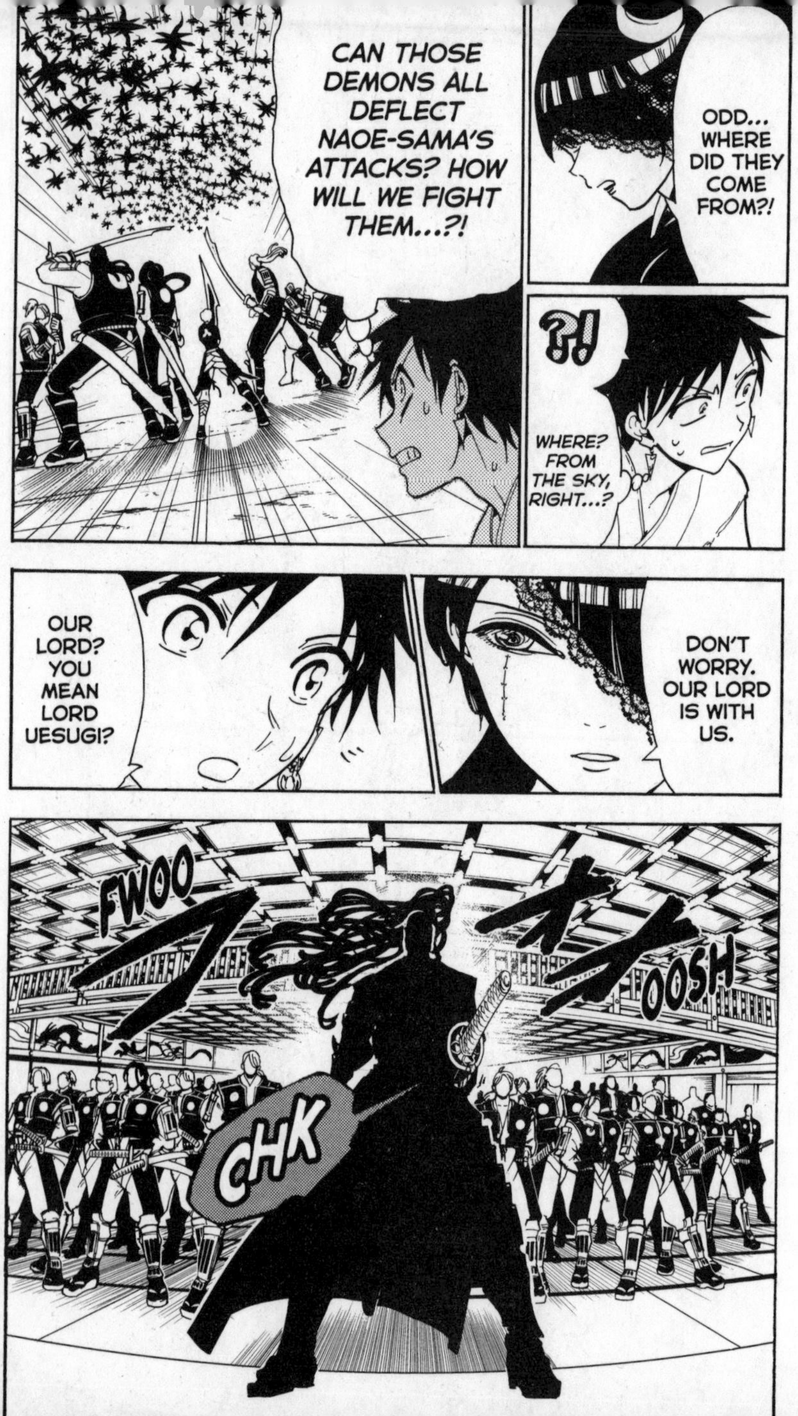
ODD... WHERE DID THEY COME FROM?!
?!
WHERE? FROM THE SKY, RIGHT...?
CAN THOSE DEMONS ALL DEFLECT NAOE-SAMA'S ATTACKS? HOW WILL WE FIGHT THEM...?!
DON'T WORRY. OUR LORD IS WITH US.
OUR LORD? YOU MEAN LORD UESUGI?
FWOO
OOSH
CHK

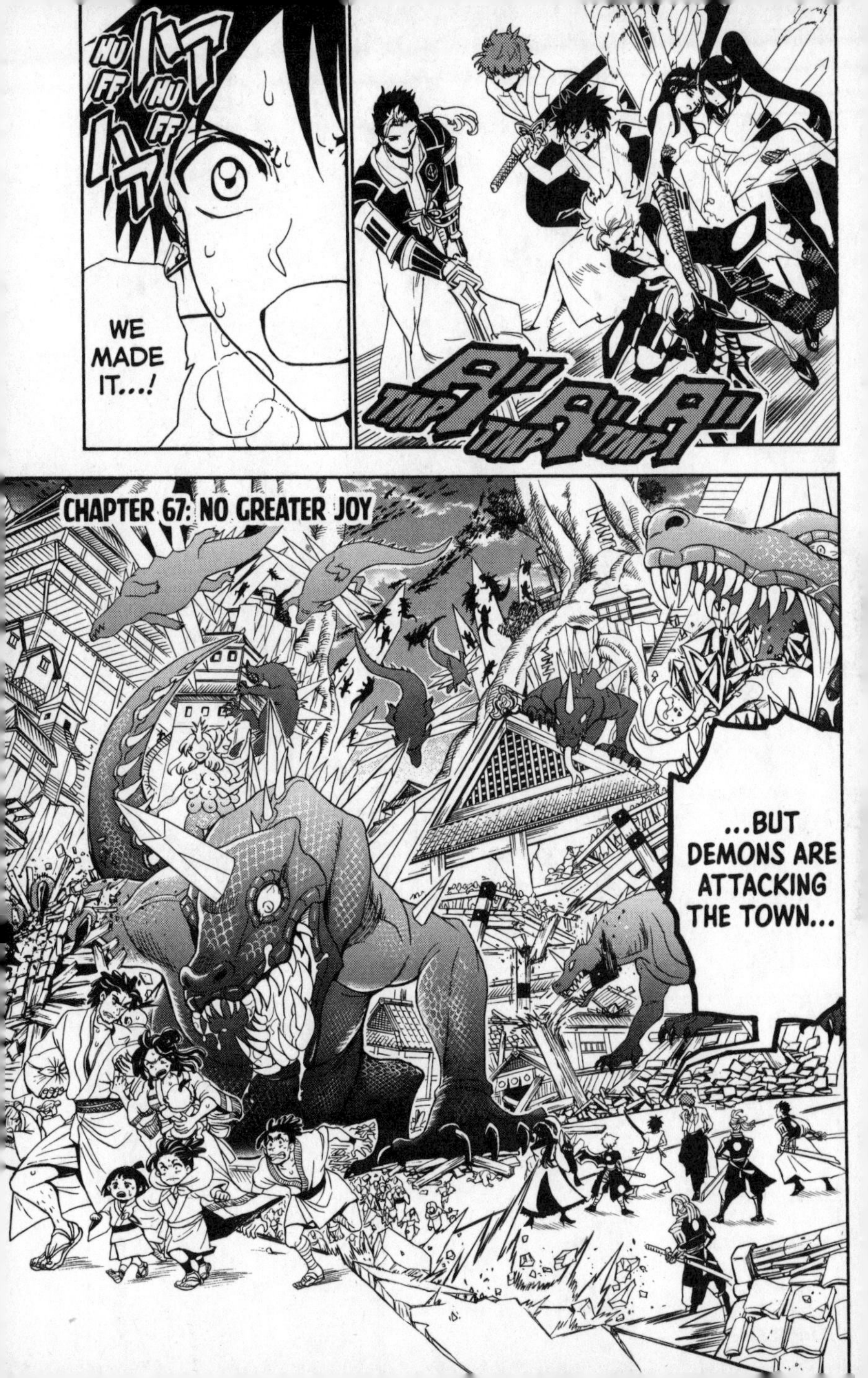
HUFF
HUFF
WE MADE IT...!
CHAPTER 67: NO GREATER JOY
...BUT DEMONS ARE ATTACKING THE TOWN...

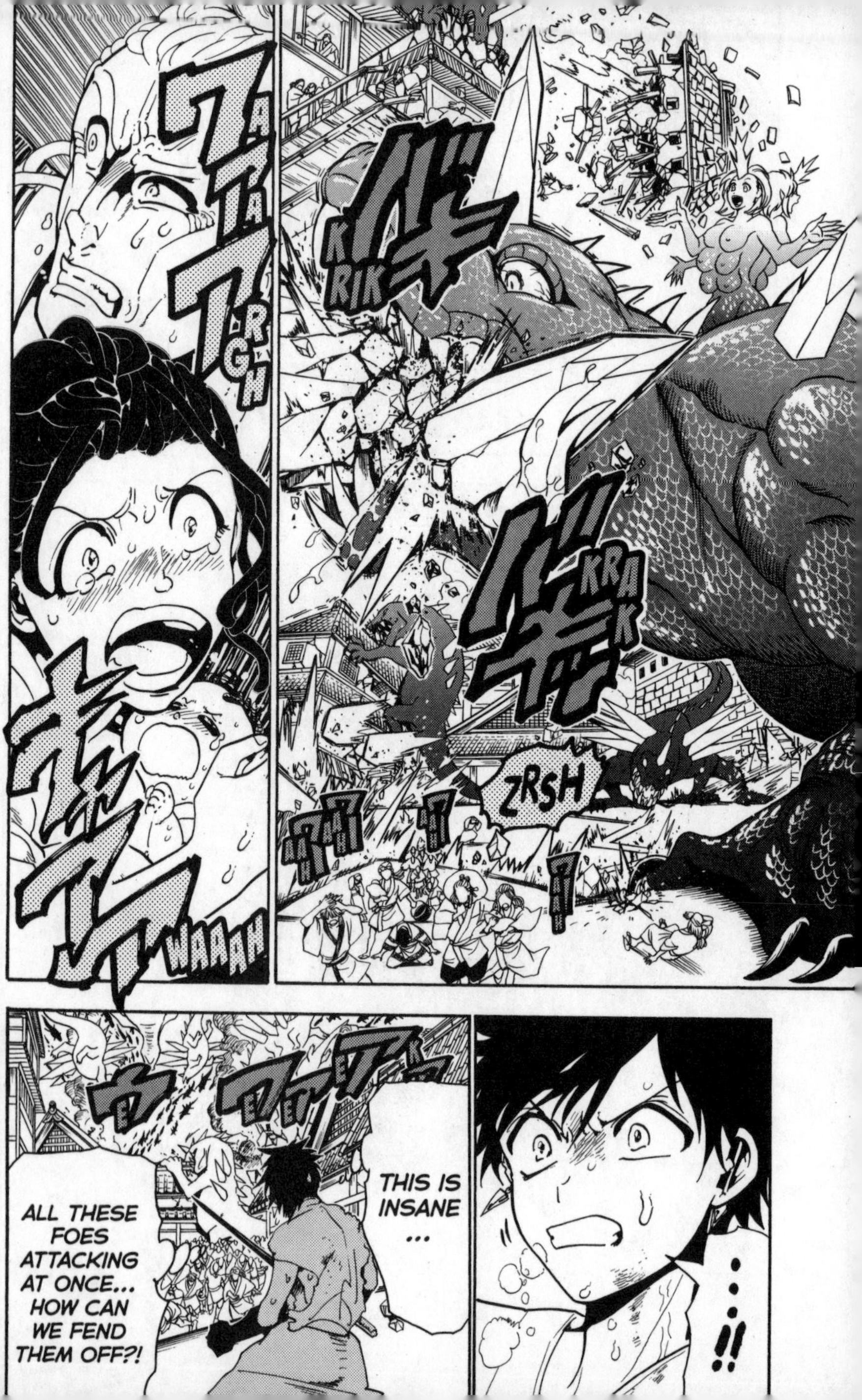
KRIK
KRAK
ZRSH
ARGH
WAAAH
...!!
THIS IS INSANE ...
ALL THESE FOES ATTACKING AT ONCE... HOW CAN WE FEND THEM OFF?!

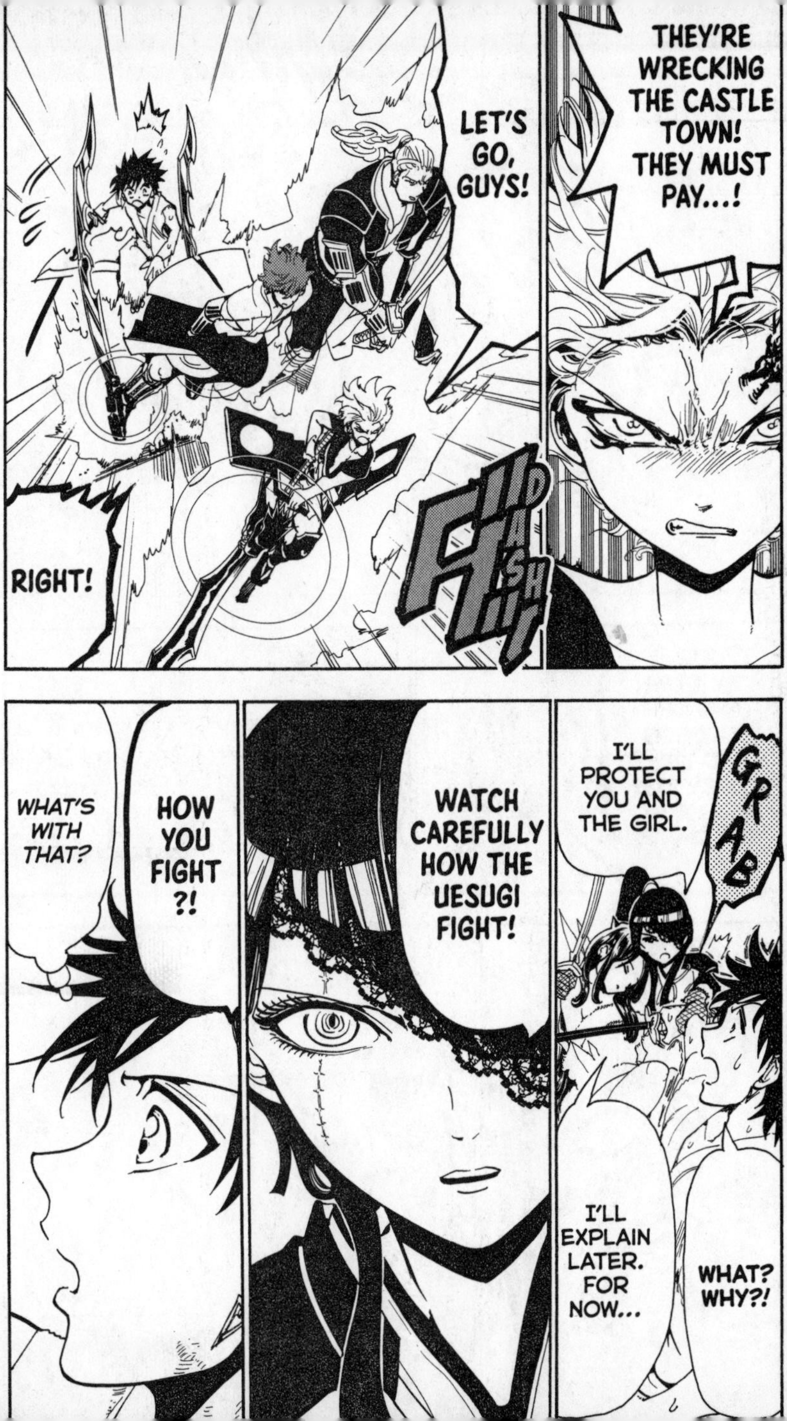
THEY'RE WRECKING THE CASTLE TOWN! THEY MUST PAY...!
LET'S GO, GUYS!
RIGHT!
GRAB
I'LL PROTECT YOU AND THE GIRL.
WHAT? WHY?!
I'LL EXPLAIN LATER. FOR NOW...
WATCH CAREFULLY HOW THE UESUGI FIGHT!
HOW YOU FIGHT?!
WHAT'S WITH THAT?

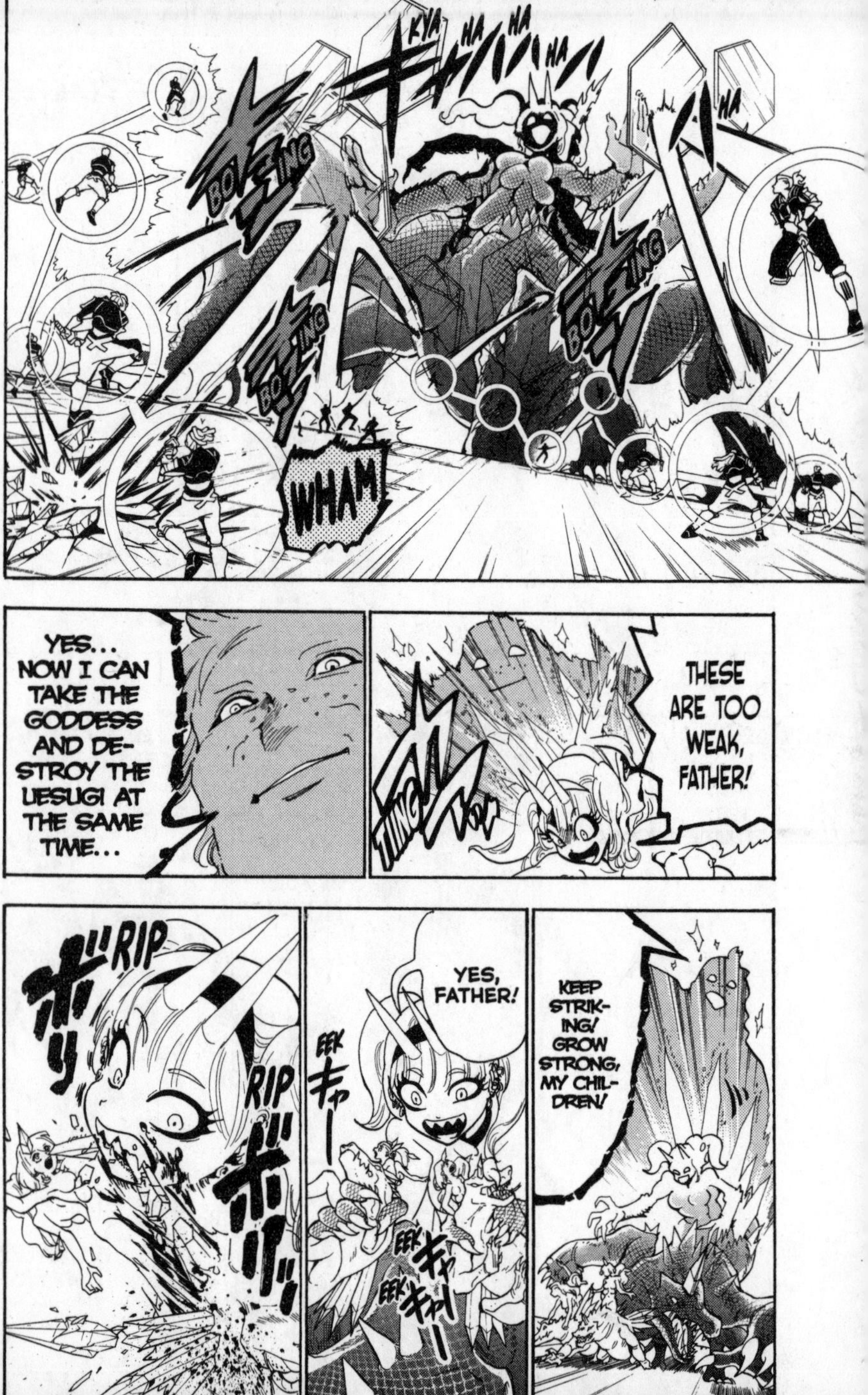
HA
KYA HA HA HA HA
BOYEING
BOYEING
BOYEING
WHAM
THESE ARE TOO WEAK, FATHER!
YES... NOW I CAN TAKE THE GODDESS AND DE-STROY THE UESUGI AT THE SAME TIME...
KEEP STRIK-ING! GROW STRONG, MY CHIL-DREN!
YES, FATHER!
EEK
EEK
EEK
RIP
RIP

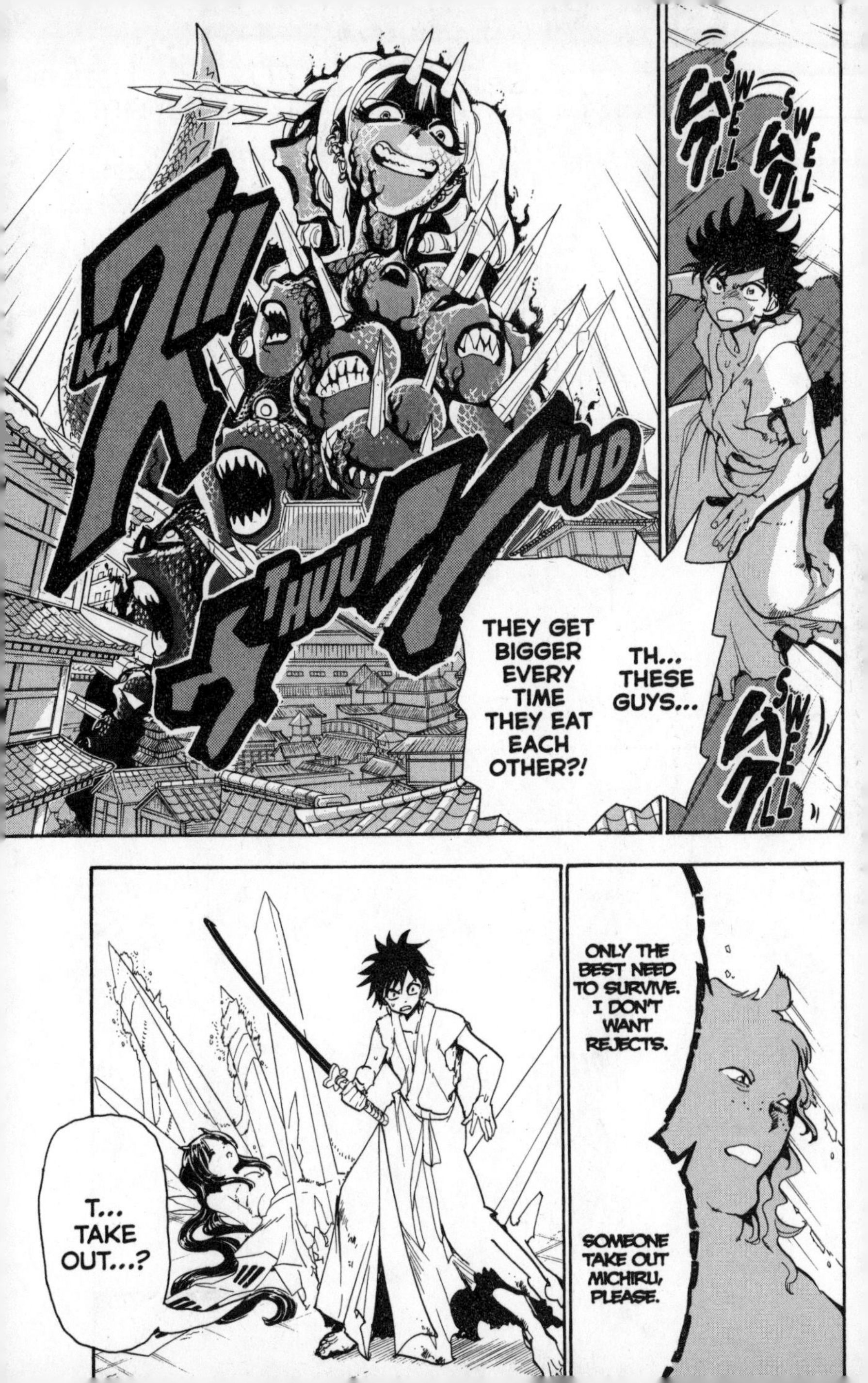
SWELL
SWELL
SWELL
TH... THESE GUYS...
THEY GET BIGGER EVERY TIME THEY EAT EACH OTHER?!
ONLY THE BEST NEED TO SURVIVE. I DON'T WANT REJECTS.
SOMEONE TAKE OUT MICHIRU, PLEASE.
T... TAKE OUT...?

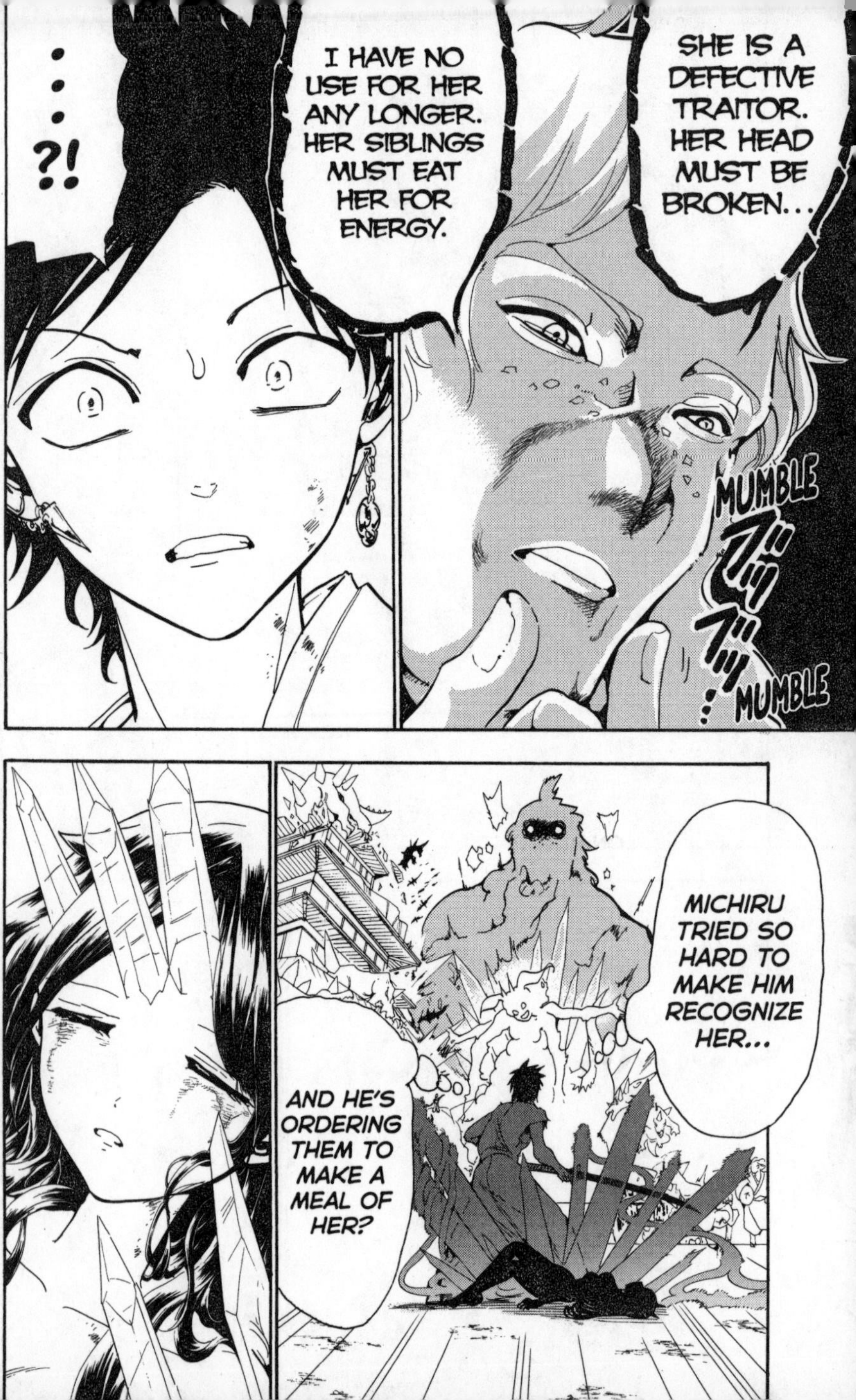
SHE IS A DEFECTIVE TRAITOR. HER HEAD MUST BE BROKEN...
I HAVE NO USE FOR HER ANY LONGER. HER SIBLINGS MUST EAT HER FOR ENERGY.
MUMBLE
ブツブツ...
MUMBLE
...?!
MICHIRU TRIED SO HARD TO MAKE HIM RECOGNIZE HER...
AND HE'S ORDERING THEM TO MAKE A MEAL OF HER?

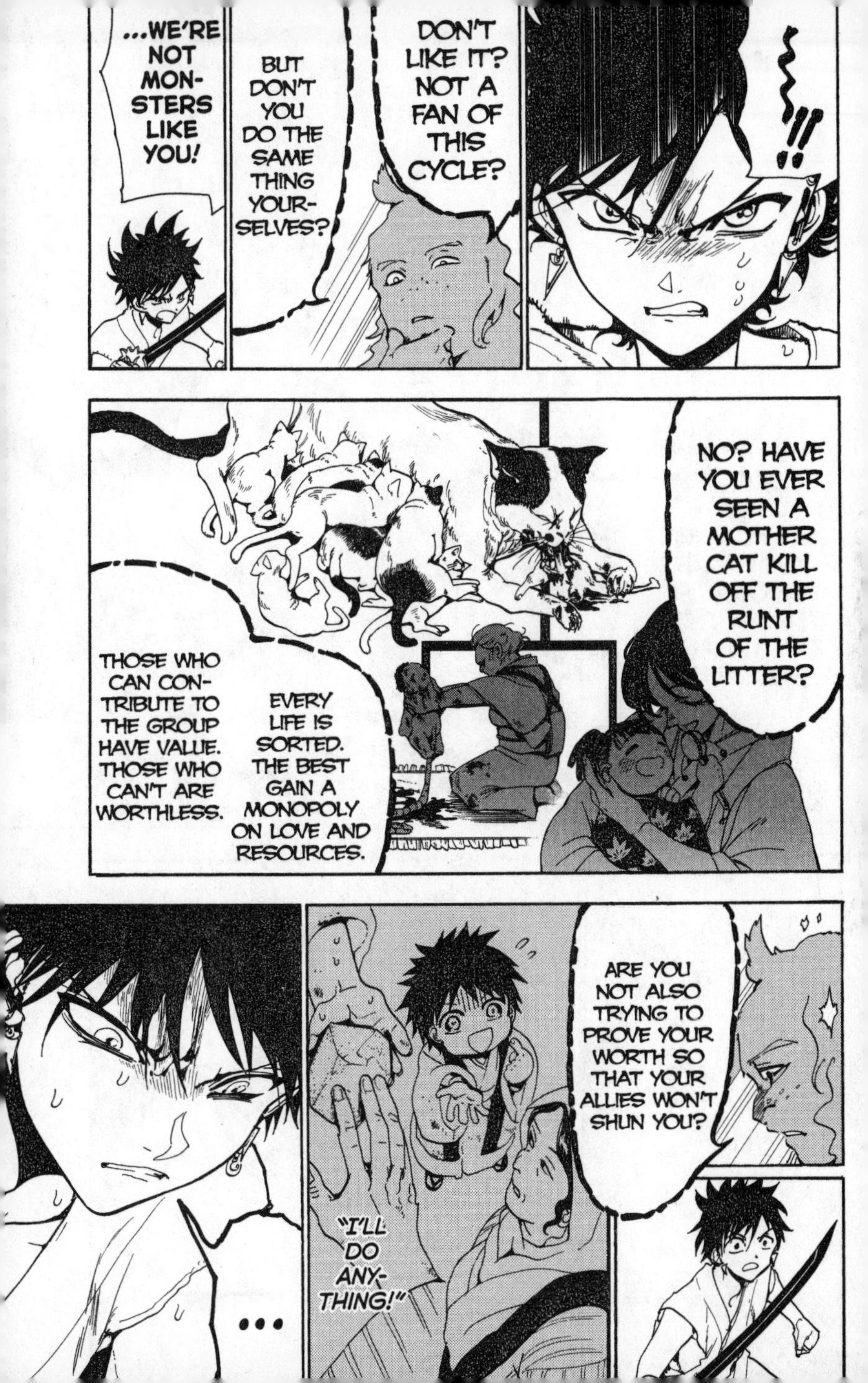
!!
DON'T LIKE IT? NOT A FAN OF THIS CYCLE?
BUT DON'T YOU DO THE SAME THING YOURSELVES?
...WE'RE NOT MONSTERS LIKE YOU!
NO? HAVE YOU EVER SEEN A MOTHER CAT KILL OFF THE RUNT OF THE LITTER?
EVERY LIFE IS SORTED. THE BEST GAIN A MONOPOLY ON LOVE AND RESOURCES.
THOSE WHO CAN CONTRIBUTE TO THE GROUP HAVE VALUE. THOSE WHO CAN'T ARE WORTHLESS.
ARE YOU NOT ALSO TRYING TO PROVE YOUR WORTH SO THAT YOUR ALLIES WON'T SHUN YOU?
"I'LL DO ANYTHING!"
...

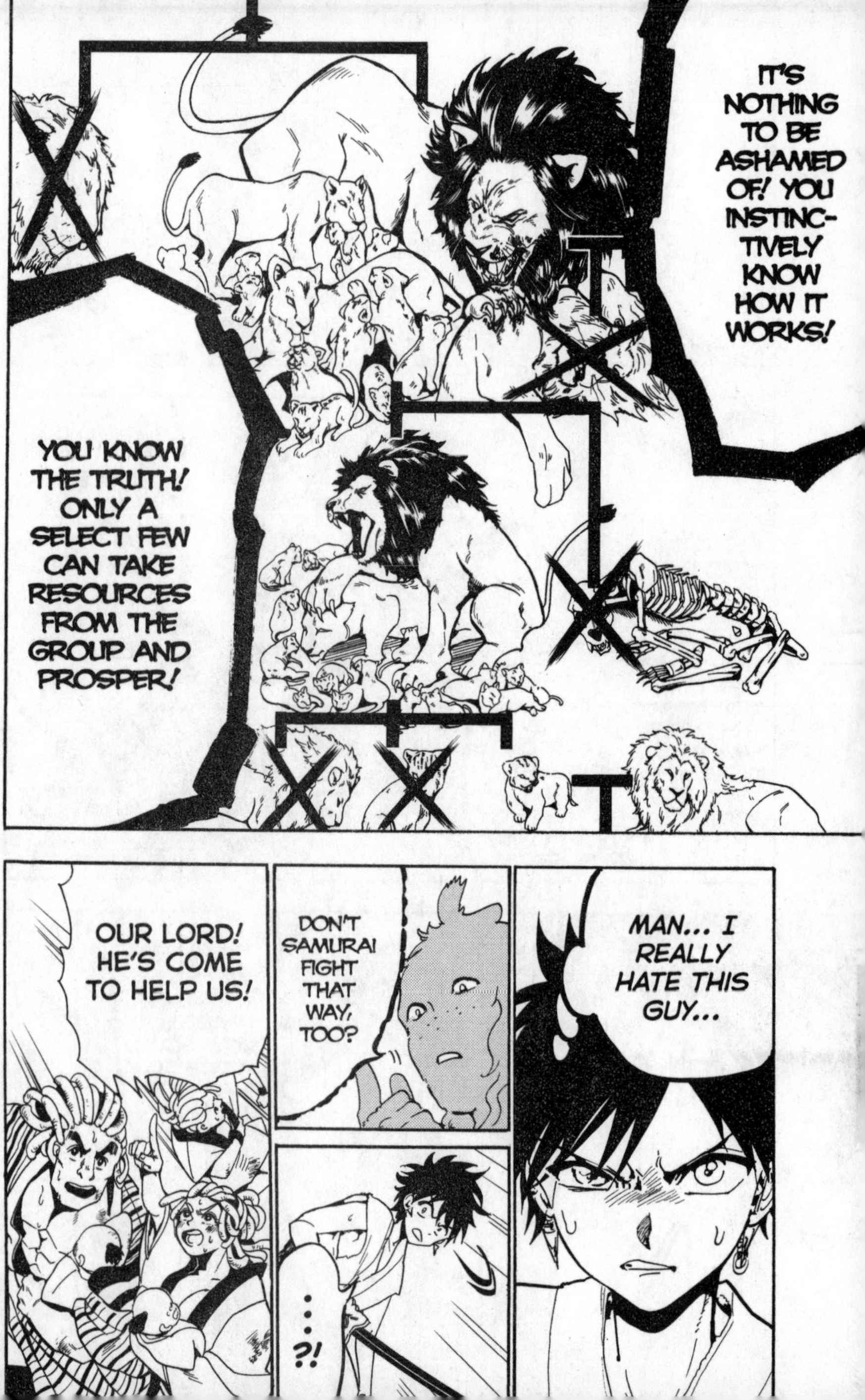
IT'S NOTHING TO BE ASHAMED OF! YOU INSTINCTIVELY KNOW HOW IT WORKS!
YOU KNOW THE TRUTH! ONLY A SELECT FEW CAN TAKE RESOURCES FROM THE GROUP AND PROSPER!
MAN... I REALLY HATE THIS GUY...
DON'T SAMURAI FIGHT THAT WAY, TOO?
...?!
OUR LORD! HE'S COME TO HELP US!

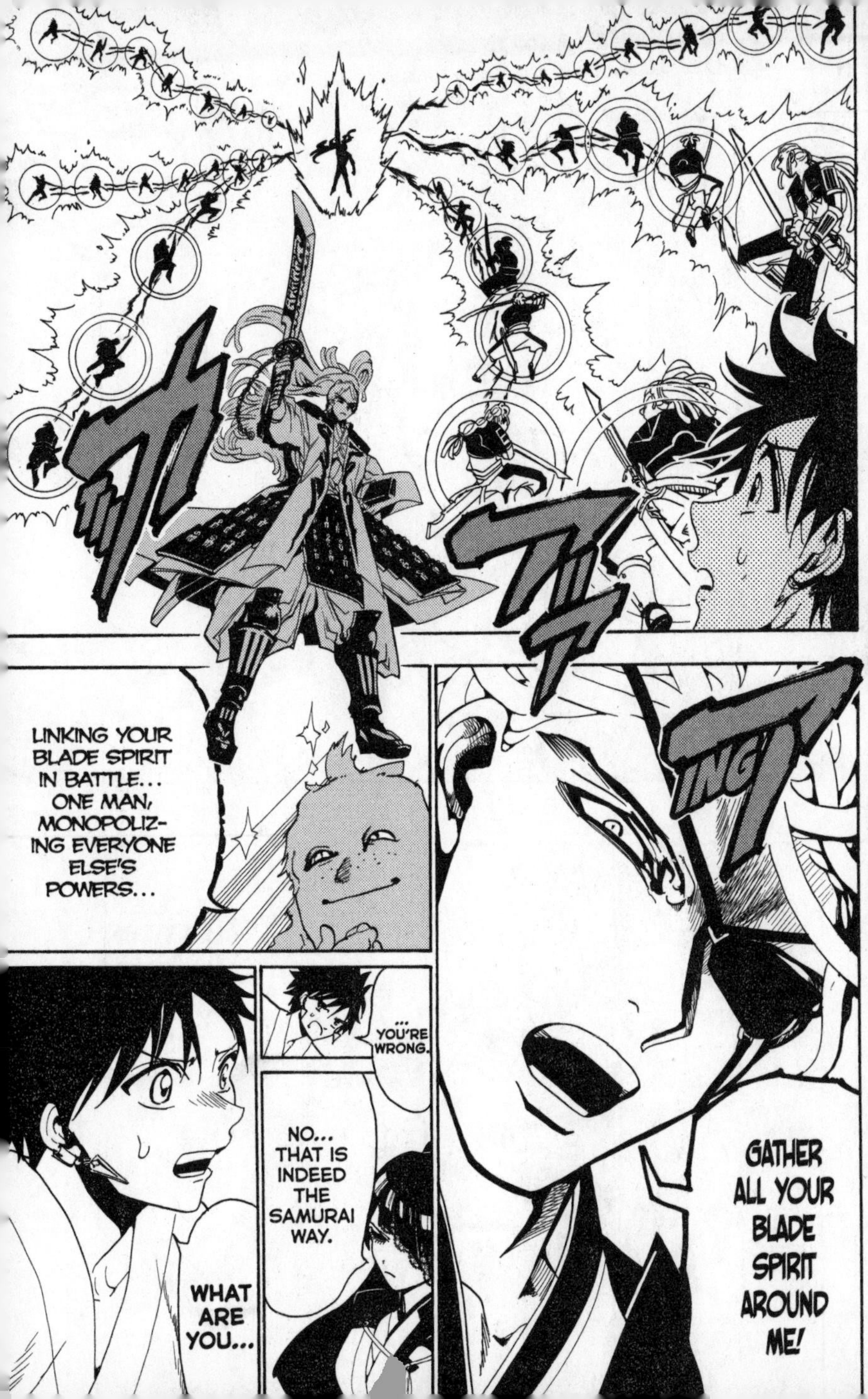
ING
GATHER ALL YOUR BLADE SPIRIT AROUND ME!
LINKING YOUR BLADE SPIRIT IN BATTLE... ONE MAN, MONOPOLIZ-ING EVERYONE ELSE'S POWERS...
...YOU'RE WRONG.
NO... THAT IS INDEED THE SAMURAI WAY.
WHAT ARE YOU...

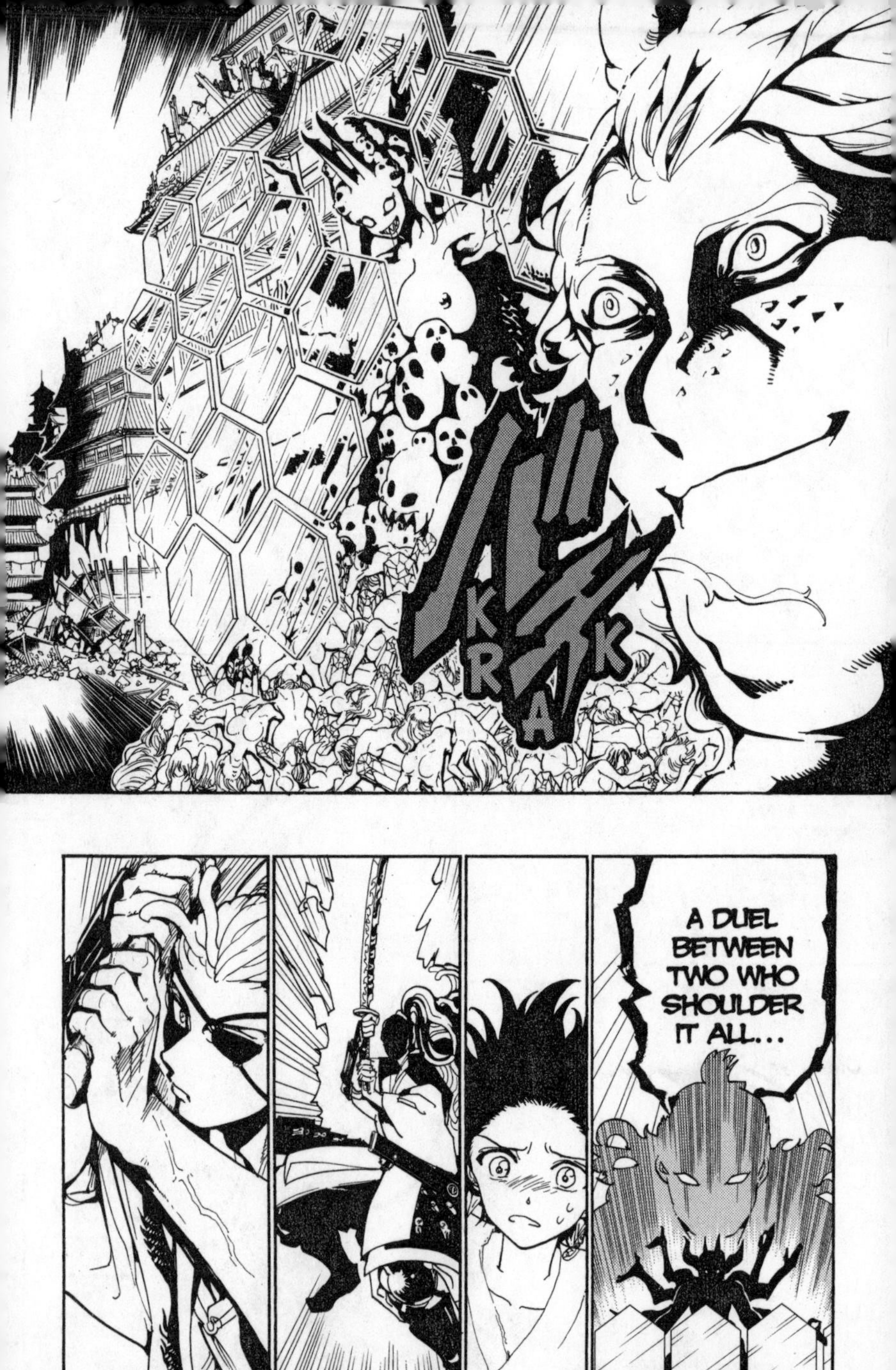
KRAK
A DUEL BETWEEN TWO WHO SHOULDER IT ALL...

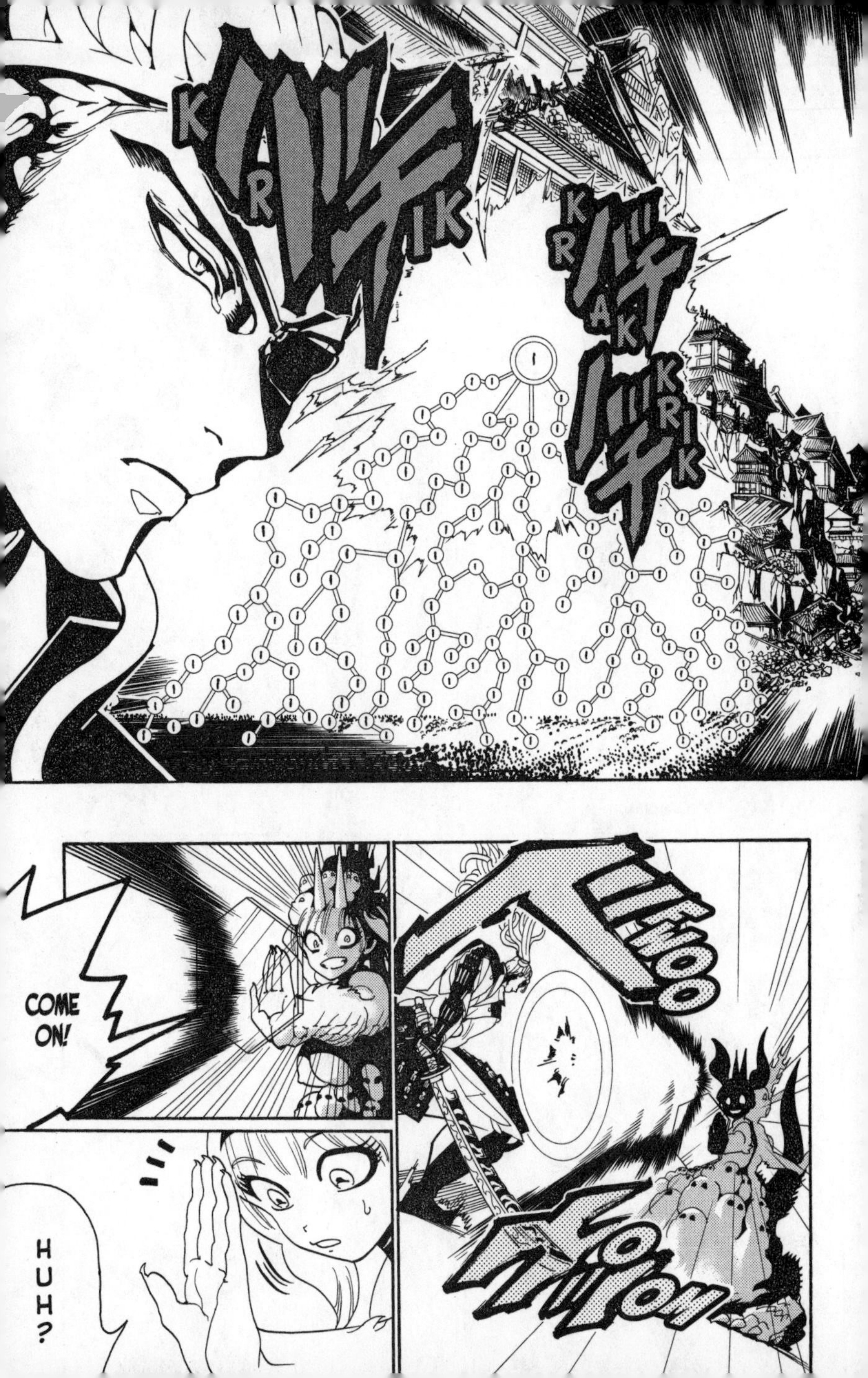
KRIK
KRAK KRIK
KRIK
FWOO
COME ON!
HUH?

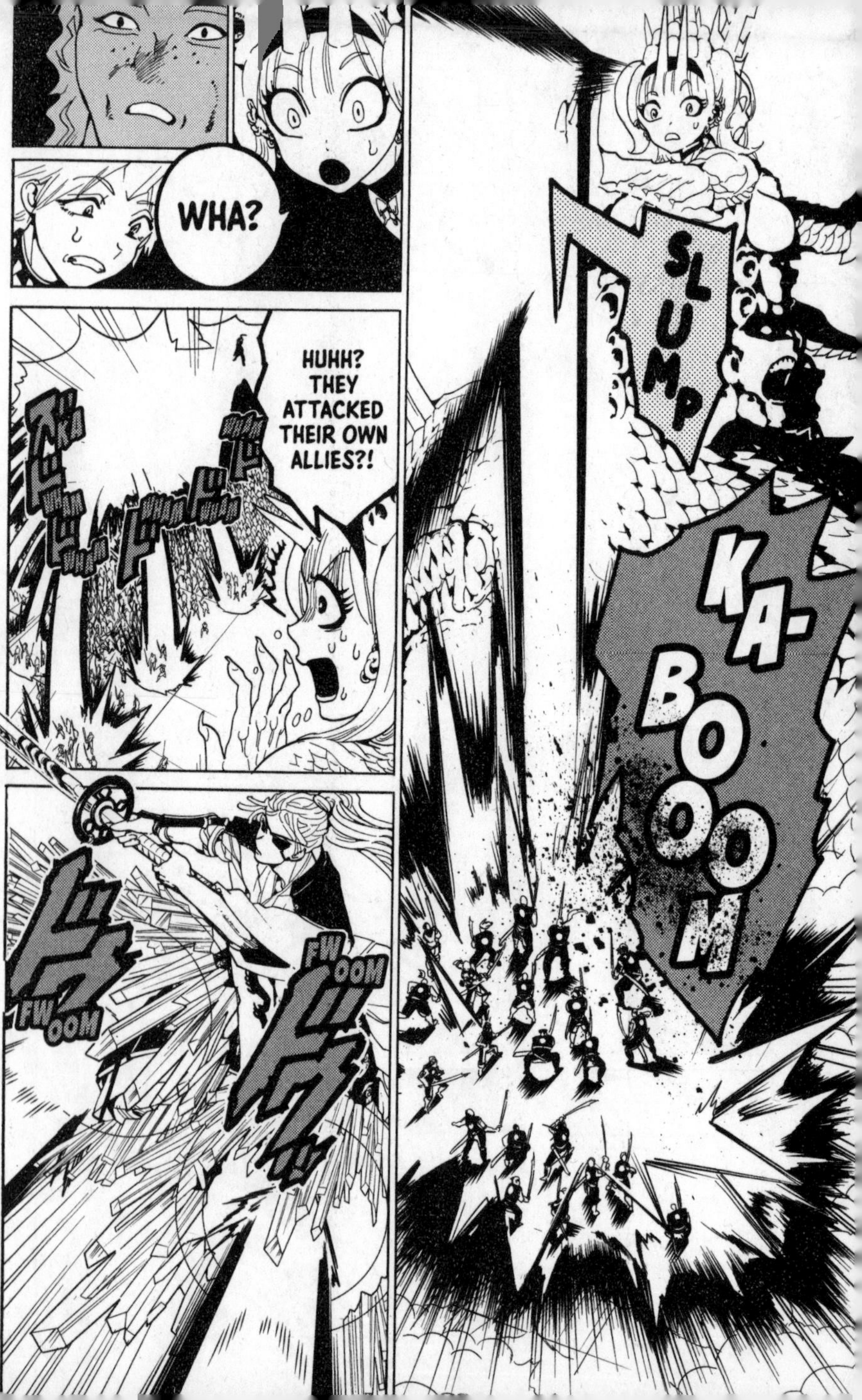
SLUMP
KA-BOOM
WHA?
HUHH? THEY ATTACKED THEIR OWN ALLIES?!
FWOOM
FWOOM

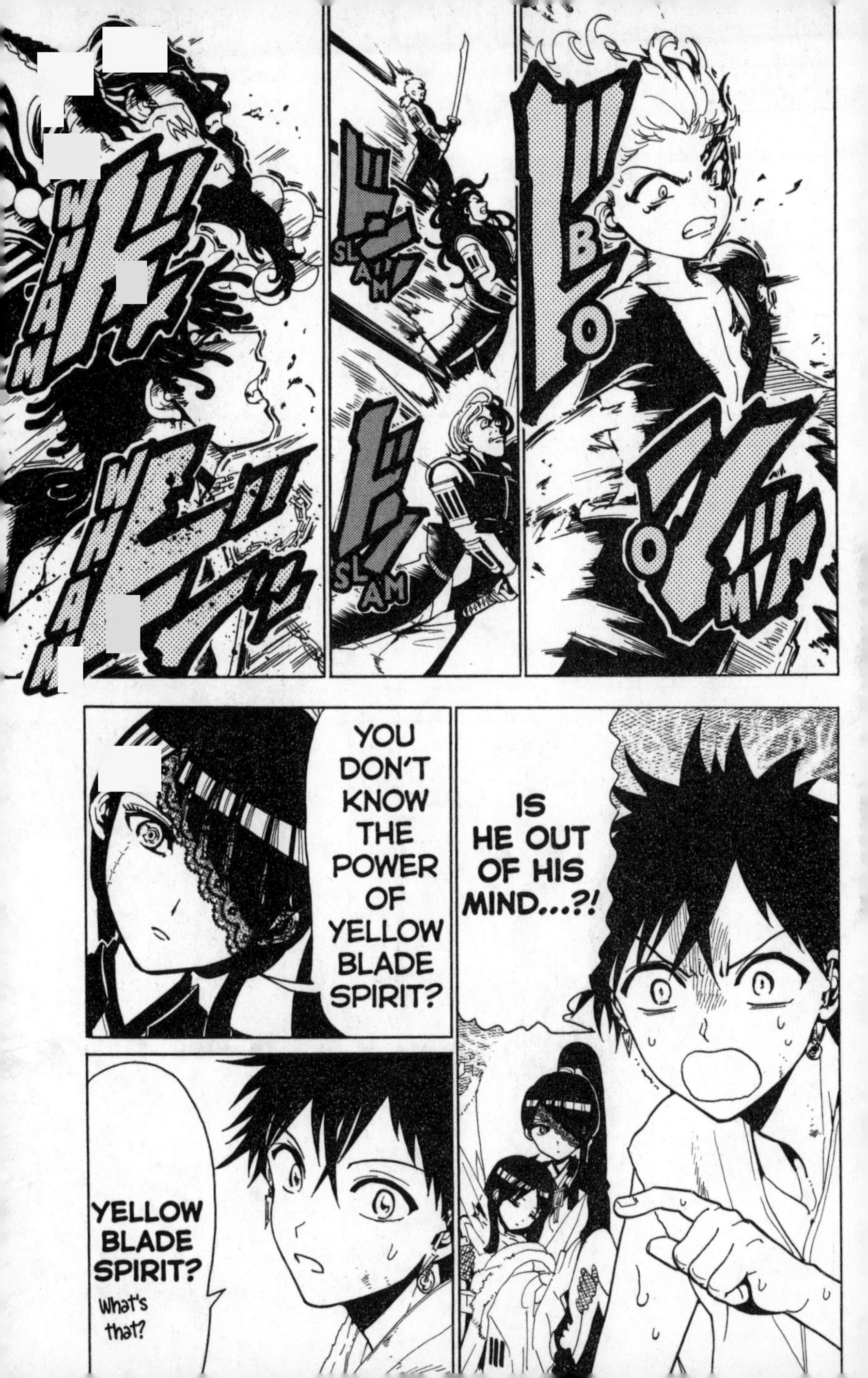
BOOM
SLAM
SLAM
WHAM
WHAM
IS HE OUT OF HIS MIND...?!
YOU DON'T KNOW THE POWER OF YELLOW BLADE SPIRIT?
YELLOW BLADE SPIRIT?
What's that?

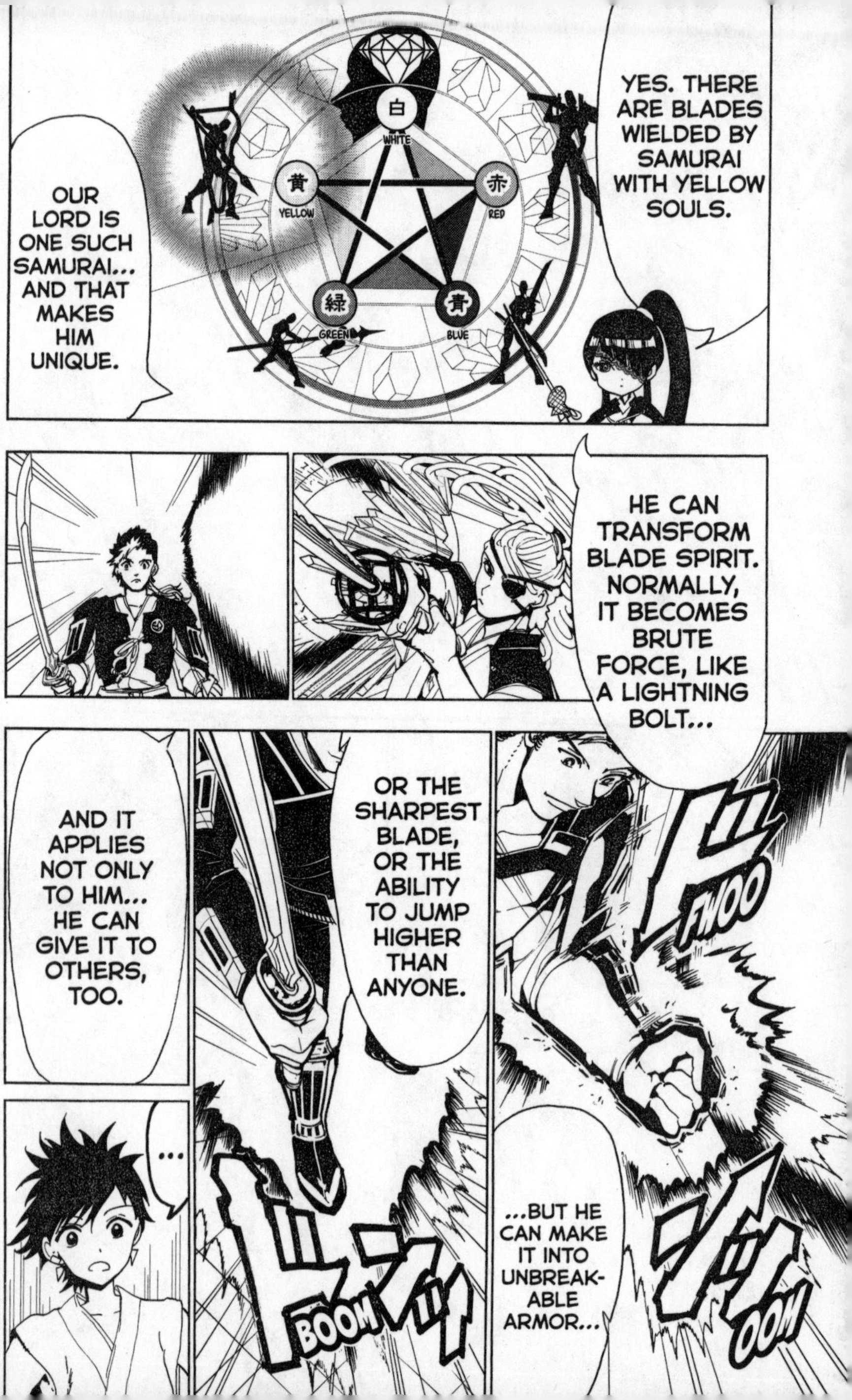
YES. THERE ARE BLADES WIELDED BY SAMURAI WITH YELLOW SOULS.
白
WHITE
赤
RED
黄
YELLOW
青
BLUE
緑
GREEN
OUR LORD IS ONE SUCH SAMURAI... AND THAT MAKES HIM UNIQUE.
HE CAN TRANSFORM BLADE SPIRIT. NORMALLY, IT BECOMES BRUTE FORCE, LIKE A LIGHTNING BOLT...
FWOO
...BUT HE CAN MAKE IT INTO UNBREAKABLE ARMOR...
OOM
OR THE SHARPEST BLADE, OR THE ABILITY TO JUMP HIGHER THAN ANYONE.
BOOM
AND IT APPLIES NOT ONLY TO HIM... HE CAN GIVE IT TO OTHERS, TOO.
...

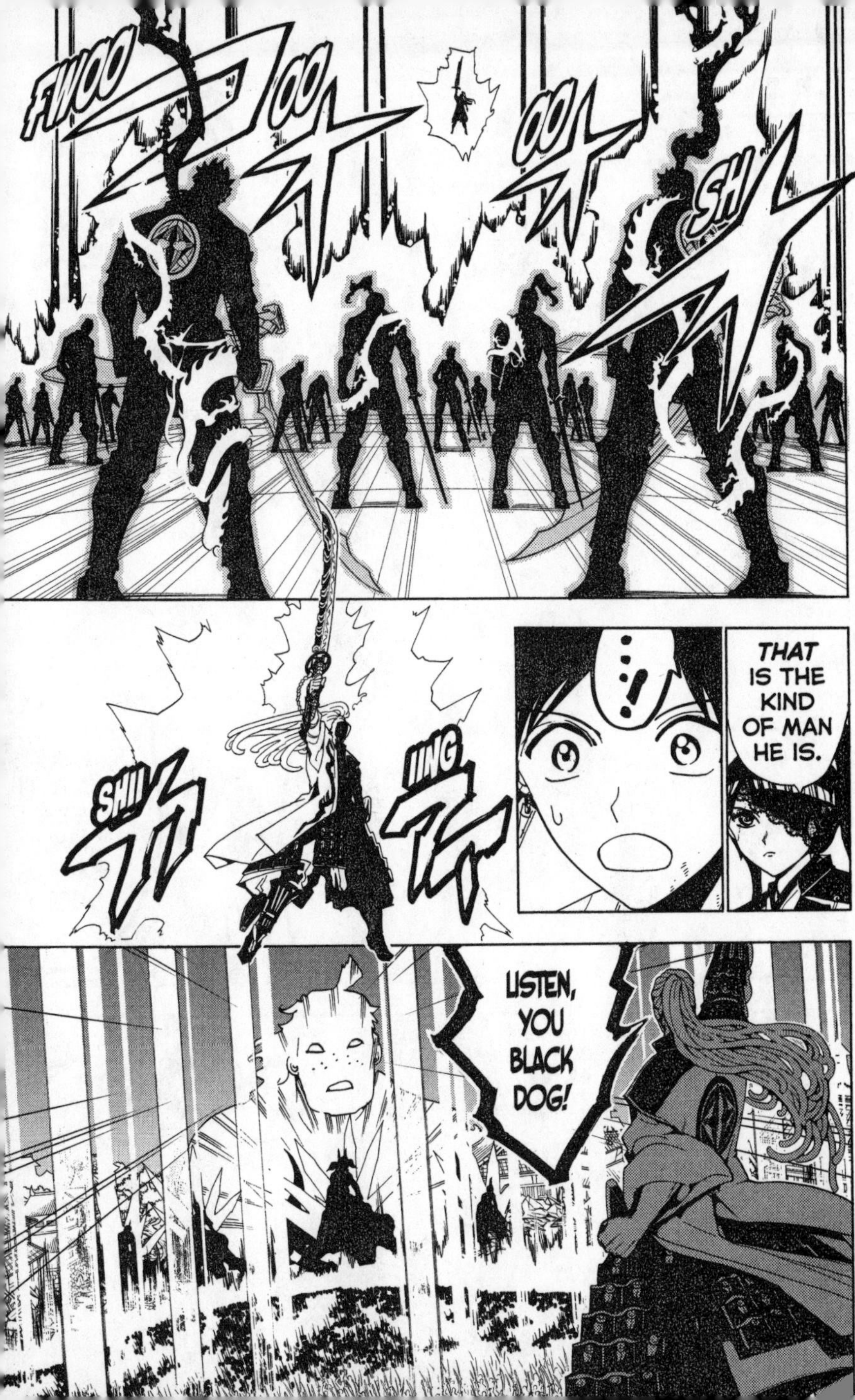
FWOO
OO
OO
SH
THAT IS THE KIND OF MAN HE IS.
...!
SHII
IING
LISTEN, YOU BLACK DOG!

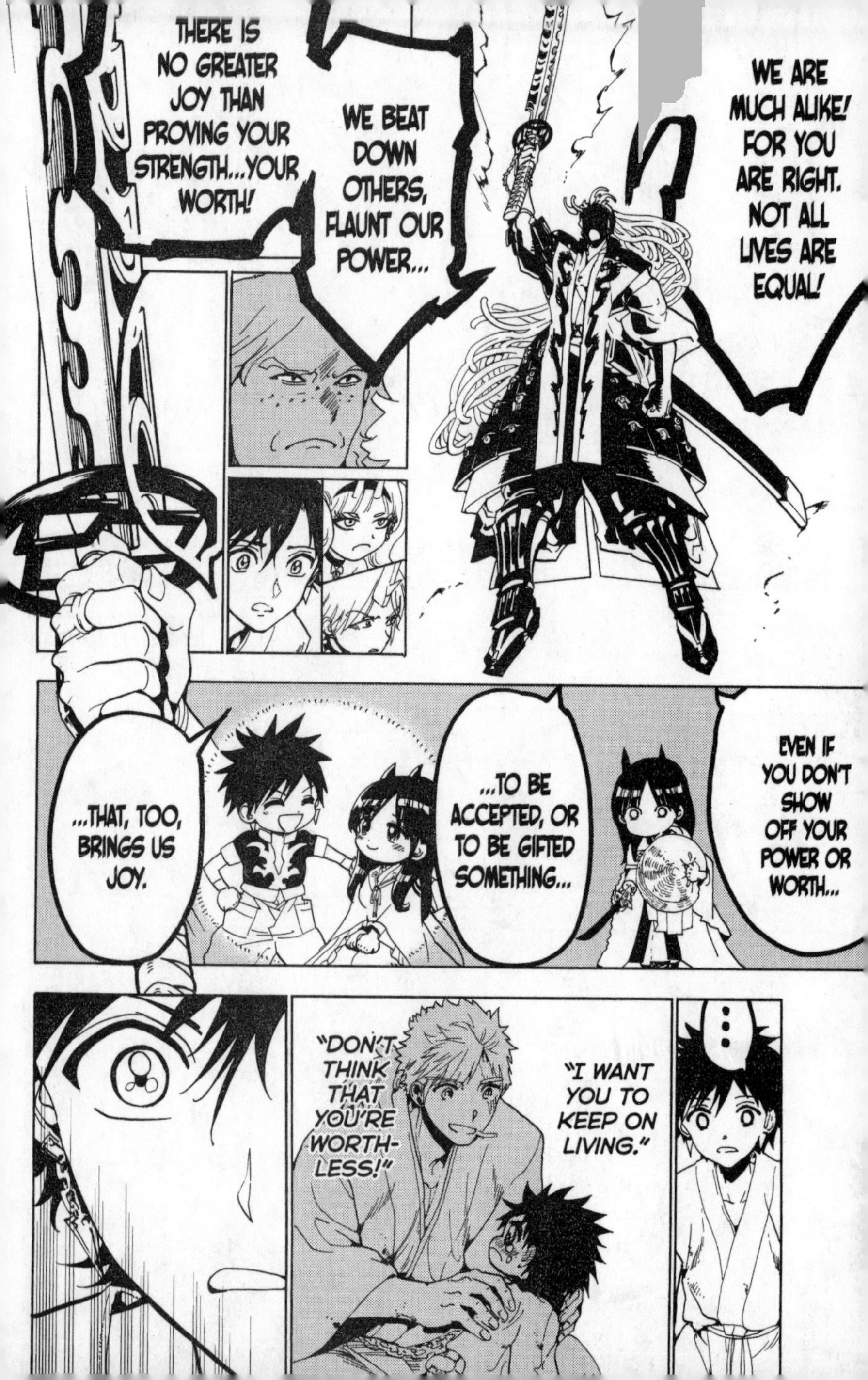
WE ARE MUCH ALIKE! FOR YOU ARE RIGHT. NOT ALL LIVES ARE EQUAL!
WE BEAT DOWN OTHERS, FLAUNT OUR POWER...
THERE IS NO GREATER JOY THAN PROVING YOUR STRENGTH...YOUR WORTH!
EVEN IF YOU DON'T SHOW OFF YOUR POWER OR WORTH...
...TO BE ACCEPTED, OR TO BE GIFTED SOMETHING...
...THAT, TOO, BRINGS US JOY.
...
"I WANT YOU TO KEEP ON LIVING."
"DON'T THINK THAT YOU'RE WORTH-LESS!"

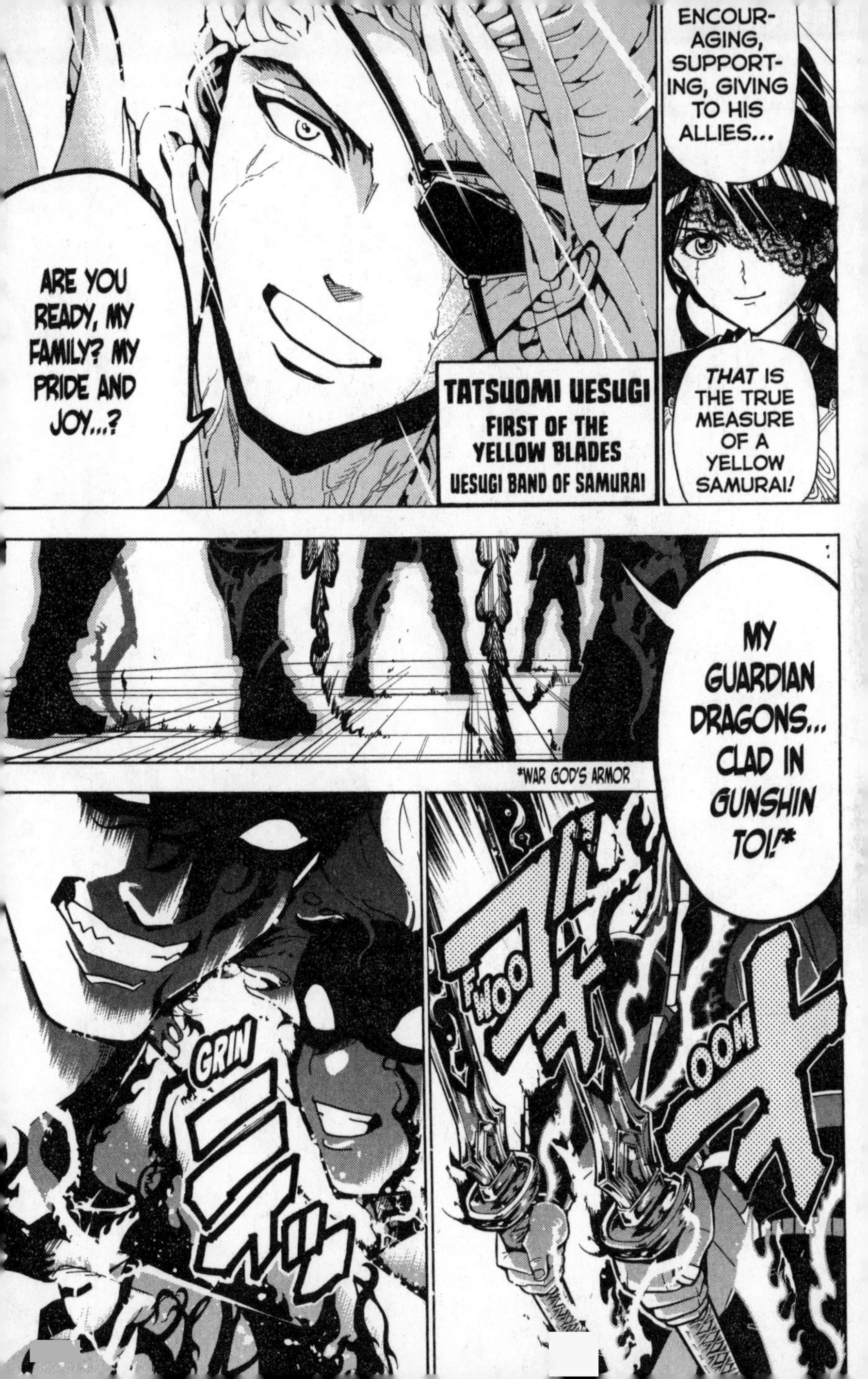
ENCOURAGING, SUPPORTING, GIVING TO HIS ALLIES...
THAT IS THE TRUE MEASURE OF A YELLOW SAMURAI!
ARE YOU READY, MY FAMILY? MY PRIDE AND JOY...?
TATSUOMI UESUGI
FIRST OF THE YELLOW BLADES
UESUGI BAND OF SAMURAI
MY GUARDIAN DRAGONS... CLAD IN GUNSHIN TOI!*
*WAR GOD'S ARMOR
FWOO
OOM
GRIN

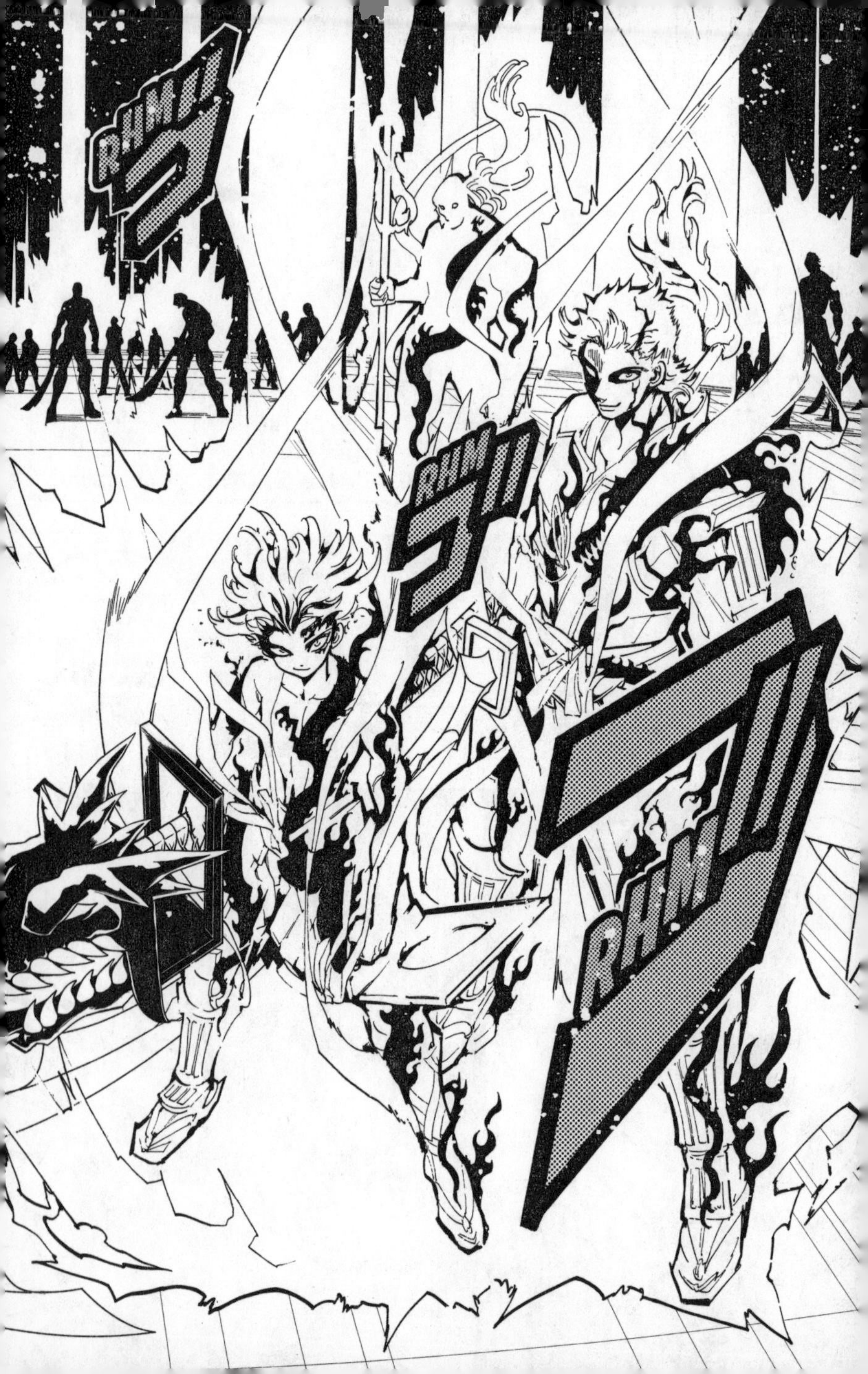
RHM
RHM
RHM

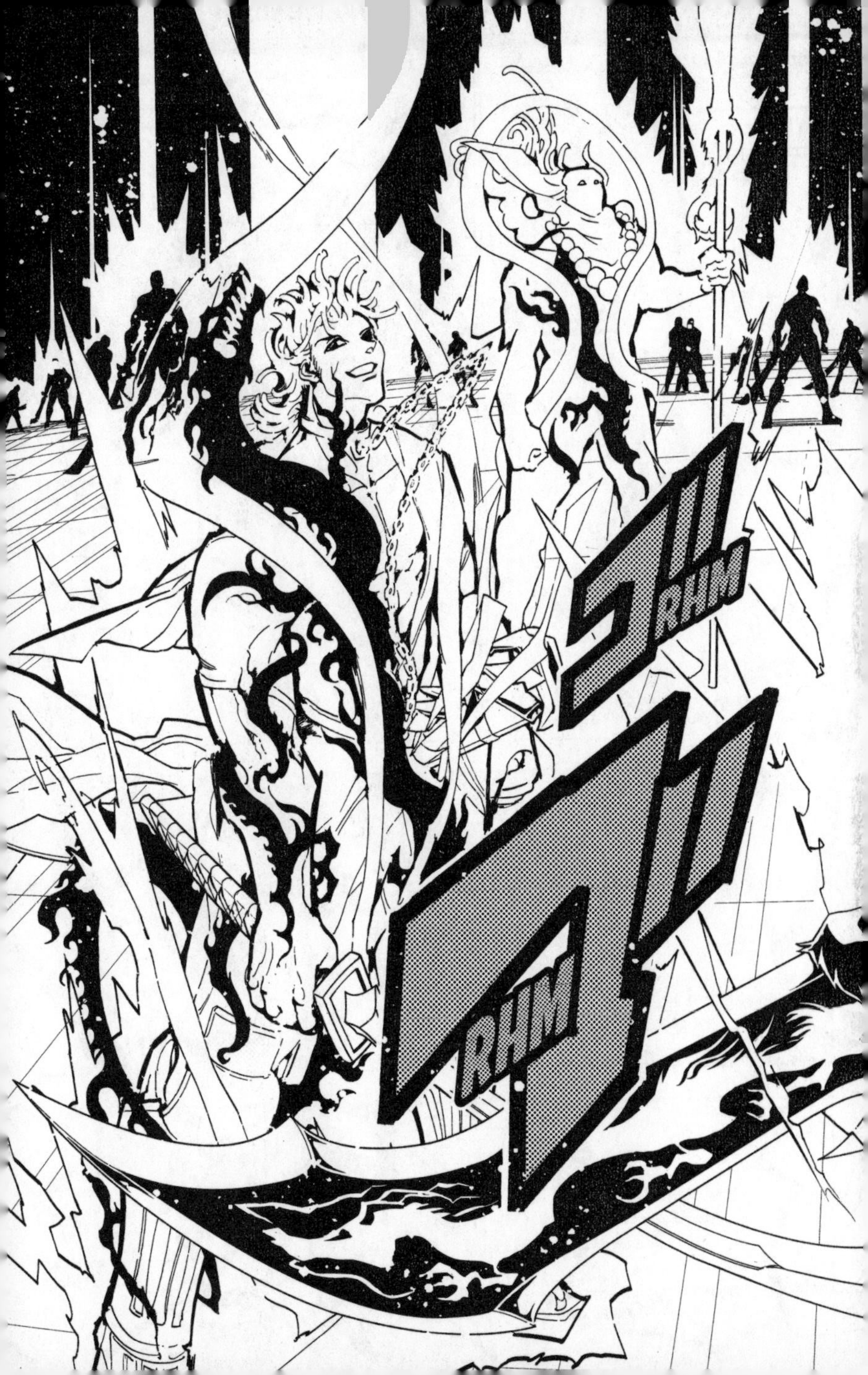
RHM
RHM

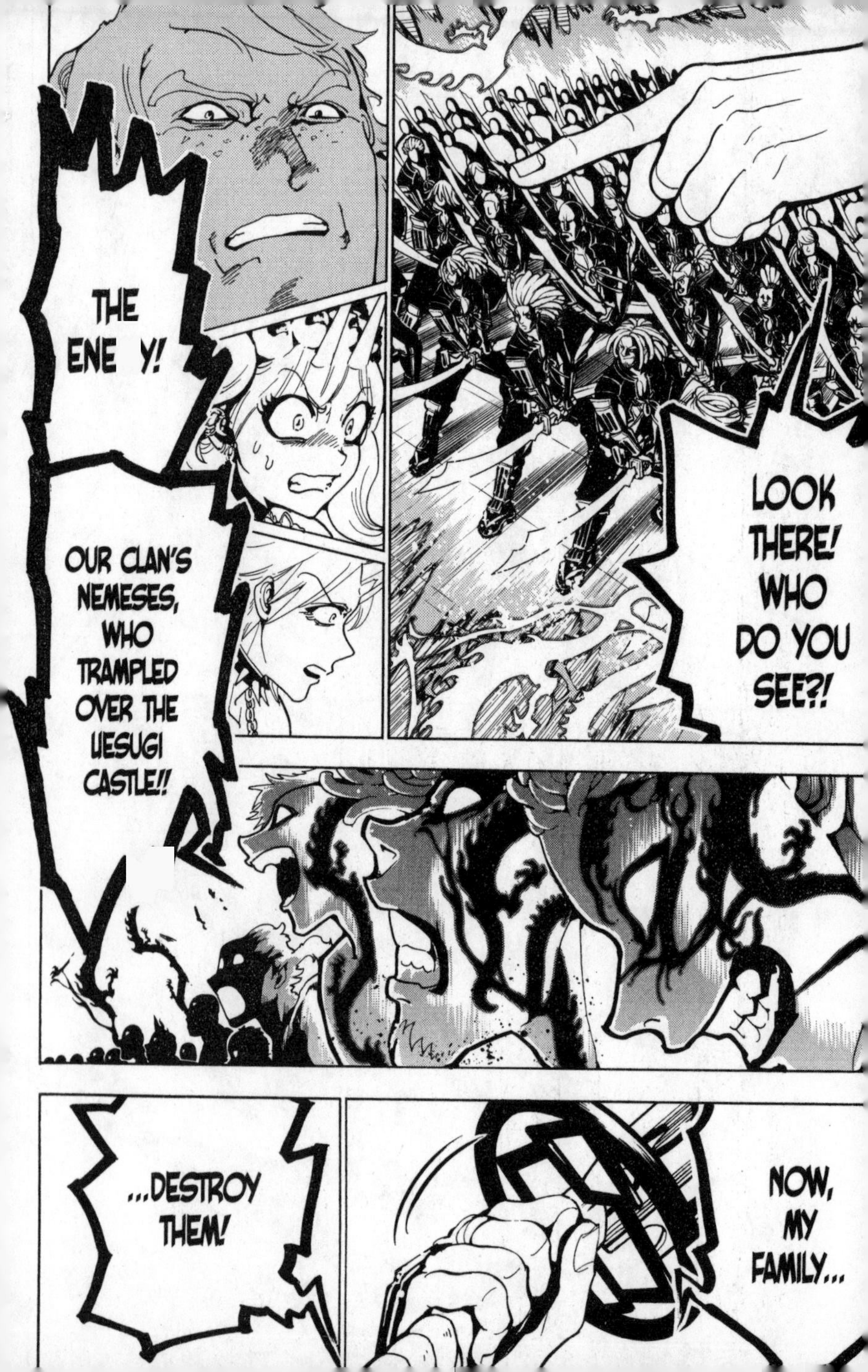
LOOK THERE! WHO DO YOU SEE?!
THE ENE Y!
OUR CLAN'S NEMESES, WHO TRAMPLED OVER THE UESUGI CASTLE!!
NOW, MY FAMILY...
...DESTROY THEM!

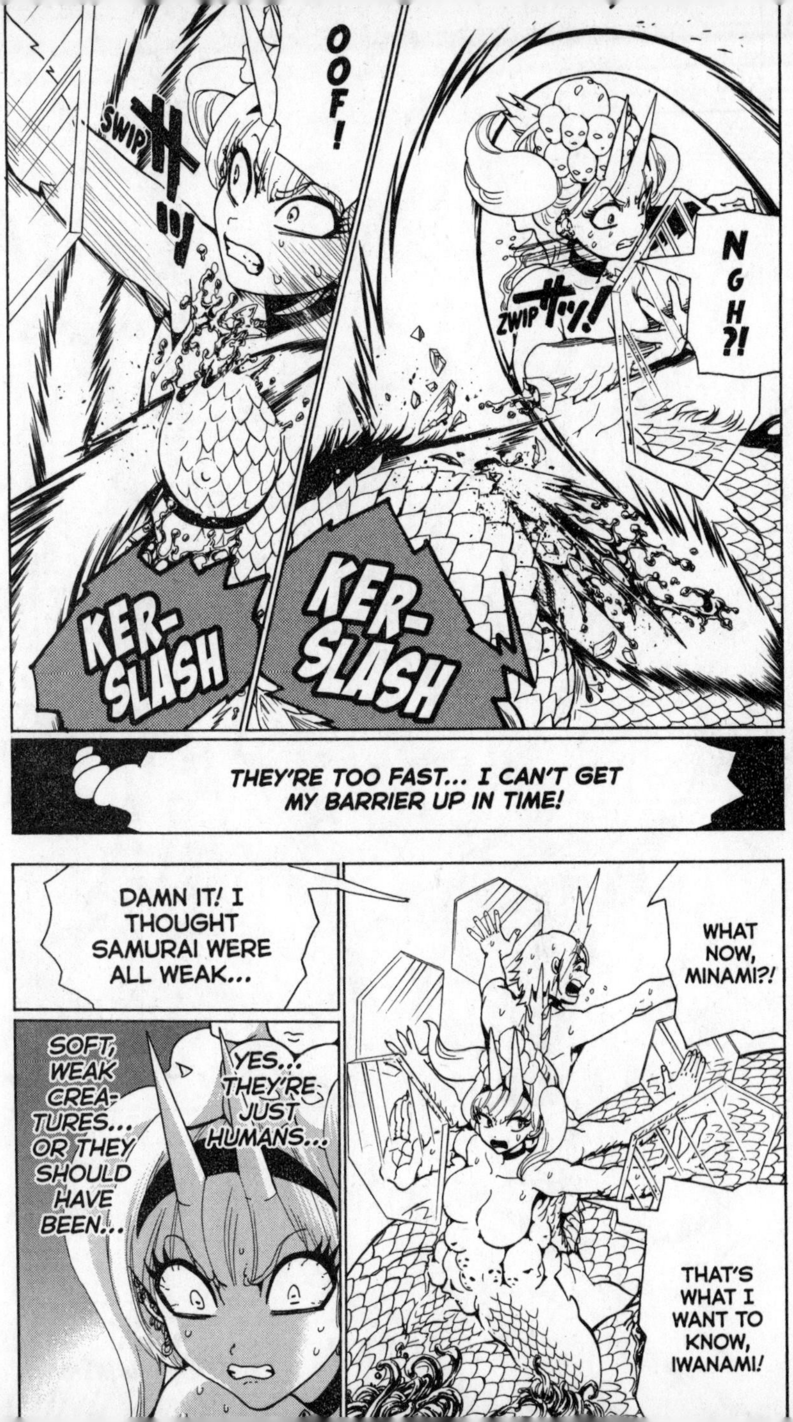
NGH?!
ZWIP
OOF!
SWIP
KER-SLASH
KER-SLASH
THEY'RE TOO FAST... I CAN'T GET MY BARRIER UP IN TIME!
WHAT NOW, MINAMI?!
THAT'S WHAT I WANT TO KNOW, IWANAMI!
DAMN IT! I THOUGHT SAMURAI WERE ALL WEAK...
YES... THEY'RE JUST HUMANS...
SOFT, WEAK CREA-TURES... OR THEY SHOULD HAVE BEEN...

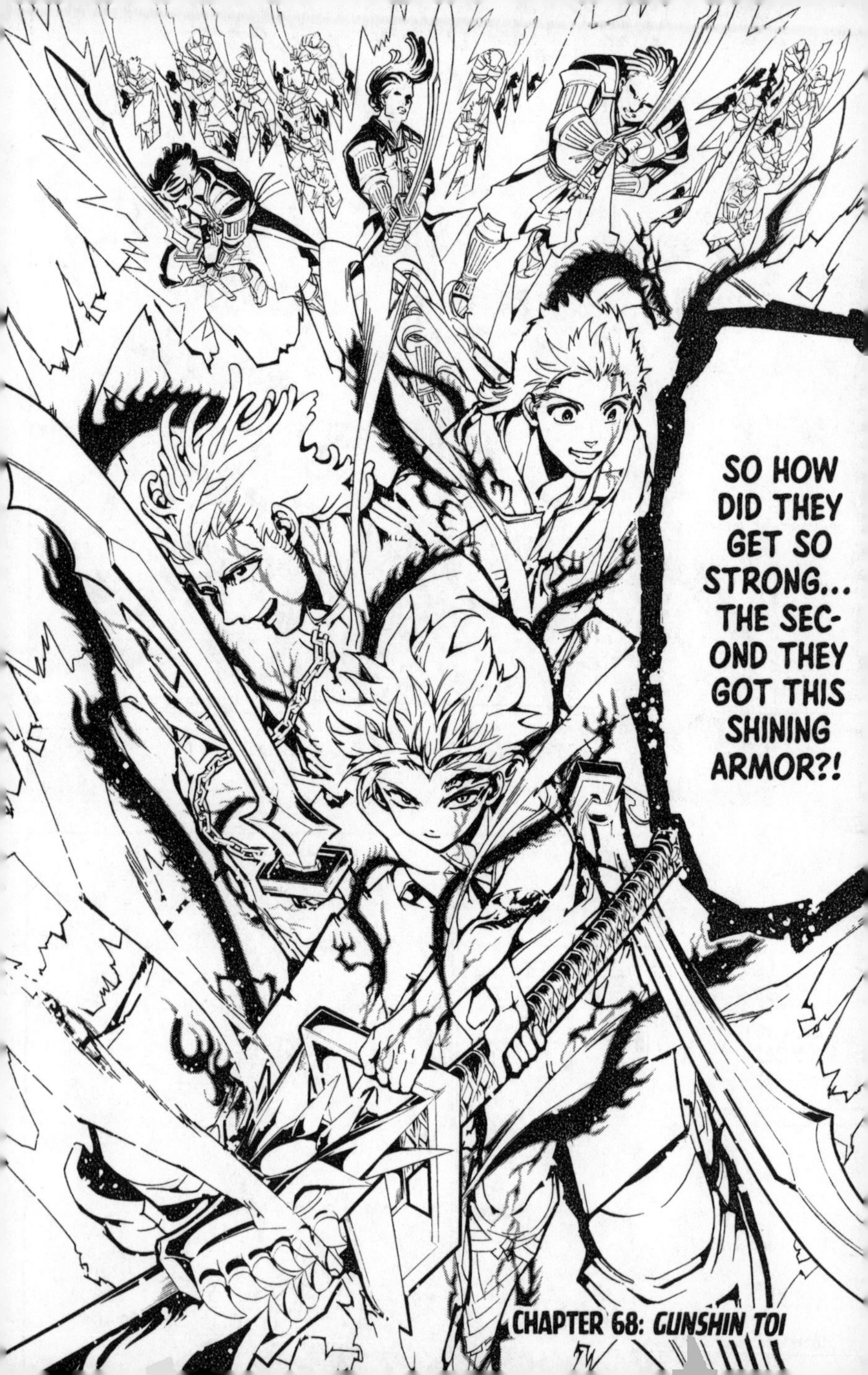
SO HOW DID THEY GET SO STRONG... THE SEC-OND THEY GOT THIS SHINING ARMOR?!
CHAPTER 68: GUNSHIN TOI

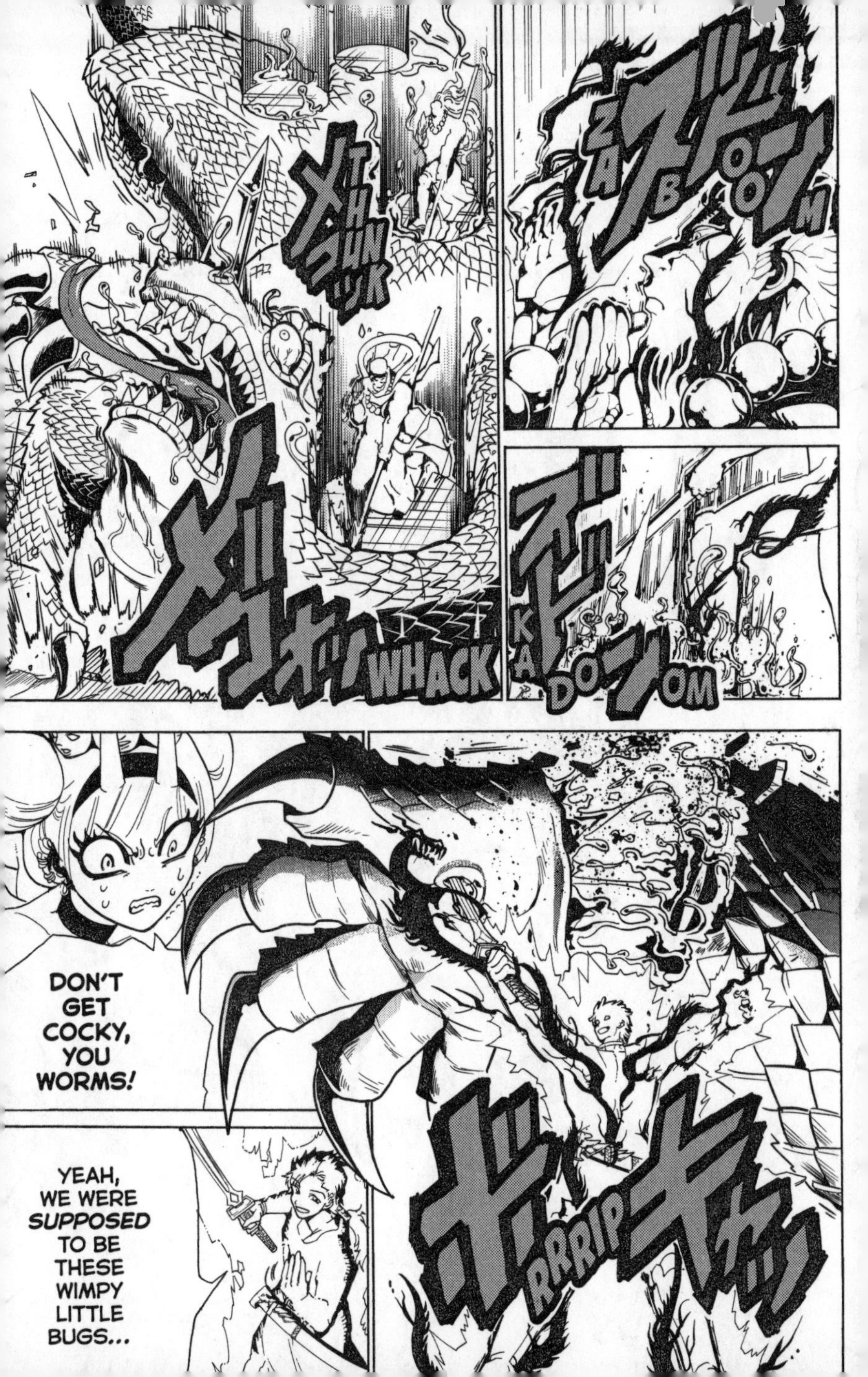
ZABOOM
KADOOM
THUNK
WHACK
RRRIP
DON'T GET COCKY, YOU WORMS!
YEAH, WE WERE *SUPPOSED* TO BE THESE WIMPY LITTLE BUGS...

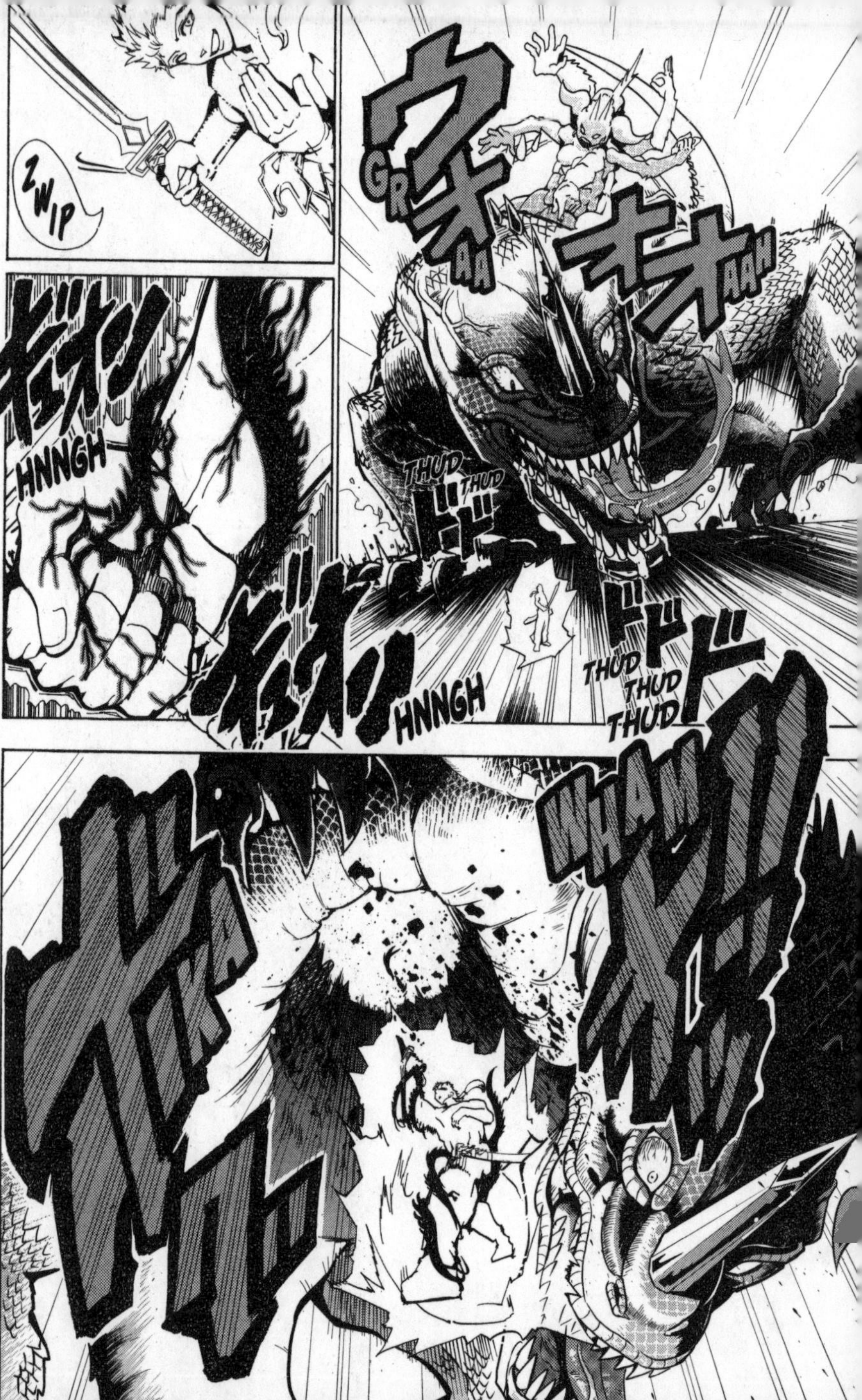
GRAAAAH
THUD THUD
THUD THUD THUD
ZWIP
HNNGH
HNNGH
WHAM!!

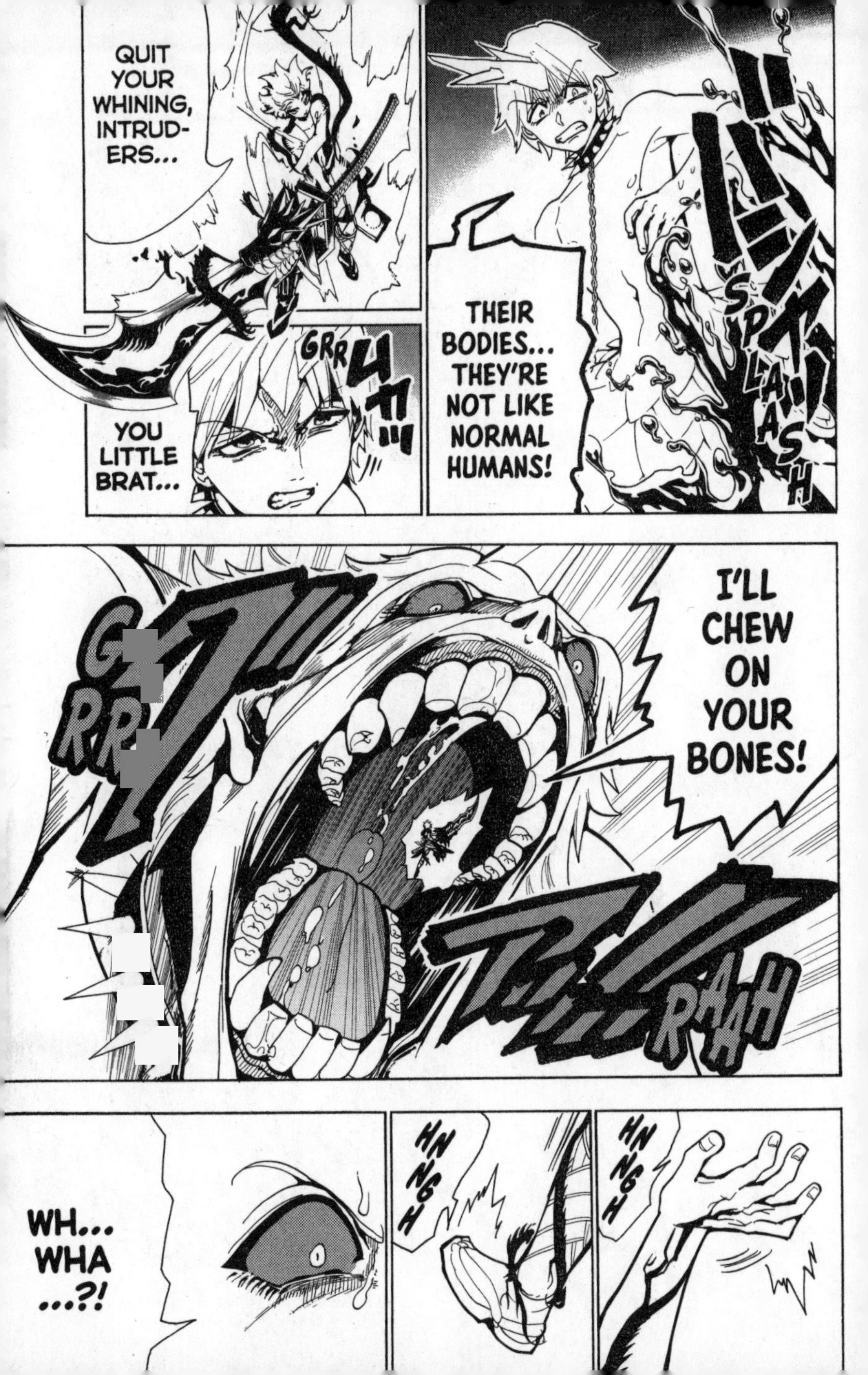
SPLASH
THEIR BODIES... THEY'RE NOT LIKE NORMAL HUMANS!
QUIT YOUR WHINING, INTRUDERS...
GRR
YOU LITTLE BRAT...
I'LL CHEW ON YOUR BONES!
RAAH
HNNGH
HNNGH
WH... WHA ...?!

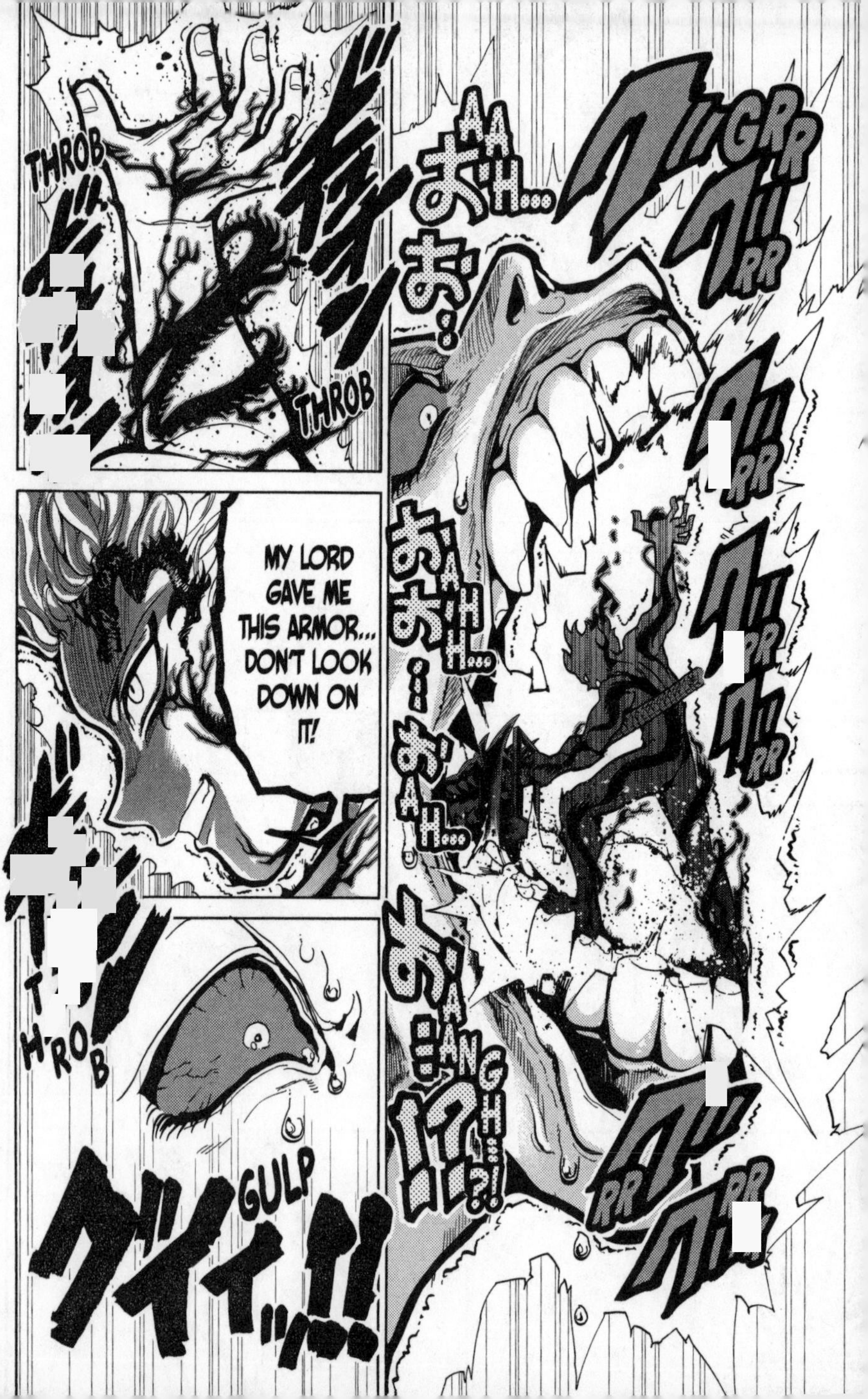
GRR
RR
AAH...
AAHH...
AH...
AANGH...?!
THROB
THROB
MY LORD GAVE ME THIS ARMOR... DON'T LOOK DOWN ON IT!
THROB
GULP

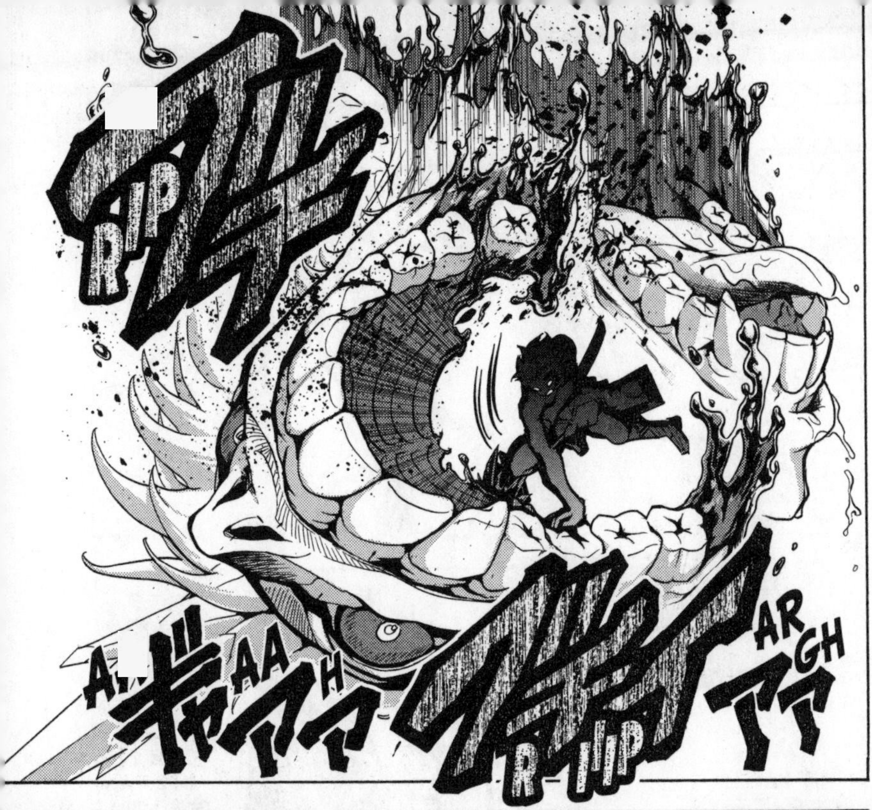
RIP
ARGH
RIP
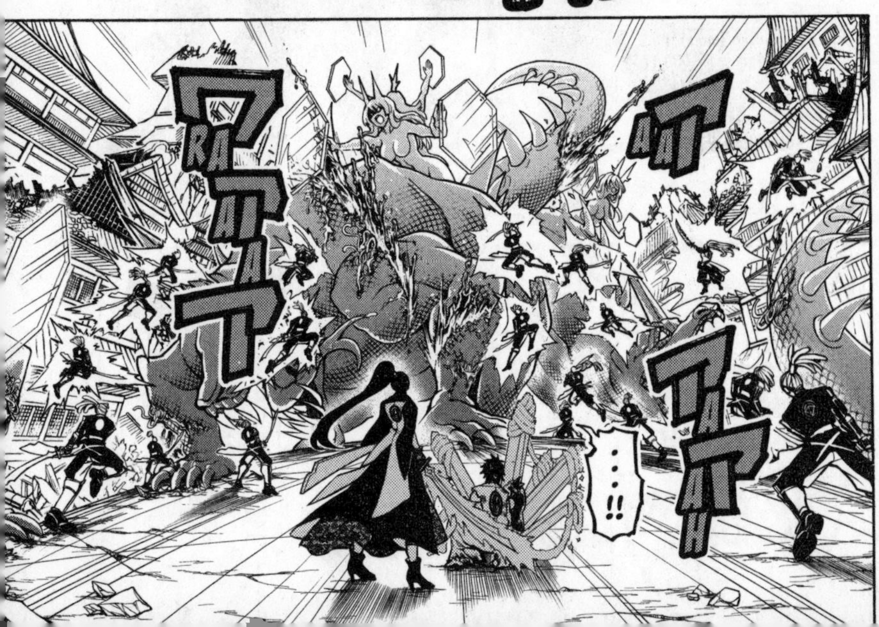
...!!

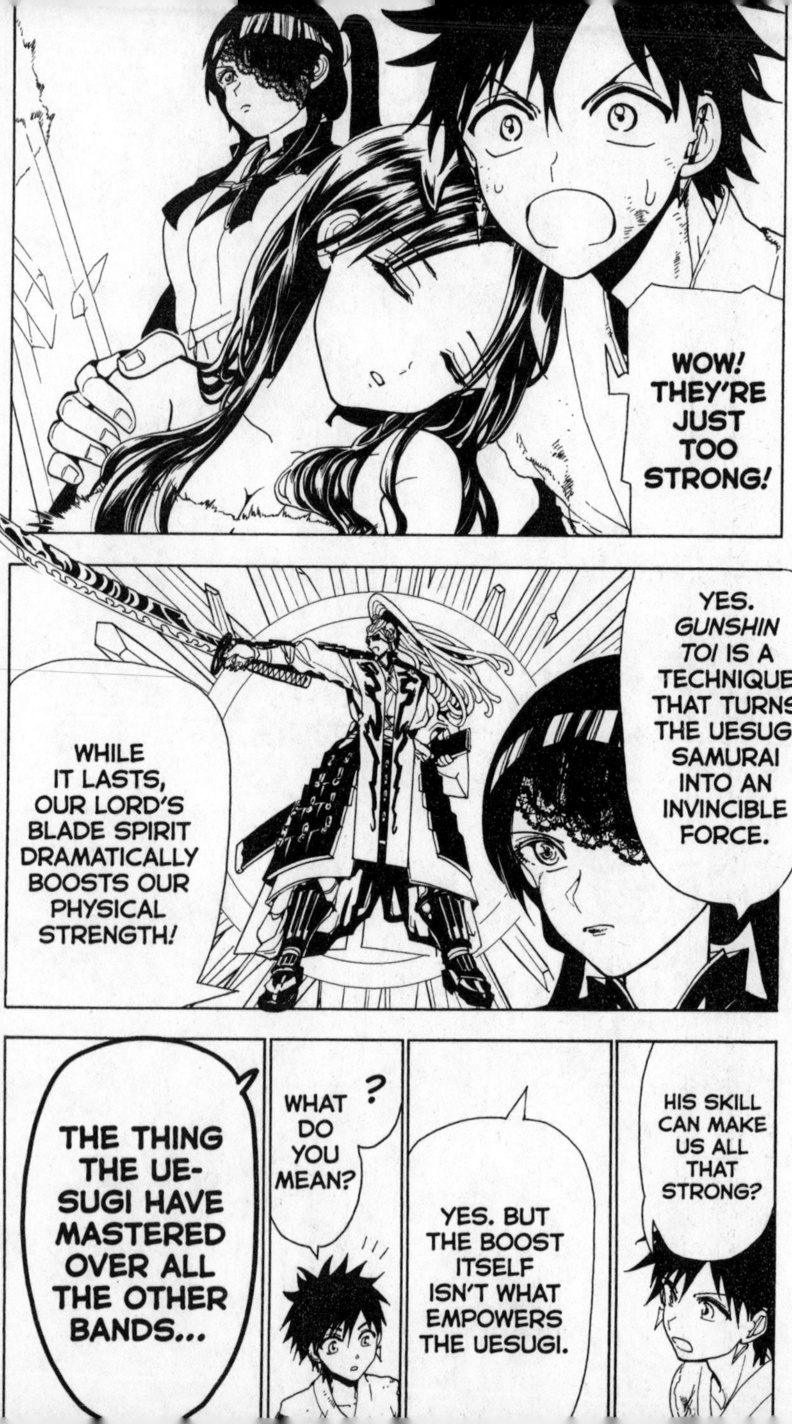
WOW! THEY'RE JUST TOO STRONG!
YES. GUNSHIN TOI IS A TECHNIQUE THAT TURNS THE UESUGI SAMURAI INTO AN INVINCIBLE FORCE.
WHILE IT LASTS, OUR LORD'S BLADE SPIRIT DRAMATICALLY BOOSTS OUR PHYSICAL STRENGTH!
HIS SKILL CAN MAKE US ALL THAT STRONG?
YES. BUT THE BOOST ITSELF ISN'T WHAT EMPOWERS THE UESUGI.
WHAT DO YOU MEAN?
THE THING THE UE-SUGI HAVE MASTERED OVER ALL THE OTHER BANDS...

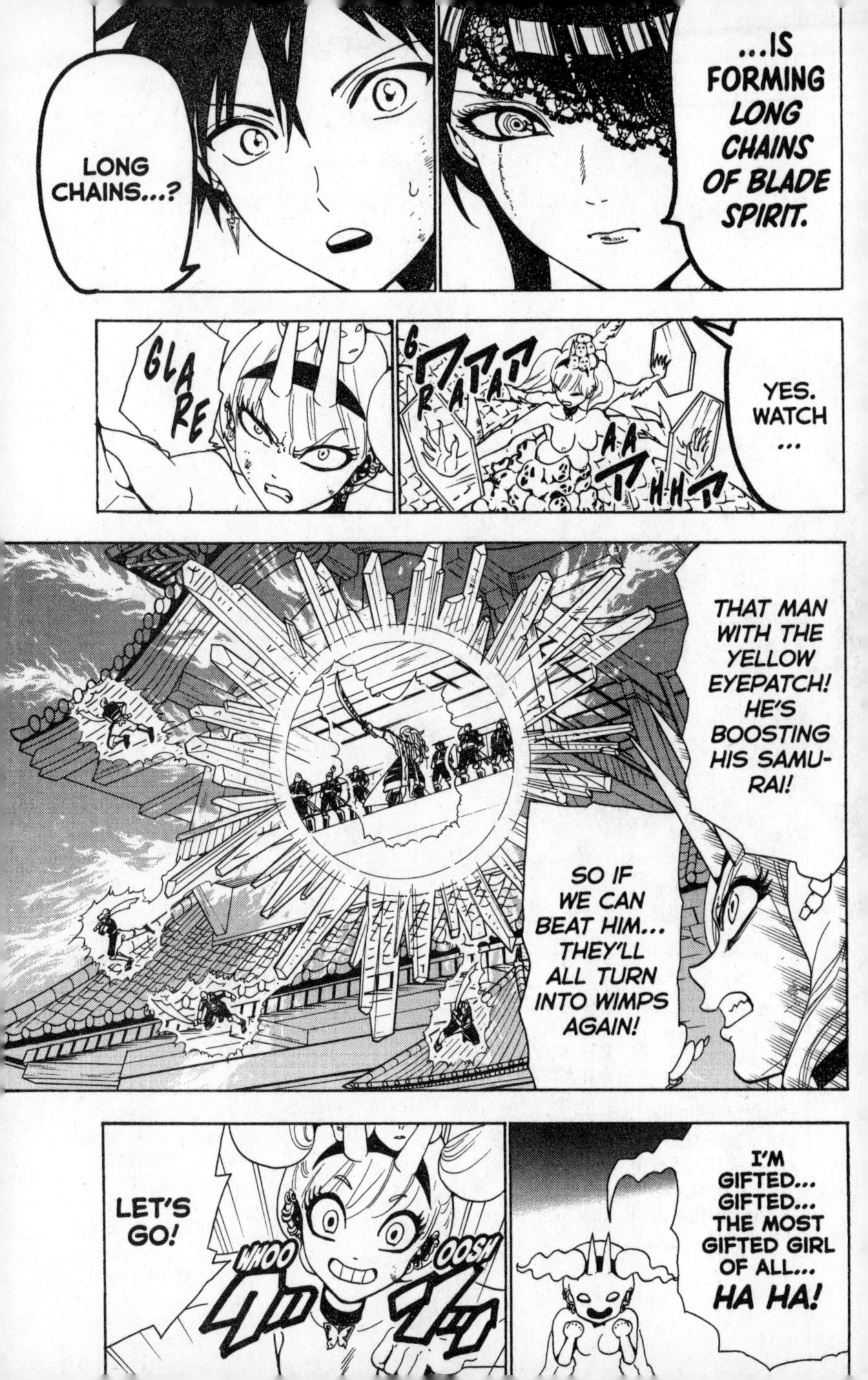
...IS FORMING LONG CHAINS OF BLADE SPIRIT.
LONG CHAINS...?
YES. WATCH ...
GLARE
THAT MAN WITH THE YELLOW EYEPATCH! HE'S BOOSTING HIS SAMURAI!
SO IF WE CAN BEAT HIM... THEY'LL ALL TURN INTO WIMPS AGAIN!
I'M GIFTED... GIFTED... THE MOST GIFTED GIRL OF ALL... HA HA!
LET'S GO!
WHOO OOSH

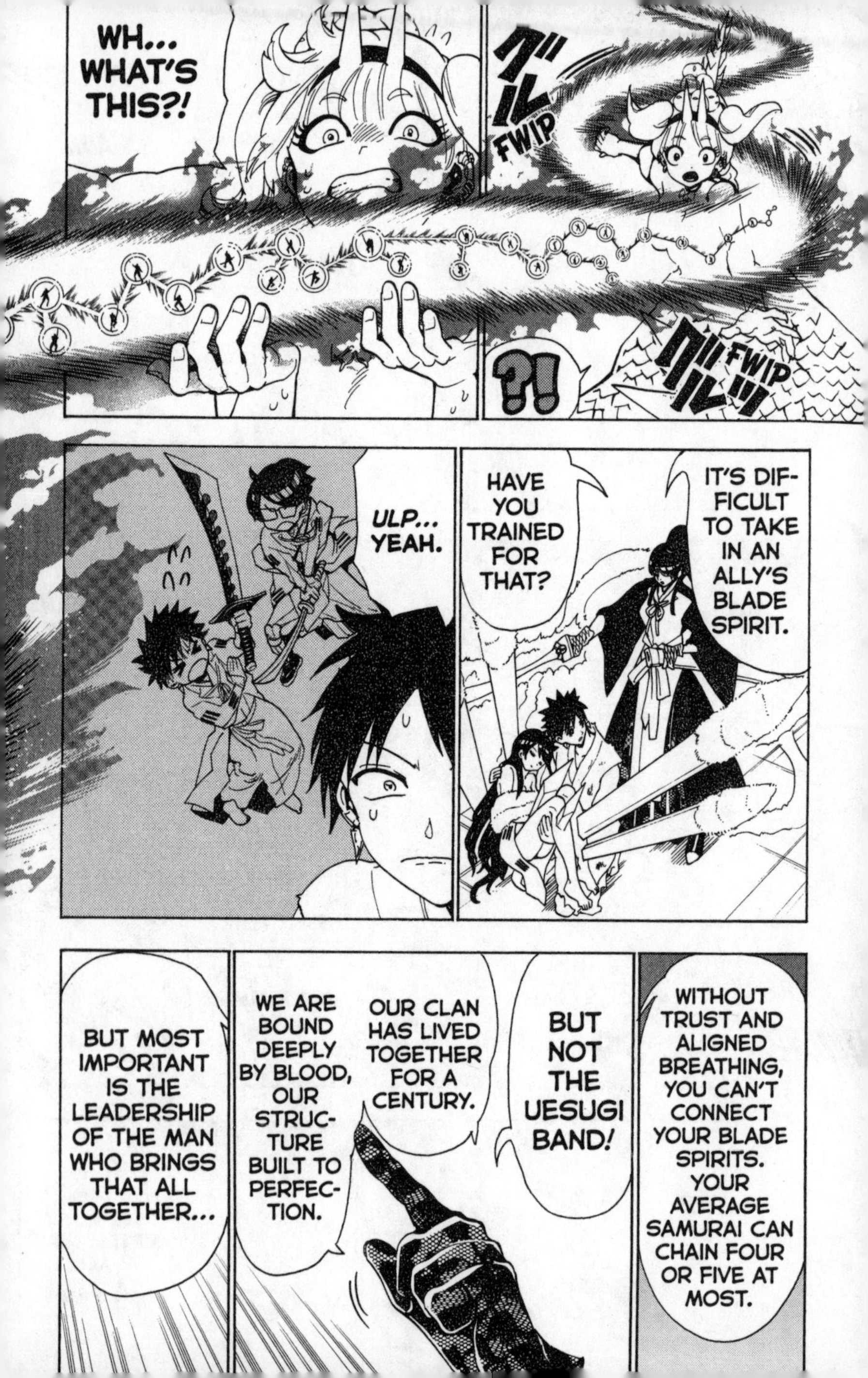
FWIP
?!
FWIP
WH... WHAT'S THIS?!
IT'S DIFFICULT TO TAKE IN AN ALLY'S BLADE SPIRIT.
HAVE YOU TRAINED FOR THAT?
ULP... YEAH.
WITHOUT TRUST AND ALIGNED BREATHING, YOU CAN'T CONNECT YOUR BLADE SPIRITS. YOUR AVERAGE SAMURAI CAN CHAIN FOUR OR FIVE AT MOST.
BUT NOT THE UESUGI BAND!
OUR CLAN HAS LIVED TOGETHER FOR A CENTURY.
WE ARE BOUND DEEPLY BY BLOOD, OUR STRUCTURE BUILT TO PERFECTION.
BUT MOST IMPORTANT IS THE LEADERSHIP OF THE MAN WHO BRINGS THAT ALL TOGETHER...

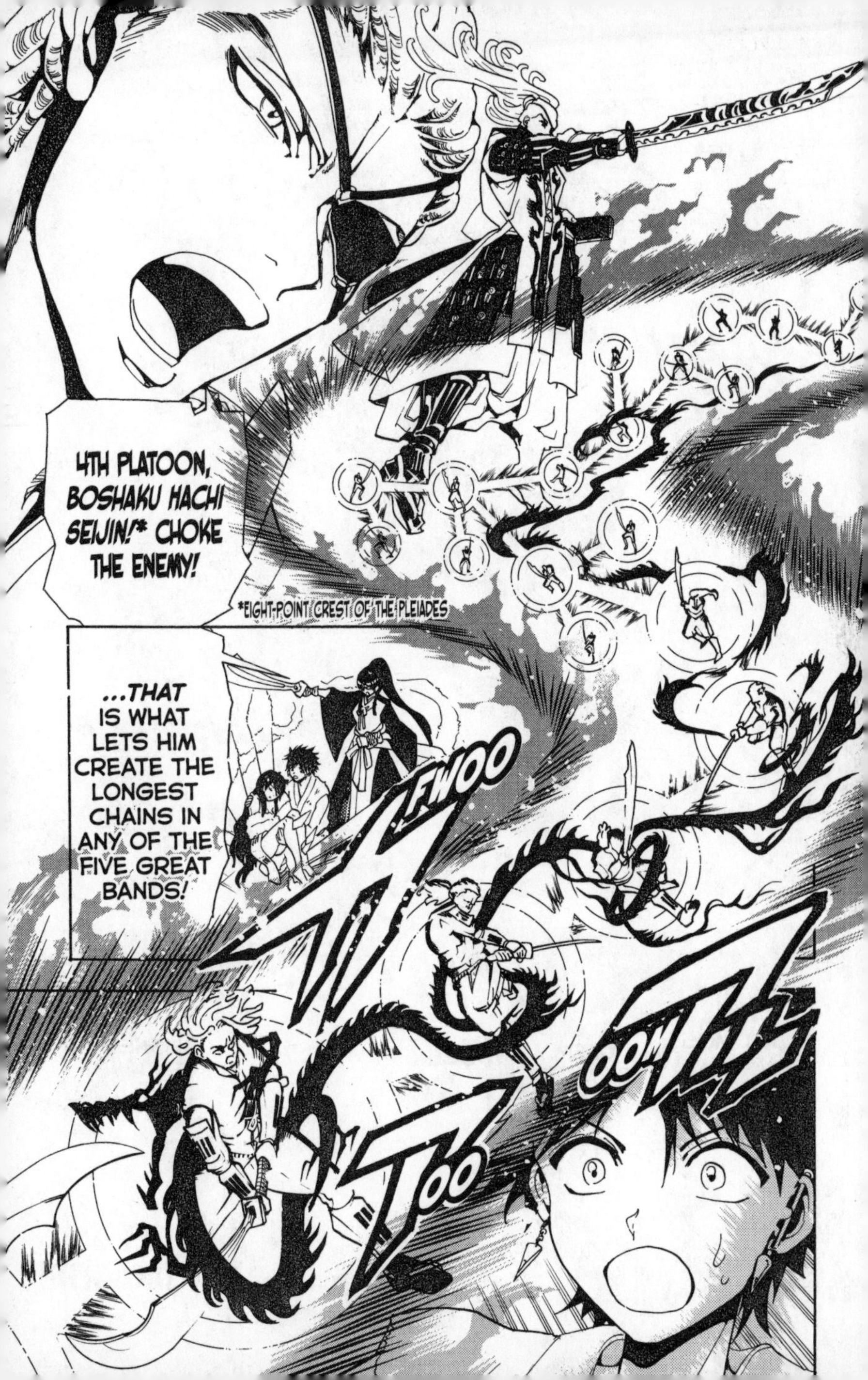
4TH PLATOON, BOSHAKU HACHI SEIJIN!* CHOKE THE ENEMY!
*EIGHT-POINT CREST OF THE PLEIADES
...THAT IS WHAT LETS HIM CREATE THE LONGEST CHAINS IN ANY OF THE FIVE GREAT BANDS!
FWOO
OOM
FOO

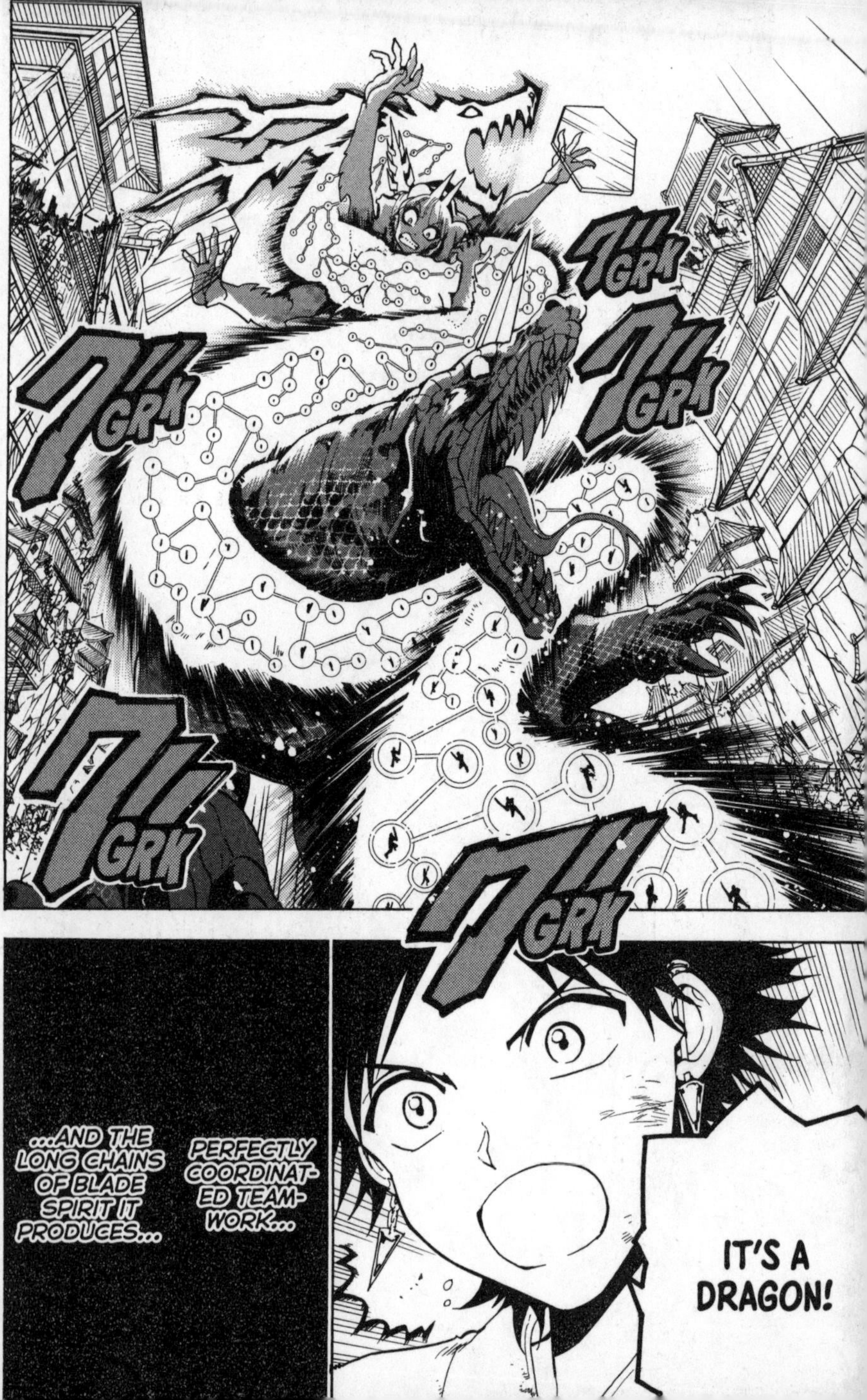
GRK
GRK
GRK
GRK
GRK
GRK
IT'S A DRAGON!
PERFECTLY COORDINATED TEAMWORK...
...AND THE LONG CHAINS OF BLADE SPIRIT IT PRODUCES...

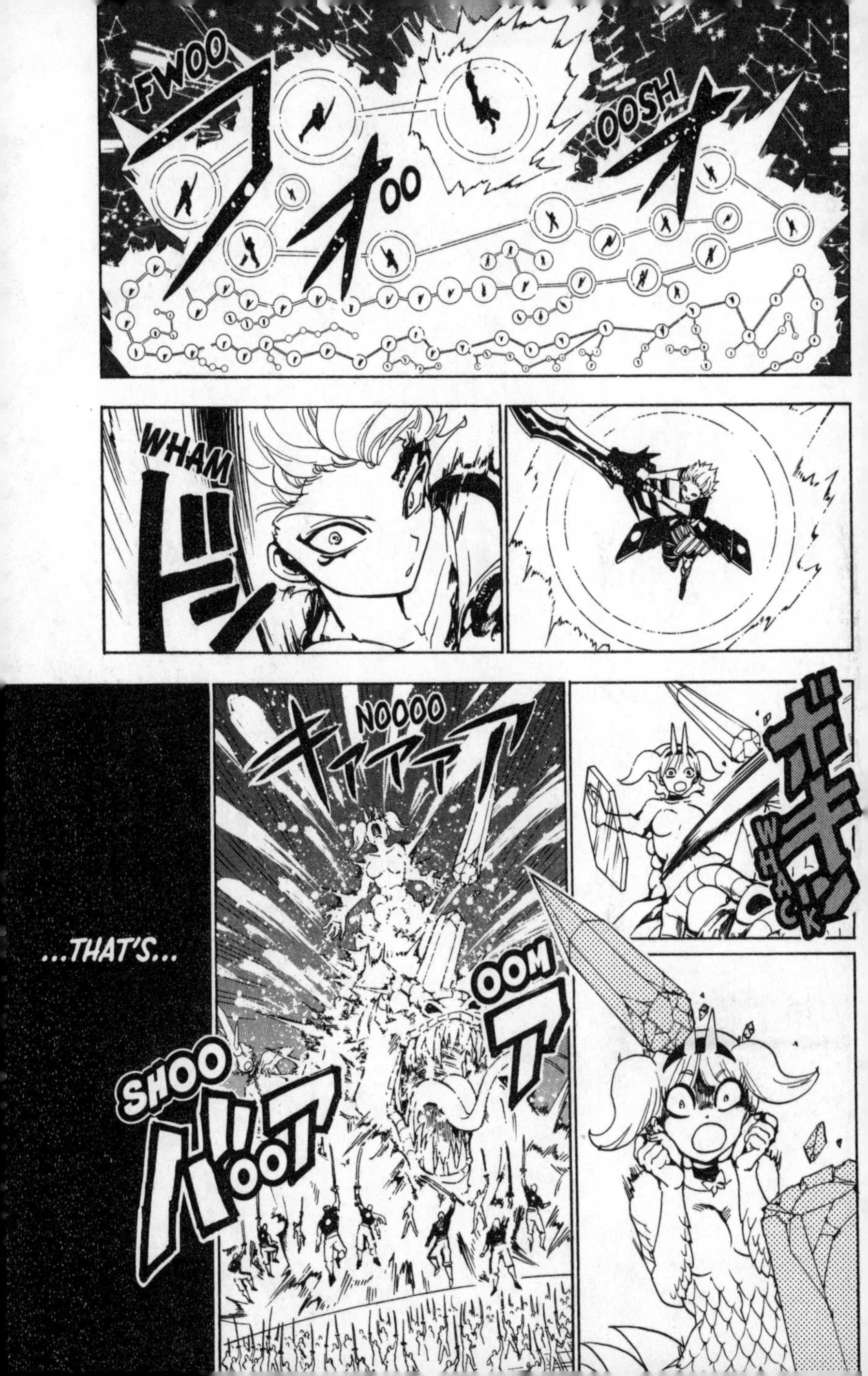
FWOO
OO
OOSH
WHAM
WHACK
NOOOO
OOM
SHOO
OOT
...THAT'S...

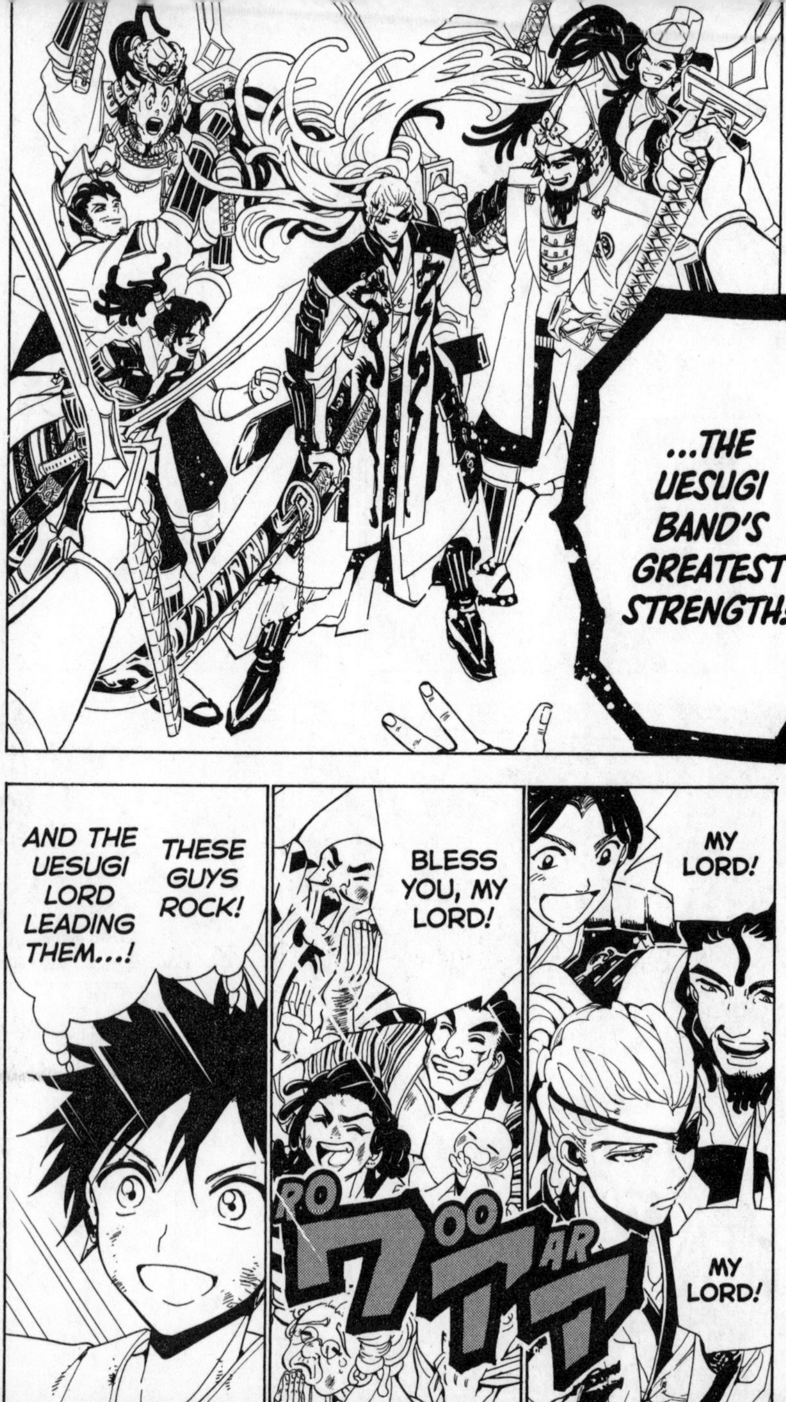
...THE UESUGI BAND'S GREATEST STRENGTH!
MY LORD!
MY LORD!
BLESS YOU, MY LORD!
ROOOAR
THESE GUYS ROCK!
AND THE UESUGI LORD LEADING THEM...!

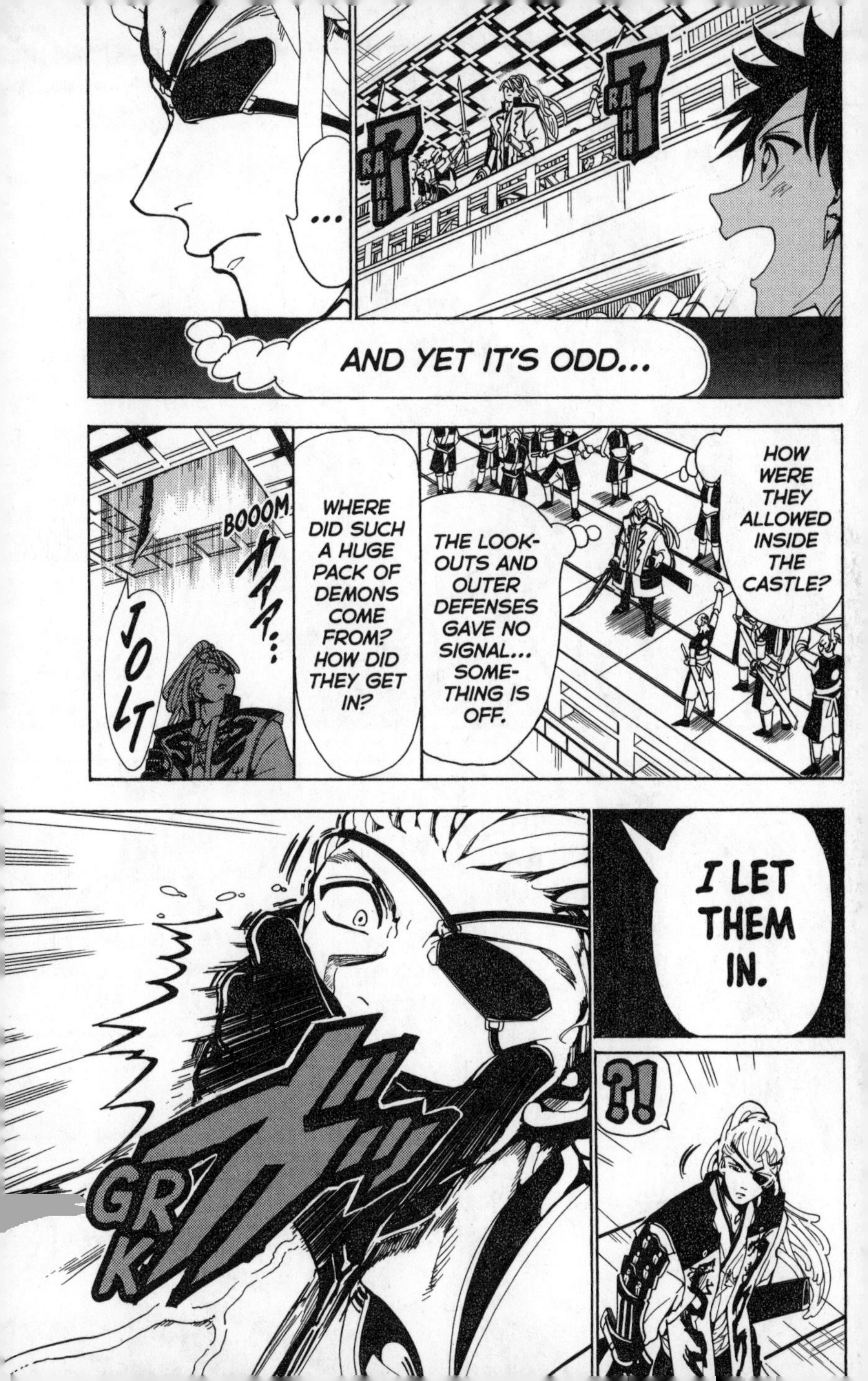
RAHH
RAHH
...
AND YET IT'S ODD...
HOW WERE THEY ALLOWED INSIDE THE CASTLE?
THE LOOK-OUTS AND OUTER DEFENSES GAVE NO SIGNAL... SOMETHING IS OFF.
WHERE DID SUCH A HUGE PACK OF DEMONS COME FROM? HOW DID THEY GET IN?
BOOOM
HAA...
JOLT
I LET THEM IN.
?!
GRK

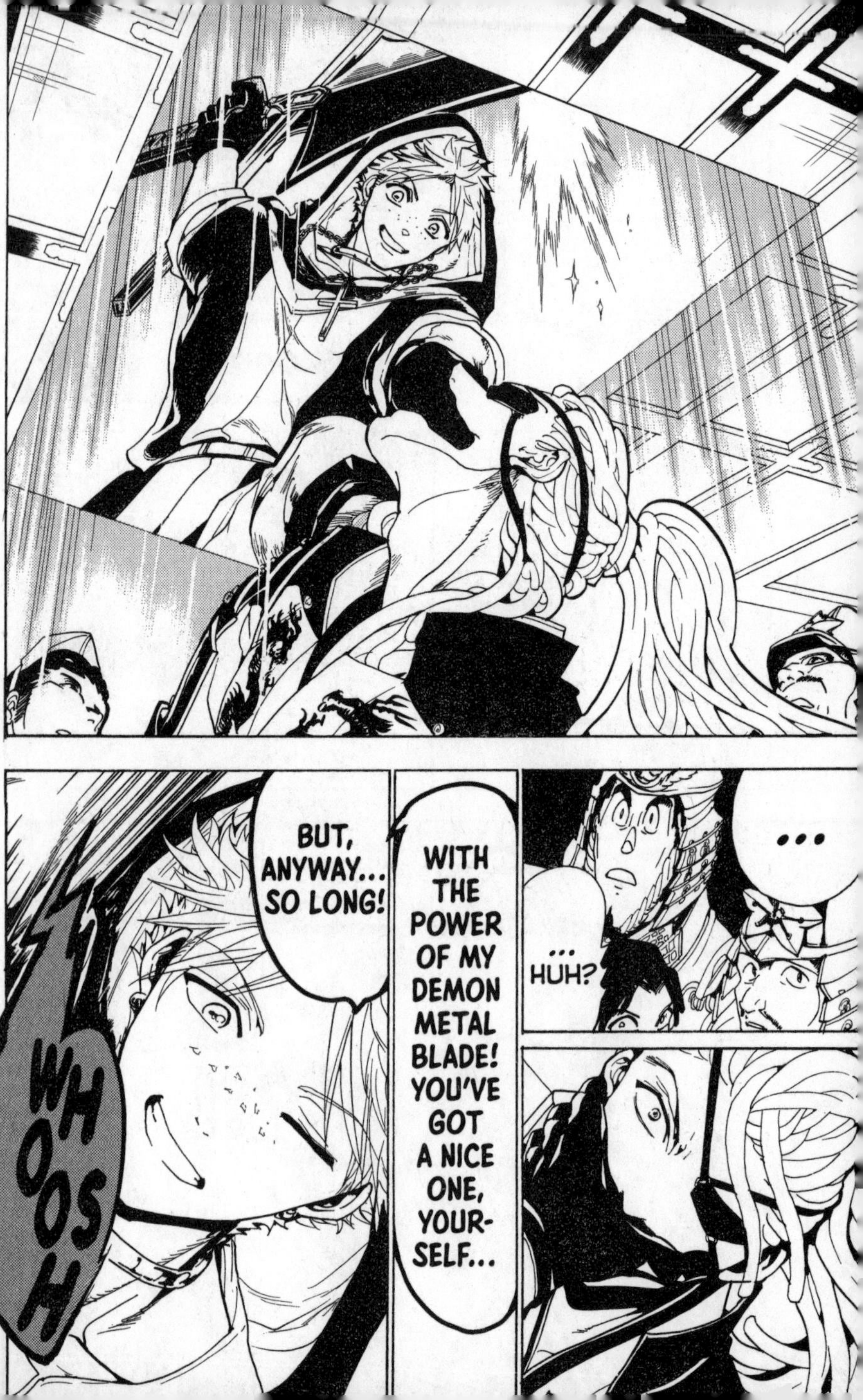
...
... HUH?
WITH THE POWER OF MY DEMON METAL BLADE! YOU'VE GOT A NICE ONE, YOURSELF...
BUT, ANYWAY... SO LONG!
WHOOSH

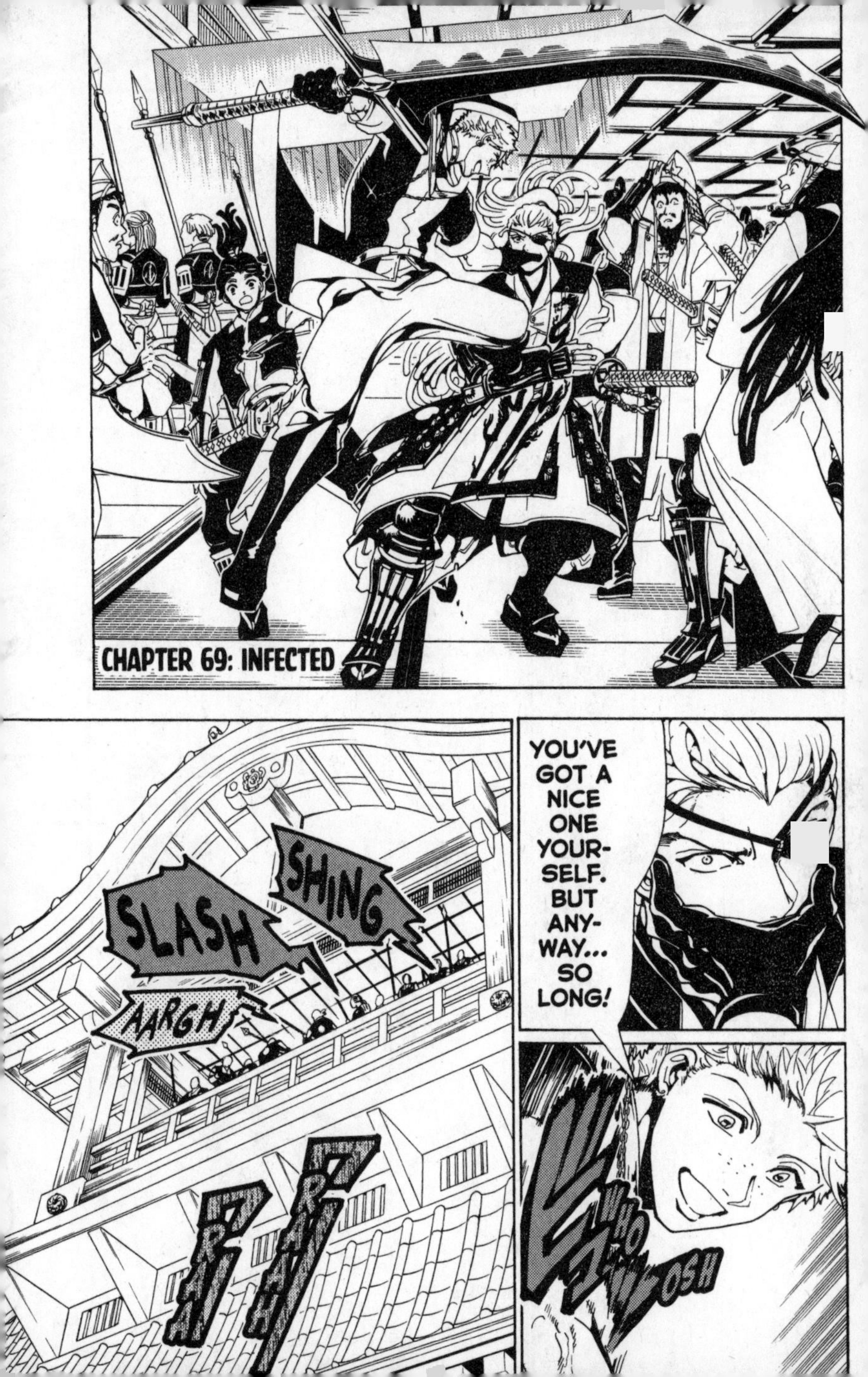
CHAPTER 69: INFECTED
YOU'VE GOT A NICE ONE YOURSELF. BUT ANYWAY... SO LONG!
WHOOSH
SHING
SLASH
AARGH
RAAH
RAAH

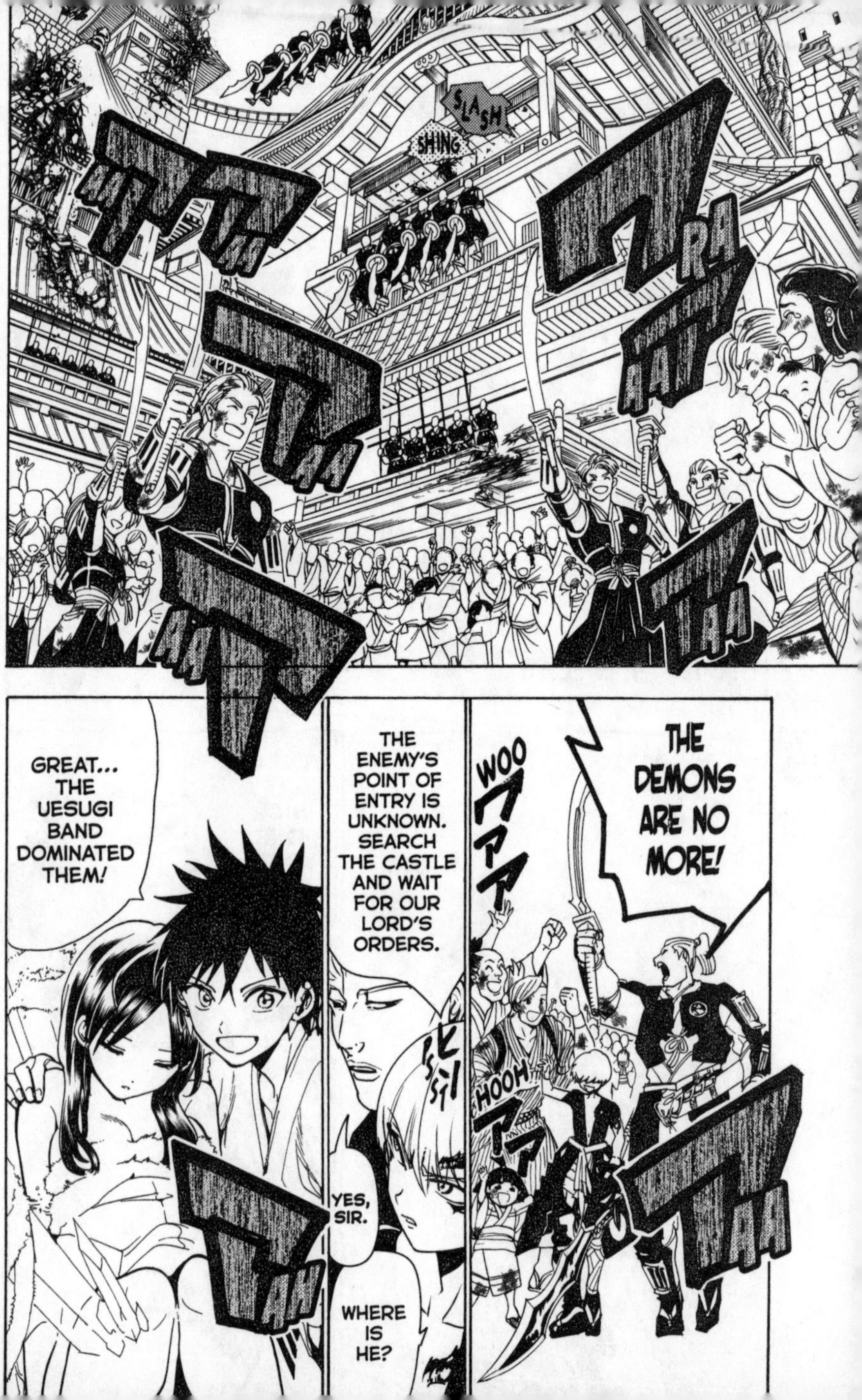
SLASH
SHING
THE DEMONS ARE NO MORE!
WOO
HOOH
THE ENEMY'S POINT OF ENTRY IS UNKNOWN. SEARCH THE CASTLE AND WAIT FOR OUR LORD'S ORDERS.
YES, SIR.
PSST
WHERE IS HE?
GREAT... THE UESUGI BAND DOMINATED THEM!

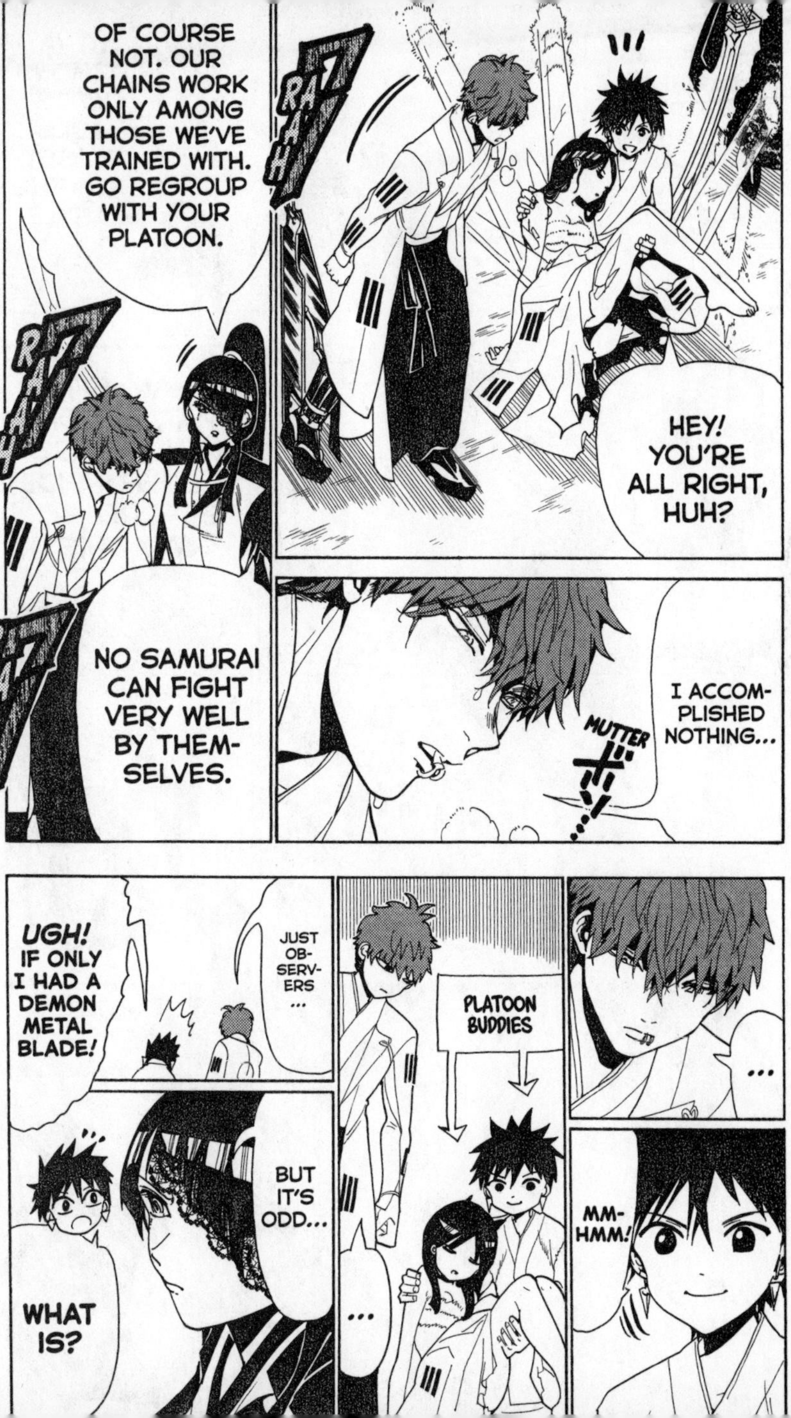

RAAAH
HEY! YOU'RE ALL RIGHT, HUH?
MUTTER
I ACCOM-PLISHED NOTHING...
OF COURSE NOT. OUR CHAINS WORK ONLY AMONG THOSE WE'VE TRAINED WITH. GO REGROUP WITH YOUR PLATOON.
RAAAH
NO SAMURAI CAN FIGHT VERY WELL BY THEM-SELVES.
RAAAH
...
MM-HMM!
PLATOON BUDDIES
...
JUST OB-SERV-ERS ...
UGH! IF ONLY I HAD A DEMON METAL BLADE!
BUT IT'S ODD...
WHAT IS?

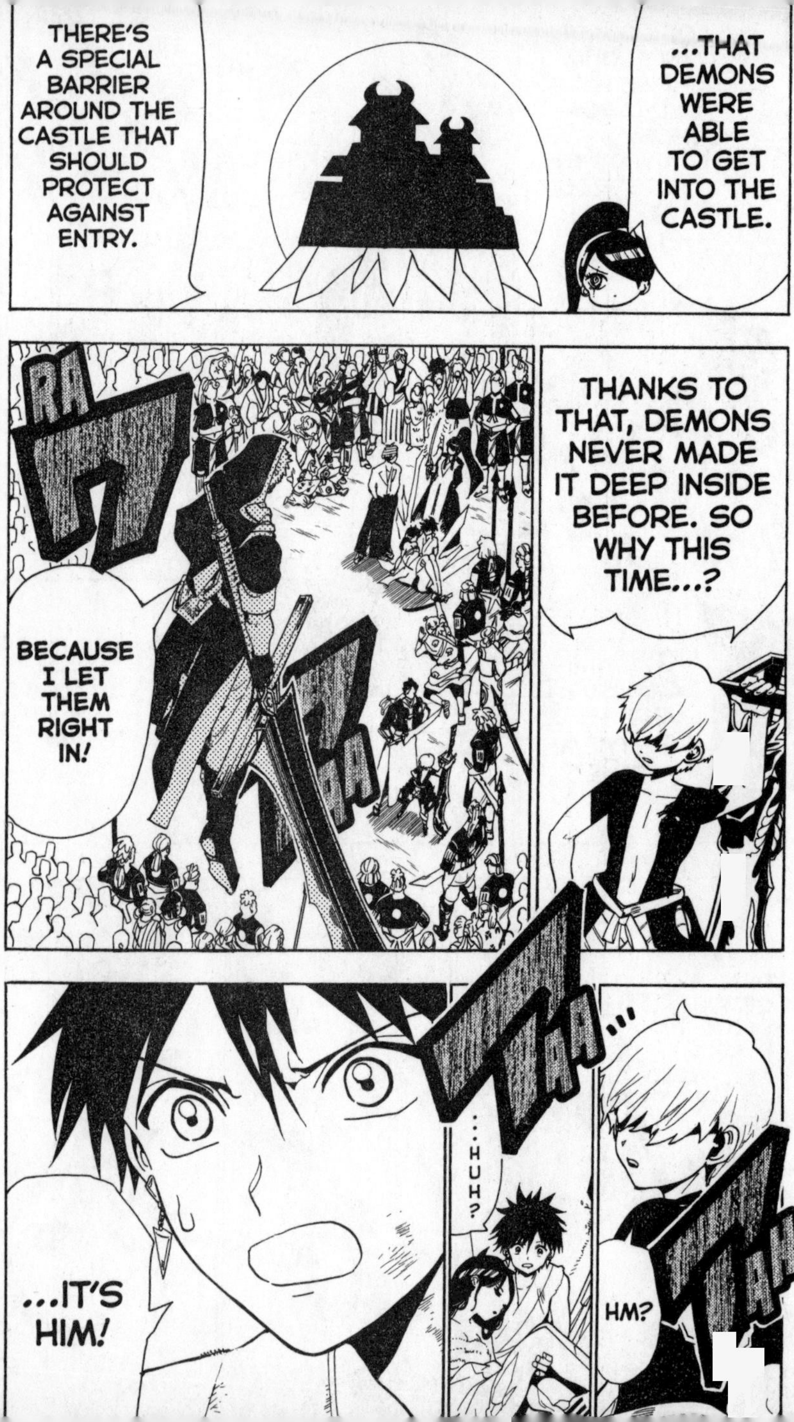
...THAT DEMONS WERE ABLE TO GET INTO THE CASTLE.
THERE'S A SPECIAL BARRIER AROUND THE CASTLE THAT SHOULD PROTECT AGAINST ENTRY.
THANKS TO THAT, DEMONS NEVER MADE IT DEEP INSIDE BEFORE. SO WHY THIS TIME...?
RA
BECAUSE I LET THEM RIGHT IN!
AA
HM?
...HUH?
AA...
...IT'S HIM!

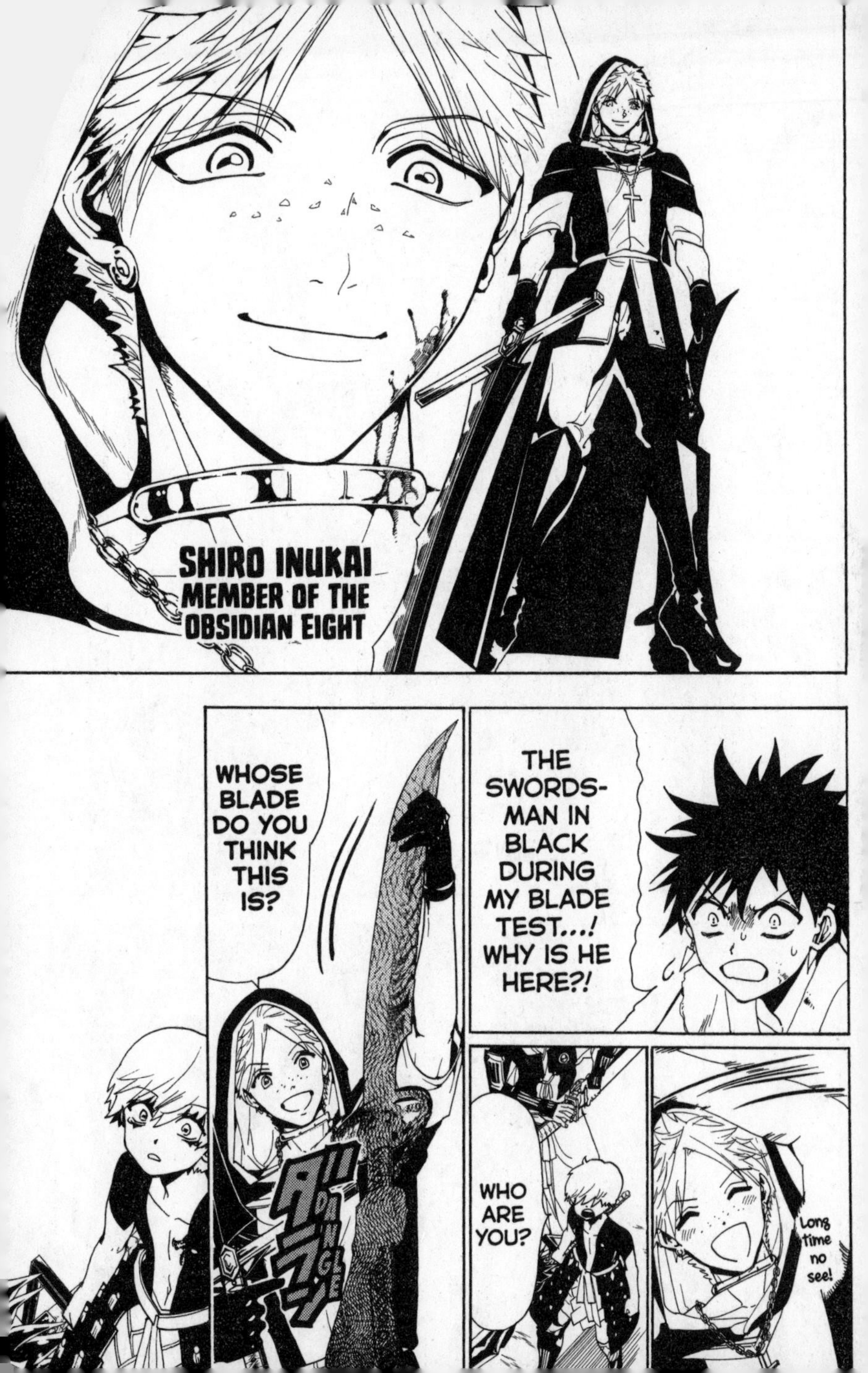

SHIRO INUKAI
MEMBER OF THE OBSIDIAN EIGHT
THE SWORDS-MAN IN BLACK DURING MY BLADE TEST...! WHY IS HE HERE?!
Long time no see!
WHO ARE YOU?
WHOSE BLADE DO YOU THINK THIS IS?
DANGLE

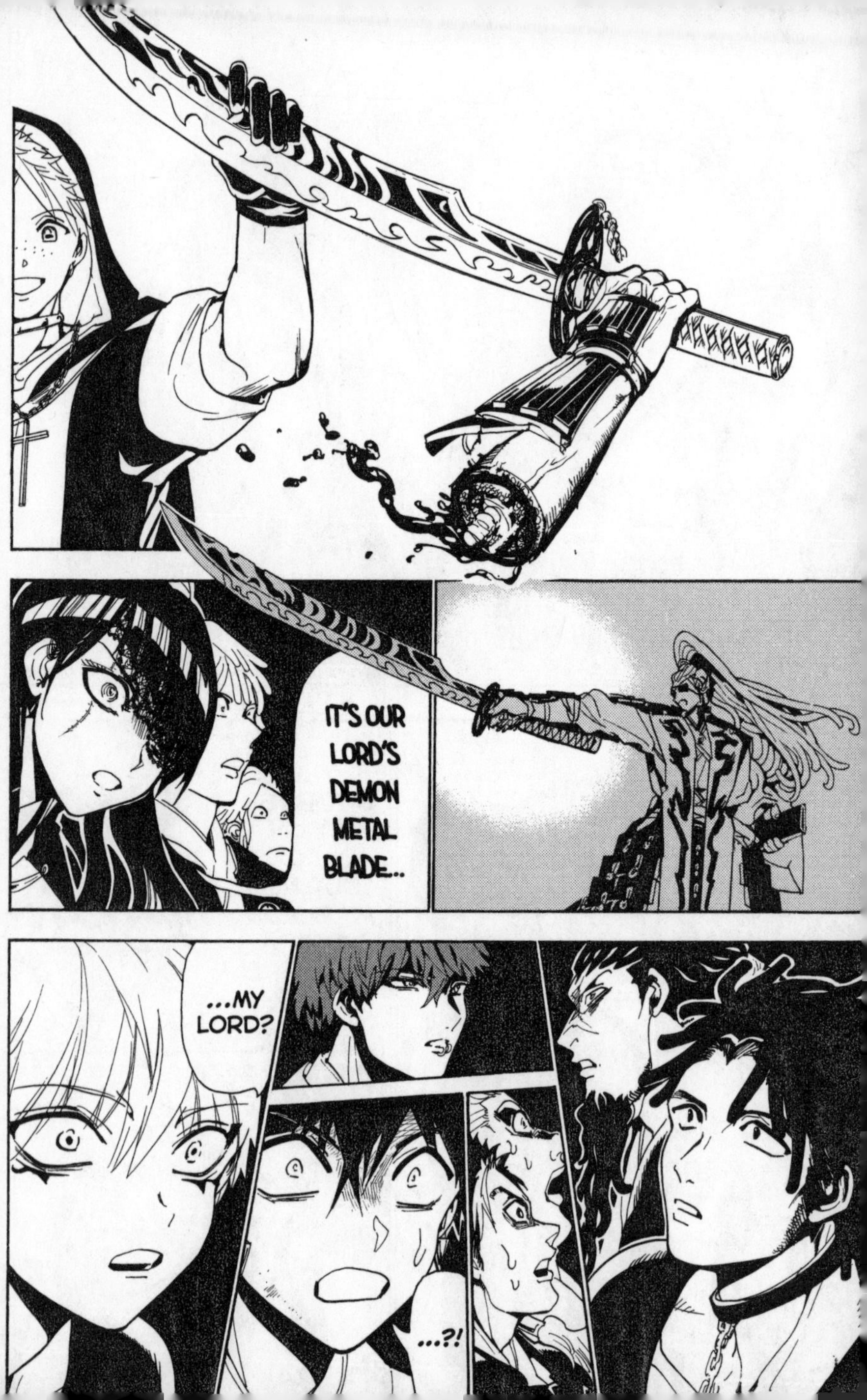
IT'S OUR LORD'S DEMON METAL BLADE...
...?!
...MY LORD?

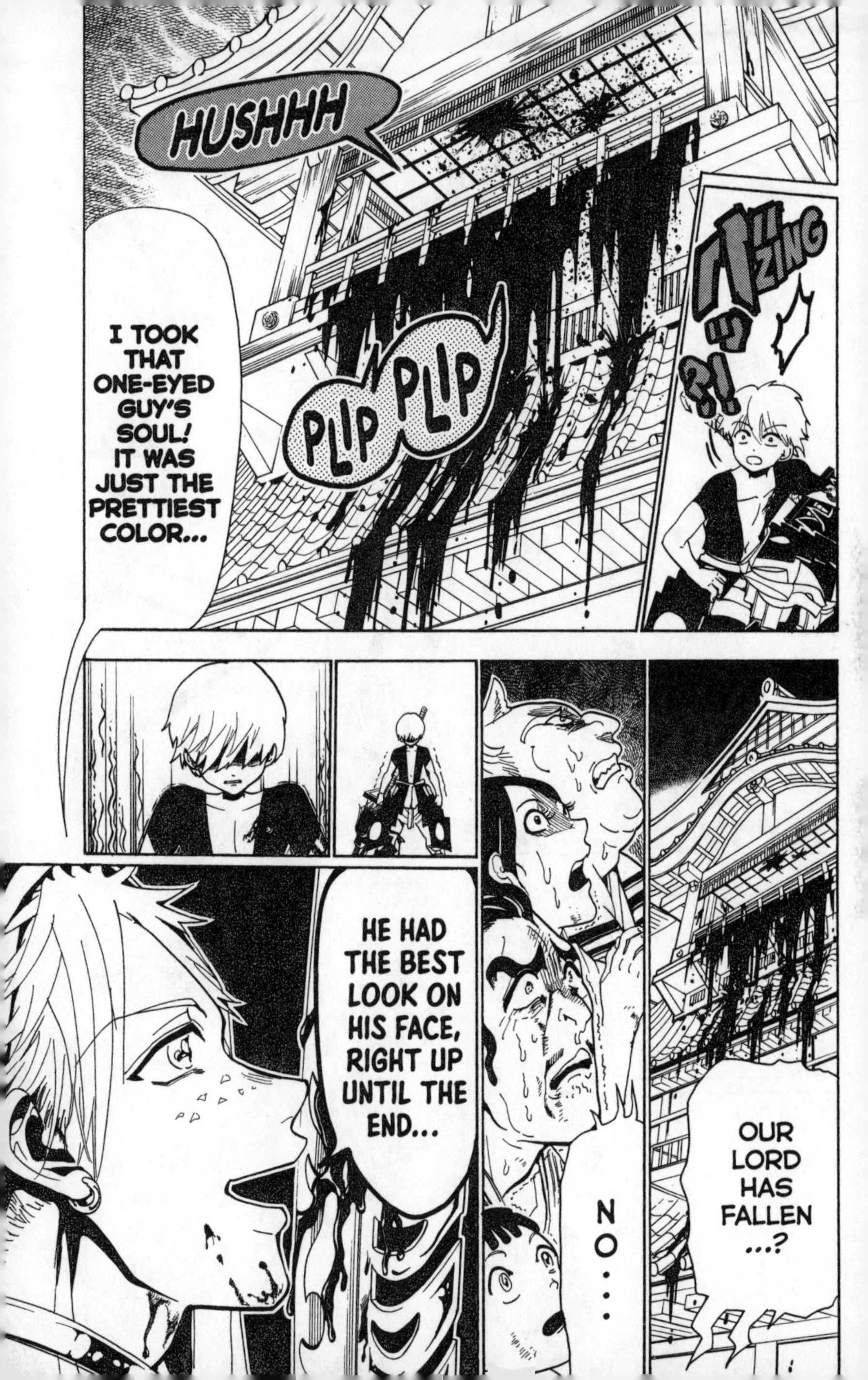
HUSHHH
PLIP PLIP
ZING
?!
I TOOK THAT ONE-EYED GUY'S SOUL! IT WAS JUST THE PRETTIEST COLOR...
OUR LORD HAS FALLEN...?
NO...
HE HAD THE BEST LOOK ON HIS FACE, RIGHT UP UNTIL THE END...

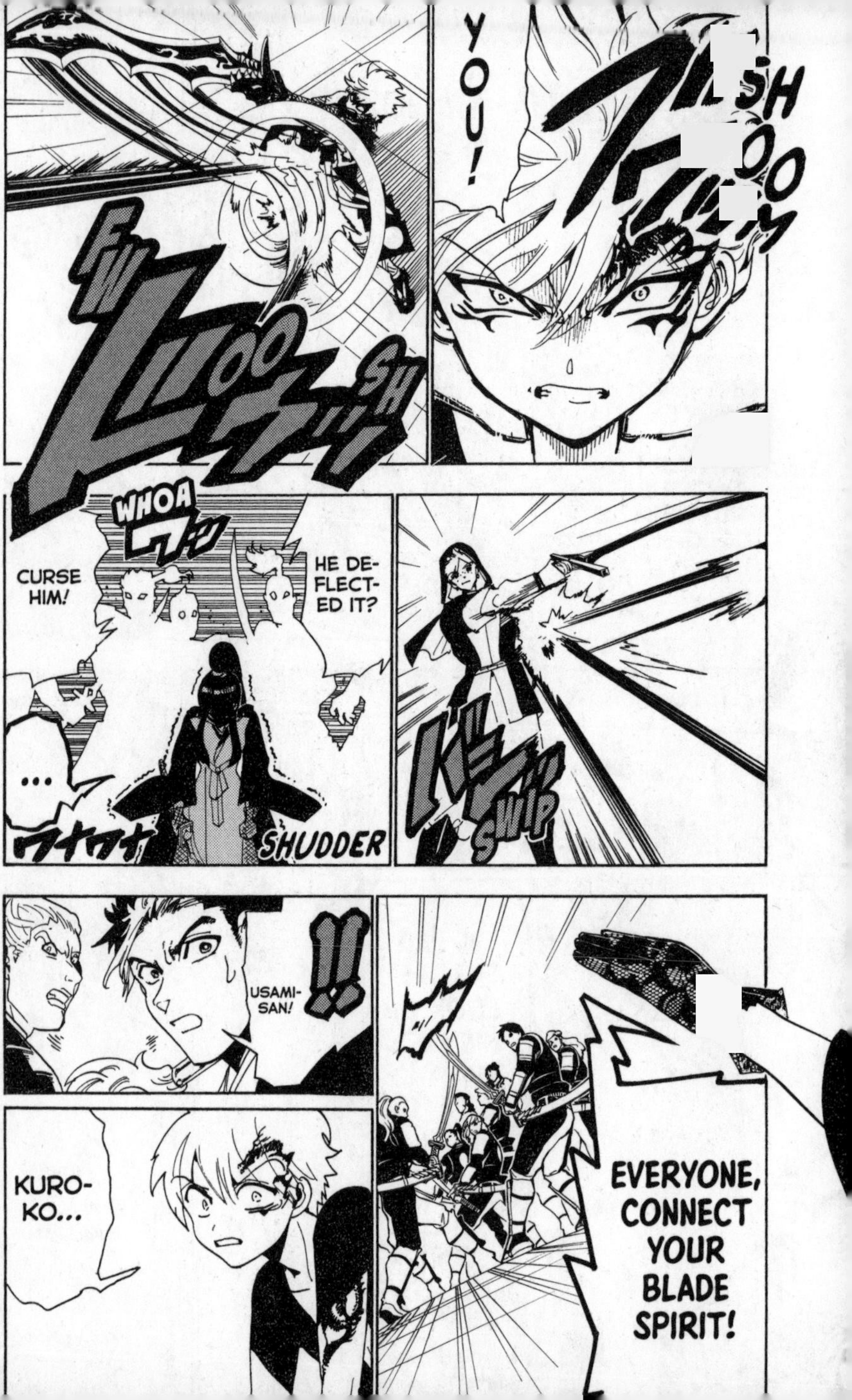
YOU!
SHOOM
FWOOSH
SWIP
HE DE-FLECTED IT?
WHOA
CURSE HIM!
...
SHUDDER
EVERYONE, CONNECT YOUR BLADE SPIRIT!
USAMI-SAN!
!!
KURO-KO...

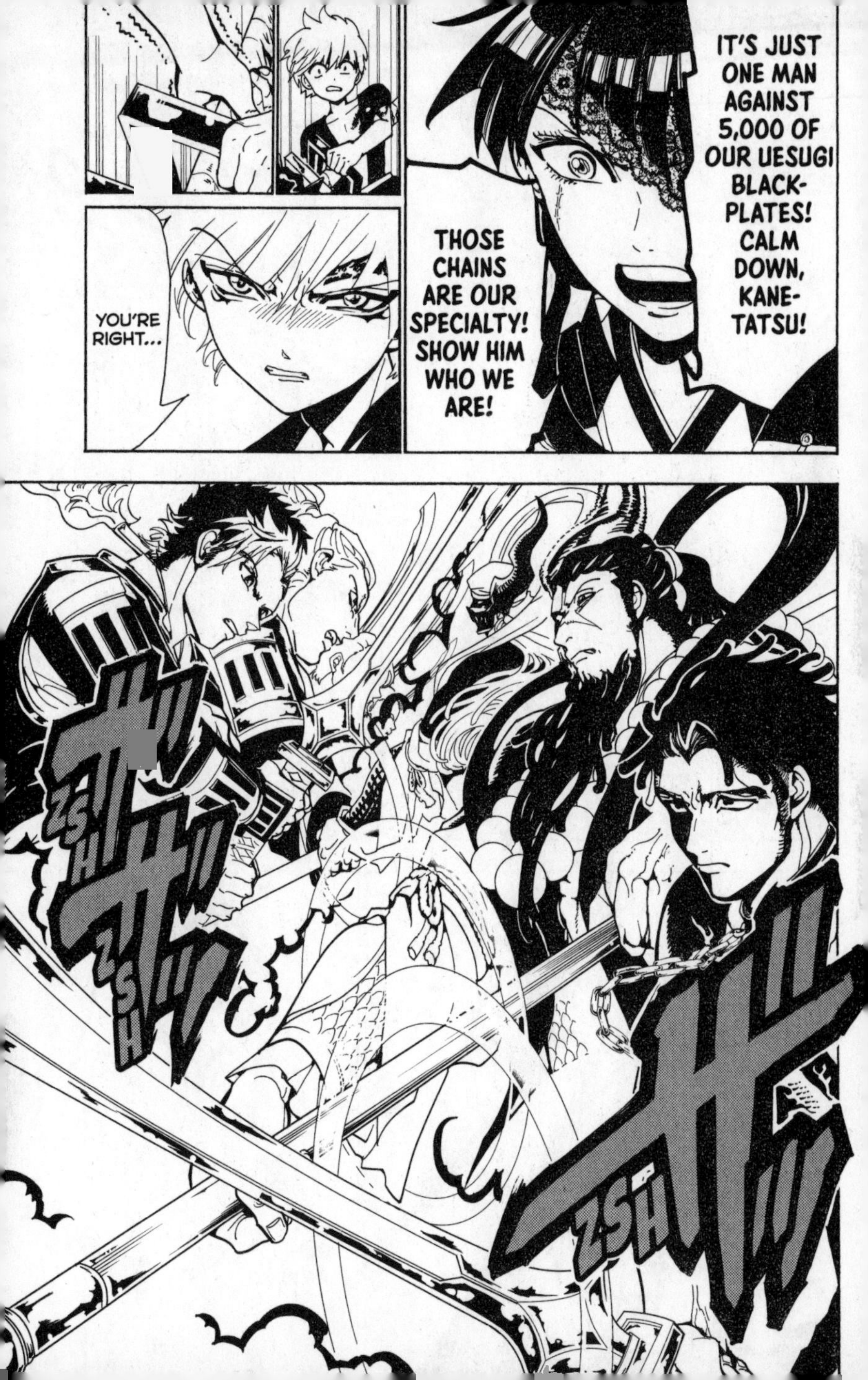

IT'S JUST ONE MAN AGAINST 5,000 OF OUR UESUGI BLACK-PLATES! CALM DOWN, KANE-TATSU!
THOSE CHAINS ARE OUR SPECIALTY! SHOW HIM WHO WE ARE!
YOU'RE RIGHT...
ZSH
ZSH
ZSH

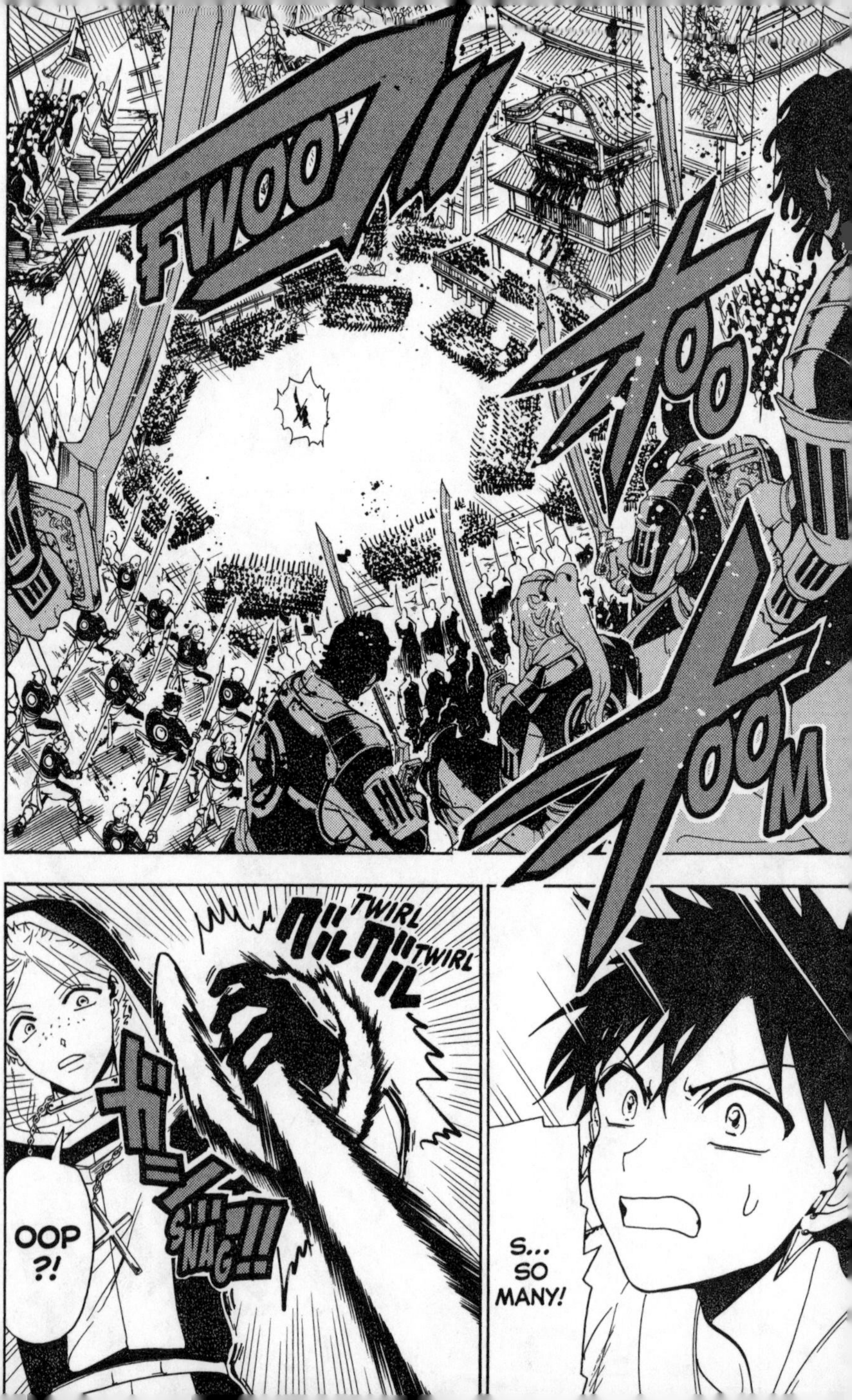
FWOO
OOM
S... SO MANY!
TWIRL TWIRL
SNAG!!
OOP ?!

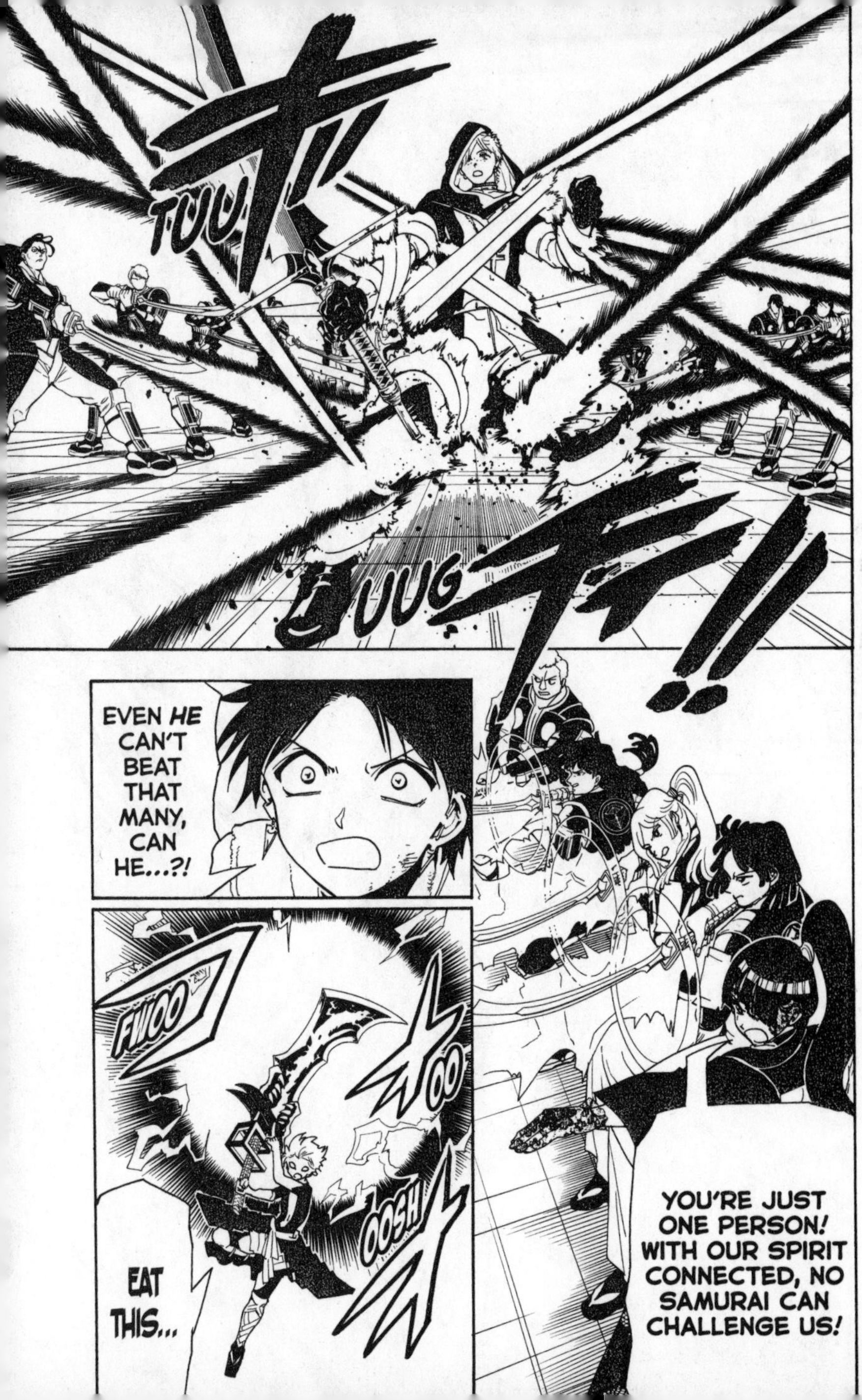
TUU
DUUG
YOU'RE JUST ONE PERSON! WITH OUR SPIRIT CONNECTED, NO SAMURAI CAN CHALLENGE US!
EVEN *HE* CAN'T BEAT THAT MANY, CAN HE...?!
FWOO
OO
OOSH
EAT THIS...

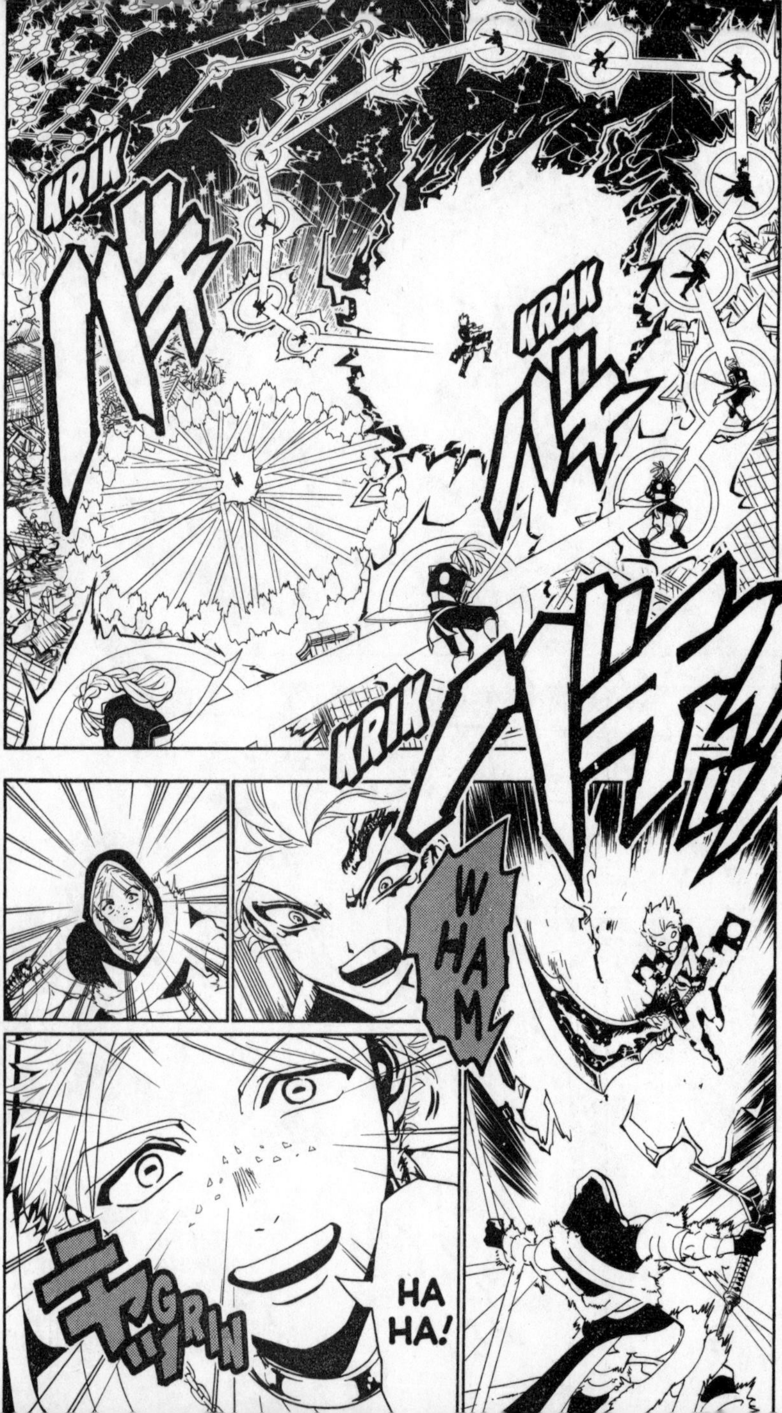
KRIK
KRAK
KRIK
WHAM
HA HA!
GRIN

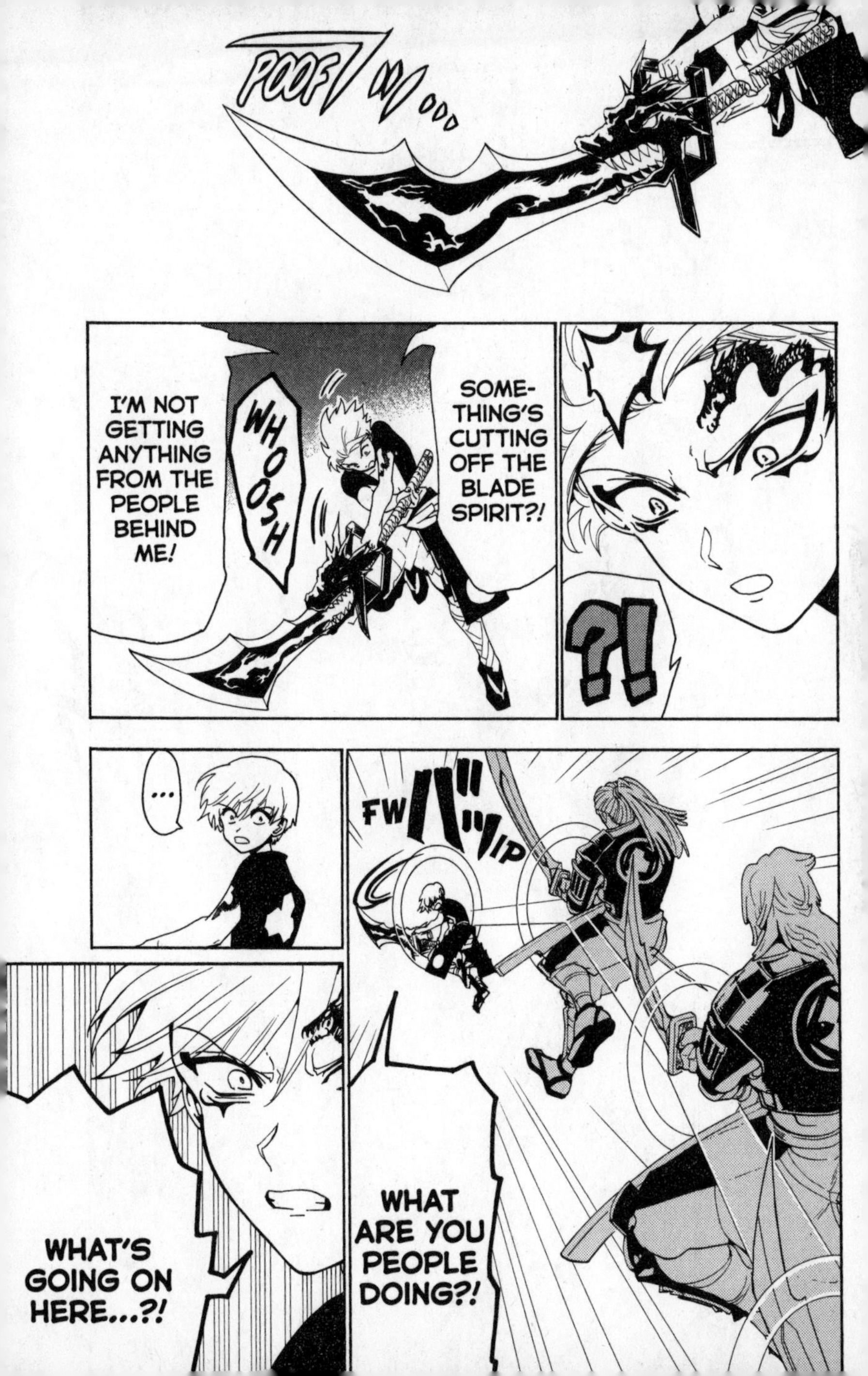
POOF
?!
SOME-THING'S CUTTING OFF THE BLADE SPIRIT?!
WHOOSH
I'M NOT GETTING ANYTHING FROM THE PEOPLE BEHIND ME!
FWIP
WHAT ARE YOU PEOPLE DOING?!
...
WHAT'S GOING ON HERE...?!

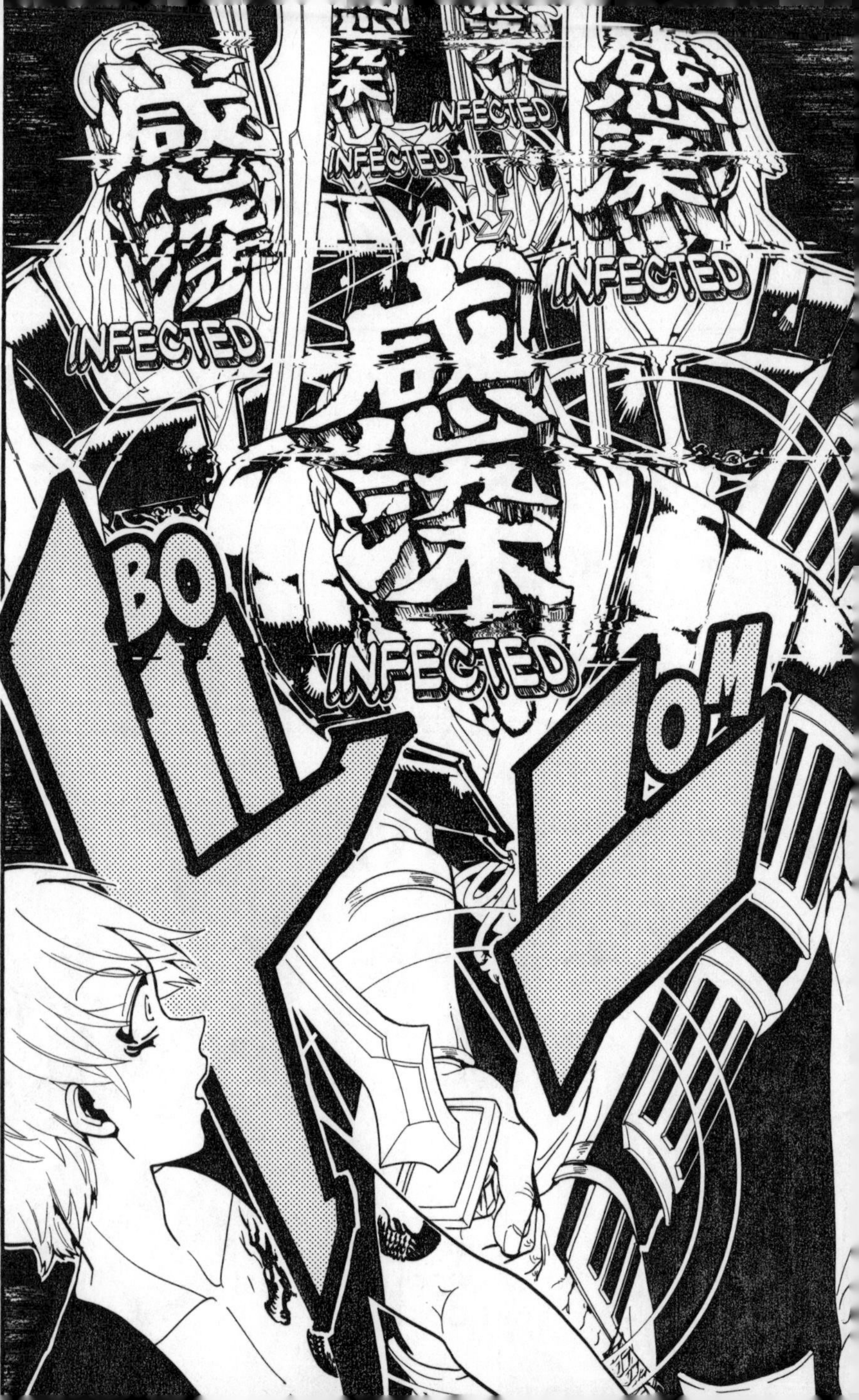
感染
INFECTED
INFECTED
感染
INFECTED
INFECTED
感染
INFECTED
BOOM

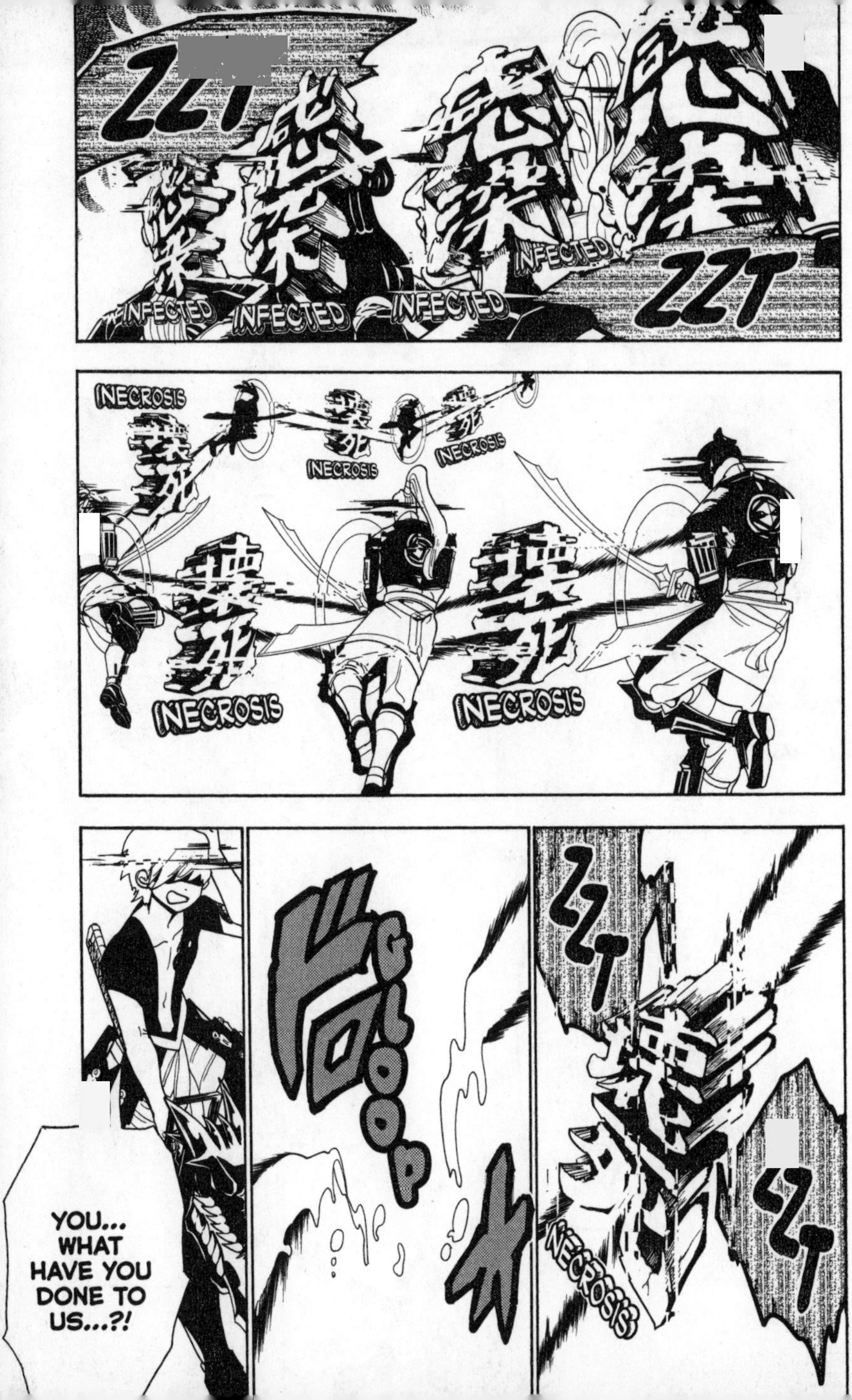
ZZT
INFECTED
INFECTED
INFECTED
INFECTED
ZZT
NECROSIS
NECROSIS
NECROSIS
NECROSIS
NECROSIS
NECROSIS
ZZT
NECROSIS
ZZT
GLOOOP
YOU... WHAT HAVE YOU DONE TO US...?!

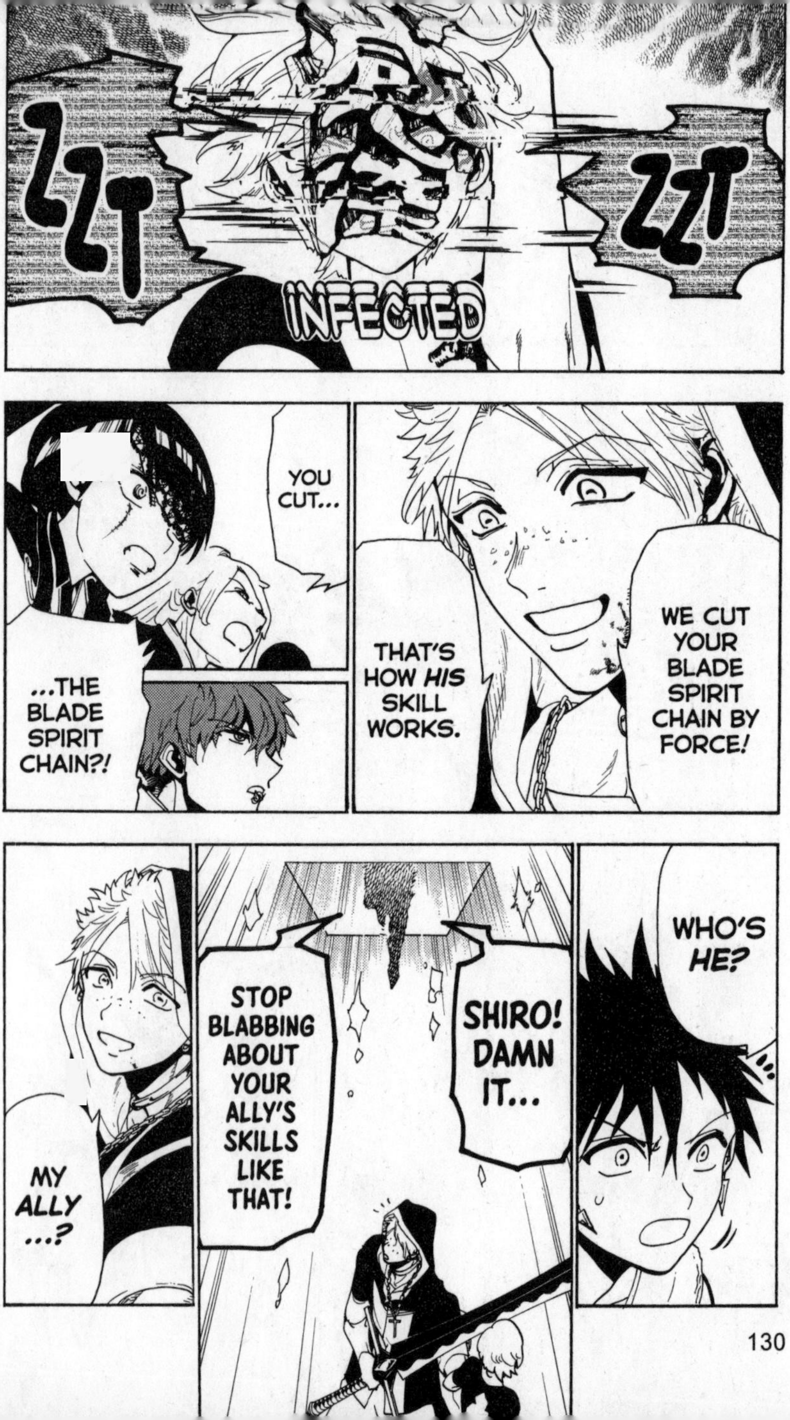
ZZT
INFECTED
ZZT
WE CUT YOUR BLADE SPIRIT CHAIN BY FORCE!
THAT'S HOW *HIS* SKILL WORKS.
YOU CUT...
...THE BLADE SPIRIT CHAIN?!
WHO'S *HE?*
SHIRO! DAMN IT...
STOP BLABBING ABOUT YOUR ALLY'S SKILLS LIKE THAT!
MY ALLY ...?

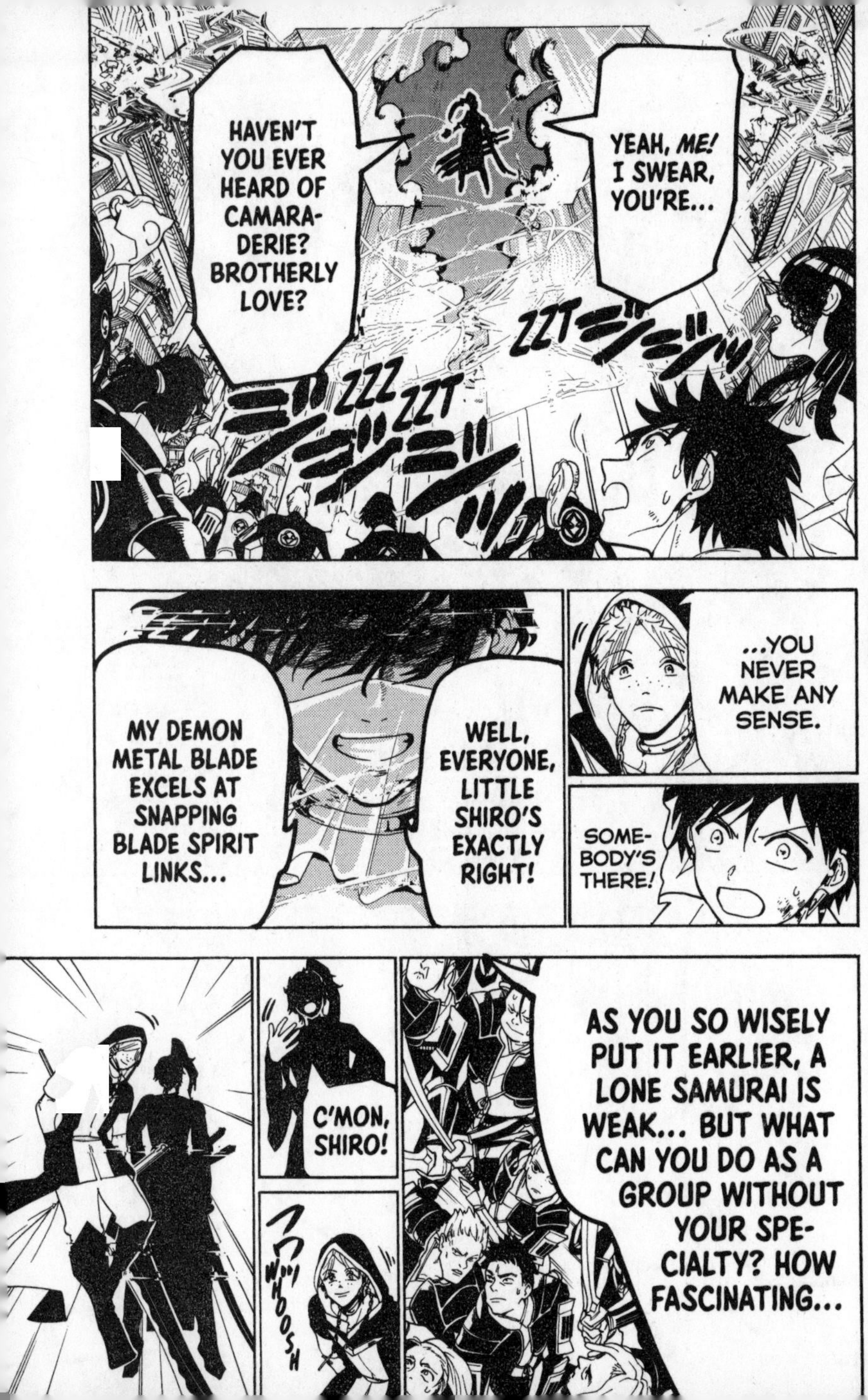
YEAH, ME! I SWEAR, YOU'RE...
HAVEN'T YOU EVER HEARD OF CAMARADERIE? BROTHERLY LOVE?
ZZT
ZZZ
ZZT
...YOU NEVER MAKE ANY SENSE.
SOMEBODY'S THERE!
WELL, EVERYONE, LITTLE SHIRO'S EXACTLY RIGHT!
MY DEMON METAL BLADE EXCELS AT SNAPPING BLADE SPIRIT LINKS...
AS YOU SO WISELY PUT IT EARLIER, A LONE SAMURAI IS WEAK... BUT WHAT CAN YOU DO AS A GROUP WITHOUT YOUR SPECIALTY? HOW FASCINATING...
C'MON, SHIRO!
WHOOSH

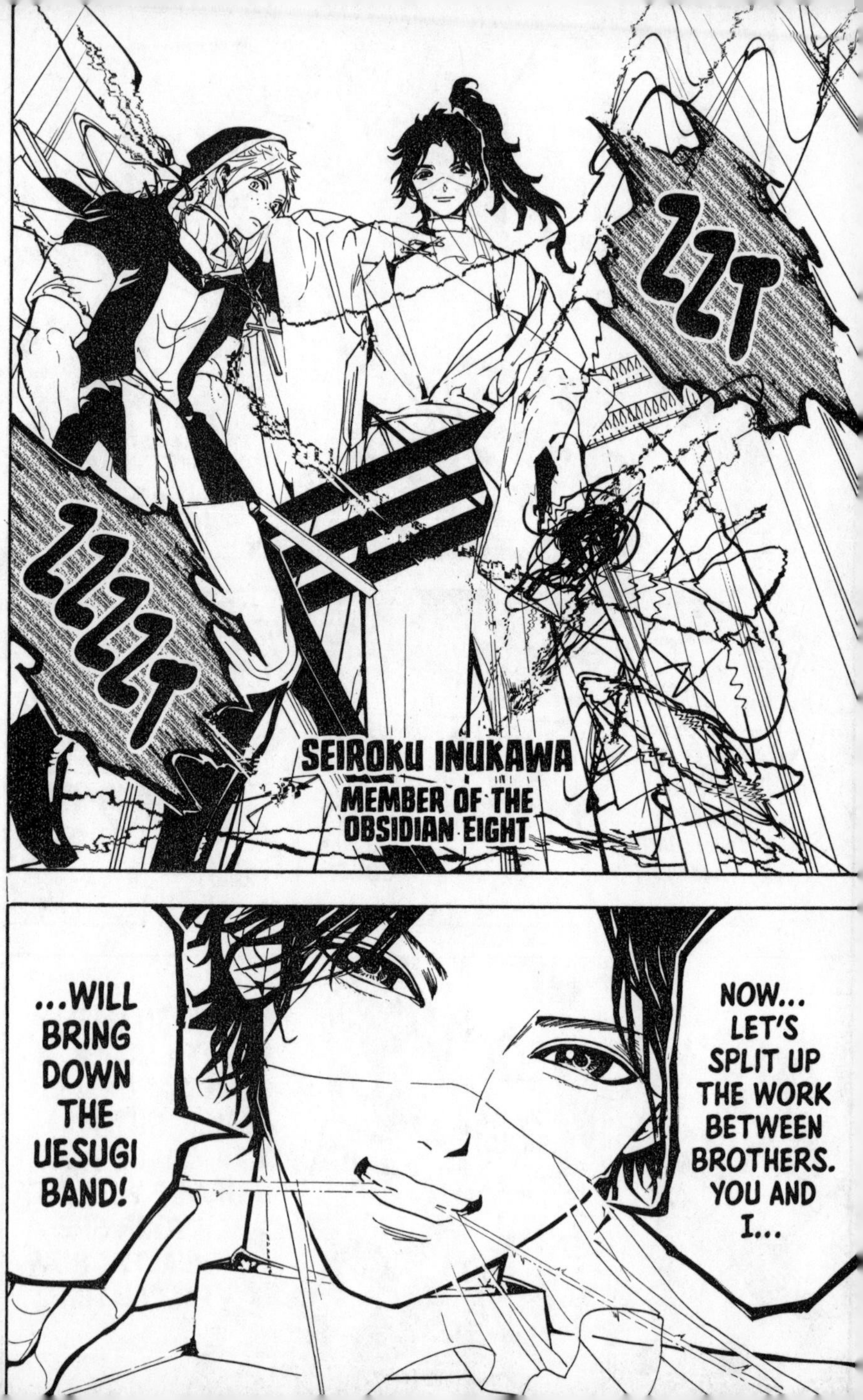
ZZT
ZZZZT
SEIROKU INUKAWA
MEMBER OF THE OBSIDIAN EIGHT
NOW... LET'S SPLIT UP THE WORK BETWEEN BROTHERS. YOU AND I...
...WILL BRING DOWN THE UESUGI BAND!

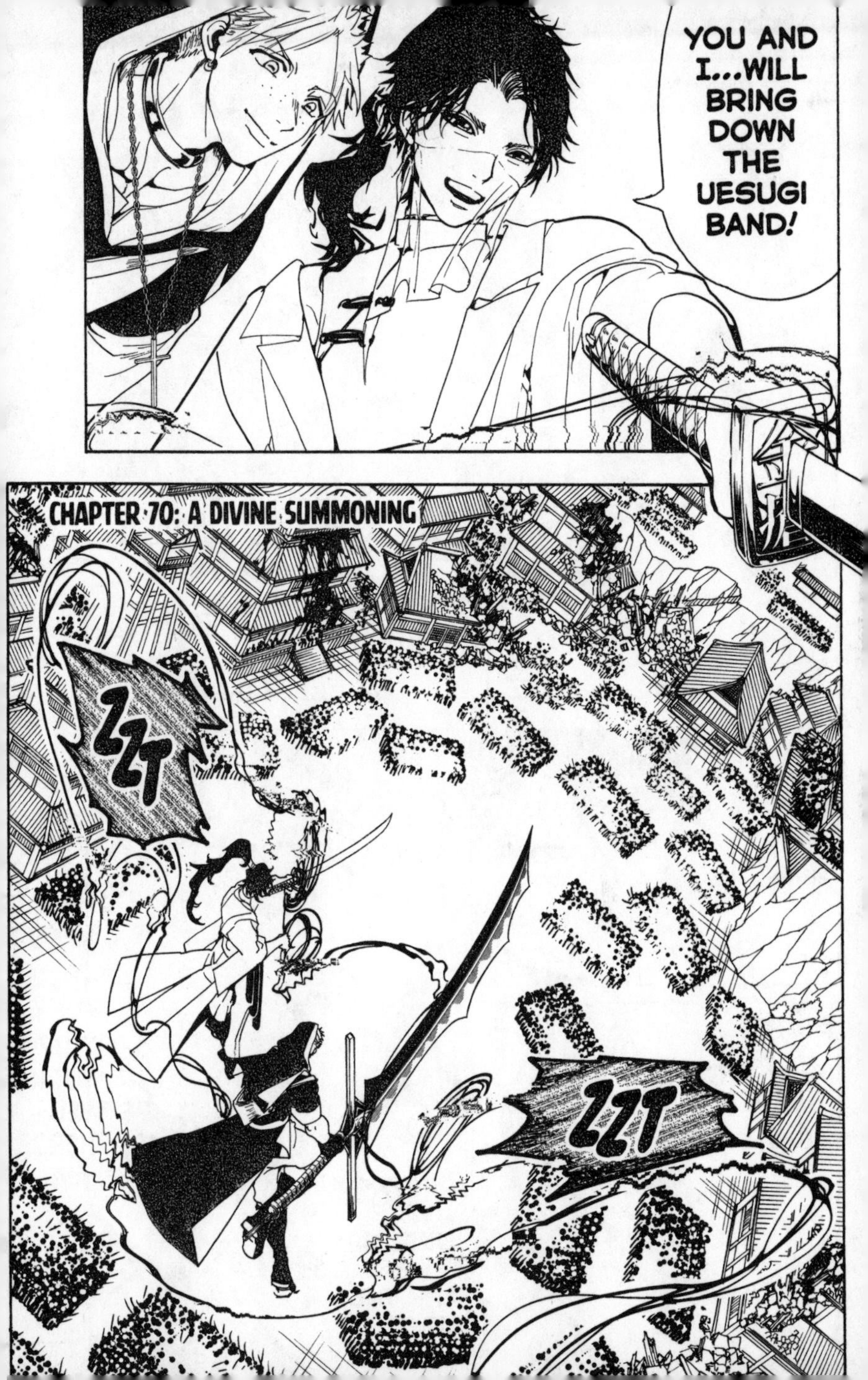
YOU AND I...WILL BRING DOWN THE UESUGI BAND!
CHAPTER 70: A DIVINE SUMMONING
ZZT
ZZT

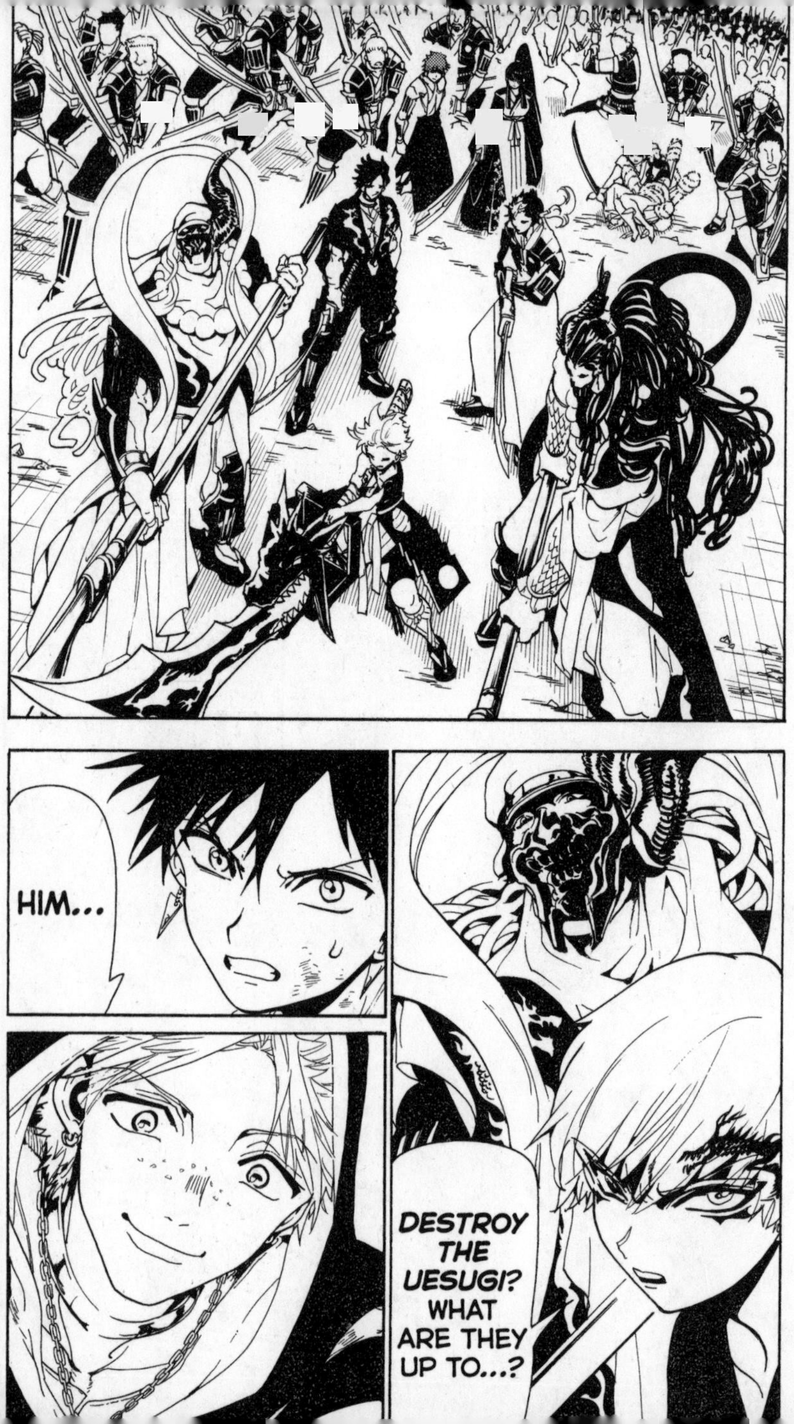
DESTROY THE UESUGI? WHAT ARE THEY UP TO...?
HIM...

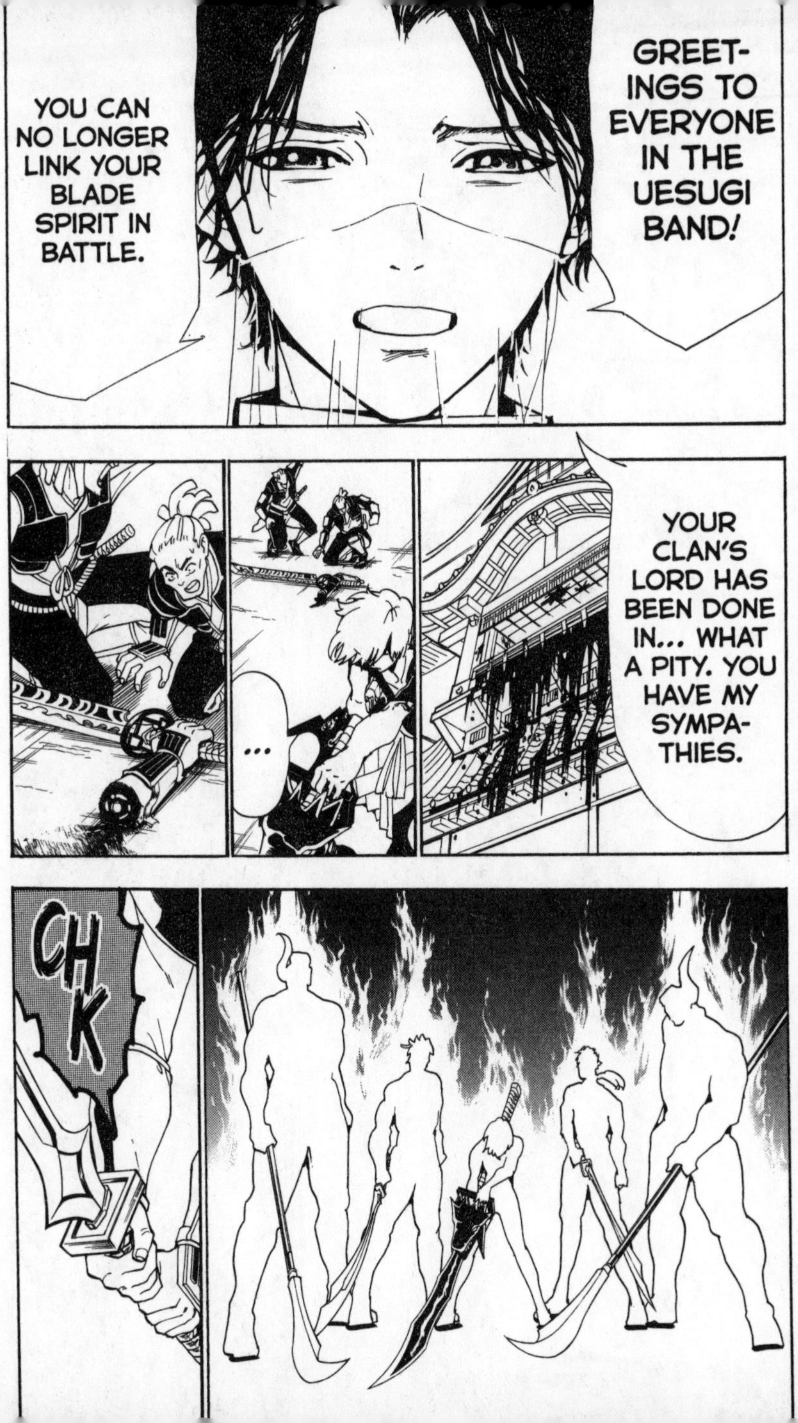
GREET-INGS TO EVERYONE IN THE UESUGI BAND!
YOU CAN NO LONGER LINK YOUR BLADE SPIRIT IN BATTLE.
YOUR CLAN'S LORD HAS BEEN DONE IN... WHAT A PITY. YOU HAVE MY SYMPA-THIES.
...
CHK

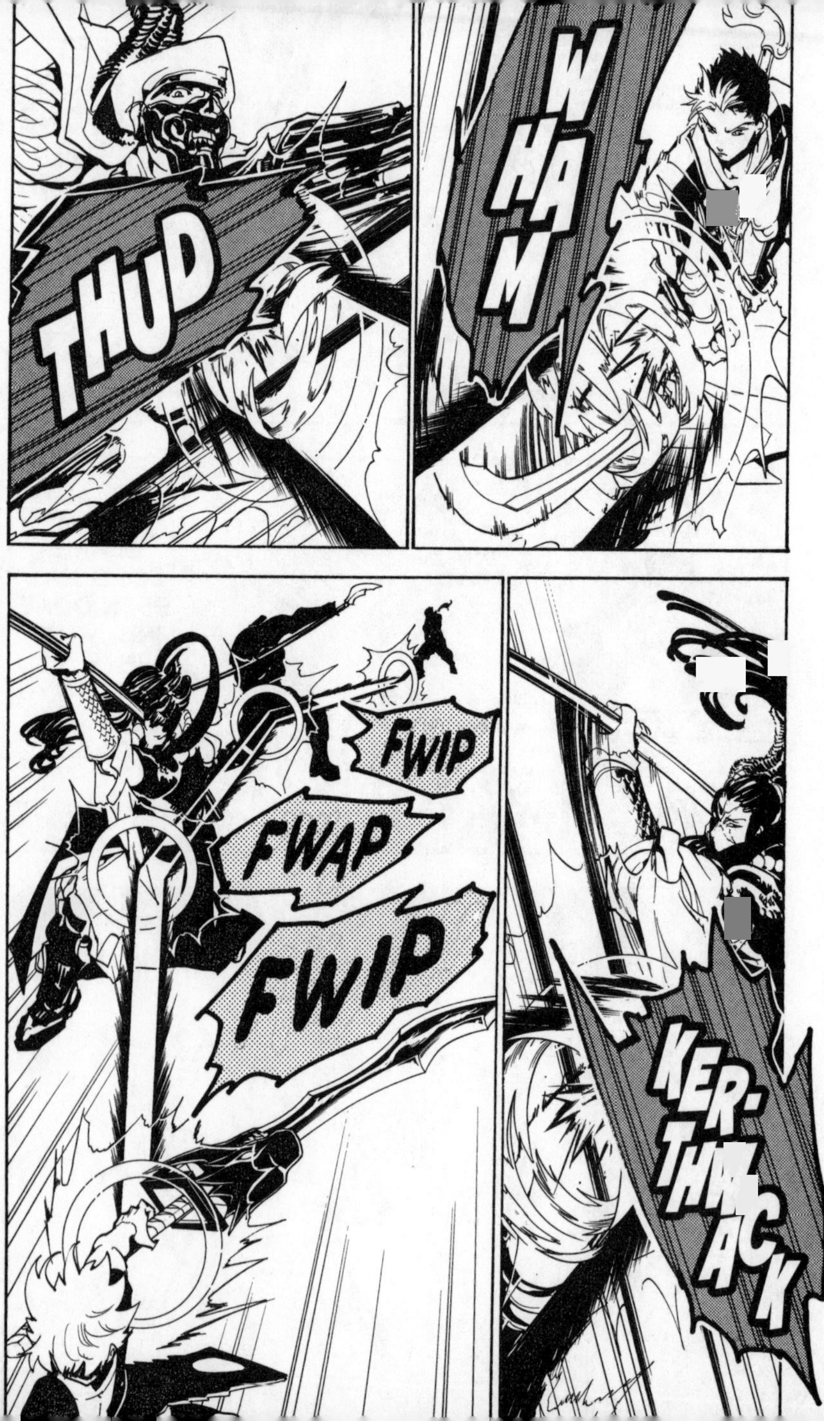
WHAM
THUD
KER-THWACK
FWIP
FWAP
FWIP

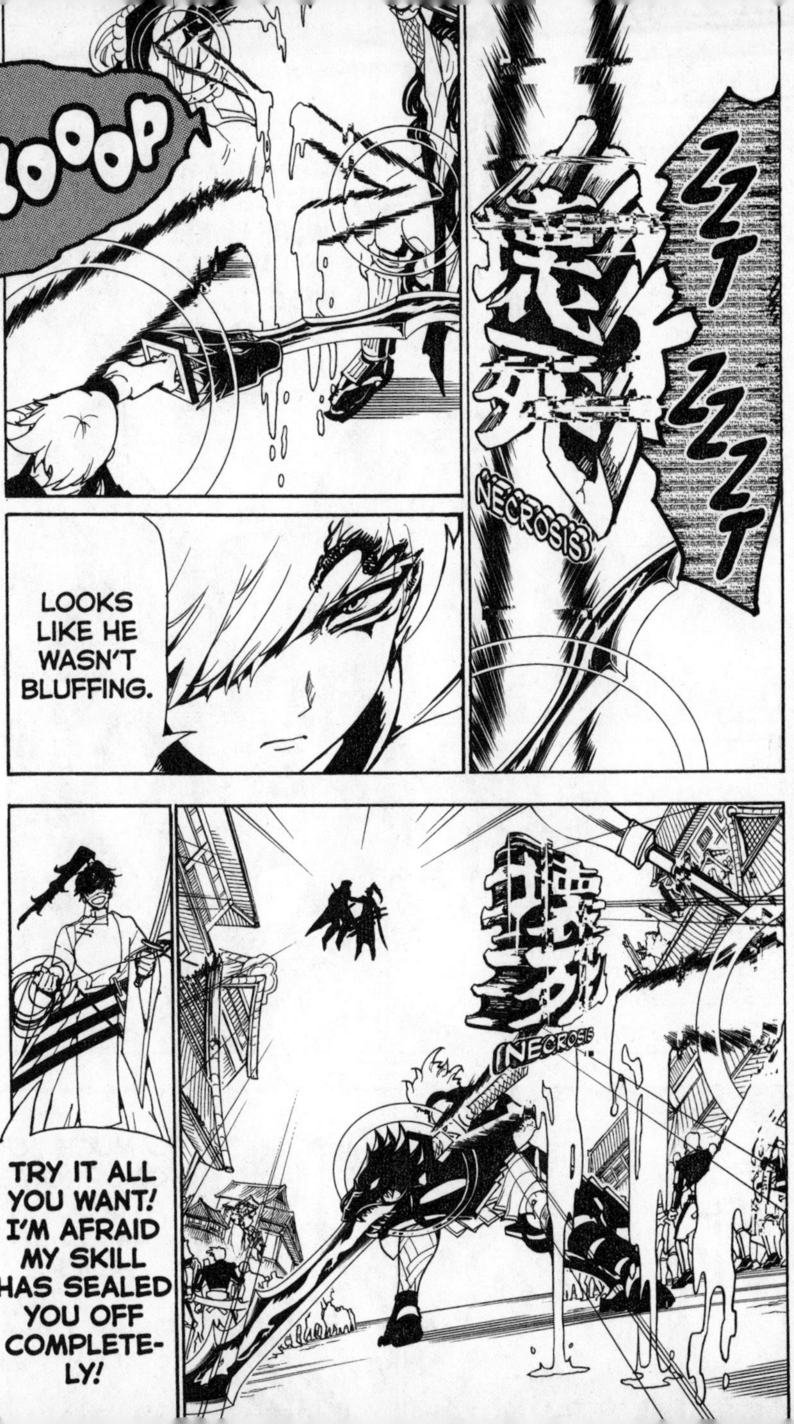
ZZZT ZZZZT
NECROSIS
GLOOOP
LOOKS LIKE HE WASN'T BLUFFING.
NECROSIS
TRY IT ALL YOU WANT! I'M AFRAID MY SKILL HAS SEALED YOU OFF COMPLETE-LY!

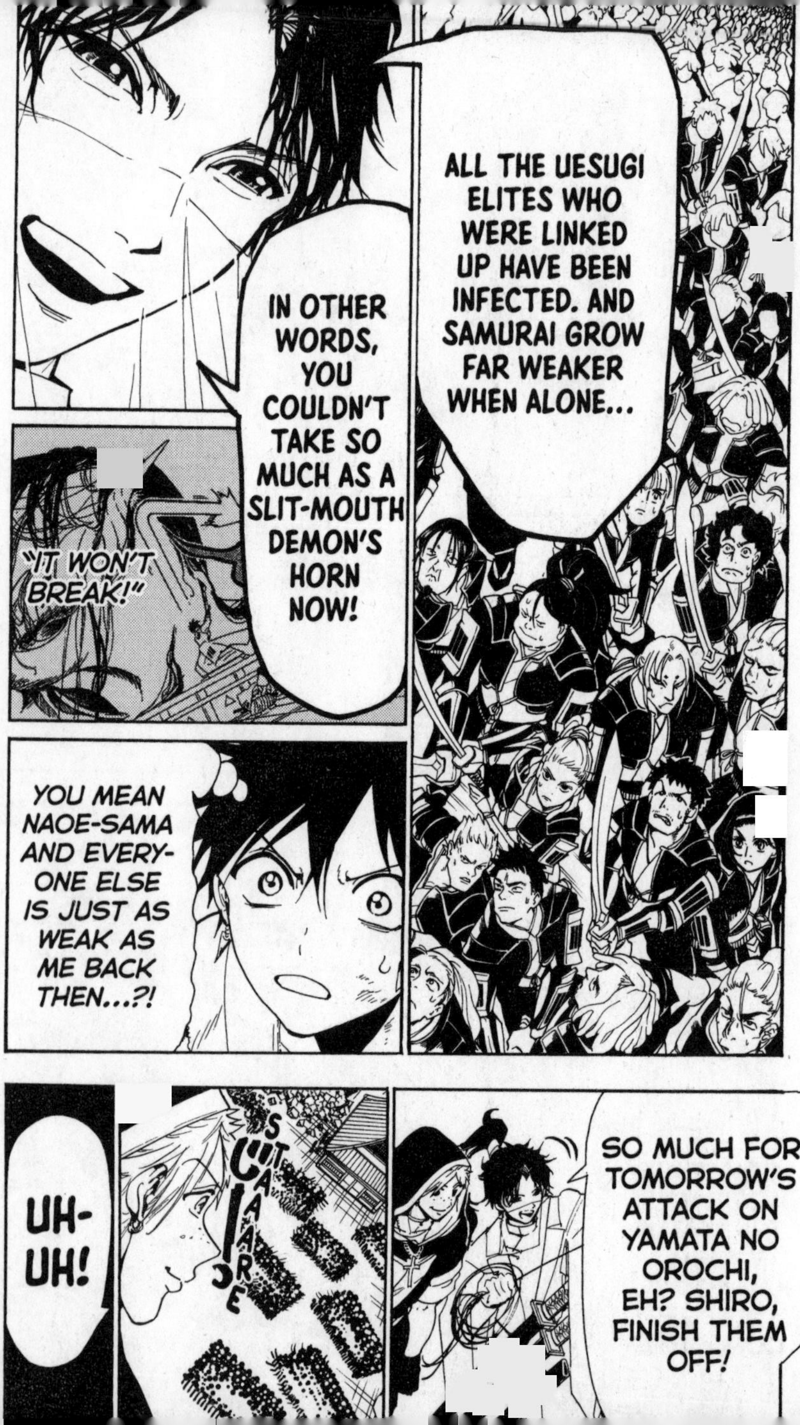
ALL THE UESUGI ELITES WHO WERE LINKED UP HAVE BEEN INFECTED. AND SAMURAI GROW FAR WEAKER WHEN ALONE...
IN OTHER WORDS, YOU COULDN'T TAKE SO MUCH AS A SLIT-MOUTH DEMON'S HORN NOW!
"IT WON'T BREAK!"
YOU MEAN NAOE-SAMA AND EVERY-ONE ELSE IS JUST AS WEAK AS ME BACK THEN...?!
SO MUCH FOR TOMORROW'S ATTACK ON YAMATA NO OROCHI, EH? SHIRO, FINISH THEM OFF!
UH-UH!

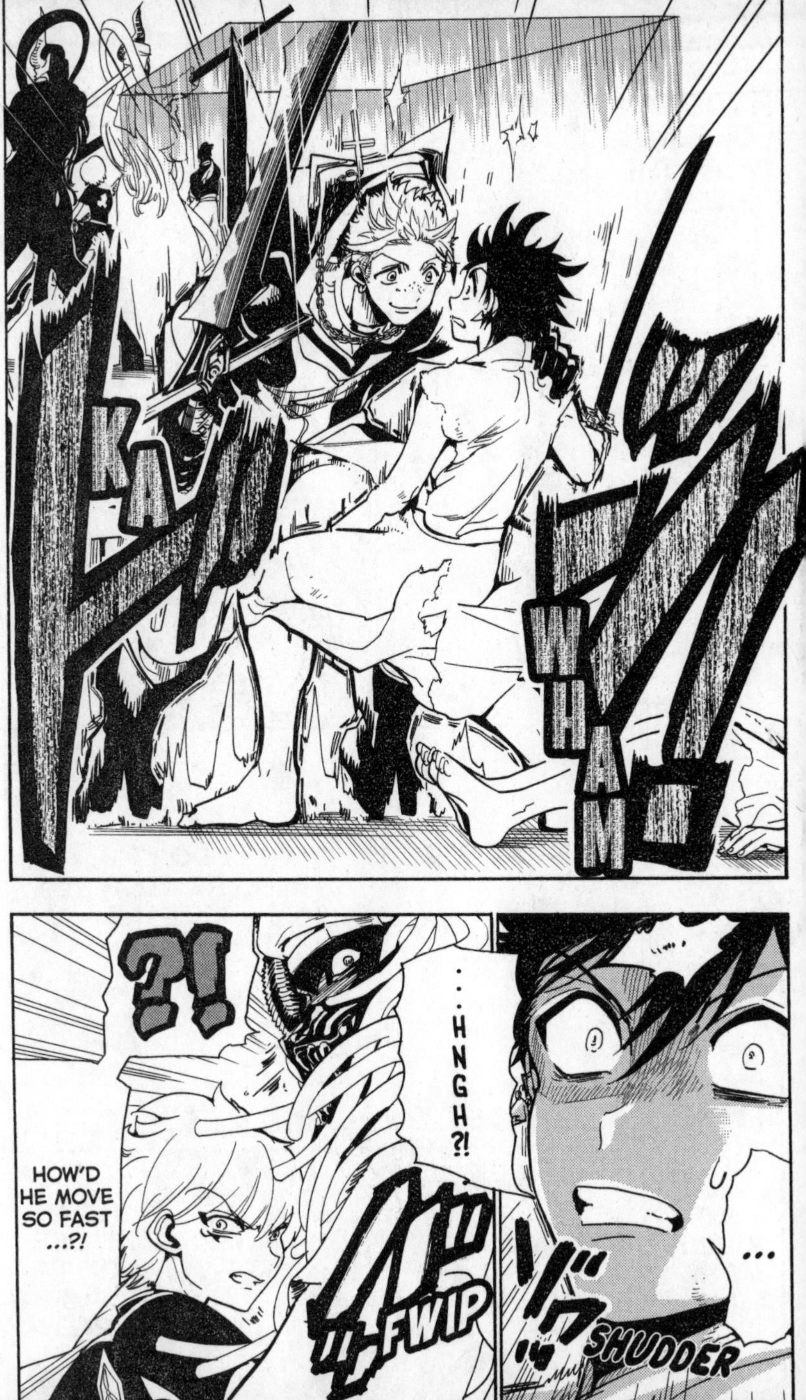
WHAM
KA
...HNGH?!
...
SHUDDER
?!
HOW'D HE MOVE SO FAST ...?!
FWIP

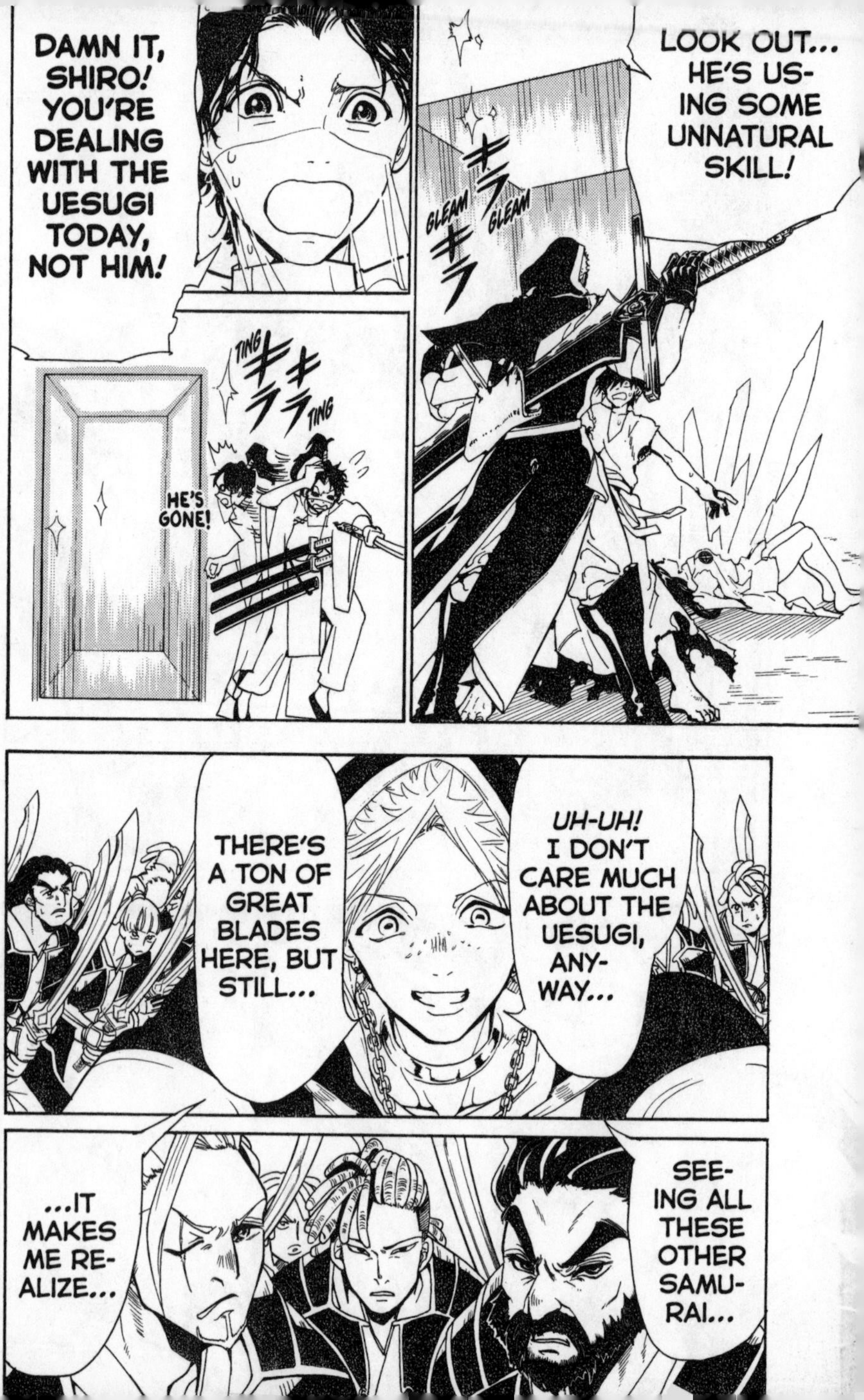
LOOK OUT... HE'S US-ING SOME UNNATURAL SKILL!
キラ GLEAM
キラ GLEAM
DAMN IT, SHIRO! YOU'RE DEALING WITH THE UESUGI TODAY, NOT HIM!
キラ TING
キラ TING
HE'S GONE!
UH-UH! I DON'T CARE MUCH ABOUT THE UESUGI, ANY-WAY...
THERE'S A TON OF GREAT BLADES HERE, BUT STILL...
SEE-ING ALL THESE OTHER SAMU-RAI...
...IT MAKES ME RE-ALIZE...

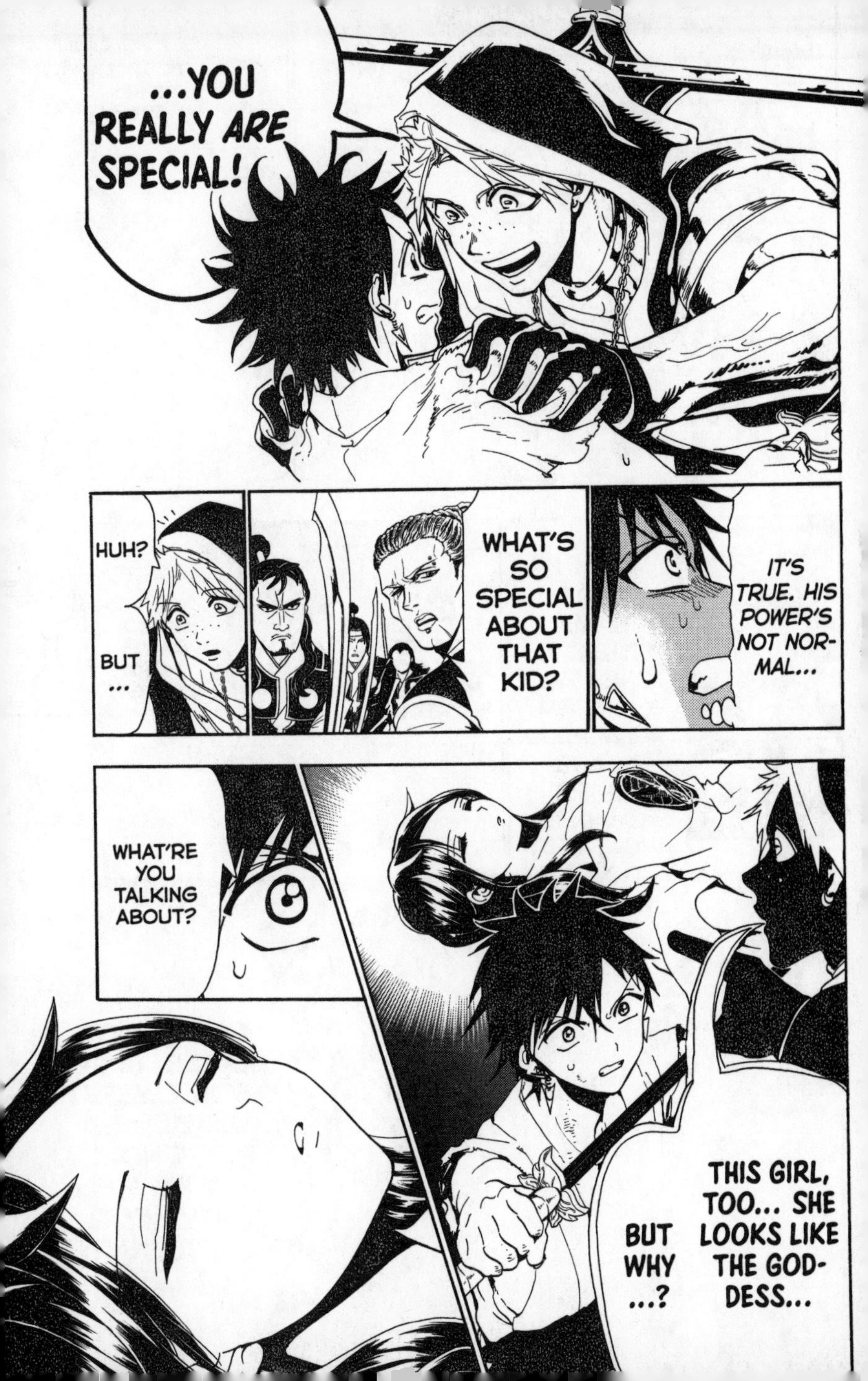
...YOU REALLY ARE SPECIAL!
IT'S TRUE. HIS POWER'S NOT NOR-MAL...
WHAT'S SO SPECIAL ABOUT THAT KID?
HUH?
BUT ...
THIS GIRL, TOO... SHE LOOKS LIKE THE GOD-DESS...
BUT WHY ...?
WHAT'RE YOU TALKING ABOUT?

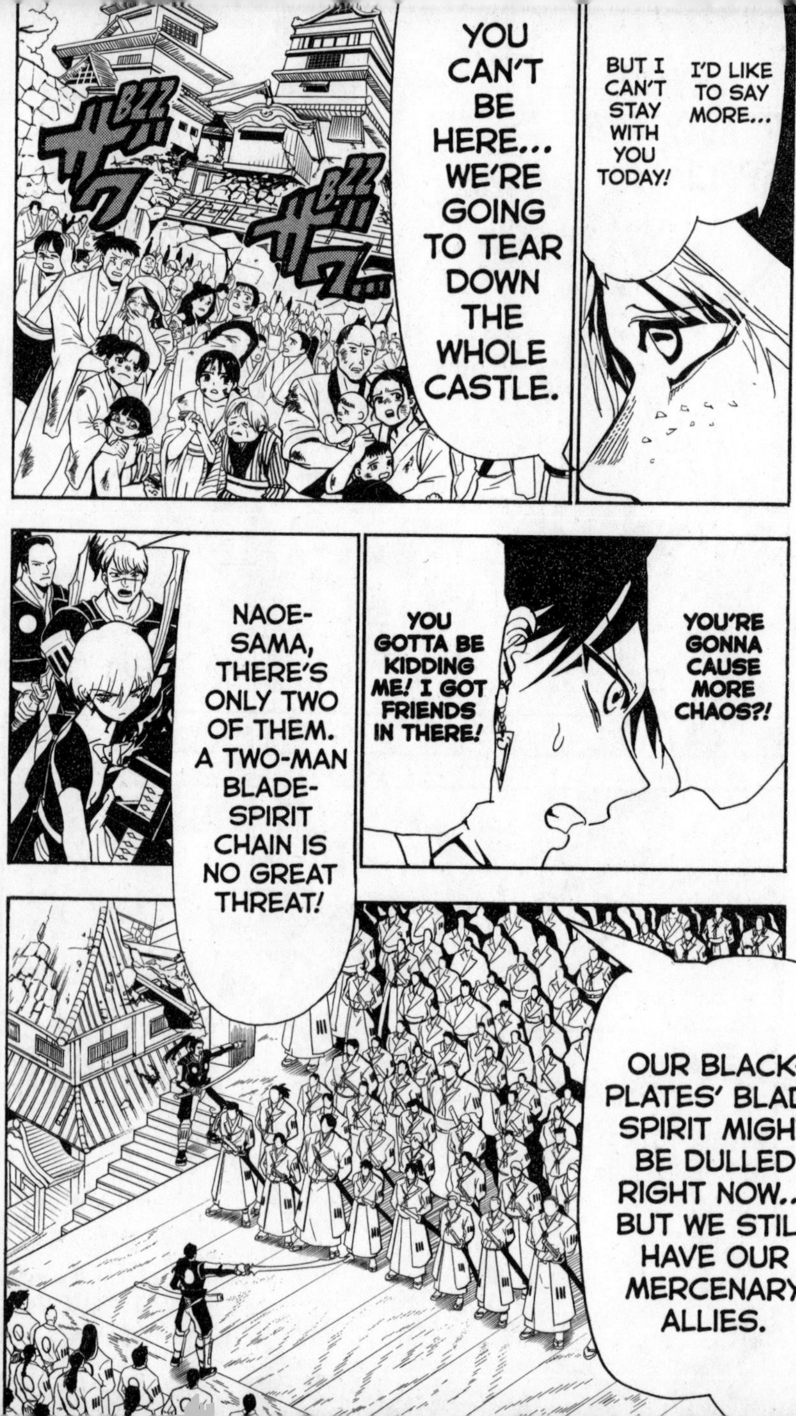
I'D LIKE TO SAY MORE...
BUT I CAN'T STAY WITH YOU TODAY!
YOU CAN'T BE HERE... WE'RE GOING TO TEAR DOWN THE WHOLE CASTLE.
BZZ
BZZ
YOU'RE GONNA CAUSE MORE CHAOS?!
YOU GOTTA BE KIDDING ME! I GOT FRIENDS IN THERE!
NAOE-SAMA, THERE'S ONLY TWO OF THEM. A TWO-MAN BLADE-SPIRIT CHAIN IS NO GREAT THREAT!
OUR BLACK-PLATES' BLADE SPIRIT MIGHT BE DULLED RIGHT NOW... BUT WE STILL HAVE OUR MERCENARY ALLIES.

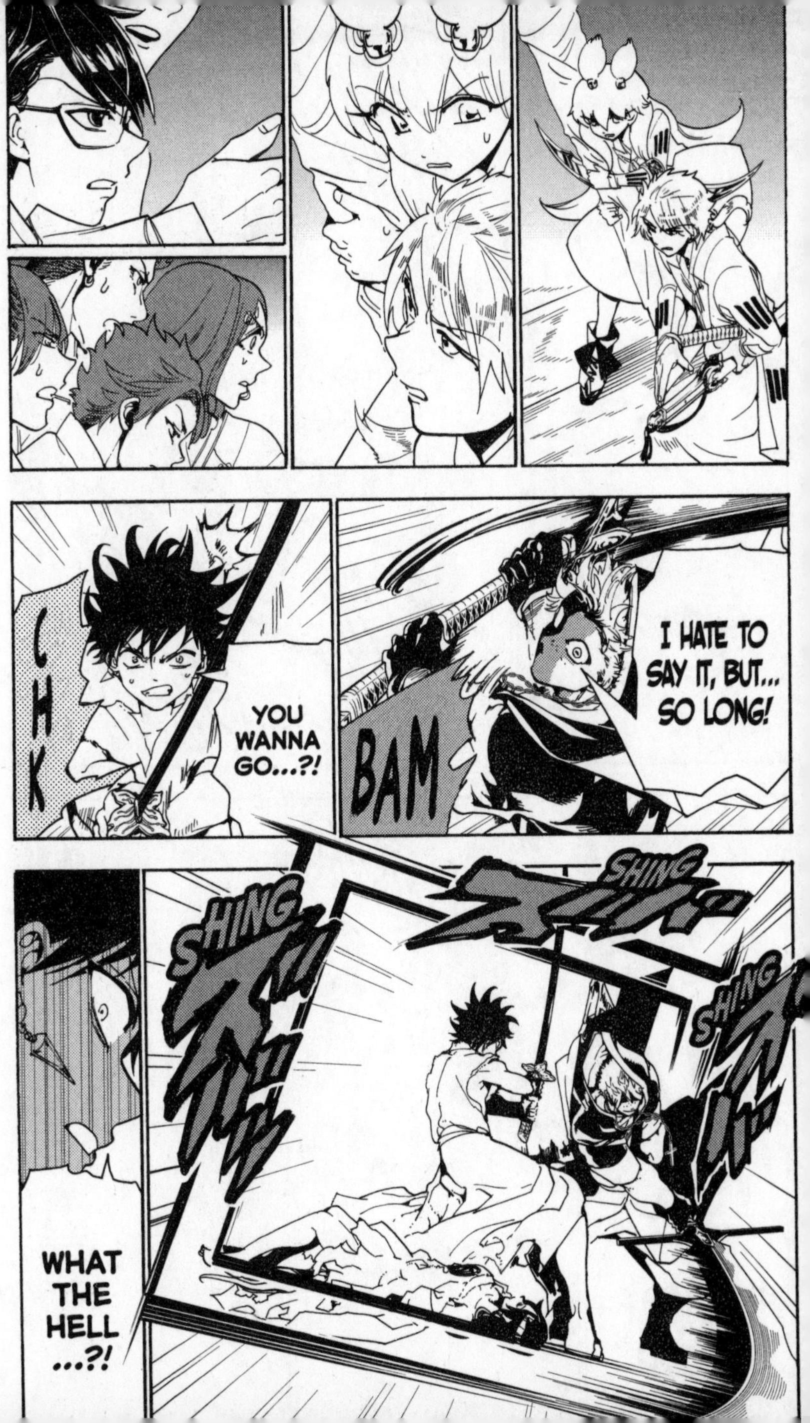
I HATE TO SAY IT, BUT... SO LONG!
BAM
YOU WANNA GO...?!
CHK
SHING
SHING
SHING
WHAT THE HELL ...?!

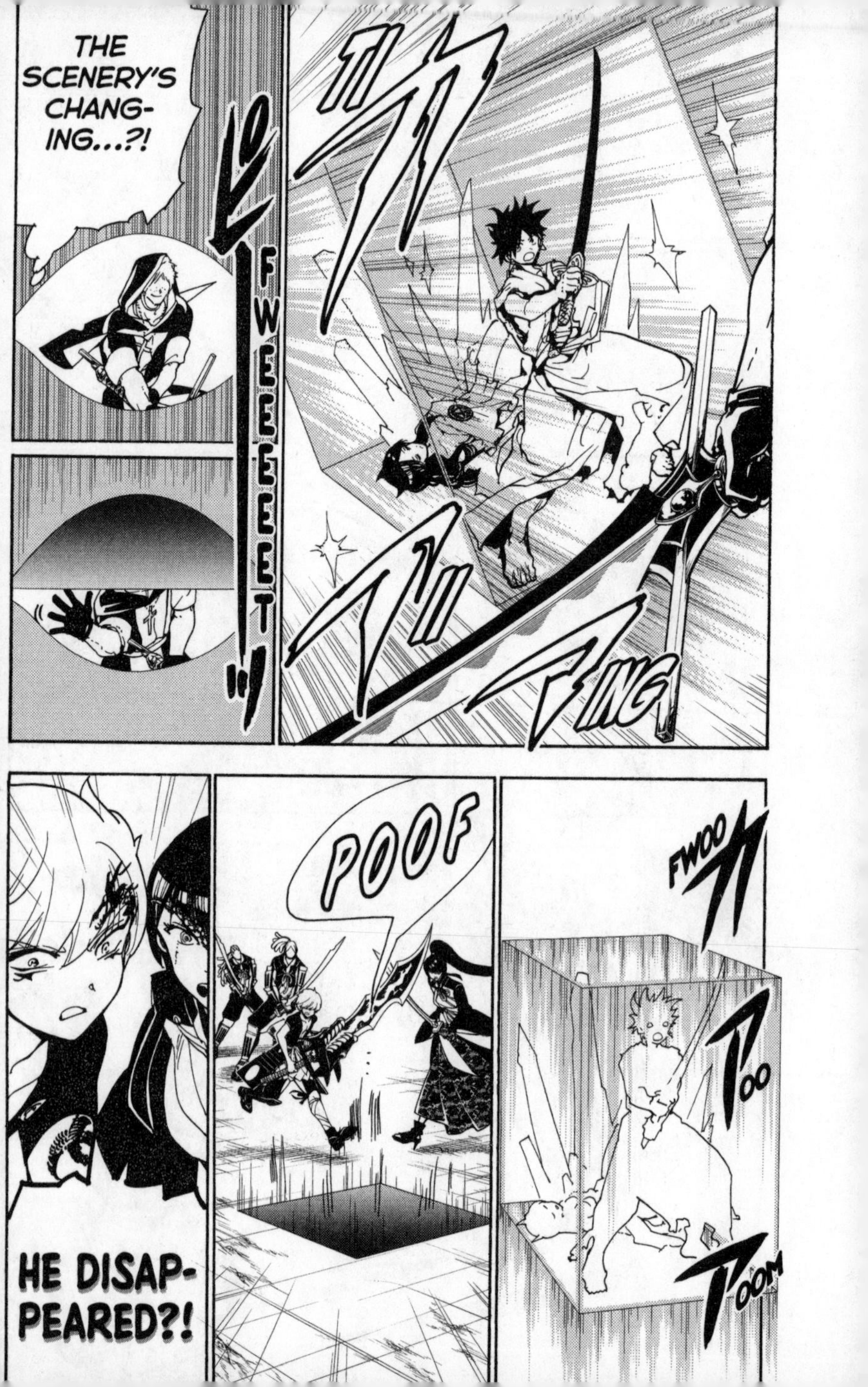
FWEEEEET!!
THE SCENERY'S CHANGING...?!
FWOOM
TOOOM
POOF
HE DISAPPEARED?!

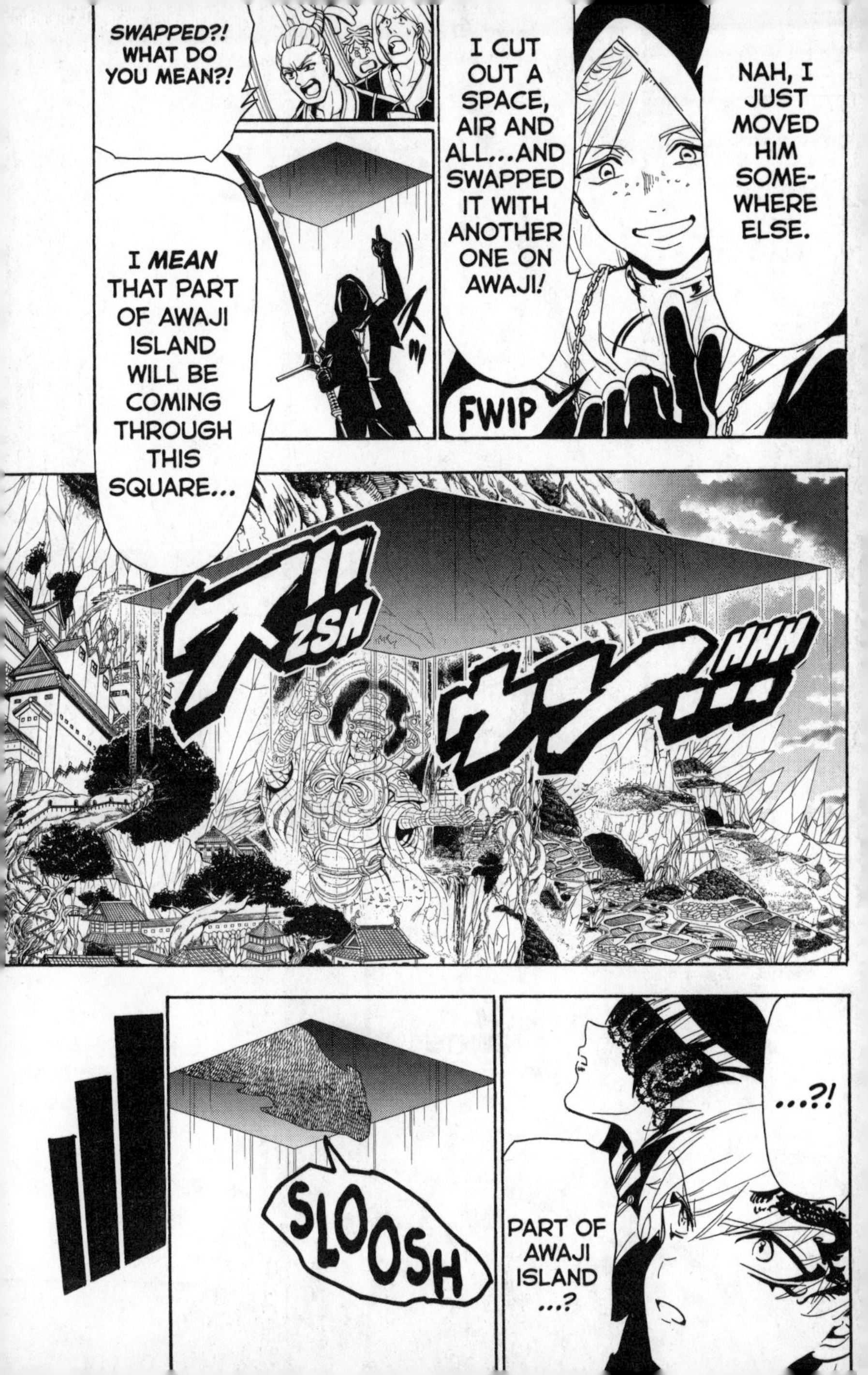
NAH, I JUST MOVED HIM SOME-WHERE ELSE.
I CUT OUT A SPACE, AIR AND ALL...AND SWAPPED IT WITH ANOTHER ONE ON AWAJI!
FWIP
SWAPPED?! WHAT DO YOU MEAN?!
I MEAN THAT PART OF AWAJI ISLAND WILL BE COMING THROUGH THIS SQUARE...
ZSH
HHH
...?!
PART OF AWAJI ISLAND ...?
SLOOSH

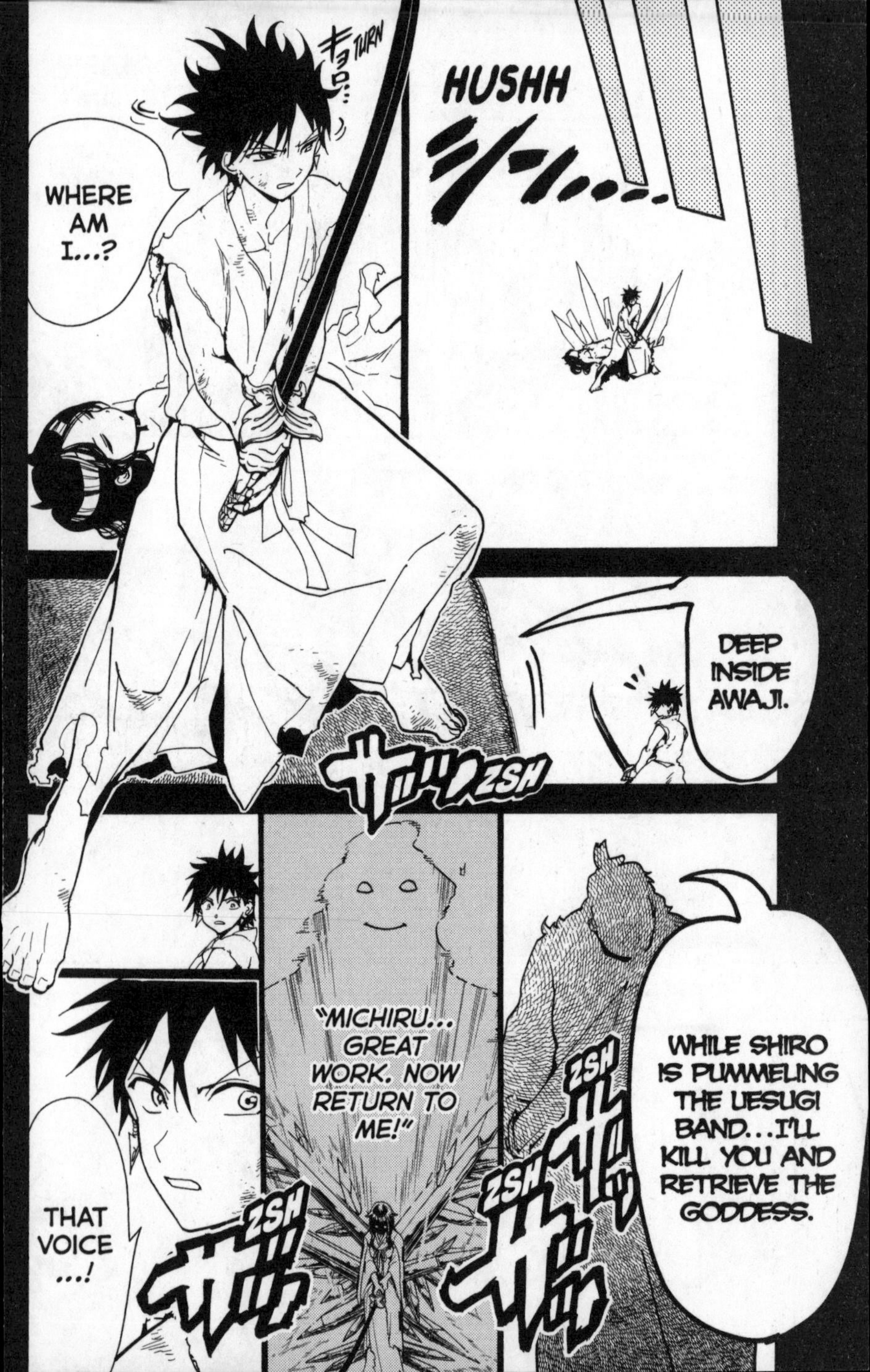
HUSHH
TURN
WHERE AM I...?
DEEP INSIDE AWAJI.
ZSH
WHILE SHIRO IS PUMMELING THE UESUGI BAND...I'LL KILL YOU AND RETRIEVE THE GODDESS.
ZSH
ZSH
"MICHIRU... GREAT WORK. NOW RETURN TO ME!"
ZSH
THAT VOICE ...!

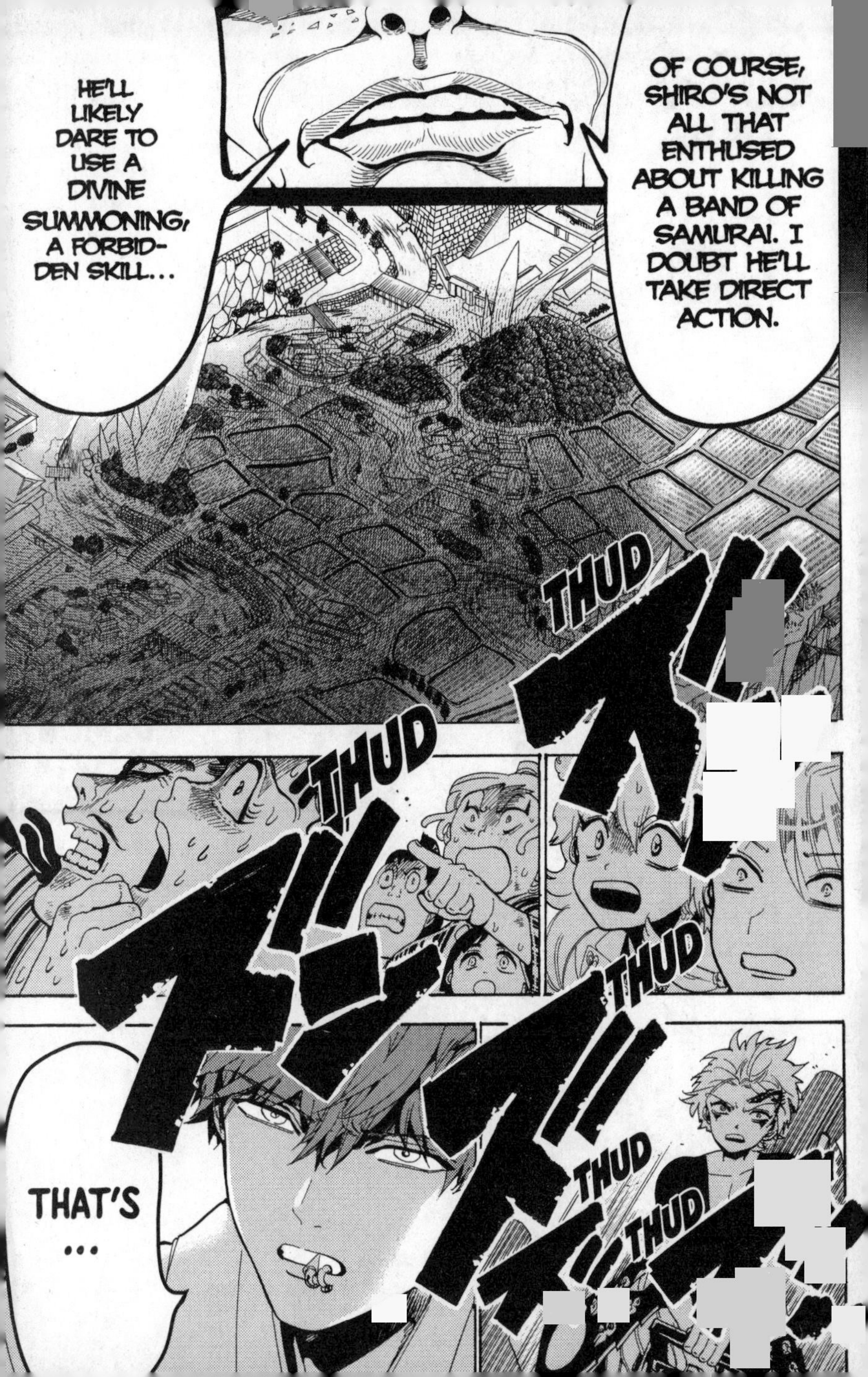
OF COURSE, SHIRO'S NOT ALL THAT ENTHUSED ABOUT KILLING A BAND OF SAMURAI. I DOUBT HE'LL TAKE DIRECT ACTION.
HE'LL LIKELY DARE TO USE A DIVINE SUMMONING, A FORBID-DEN SKILL...
THUD
THUD
THUD
THUD
THUD
THAT'S ...

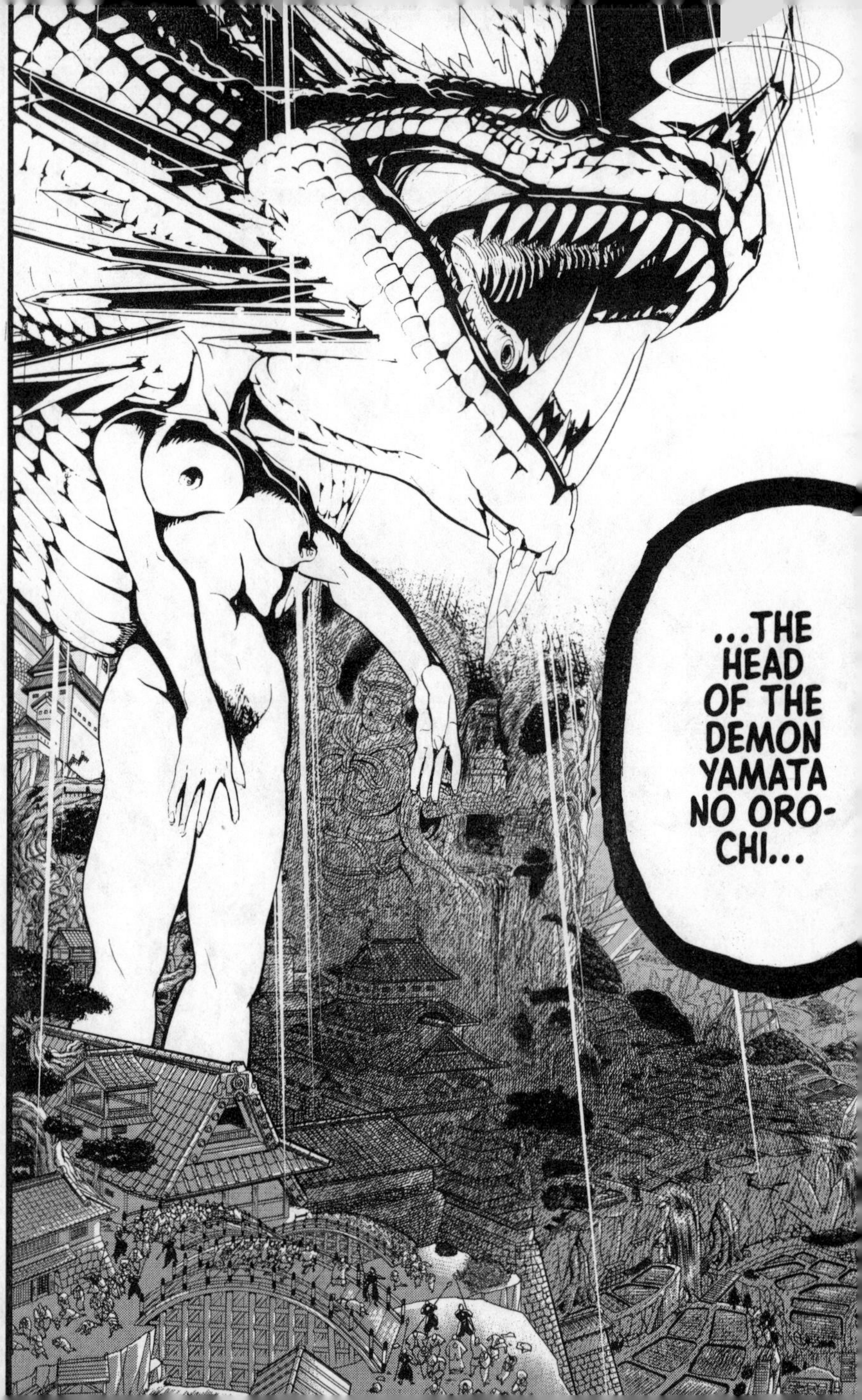
...THE HEAD OF THE DEMON YAMATA NO ORO-CHI...

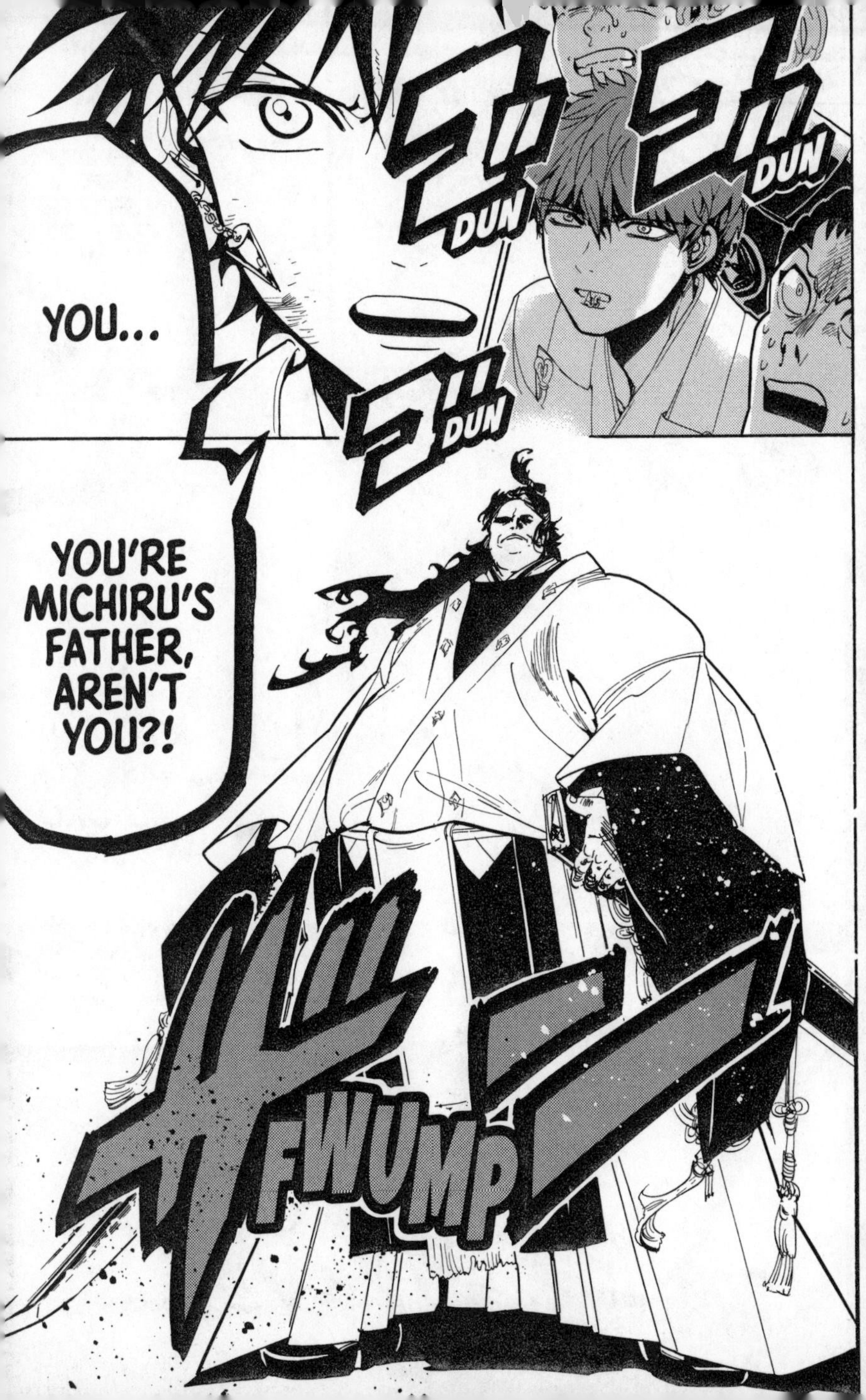
DUN
DUN
DUN
YOU...
YOU'RE MICHIRU'S FATHER, AREN'T YOU?!
FWUMP

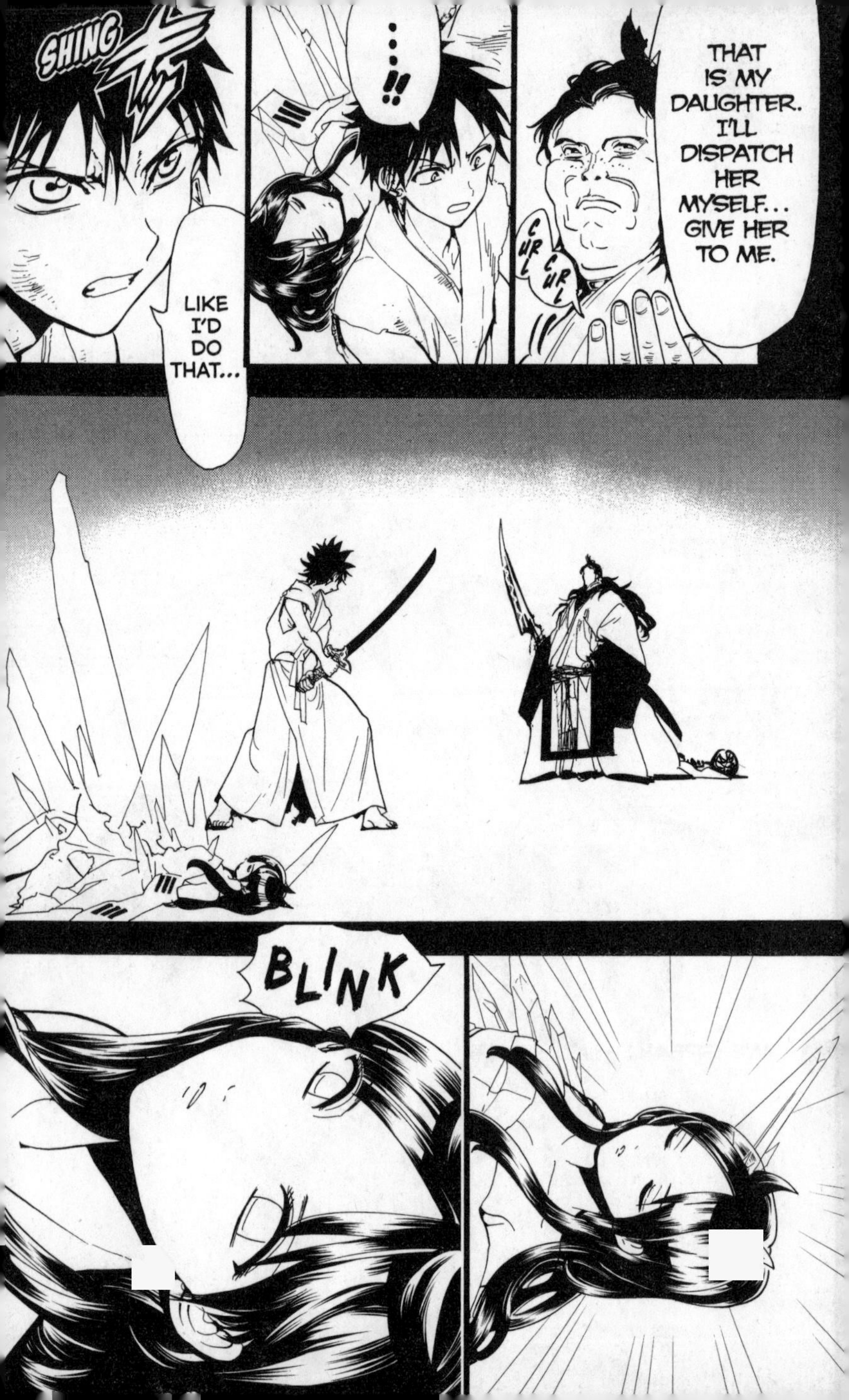

THAT IS MY DAUGHTER. I'LL DISPATCH HER MYSELF... GIVE HER TO ME.
CURL CURL
...!!
SHING
LIKE I'D DO THAT...
BLINK

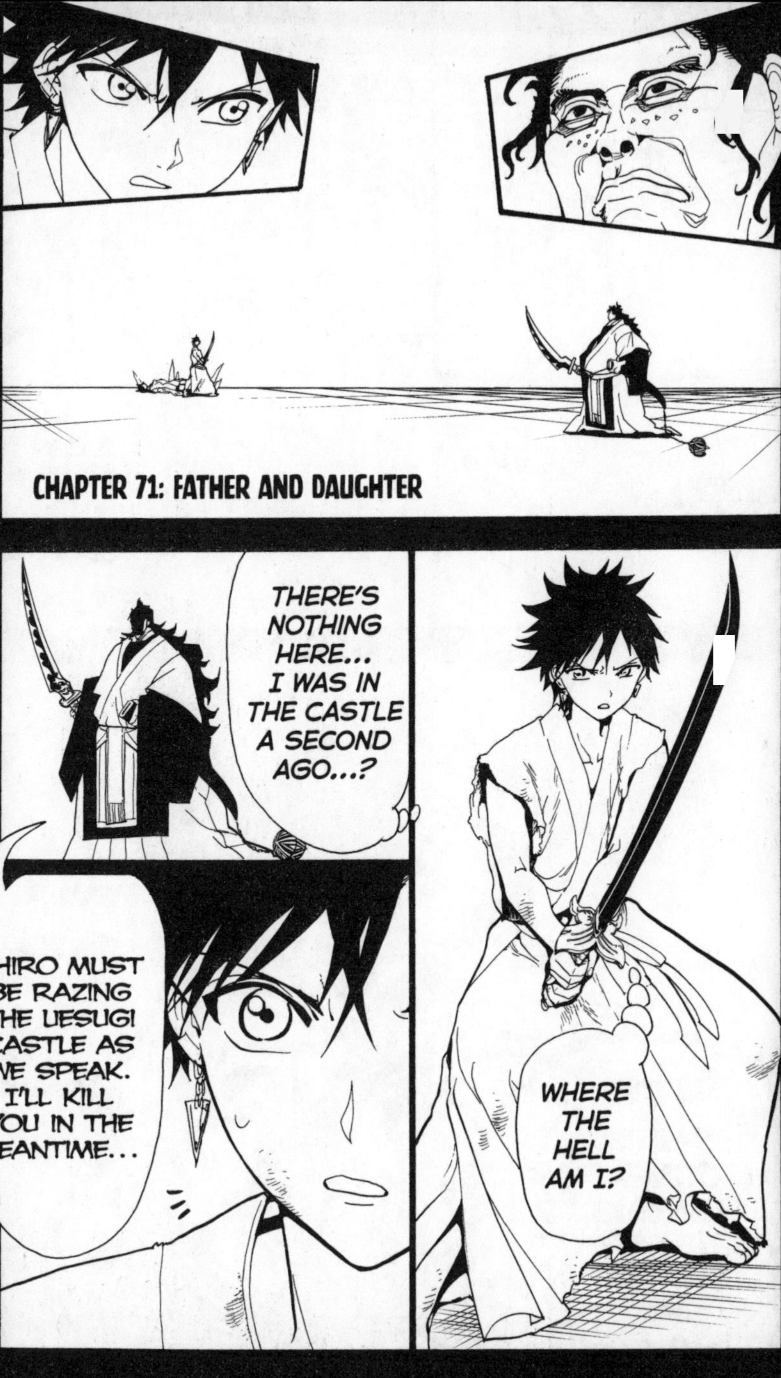
CHAPTER 71: FATHER AND DAUGHTER
WHERE THE HELL AM I?
THERE'S NOTHING HERE... I WAS IN THE CASTLE A SECOND AGO...?
SHIRO MUST BE RAZING THE UESUGI CASTLE AS WE SPEAK. I'LL KILL YOU IN THE MEANTIME...

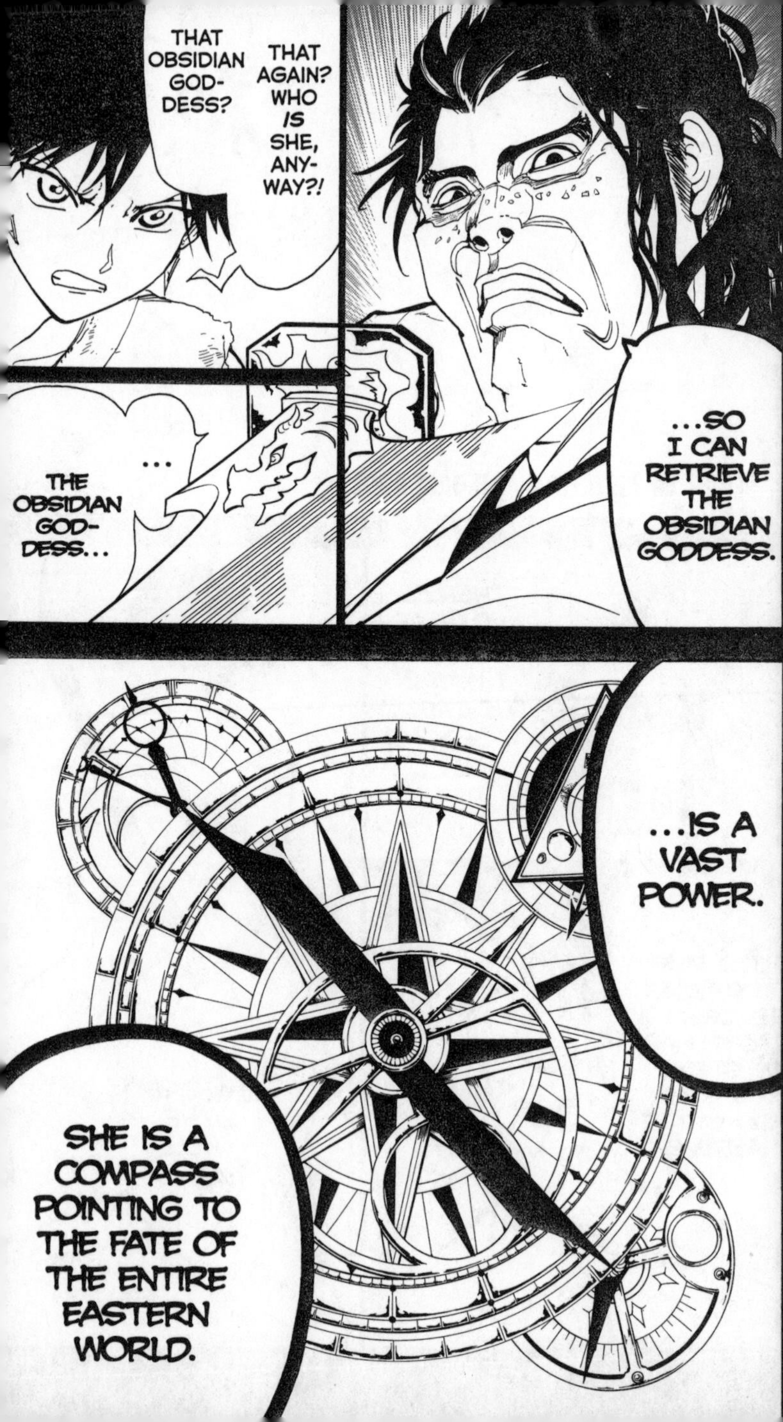
...SO I CAN RETRIEVE THE OBSIDIAN GODDESS.
THAT AGAIN? WHO *IS* SHE, ANYWAY?!
THAT OBSIDIAN GOD-DESS?
...
THE OBSIDIAN GOD-DESS...
...IS A VAST POWER.
SHE IS A COMPASS POINTING TO THE FATE OF THE ENTIRE EASTERN WORLD.

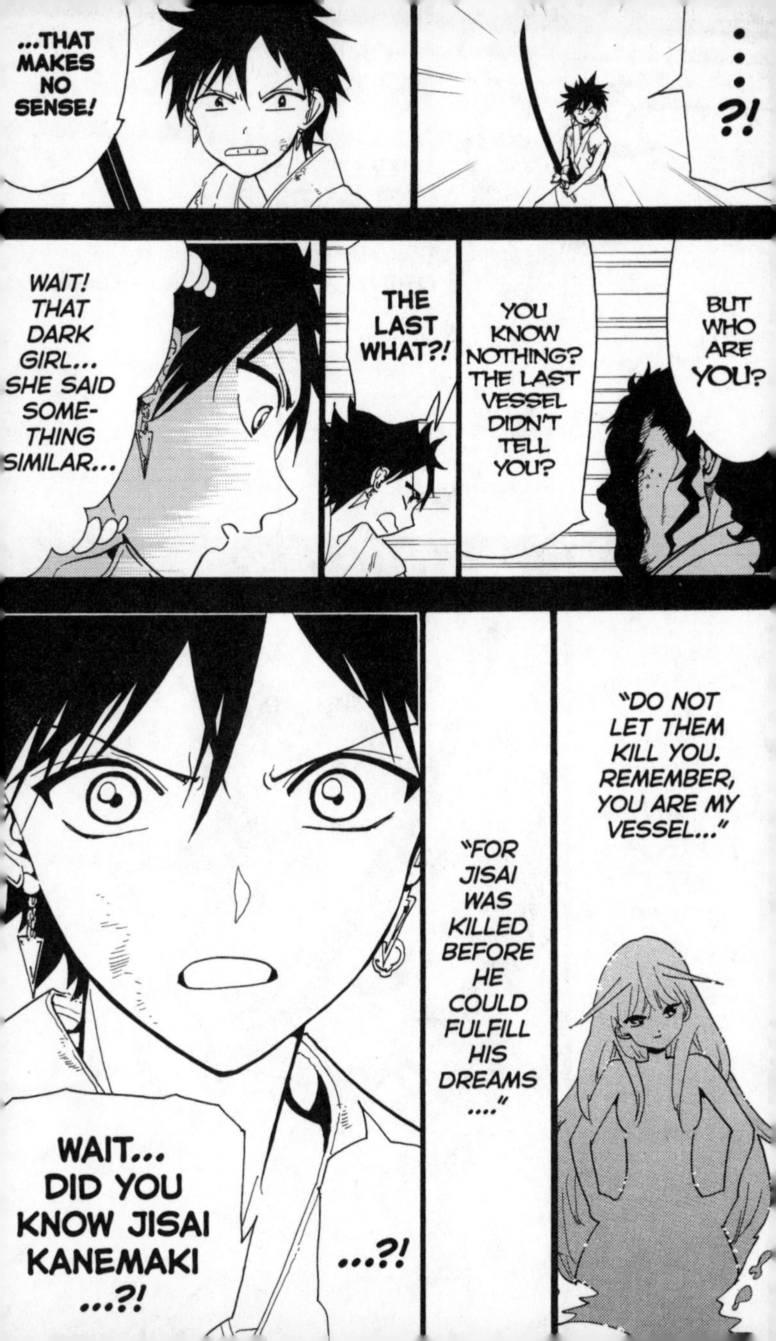

...?!
...THAT MAKES NO SENSE!
BUT WHO ARE YOU?
YOU KNOW NOTHING? THE LAST VESSEL DIDN'T TELL YOU?
THE LAST WHAT?!
WAIT! THAT DARK GIRL... SHE SAID SOME-THING SIMILAR...
"DO NOT LET THEM KILL YOU. REMEMBER, YOU ARE MY VESSEL..."
"FOR JISAI WAS KILLED BEFORE HE COULD FULFILL HIS DREAMS ...."
...?!
WAIT... DID YOU KNOW JISAI KANEMAKI ...?!

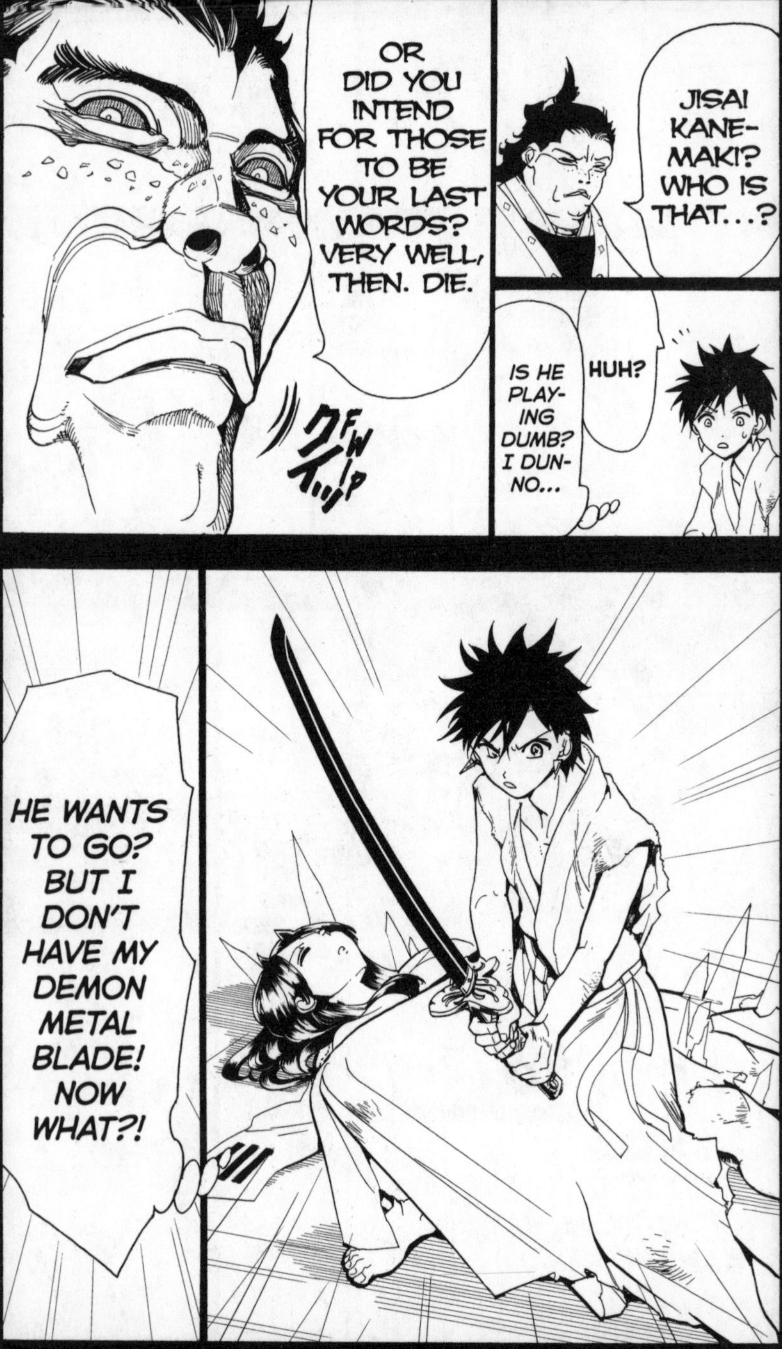
JISAI KANE-MAKI? WHO IS THAT...?
HUH?
IS HE PLAY-ING DUMB? I DUN-NO...
OR DID YOU INTEND FOR THOSE TO BE YOUR LAST WORDS? VERY WELL, THEN. DIE.
FWIP
HE WANTS TO GO? BUT I DON'T HAVE MY DEMON METAL BLADE! NOW WHAT?!

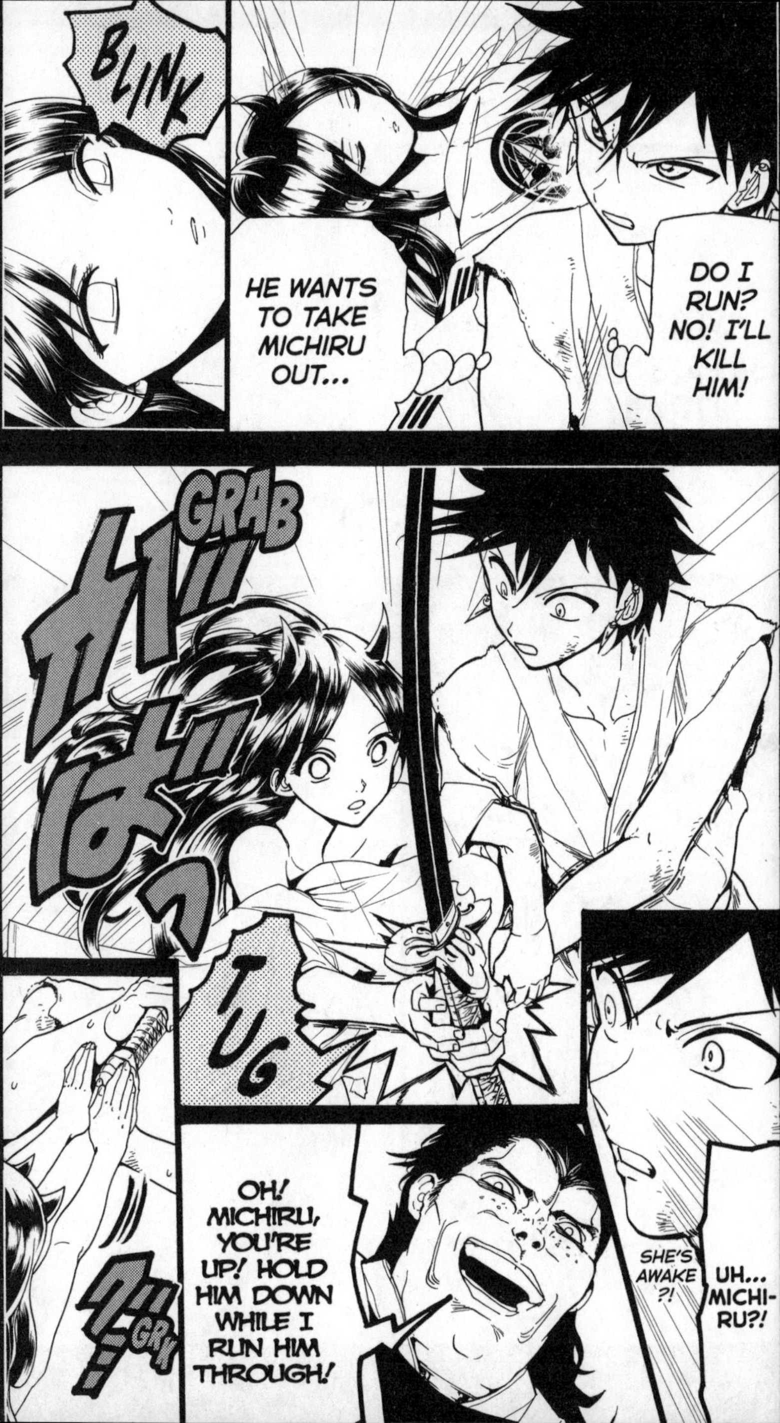
DO I RUN? NO! I'LL KILL HIM!
HE WANTS TO TAKE MICHIRU OUT...
BLINK
GRAB
TUG
UH... MICHI-RU?!
SHE'S AWAKE ?!
OH! MICHIRU, YOU'RE UP! HOLD HIM DOWN WHILE I RUN HIM THROUGH!
GRK

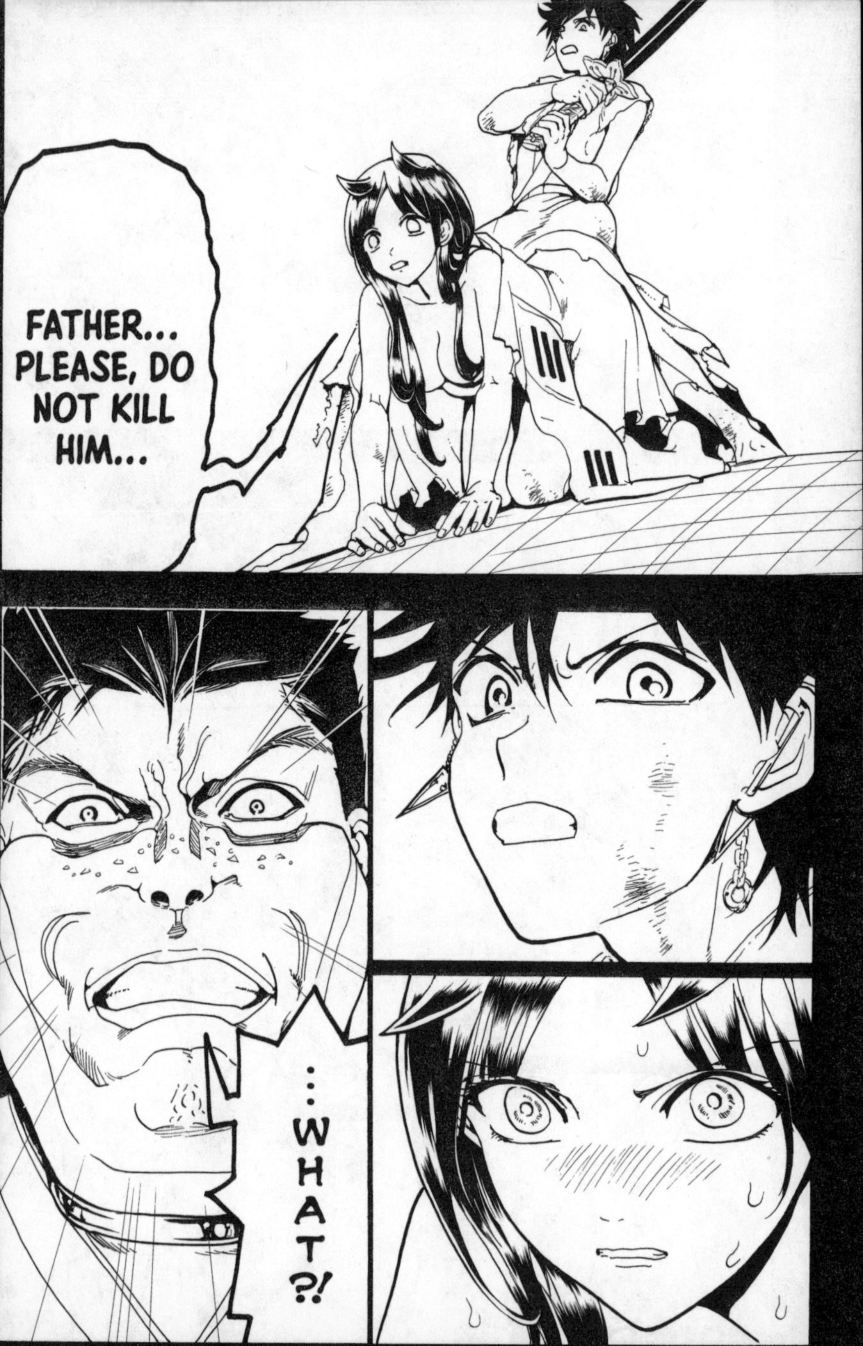
FATHER... PLEASE, DO NOT KILL HIM...
...WHAT?!

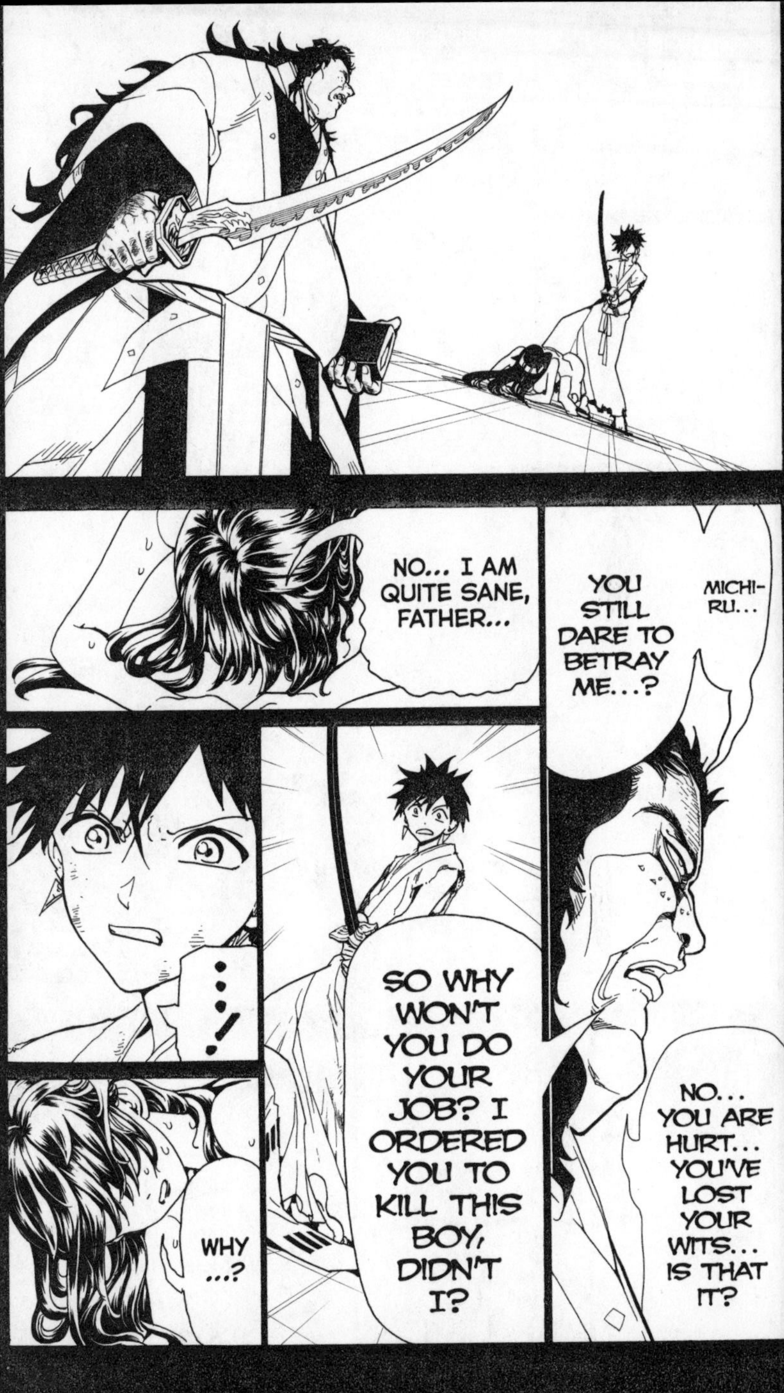
MICHI-RU...
YOU STILL DARE TO BETRAY ME...?
NO... YOU ARE HURT... YOU'VE LOST YOUR WITS... IS THAT IT?
NO... I AM QUITE SANE, FATHER...
SO WHY WON'T YOU DO YOUR JOB? I ORDERED YOU TO KILL THIS BOY, DIDN'T I?
...!
WHY ...?

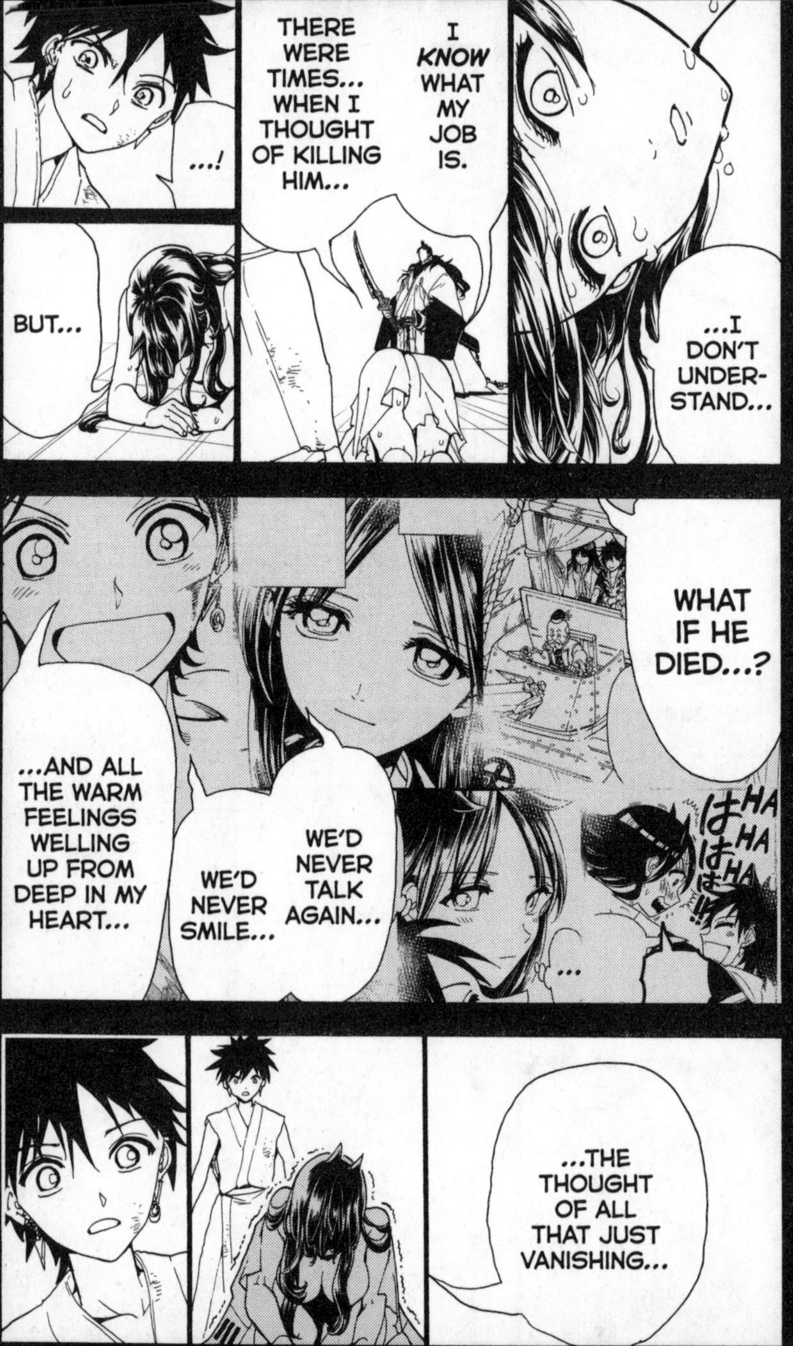
...I DON'T UNDERSTAND...
I *KNOW* WHAT MY JOB IS.
THERE WERE TIMES... WHEN I THOUGHT OF KILLING HIM...
...!
BUT...
WHAT IF HE DIED...?
ははは!!
HA HA HA
...
WE'D NEVER TALK AGAIN...
WE'D NEVER SMILE...
...AND ALL THE WARM FEELINGS WELLING UP FROM DEEP IN MY HEART...
...THE THOUGHT OF ALL THAT JUST VANISHING...

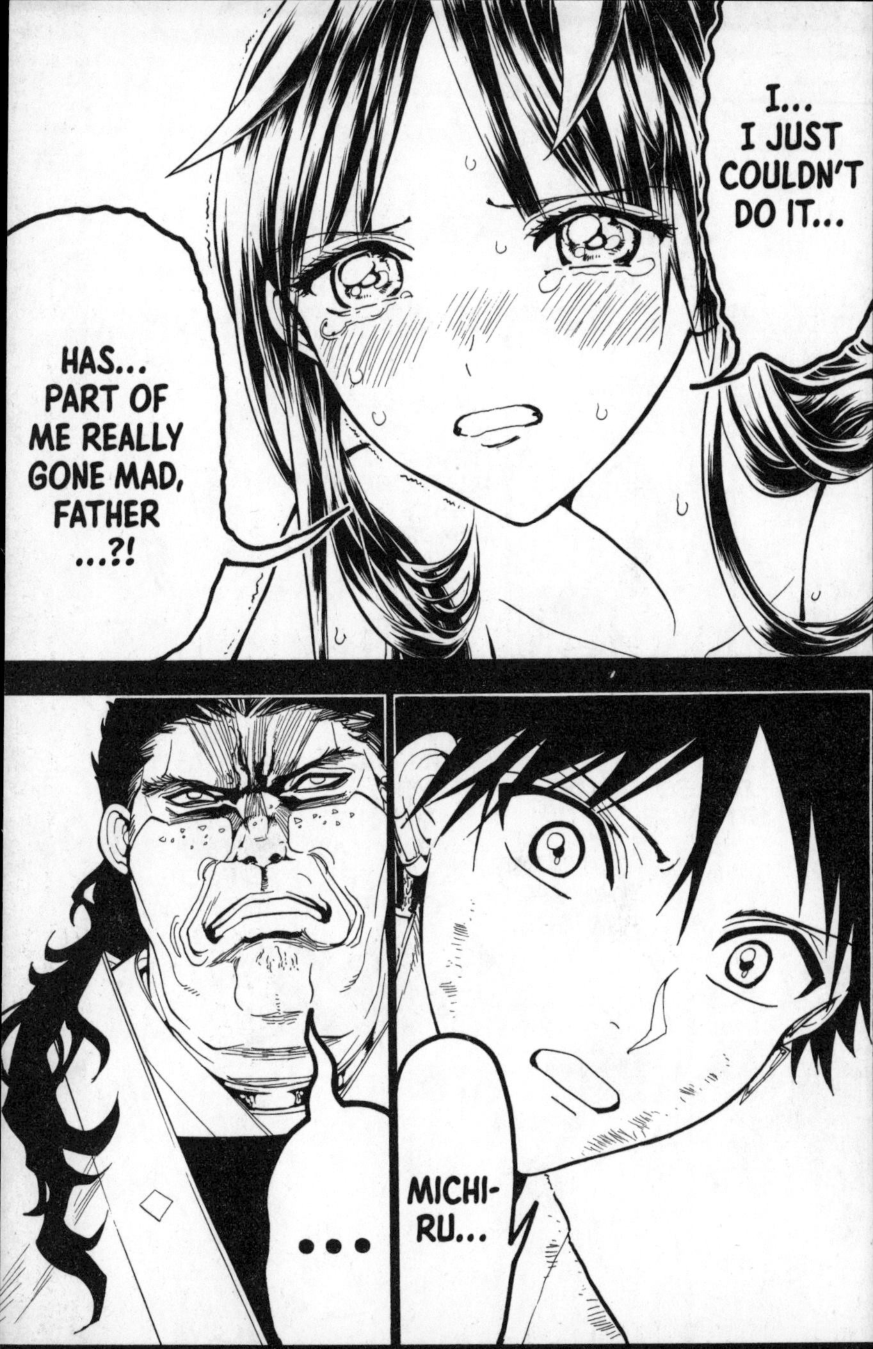
I... I JUST COULDN'T DO IT...
HAS... PART OF ME REALLY GONE MAD, FATHER ...?!
MICHI-RU...
...

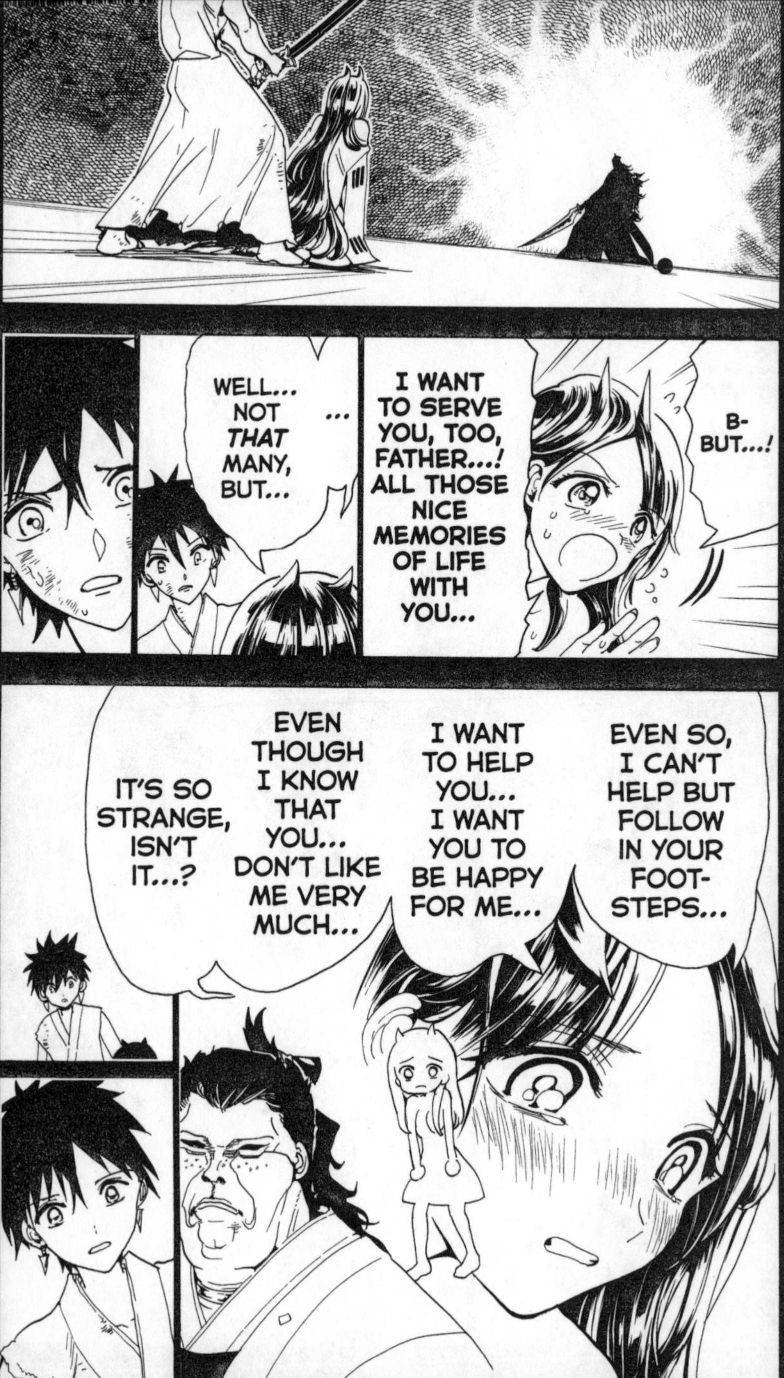

B- BUT...!
I WANT TO SERVE YOU, TOO, FATHER...! ALL THOSE NICE MEMORIES OF LIFE WITH YOU...
...
WELL... NOT *THAT* MANY, BUT...
EVEN SO, I CAN'T HELP BUT FOLLOW IN YOUR FOOT- STEPS...
I WANT TO HELP YOU... I WANT YOU TO BE HAPPY FOR ME...
EVEN THOUGH I KNOW THAT YOU... DON'T LIKE ME VERY MUCH...
IT'S SO STRANGE, ISN'T IT...?

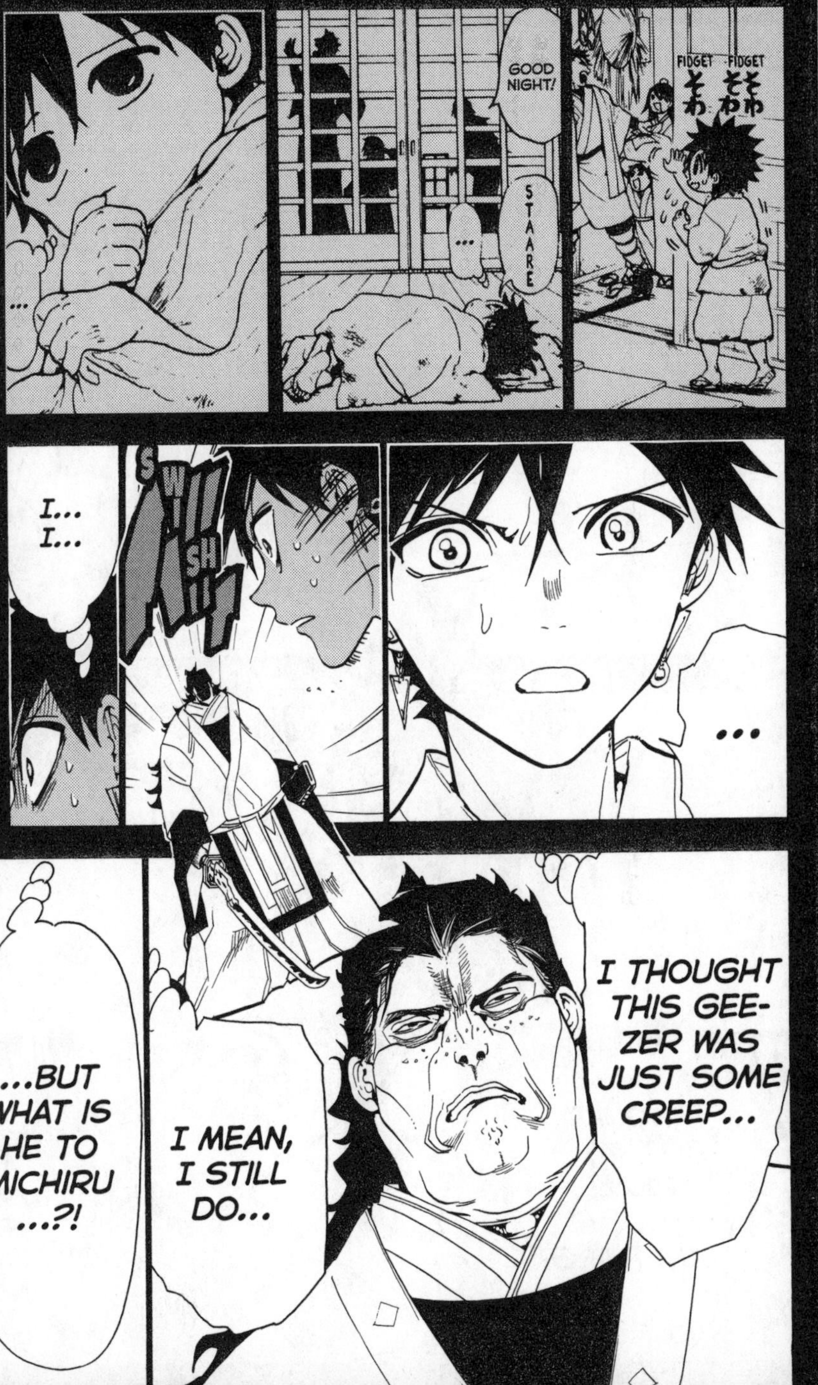
FIDGET -FIDGET
そわそわ
GOOD NIGHT!
STAARE
...
...
...
SWISH
I... I...
I THOUGHT THIS GEE-ZER WAS JUST SOME CREEP...
I MEAN, I STILL DO...
...BUT WHAT IS HE TO MICHIRU ...?!

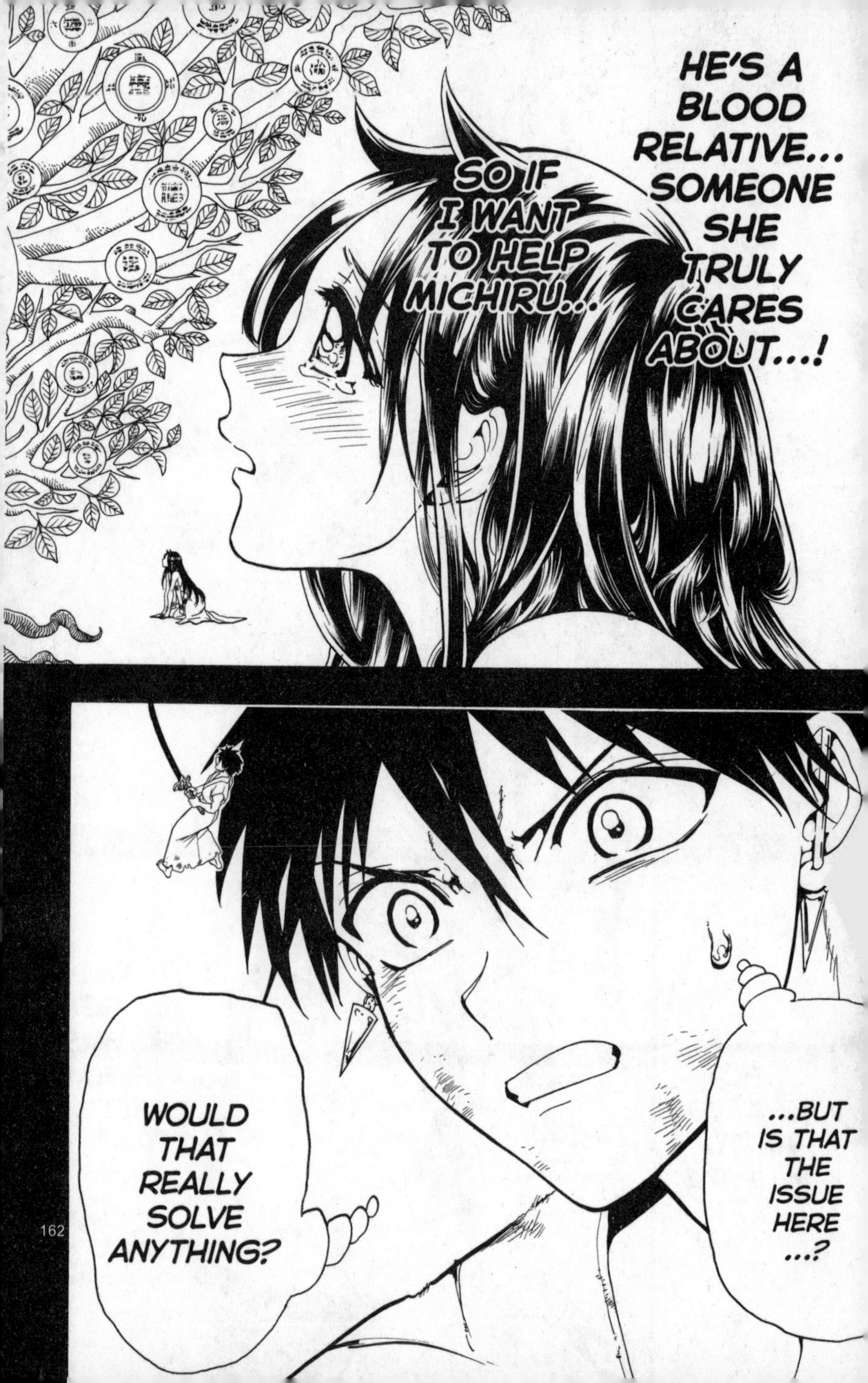
HE'S A BLOOD RELATIVE... SOMEONE SHE TRULY CARES ABOUT...!
SO IF I WANT TO HELP MICHIRU...
...BUT IS THAT THE ISSUE HERE...?
WOULD THAT REALLY SOLVE ANYTHING?

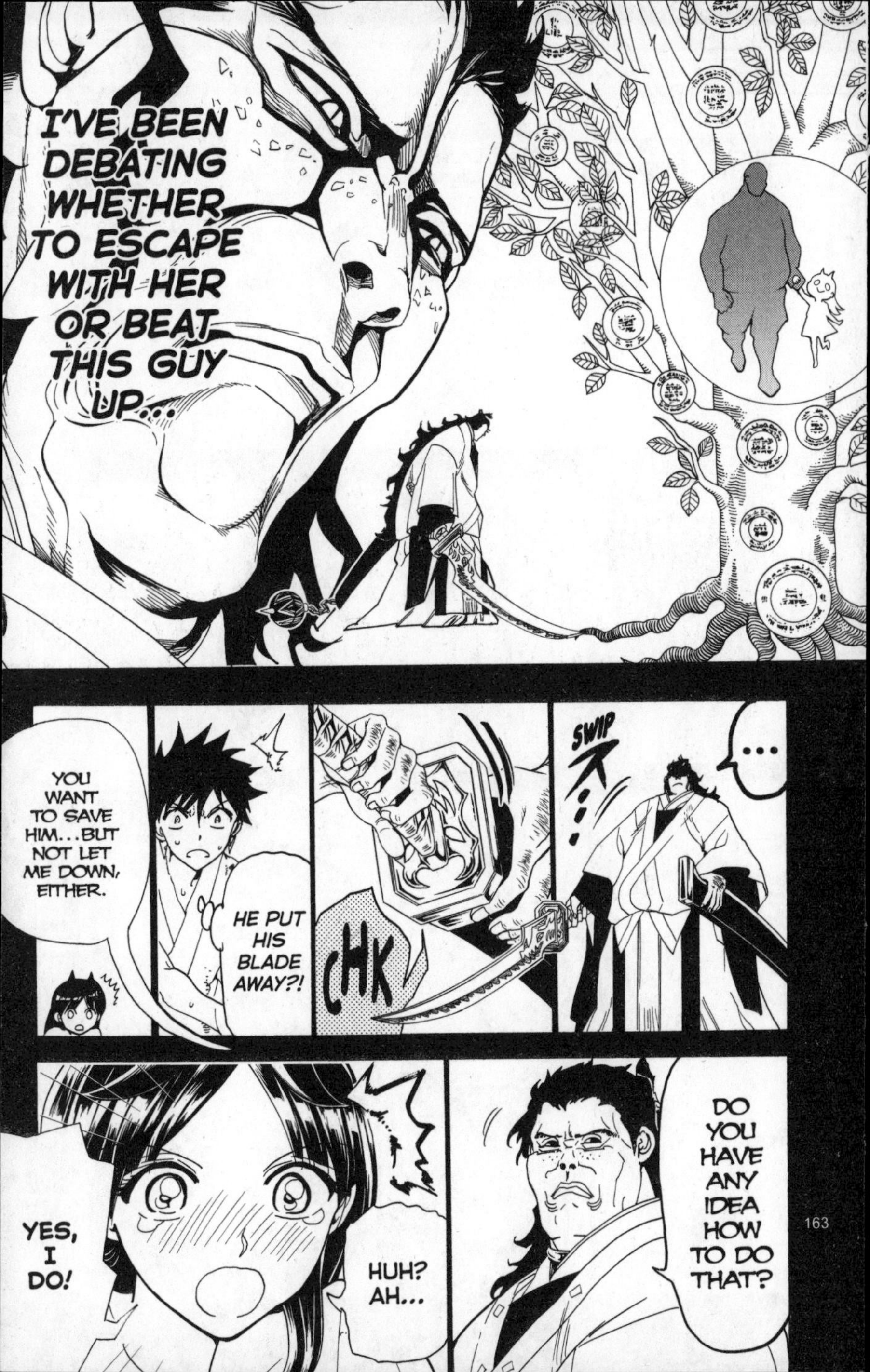
I'VE BEEN DEBATING WHETHER TO ESCAPE WITH HER OR BEAT THIS GUY UP...
...
SWIP
CHK
HE PUT HIS BLADE AWAY?!
YOU WANT TO SAVE HIM...BUT NOT LET ME DOWN, EITHER.
DO YOU HAVE ANY IDEA HOW TO DO THAT?
HUH? AH...
YES, I DO!

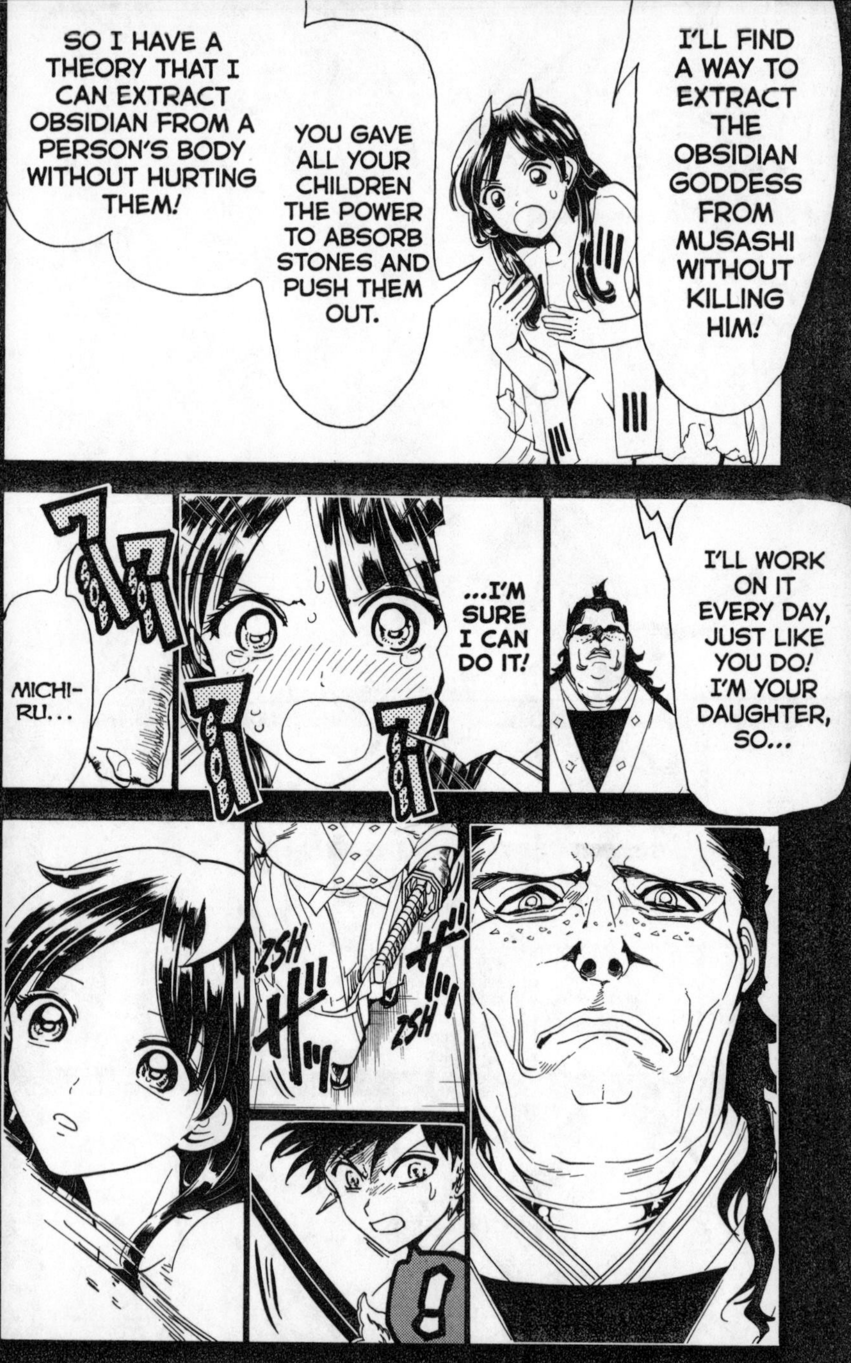
I'LL FIND A WAY TO EXTRACT THE OBSIDIAN GODDESS FROM MUSASHI WITHOUT KILLING HIM!
YOU GAVE ALL YOUR CHILDREN THE POWER TO ABSORB STONES AND PUSH THEM OUT.
SO I HAVE A THEORY THAT I CAN EXTRACT OBSIDIAN FROM A PERSON'S BODY WITHOUT HURTING THEM!
I'LL WORK ON IT EVERY DAY, JUST LIKE YOU DO! I'M YOUR DAUGHTER, SO...
...I'M SURE I CAN DO IT!
SOB
SOB
SOB
SOB
MICHI-RU...
ZSH
ZSH
!

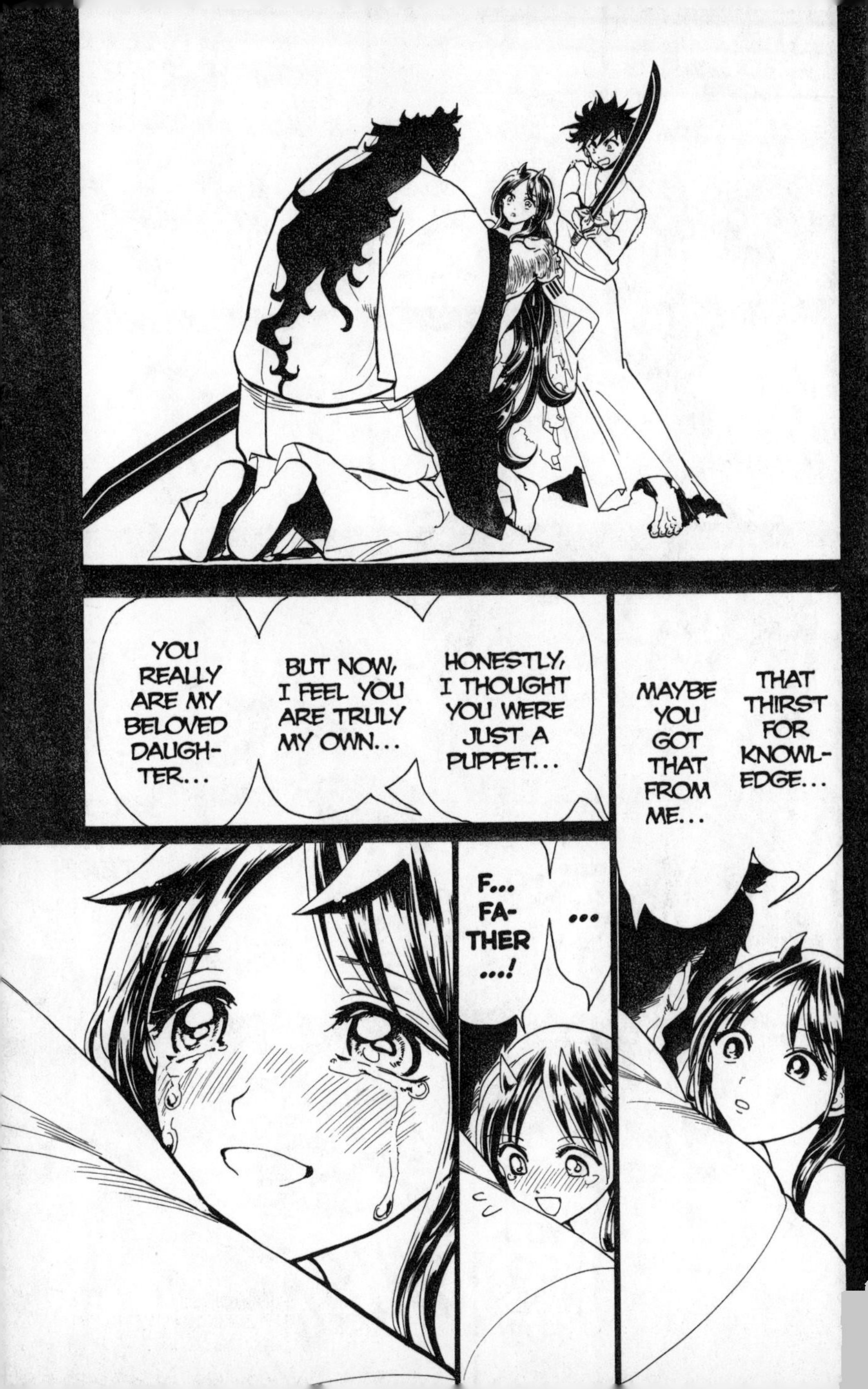
THAT THIRST FOR KNOWLEDGE...
MAYBE YOU GOT THAT FROM ME...
HONESTLY, I THOUGHT YOU WERE JUST A PUPPET...
BUT NOW, I FEEL YOU ARE TRULY MY OWN...
YOU REALLY ARE MY BELOVED DAUGHTER...
...
F... FATHER...!

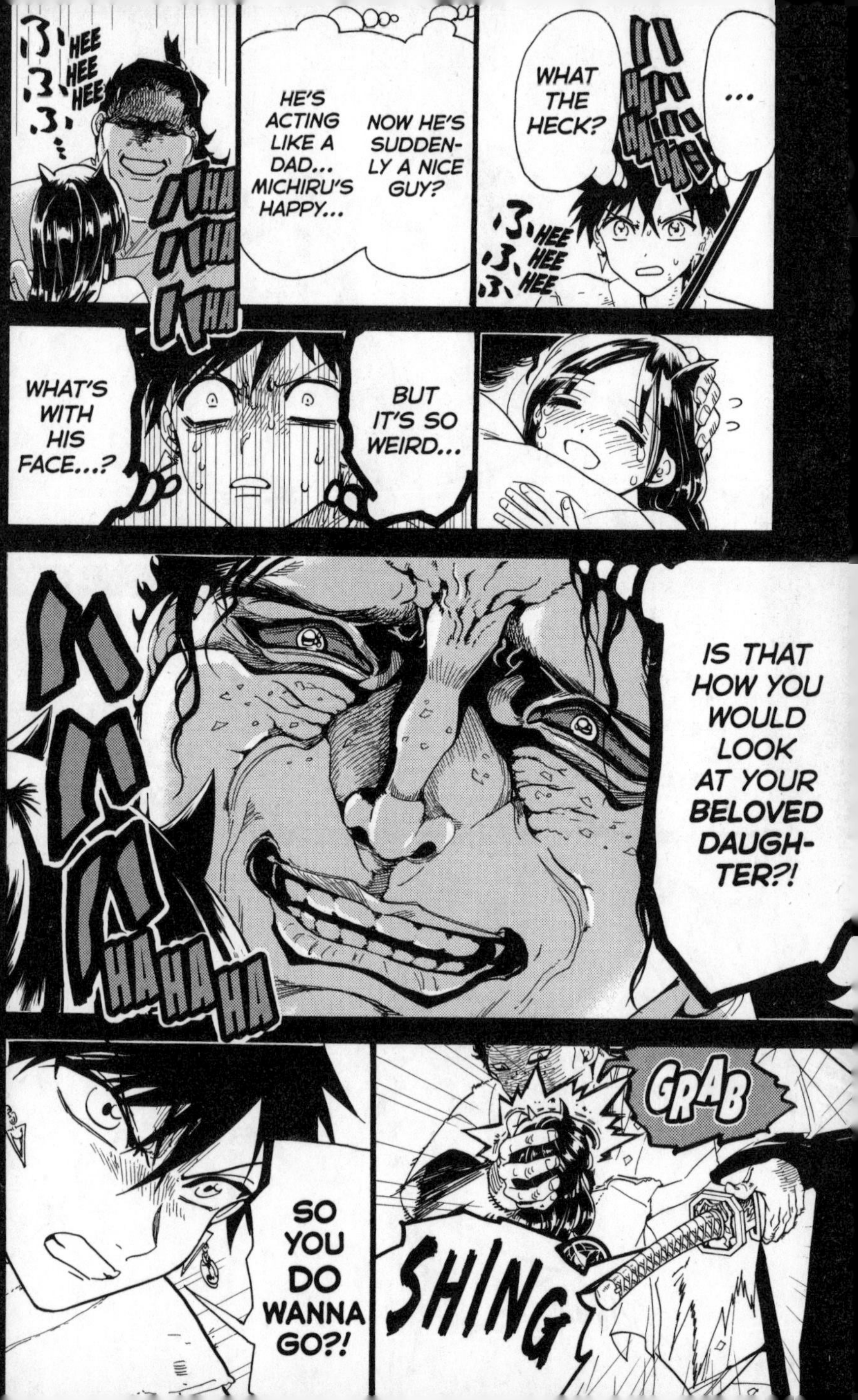

...
WHAT THE HECK?
HA HA HA
ふふふ HEE HEE HEE
NOW HE'S SUDDEN-LY A NICE GUY?
HE'S ACTING LIKE A DAD... MICHIRU'S HAPPY...
ふふふ HEE HEE HEE
HA HA HA
BUT IT'S SO WEIRD...
WHAT'S WITH HIS FACE...?
IS THAT HOW YOU WOULD LOOK AT YOUR BELOVED DAUGH-TER?!
HA HA HA HA
GRAB
SHING
SO YOU DO WANNA GO?!

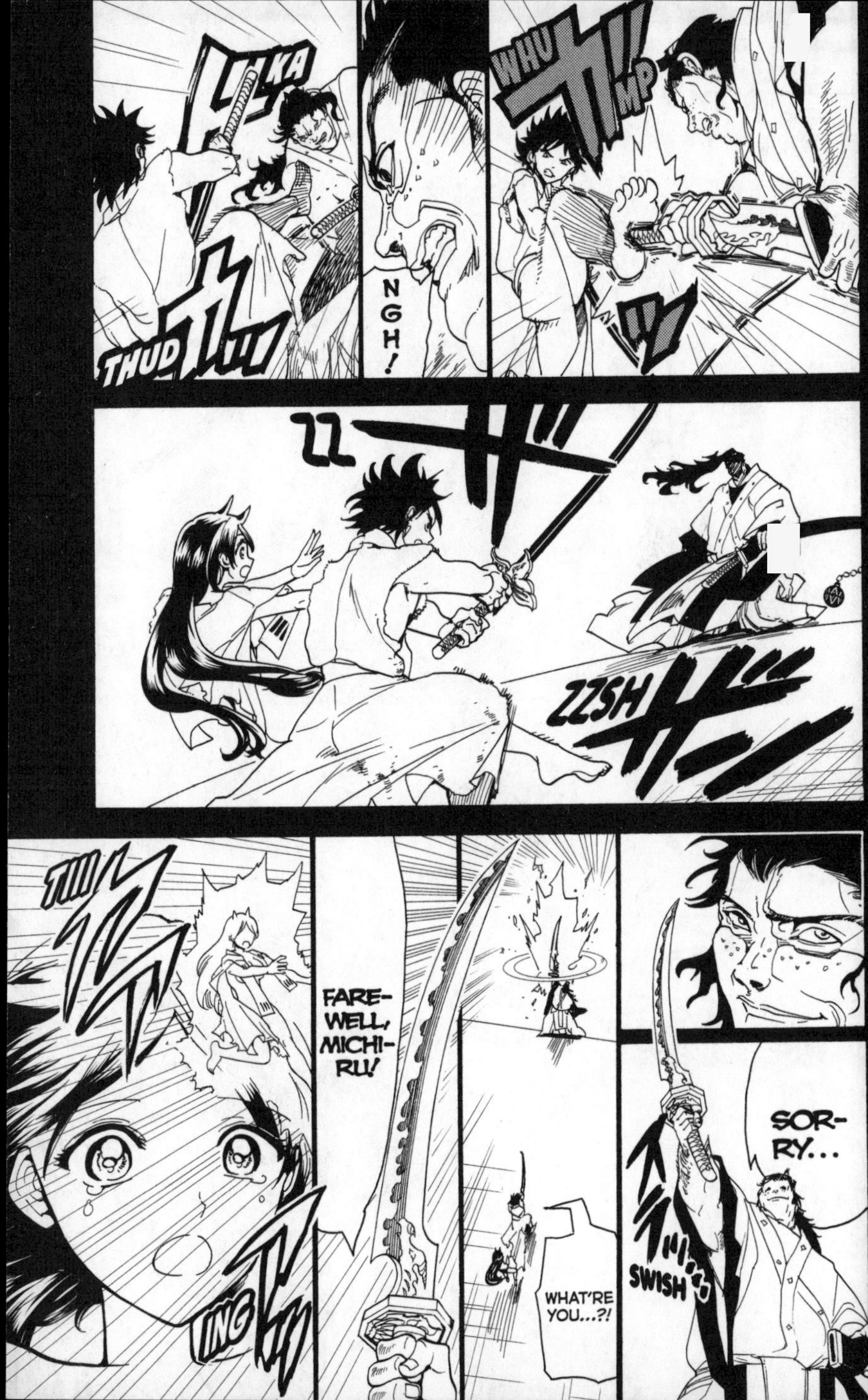
WHUMP
NGH!
KA
THUD
ZZ
ZZSH
SOR-RY...
SWISH
WHAT'RE YOU...?!
FARE-WELL, MICHI-RU!
TIII
ING

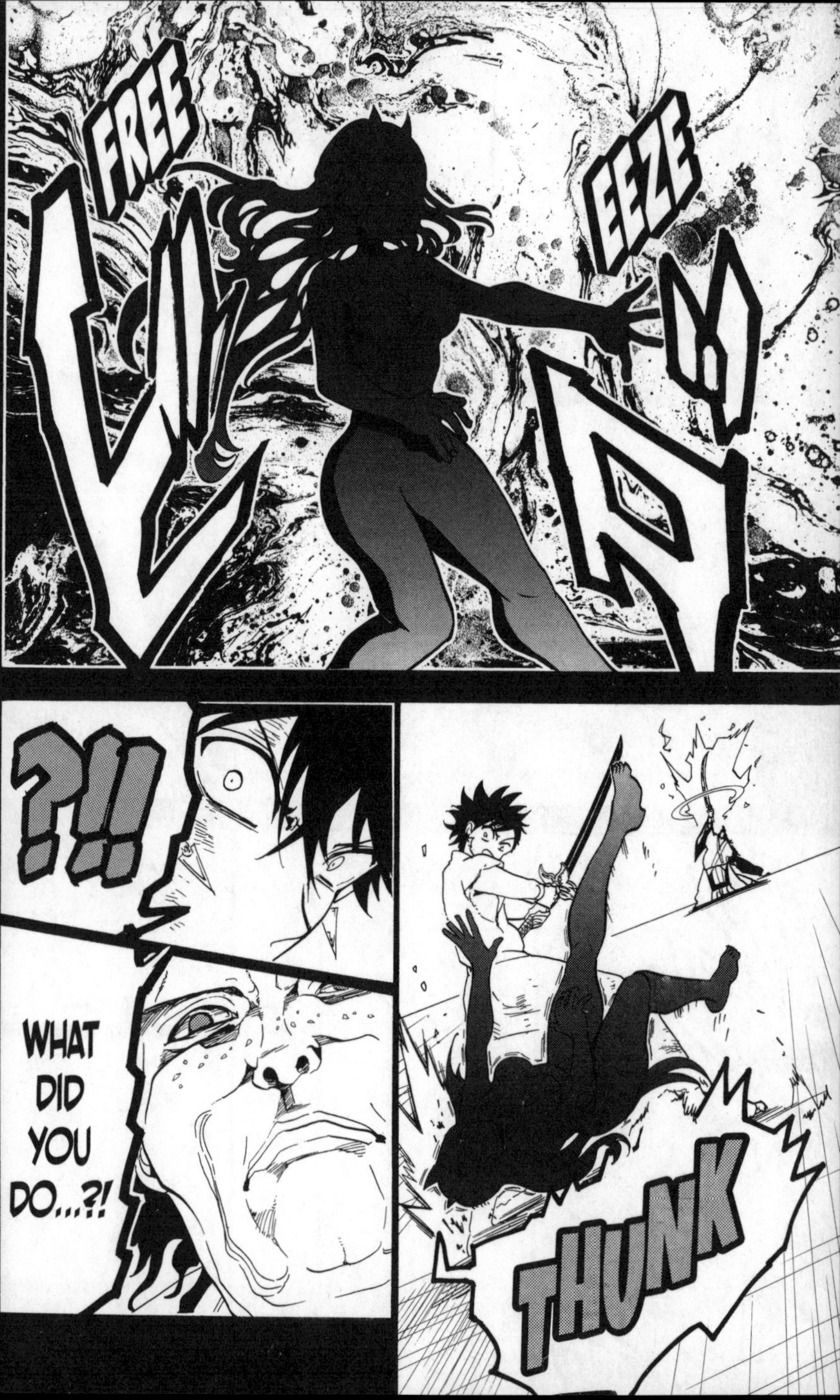
FREE
EEZE
THUNK
?!!
WHAT DID YOU DO...?!

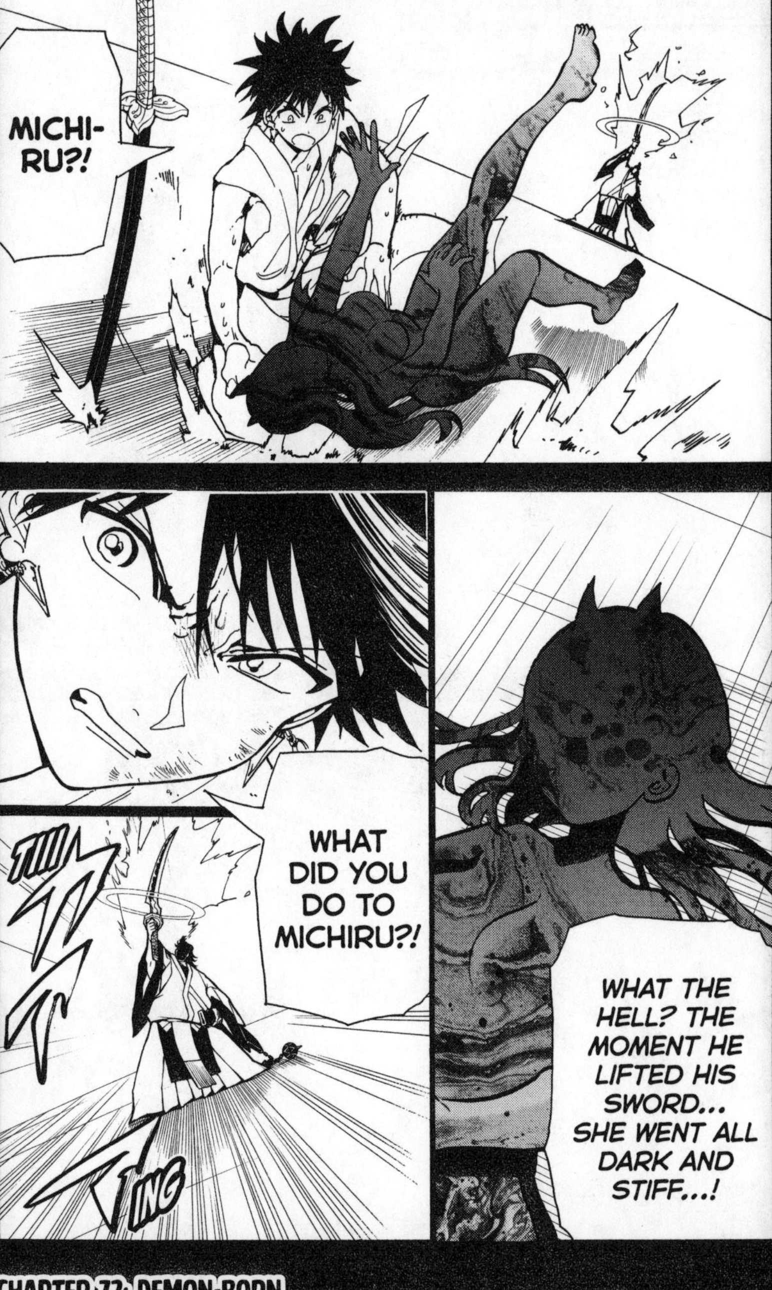
MICHI-RU?!
WHAT THE HELL? THE MOMENT HE LIFTED HIS SWORD... SHE WENT ALL DARK AND STIFF...!
WHAT DID YOU DO TO MICHIRU?!
TIII
ING

CHAPTER 72: DEMON-BORN

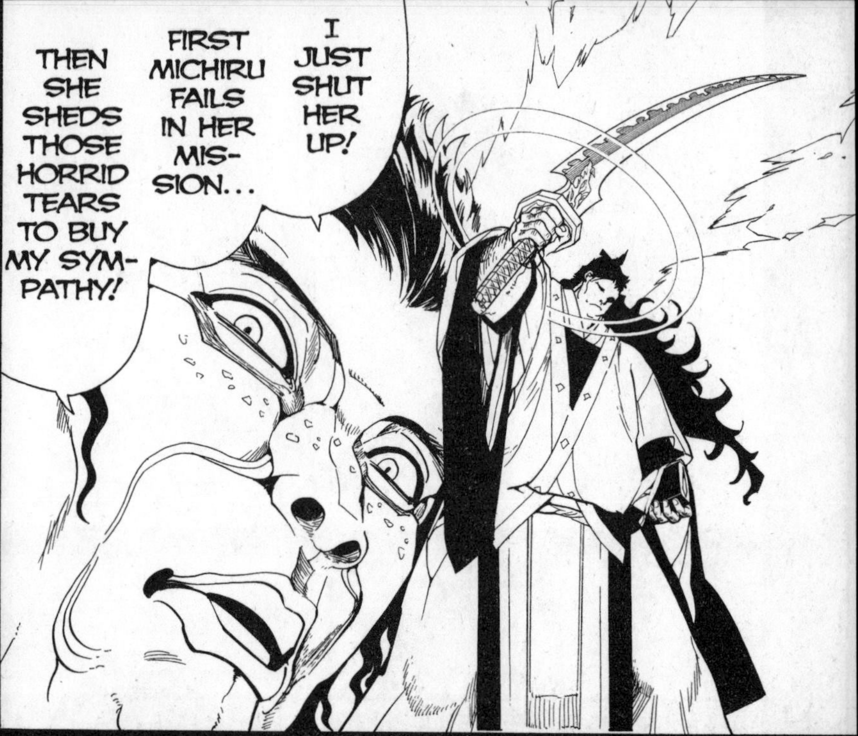
I JUST SHUT HER UP!
FIRST MICHIRU FAILS IN HER MISSION...
THEN SHE SHEDS THOSE HORRID TEARS TO BUY MY SYMPATHY!

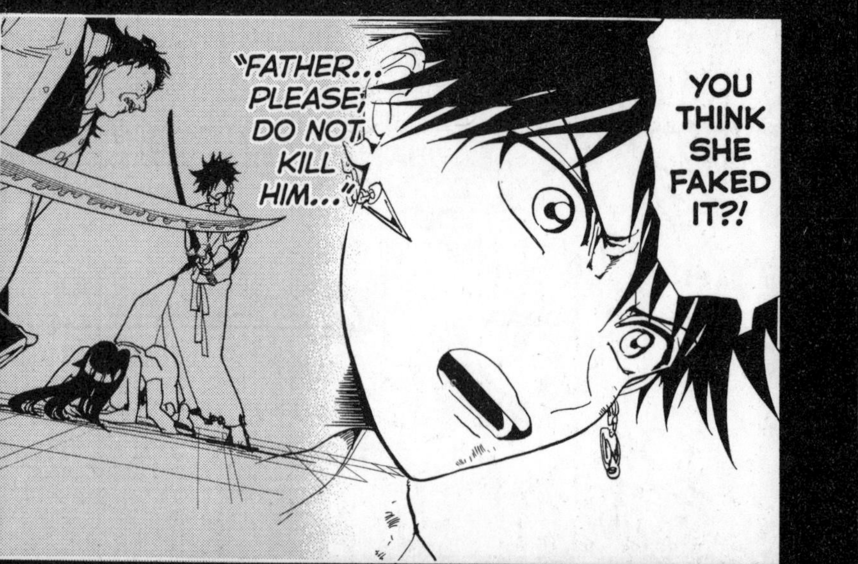
YOU THINK SHE FAKED IT?!
"FATHER... PLEASE, DO NOT KILL HIM..."

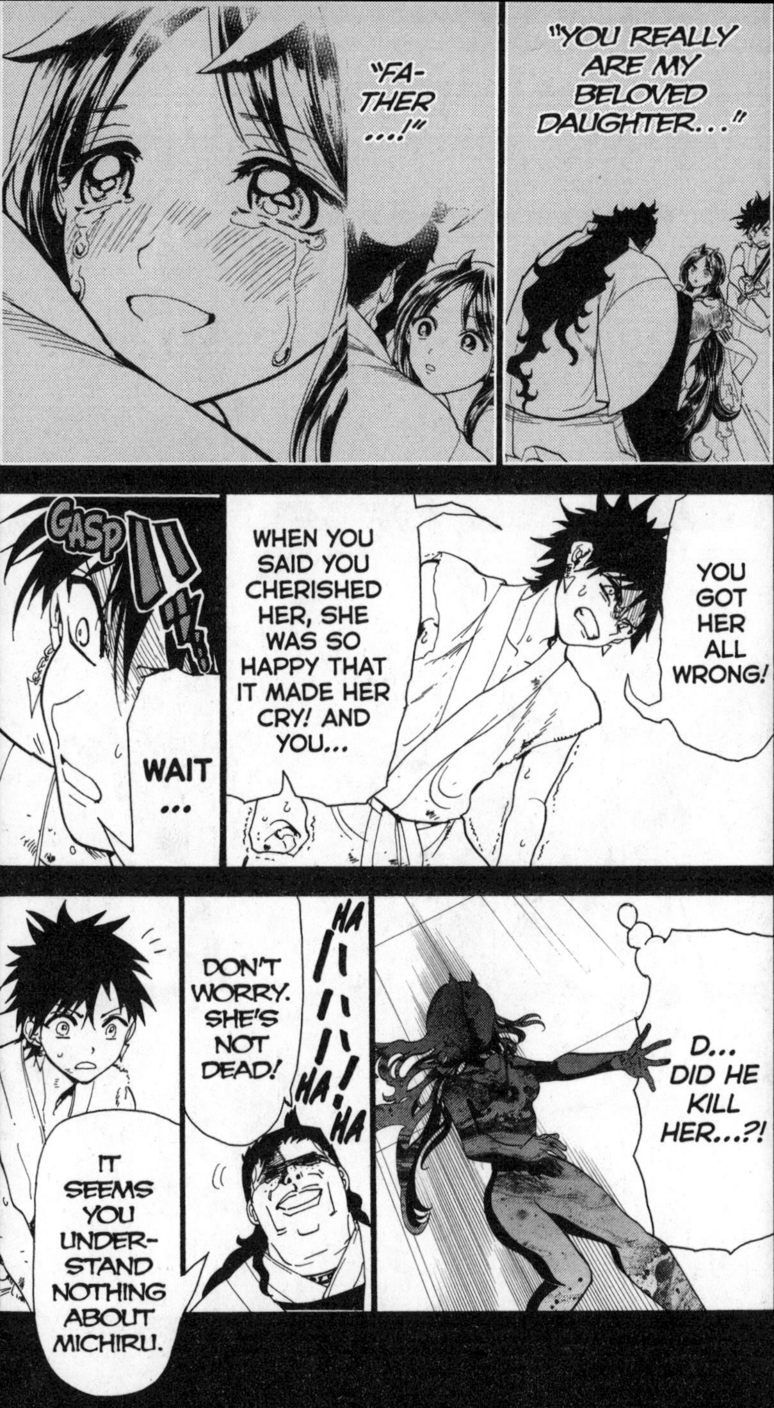
"YOU REALLY ARE MY BELOVED DAUGHTER..."
"FA-THER ...!"
YOU GOT HER ALL WRONG!
WHEN YOU SAID YOU CHERISHED HER, SHE WAS SO HAPPY THAT IT MADE HER CRY! AND YOU...
GASP
WAIT ...
D... DID HE KILL HER...?!
HA HA HA HA
DON'T WORRY. SHE'S NOT DEAD!
IT SEEMS YOU UNDERSTAND NOTHING ABOUT MICHIRU.

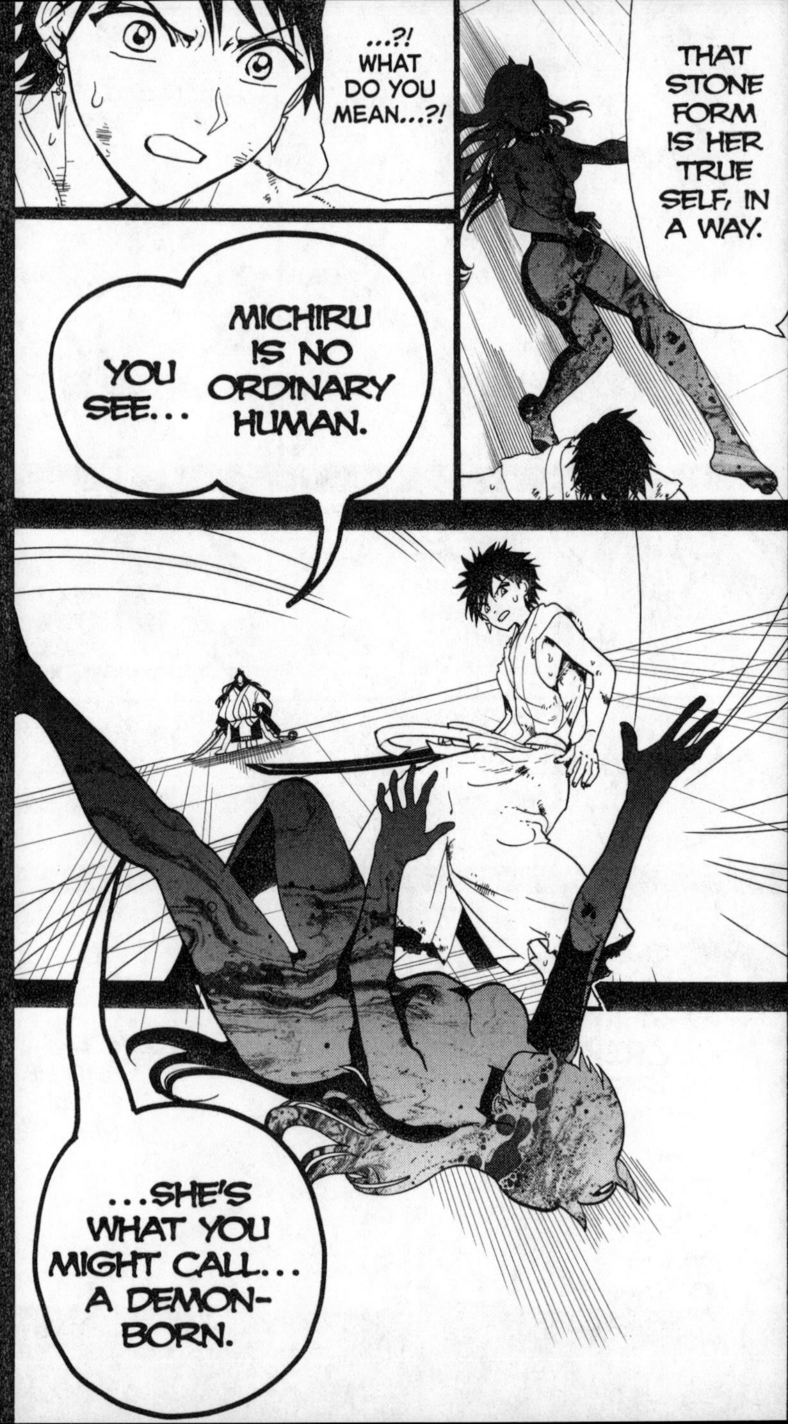
THAT STONE FORM IS HER TRUE SELF, IN A WAY.
...?! WHAT DO YOU MEAN...?!
YOU SEE... MICHIRU IS NO ORDINARY HUMAN.
...SHE'S WHAT YOU MIGHT CALL... A DEMON-BORN.

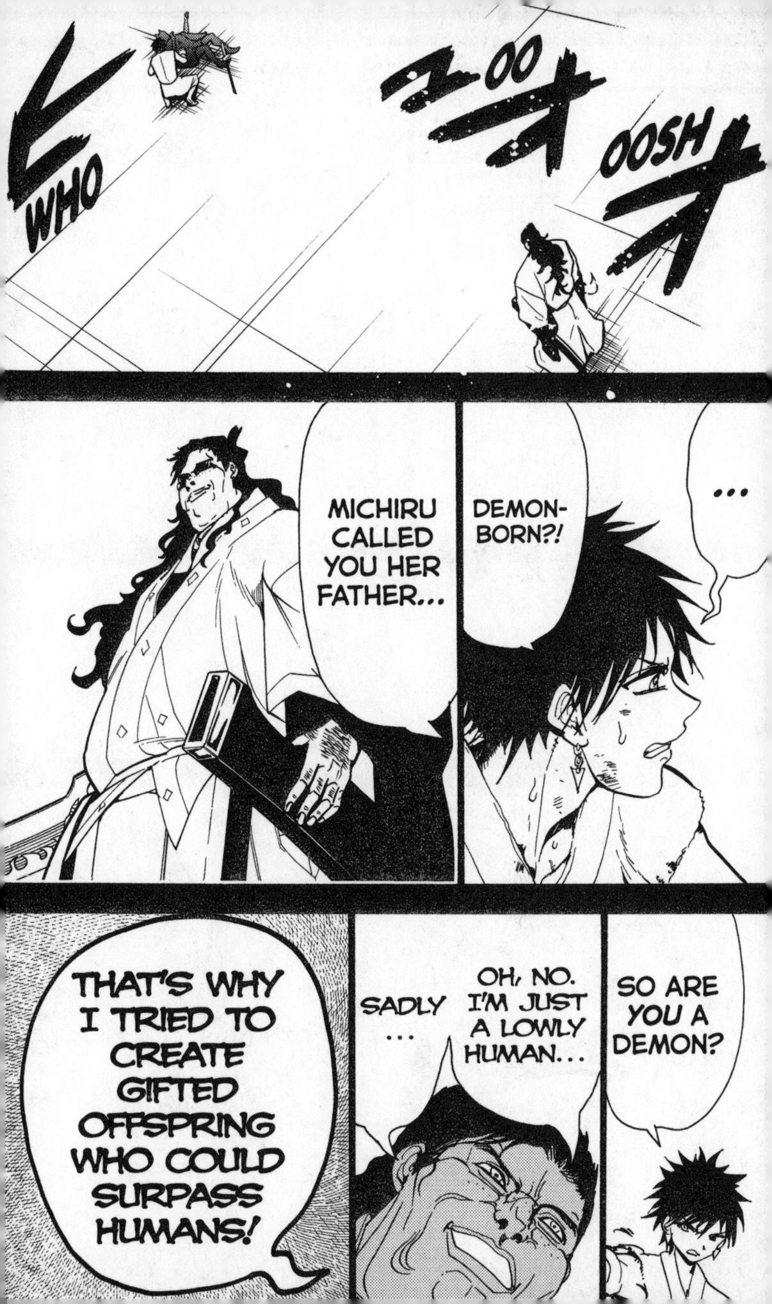
WHO OO OOSH
...
DEMON-BORN?!
MICHIRU CALLED YOU HER FATHER...
SO ARE YOU A DEMON?
OH, NO. I'M JUST A LOWLY HUMAN...
SADLY...
THAT'S WHY I TRIED TO CREATE GIFTED OFFSPRING WHO COULD SURPASS HUMANS!

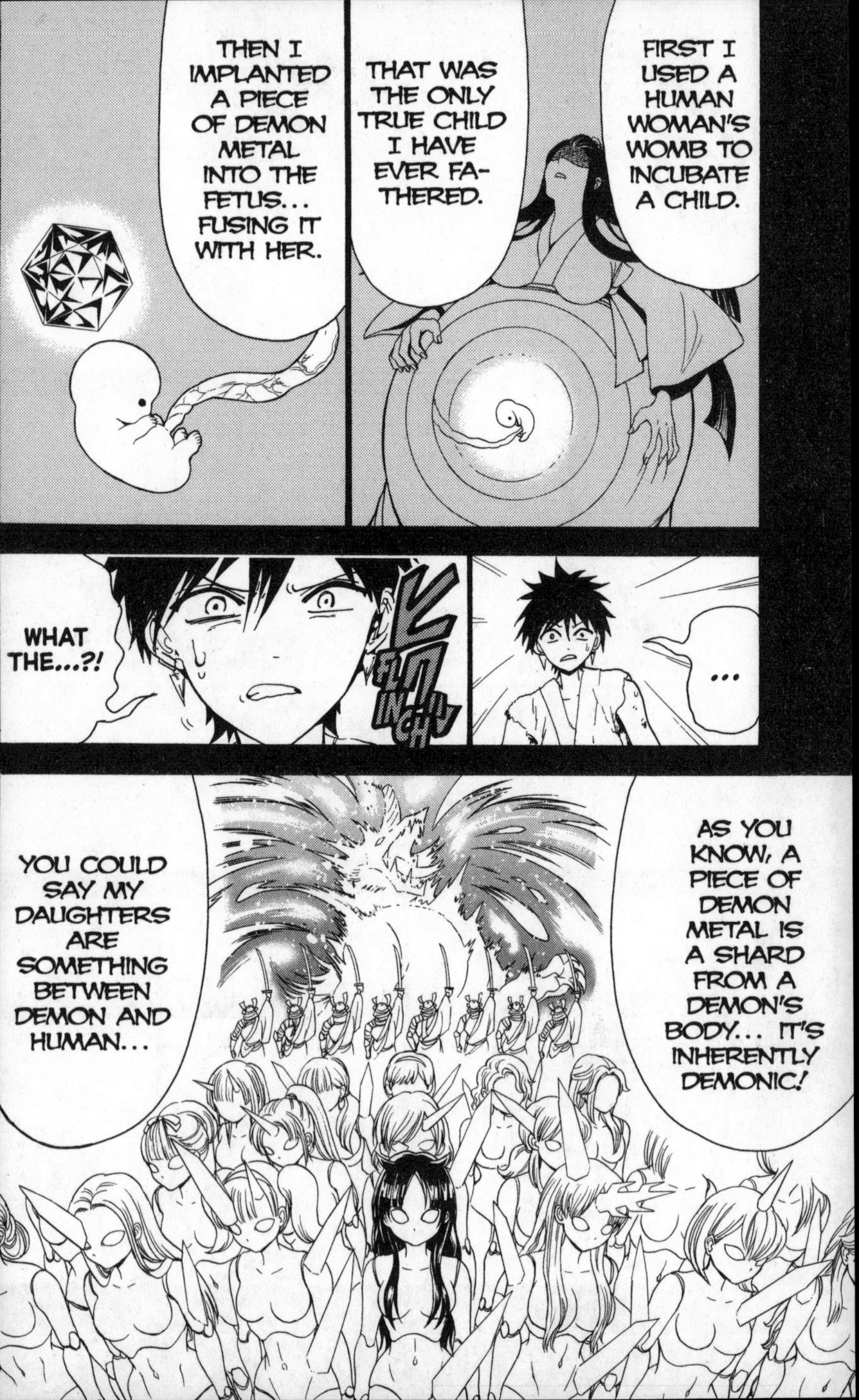
FIRST I USED A HUMAN WOMAN'S WOMB TO INCUBATE A CHILD.
THAT WAS THE ONLY TRUE CHILD I HAVE EVER FA-THERED.
THEN I IMPLANTED A PIECE OF DEMON METAL INTO THE FETUS... FUSING IT WITH HER.
...
FLINCH
WHAT THE...?!
AS YOU KNOW, A PIECE OF DEMON METAL IS A SHARD FROM A DEMON'S BODY... IT'S INHERENTLY DEMONIC!
YOU COULD SAY MY DAUGHTERS ARE SOMETHING BETWEEN DEMON AND HUMAN...

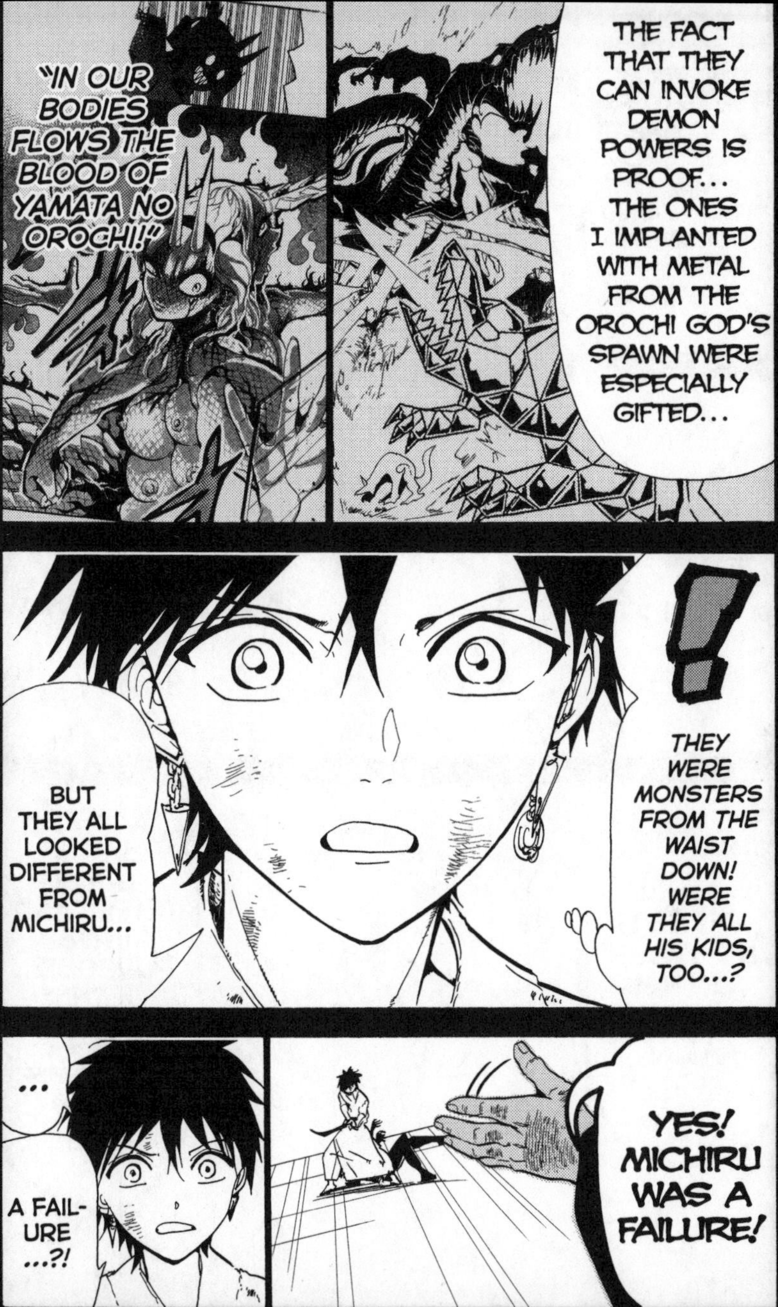
THE FACT THAT THEY CAN INVOKE DEMON POWERS IS PROOF... THE ONES I IMPLANTED WITH METAL FROM THE OROCHI GOD'S SPAWN WERE ESPECIALLY GIFTED...
"IN OUR BODIES FLOWS THE BLOOD OF YAMATA NO OROCHI!"
!
THEY WERE MONSTERS FROM THE WAIST DOWN! WERE THEY ALL HIS KIDS, TOO...?
BUT THEY ALL LOOKED DIFFERENT FROM MICHIRU...
YES! MICHIRU WAS A FAILURE!
...
A FAIL-URE ...?!

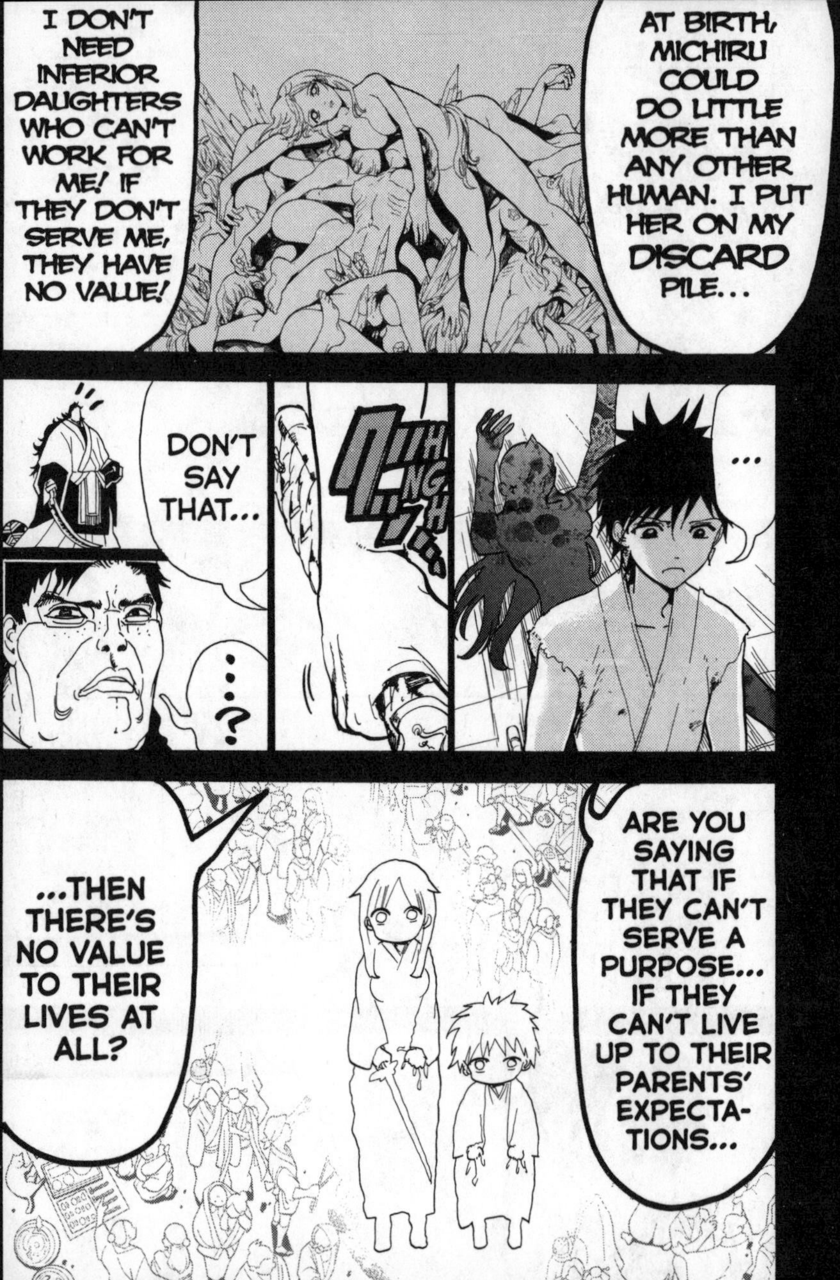
AT BIRTH, MICHIRU COULD DO LITTLE MORE THAN ANY OTHER HUMAN. I PUT HER ON MY DISCARD PILE...
I DON'T NEED INFERIOR DAUGHTERS WHO CAN'T WORK FOR ME! IF THEY DON'T SERVE ME, THEY HAVE NO VALUE!
...
DON'T SAY THAT...
...?
ARE YOU SAYING THAT IF THEY CAN'T SERVE A PURPOSE... IF THEY CAN'T LIVE UP TO THEIR PARENTS' EXPECTATIONS...
...THEN THERE'S NO VALUE TO THEIR LIVES AT ALL?

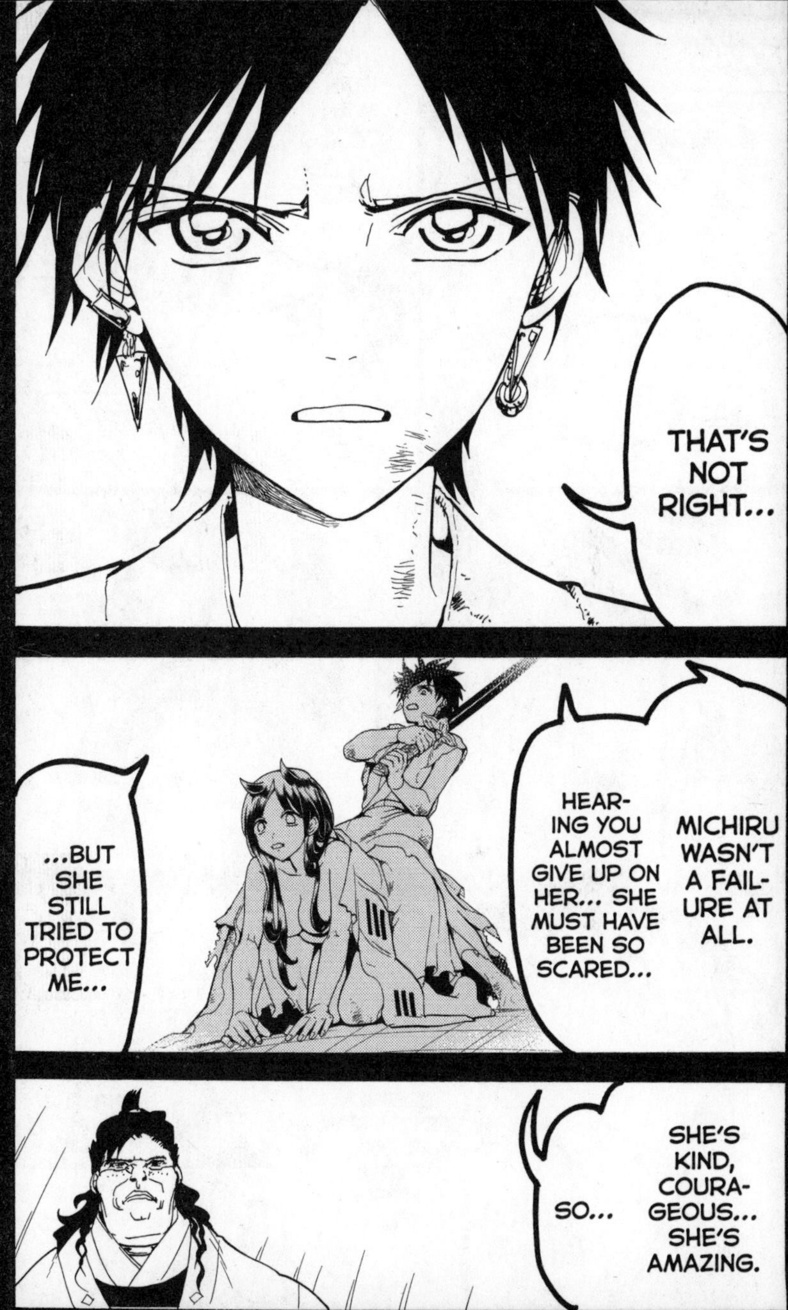
THAT'S NOT RIGHT...
MICHIRU WASN'T A FAILURE AT ALL.
HEARING YOU ALMOST GIVE UP ON HER... SHE MUST HAVE BEEN SO SCARED...
...BUT SHE STILL TRIED TO PROTECT ME...
SHE'S KIND, COURAGEOUS... SHE'S AMAZING.
SO...

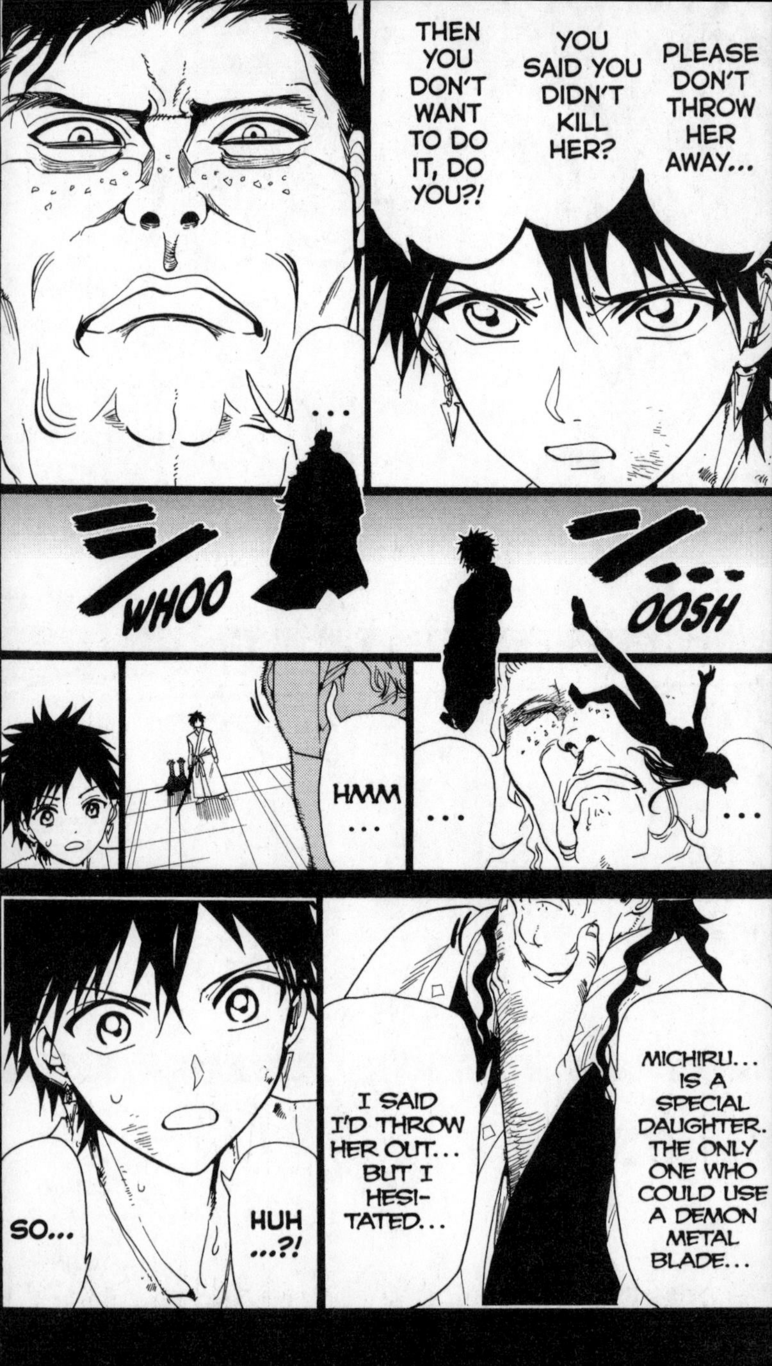
PLEASE DON'T THROW HER AWAY...
YOU SAID YOU DIDN'T KILL HER?
THEN YOU DON'T WANT TO DO IT, DO YOU?!
...
WHOO
OOSH...
...
...
HMM ...
MICHIRU... IS A SPECIAL DAUGHTER. THE ONLY ONE WHO COULD USE A DEMON METAL BLADE...
I SAID I'D THROW HER OUT... BUT I HESI-TATED...
HUH ...?!
SO...

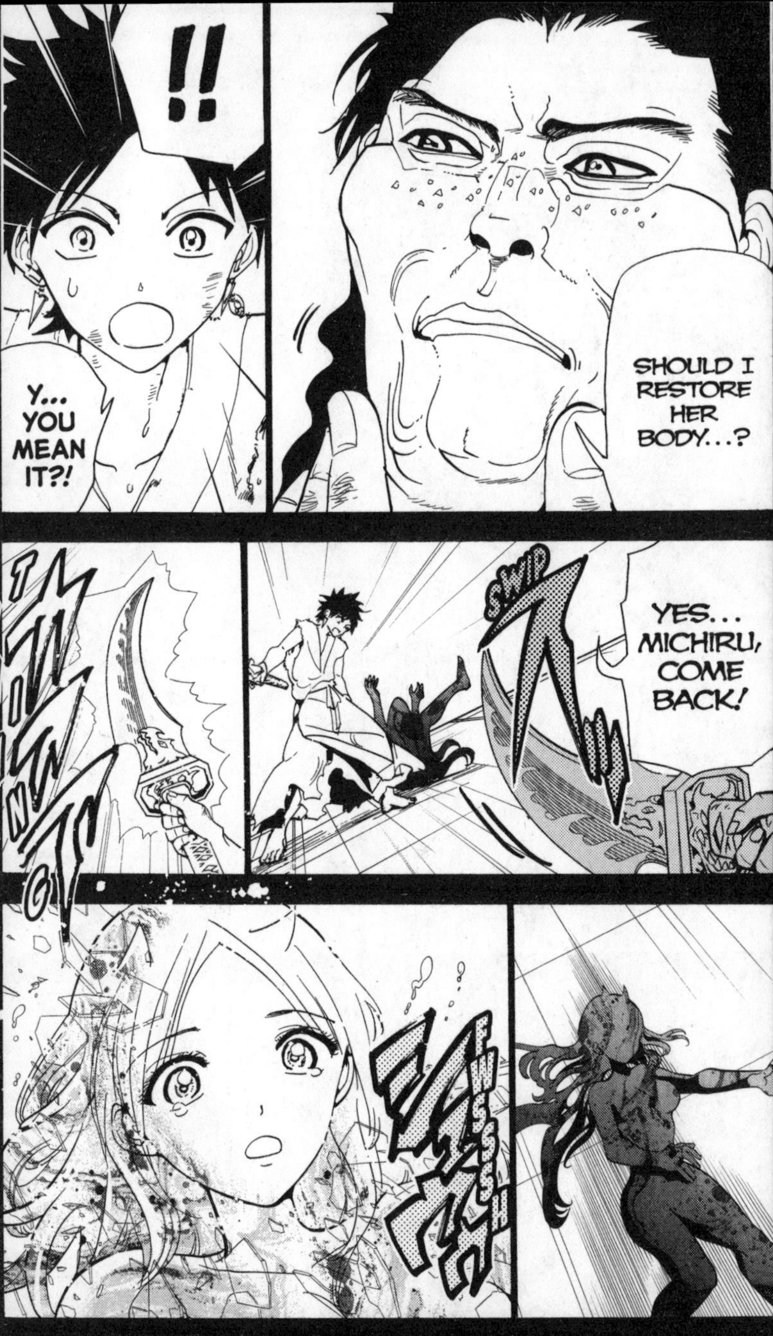
SHOULD I RESTORE HER BODY...?
!!
Y... YOU MEAN IT?!
SWIP
YES... MICHIRU, COME BACK!
TIIIING
FWSSSSH

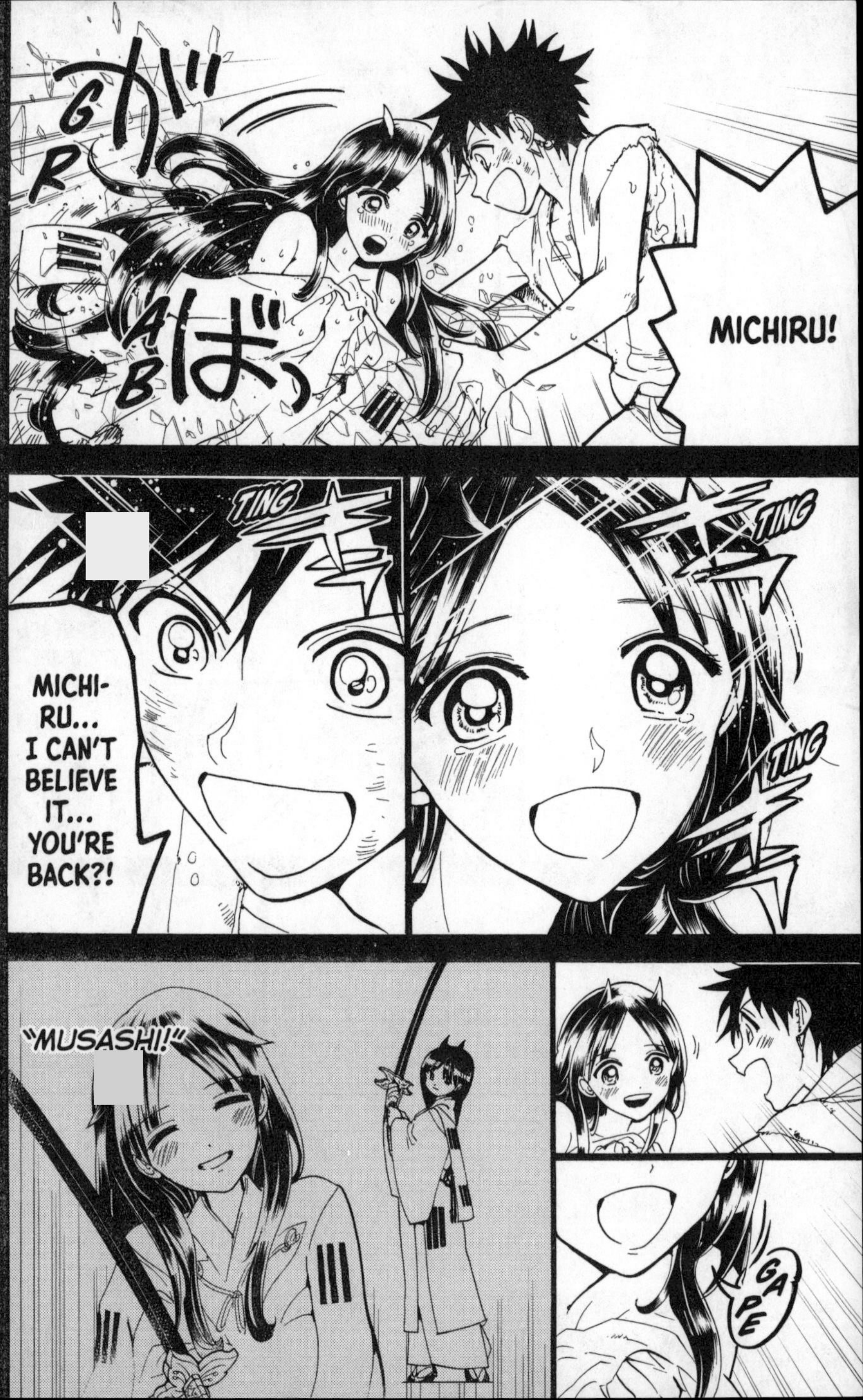
MICHIRU!
GRAB
TING
TING
TING
MICHIRU... I CAN'T BELIEVE IT... YOU'RE BACK?!
GAPE
"MUSASHI!"

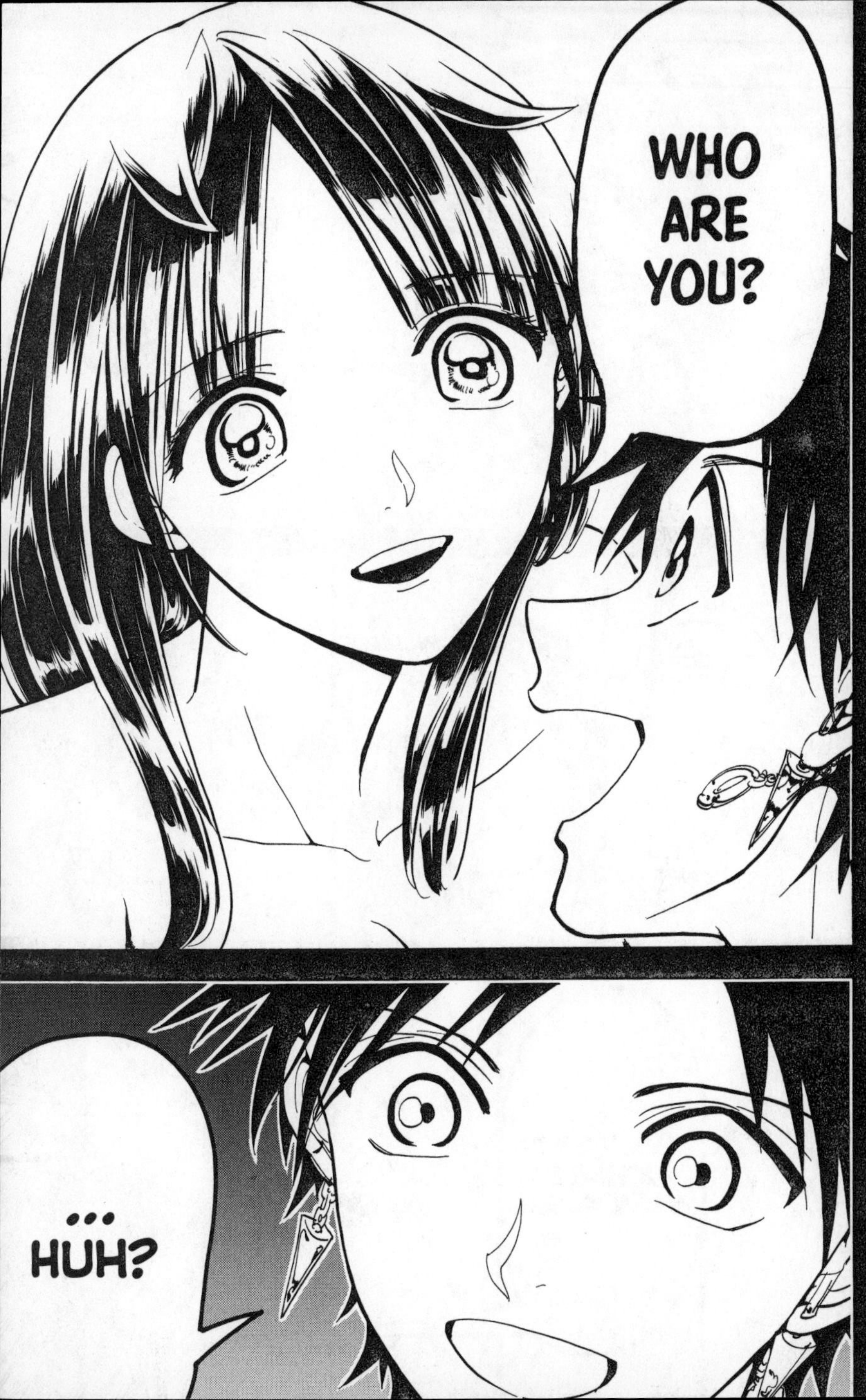
WHO ARE YOU?
...HUH?

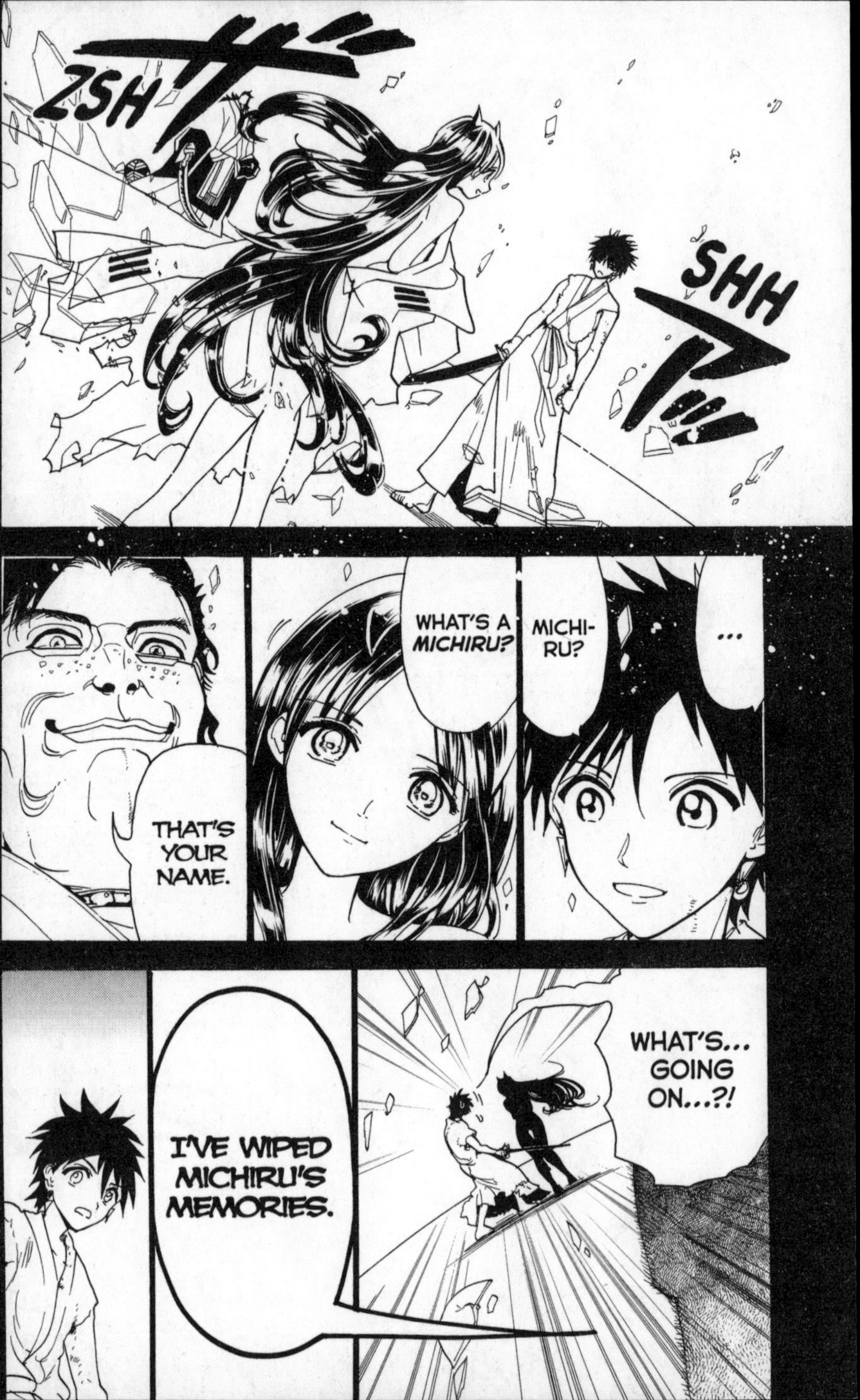
SHH
ZSH
...
MICHI-RU?
WHAT'S A MICHIRU?
THAT'S YOUR NAME.
WHAT'S... GOING ON...?!
I'VE WIPED MICHIRU'S MEMORIES.

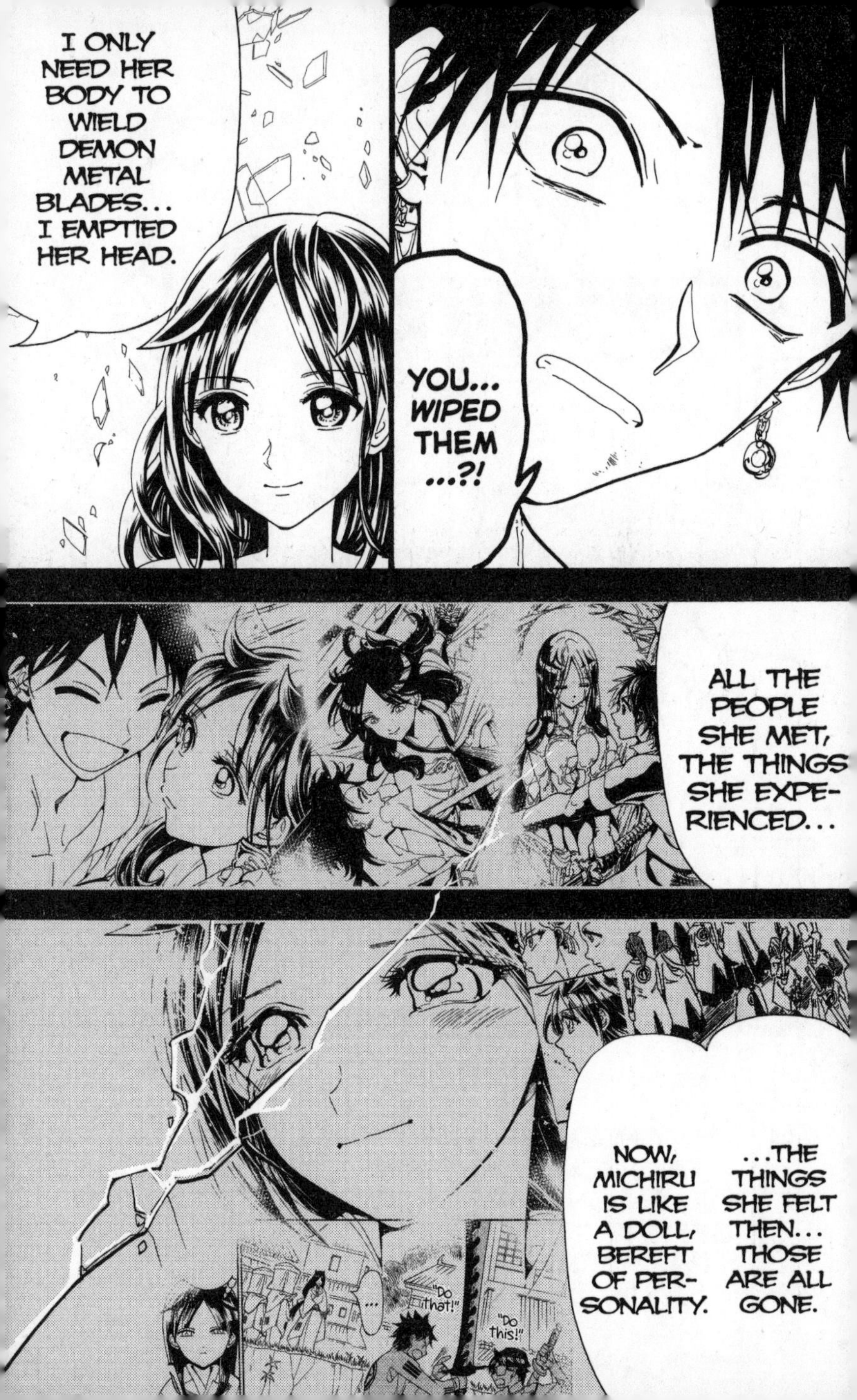
YOU... WIPED THEM ...?!
I ONLY NEED HER BODY TO WIELD DEMON METAL BLADES... I EMPTIED HER HEAD.
ALL THE PEOPLE SHE MET, THE THINGS SHE EXPE-RIENCED...
...THE THINGS SHE FELT THEN... THOSE ARE ALL GONE.
NOW, MICHIRU IS LIKE A DOLL, BEREFT OF PER-SONALITY.
"Do this!"
"Do that!"
...

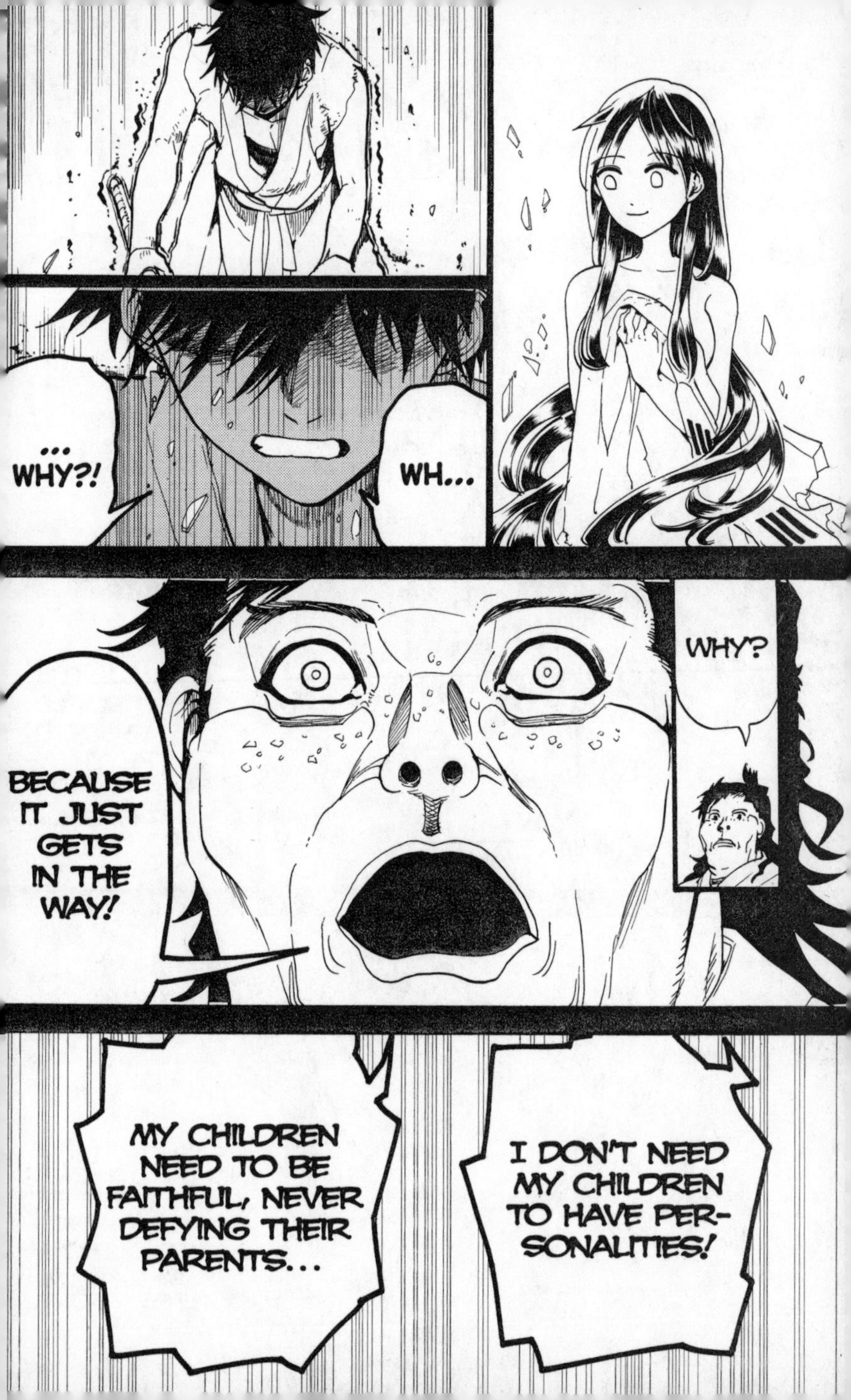
WH...
...WHY?!
WHY?
BECAUSE IT JUST GETS IN THE WAY!
I DON'T NEED MY CHILDREN TO HAVE PER-SONALITIES!
MY CHILDREN NEED TO BE FAITHFUL, NEVER DEFYING THEIR PARENTS...

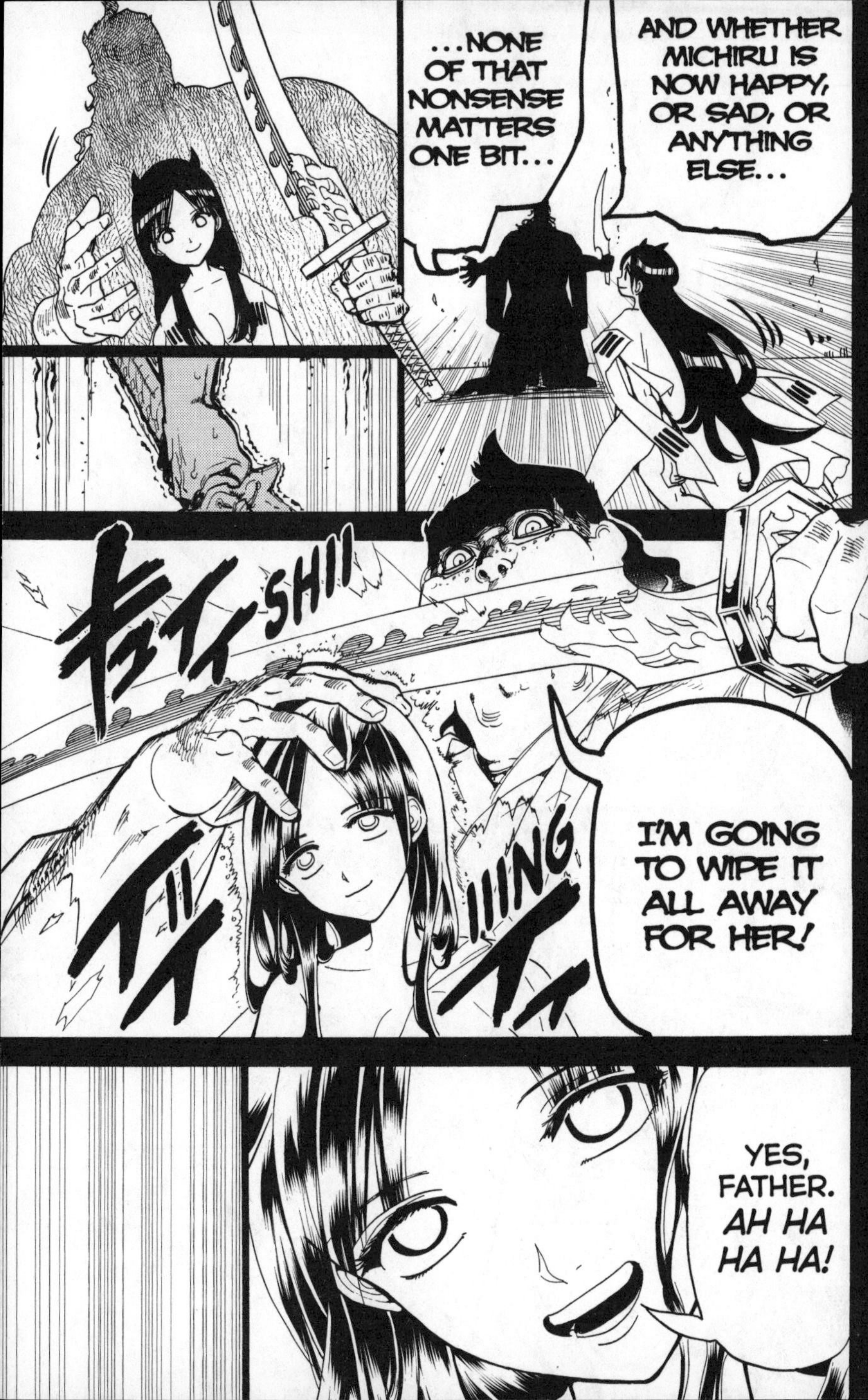
AND WHETHER MICHIRU IS NOW HAPPY, OR SAD, OR ANYTHING ELSE...
...NONE OF THAT NONSENSE MATTERS ONE BIT...
I'M GOING TO WIPE IT ALL AWAY FOR HER!
SHII
IIING
YES, FATHER. AH HA HA HA!

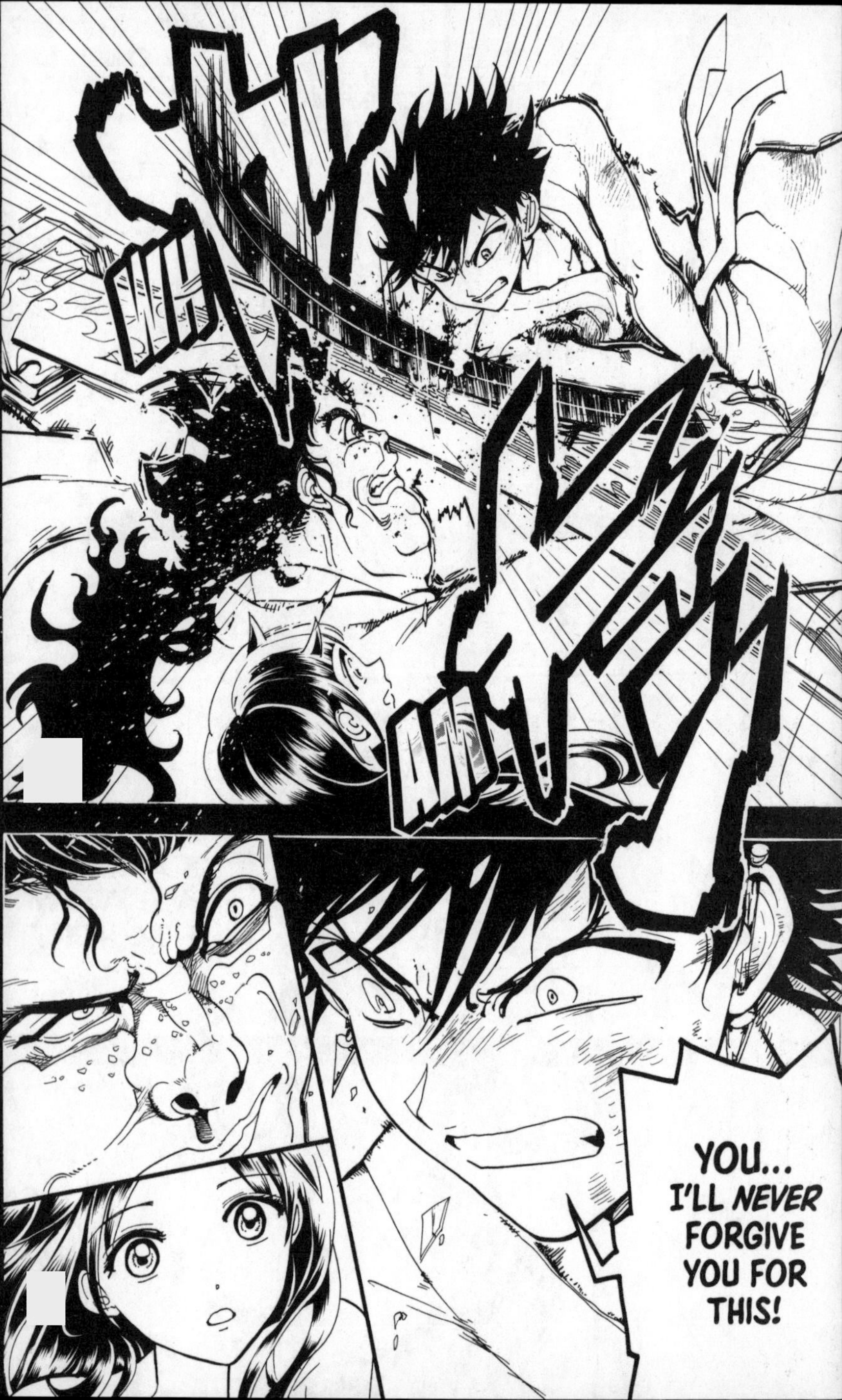
YOU... I'LL *NEVER* FORGIVE YOU FOR THIS!

❖ STAFF ❖

REGULAR ASSISTANTS

メギ
Megi

吉田 真美
Mami Yoshida

石後 千鳥
Chidori Ishigo

中村 犬彦
Inuhiko Nakamura

野方
Nogata

鈴木 莉士
Rihito Suzuki

EDITORIAL TEAM

詫摩 尚樹
Naoki Takuma

菊地 優斗
Yuto Kikuchi

長塚 雅彦
Masahiko Nagatsuka

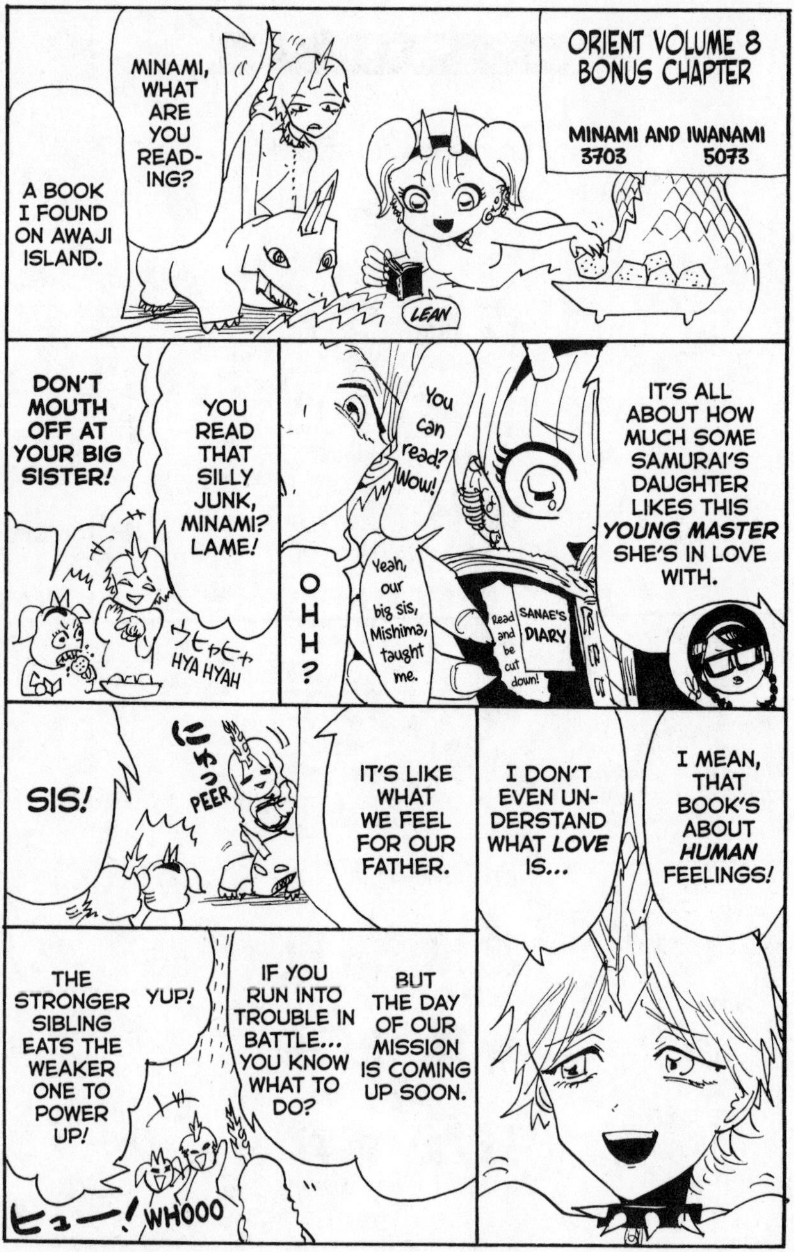
ORIENT VOLUME 8
BONUS CHAPTER
MINAMI AND IWANAMI
3703 5073
MINAMI, WHAT ARE YOU READING?
A BOOK I FOUND ON AWAJI ISLAND.
LEAN
IT'S ALL ABOUT HOW MUCH SOME SAMURAI'S DAUGHTER LIKES THIS *YOUNG MASTER* SHE'S IN LOVE WITH.
You can read? Wow!
SANAE'S DIARY
Read and be cut down!
Yeah, our big sis, Mishima, taught me.
OHH?
YOU READ THAT SILLY JUNK, MINAMI? LAME!
DON'T MOUTH OFF AT YOUR BIG SISTER!
ウヒャヒャ HYA HYAH
I MEAN, THAT BOOK'S ABOUT *HUMAN* FEELINGS!
I DON'T EVEN UNDERSTAND WHAT *LOVE* IS...
IT'S LIKE WHAT WE FEEL FOR OUR FATHER.
にゅっ PEER
SIS!
BUT THE DAY OF OUR MISSION IS COMING UP SOON.
IF YOU RUN INTO TROUBLE IN BATTLE... YOU KNOW WHAT TO DO?
YUP!
THE STRONGER SIBLING EATS THE WEAKER ONE TO POWER UP!
ヒュー! WHOOO

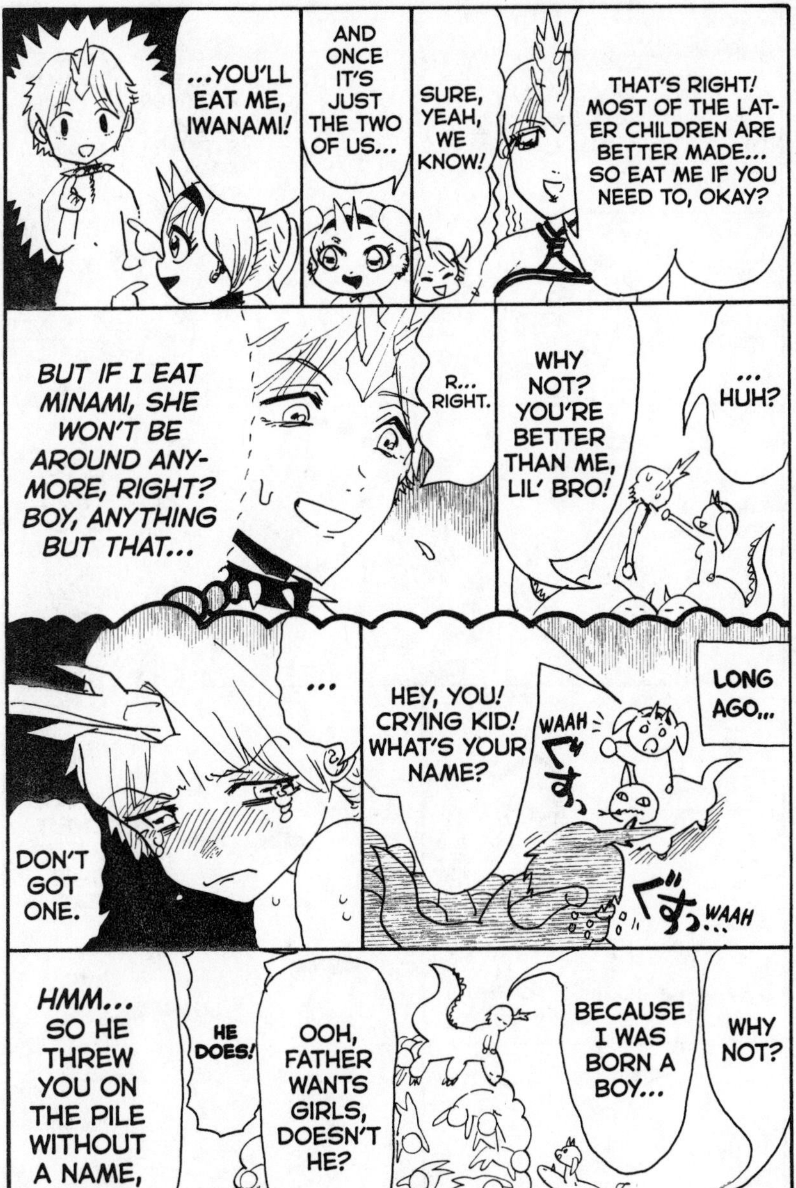
THAT'S RIGHT! MOST OF THE LATER CHILDREN ARE BETTER MADE... SO EAT ME IF YOU NEED TO, OKAY?
SURE, YEAH, WE KNOW!
AND ONCE IT'S JUST THE TWO OF US...
...YOU'LL EAT ME, IWANAMI!
... HUH?
WHY NOT? YOU'RE BETTER THAN ME, LIL' BRO!
R... RIGHT.
BUT IF I EAT MINAMI, SHE WON'T BE AROUND ANYMORE, RIGHT? BOY, ANYTHING BUT THAT...
LONG AGO...
WAAH
ぐすっ
ぐすっ
WAAH...
HEY, YOU! CRYING KID! WHAT'S YOUR NAME?
...
DON'T GOT ONE.
WHY NOT?
BECAUSE I WAS BORN A BOY...
OOH, FATHER WANTS GIRLS, DOESN'T HE?
HE DOES!
HMM... SO HE THREW YOU ON THE PILE WITHOUT A NAME, HUH?

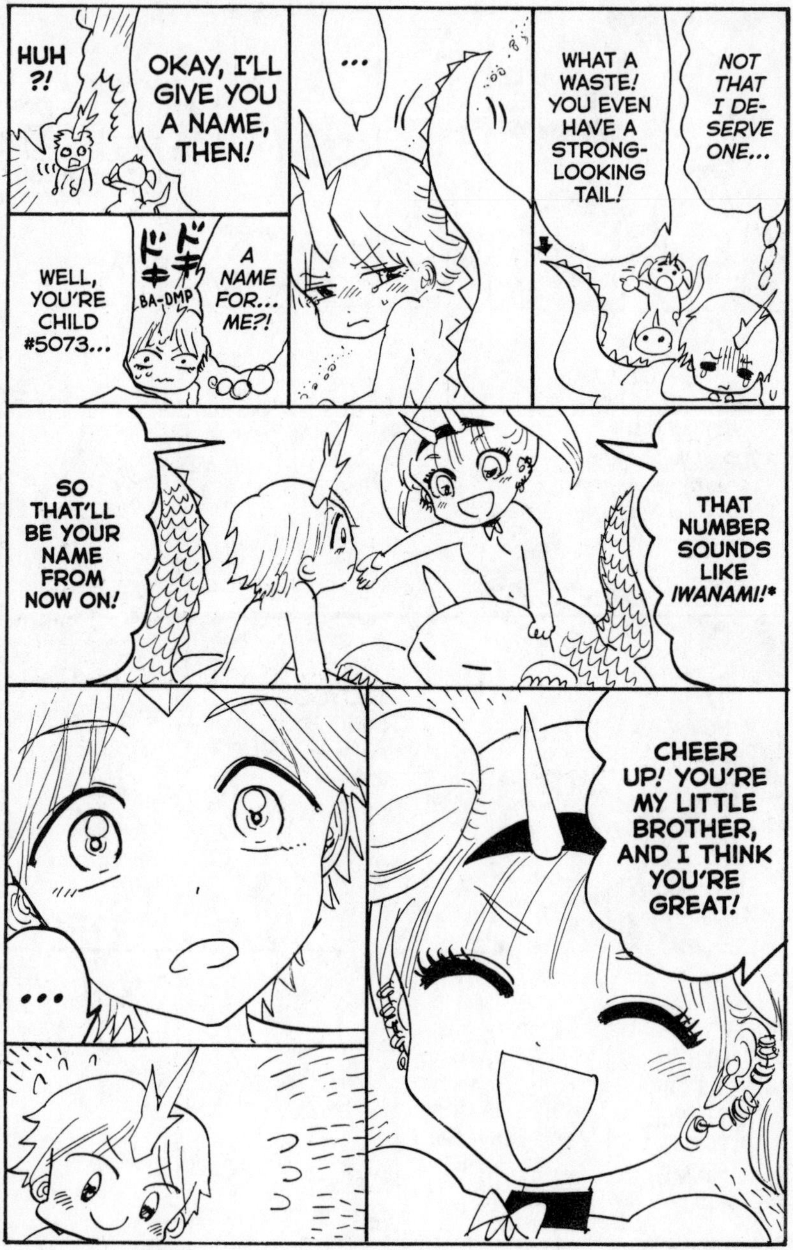
NOT THAT I DE-SERVE ONE...
WHAT A WASTE! YOU EVEN HAVE A STRONG-LOOKING TAIL!
...
OKAY, I'LL GIVE YOU A NAME, THEN!
HUH ?!
A NAME FOR... ME?!
ドキ ドキ
BA-DMP
WELL, YOU'RE CHILD #5073...
THAT NUMBER SOUNDS LIKE IWANAMI!*
SO THAT'LL BE YOUR NAME FROM NOW ON!
CHEER UP! YOU'RE MY LITTLE BROTHER, AND I THINK YOU'RE GREAT!
...

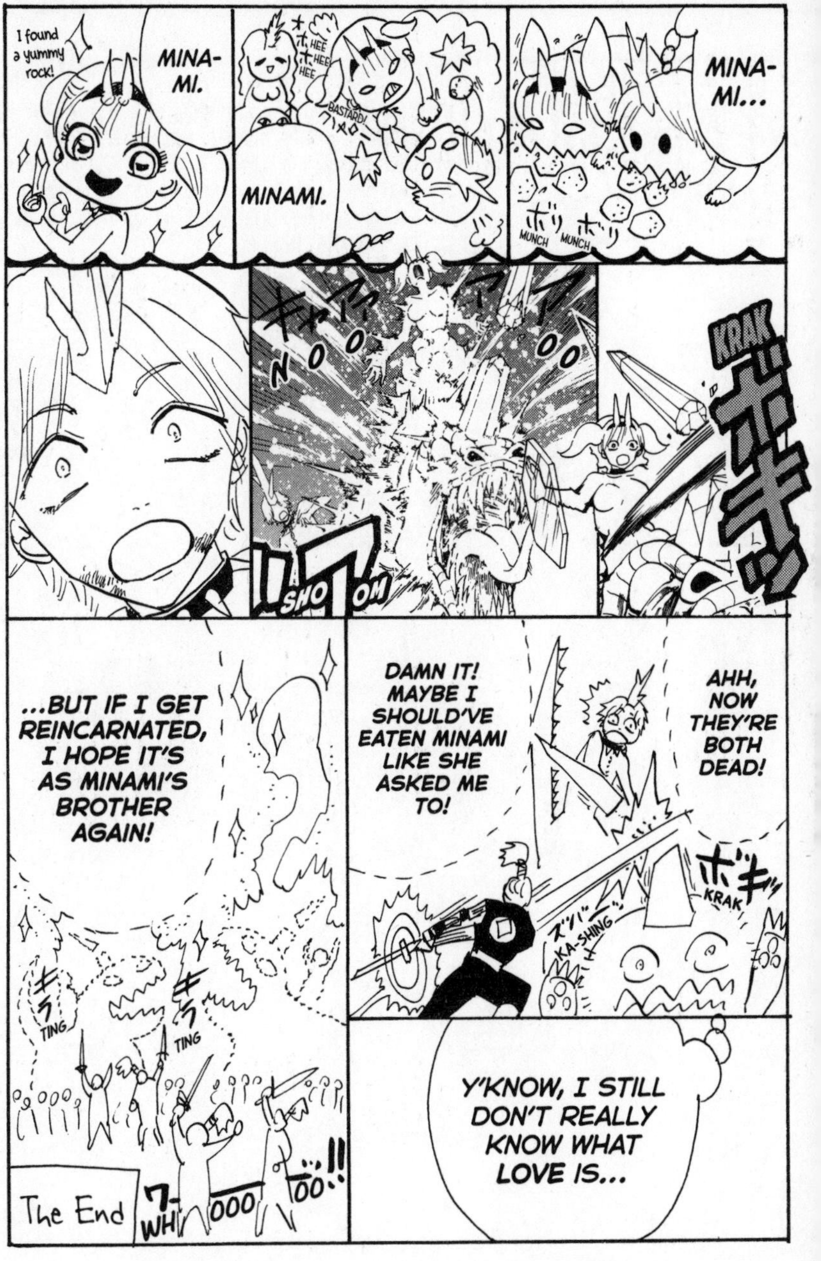
MINA-MI...
MUNCH MUNCH
MINAMI.
HEE HEE HEE
BASTARD!
MINA-MI.
I found a yummy rock!
KRAK
NOOOO
SHOOM
AHH, NOW THEY'RE BOTH DEAD!
DAMN IT! MAYBE I SHOULD'VE EATEN MINAMI LIKE SHE ASKED ME TO!
KRAK
KA-SHING
Y'KNOW, I STILL DON'T REALLY KNOW WHAT LOVE IS...
...BUT IF I GET REINCARNATED, I HOPE IT'S AS MINAMI'S BROTHER AGAIN!
TING
TING
WHOOOOO!!
The End

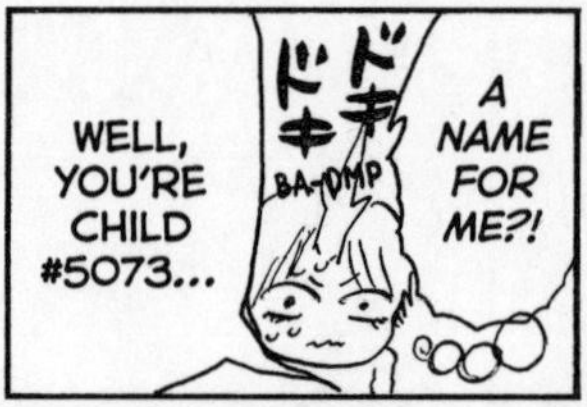
A NAME FOR ME?!
ドキドキ
BA-DMP
WELL, YOU'RE CHILD #5073...

Pg. 190, Iwanami's name

Minami is using wordplay to come up with the name Iwanami for her brother, child #5073. The numbers 5, 7, and 3 can be written individually in kanji as 五, 七, and 三. The number zero resembles a circle, which can be written in kanji as 輪. When taken together, these four kanji can be read as 五 (I) 輪 (WA) 七 (NA) 三 (MI).

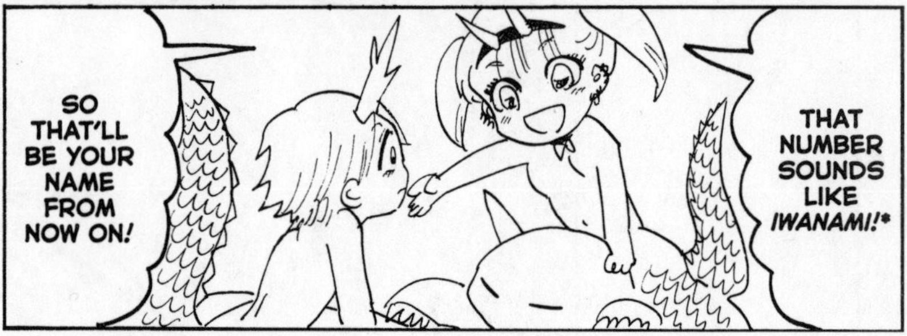
THAT NUMBER SOUNDS LIKE *IWANAMI!**
SO THAT'LL BE YOUR NAME FROM NOW ON!

ORIENT

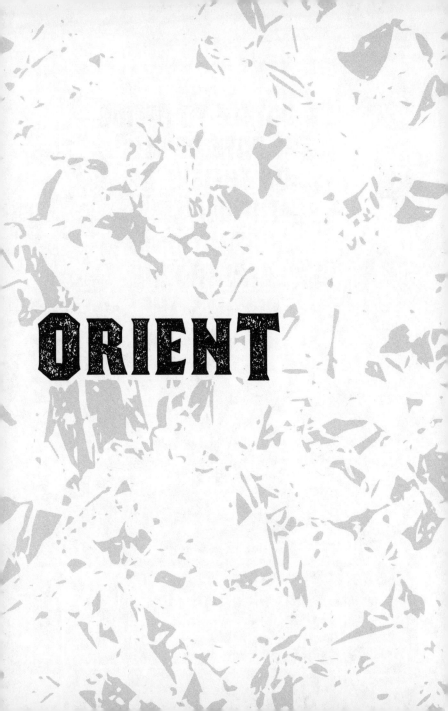

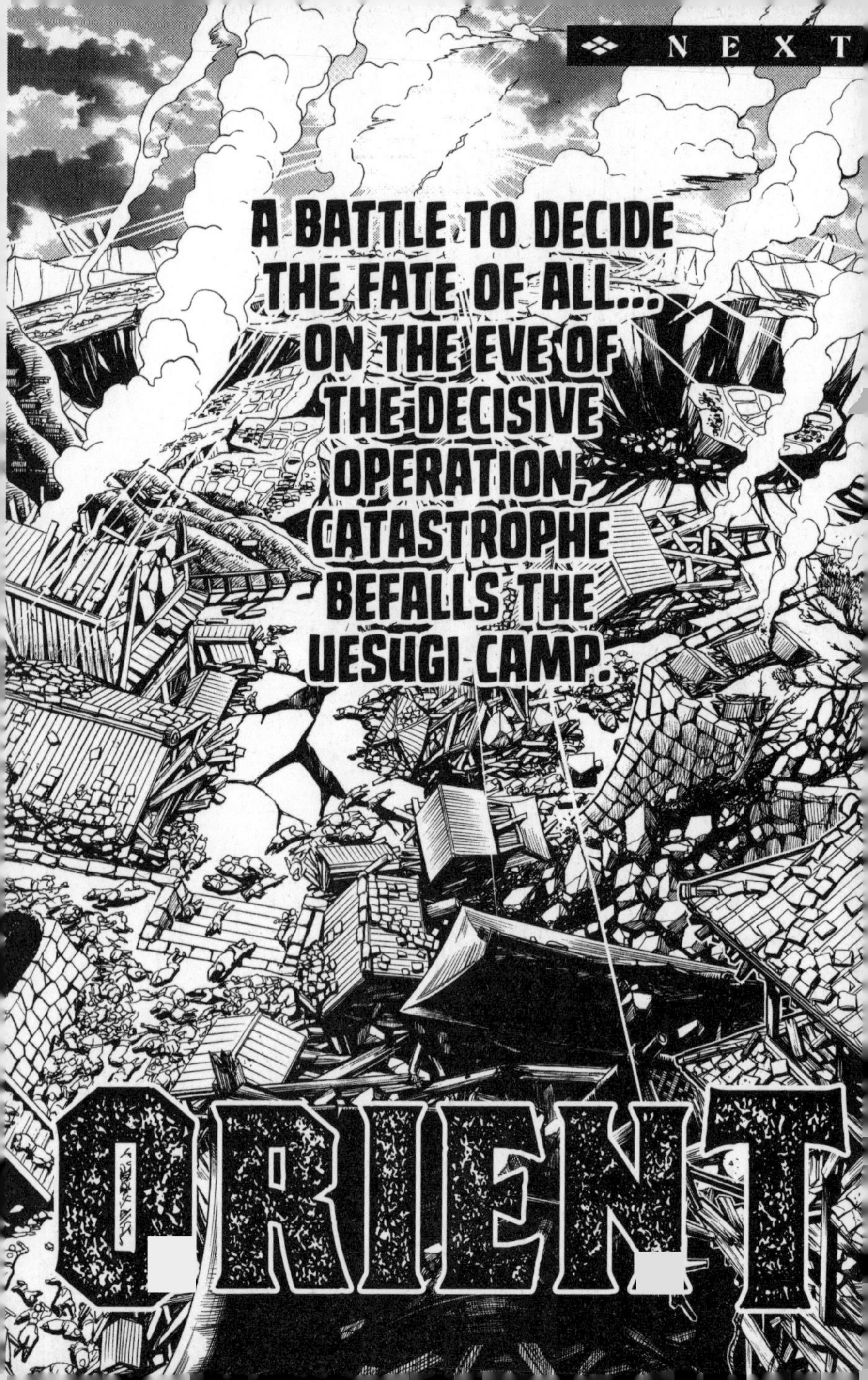
NEXT
A BATTLE TO DECIDE THE FATE OF ALL... ON THE EVE OF THE DECISIVE OPERATION, CATASTROPHE BEFALLS THE UESUGI CAMP.
ORIENT

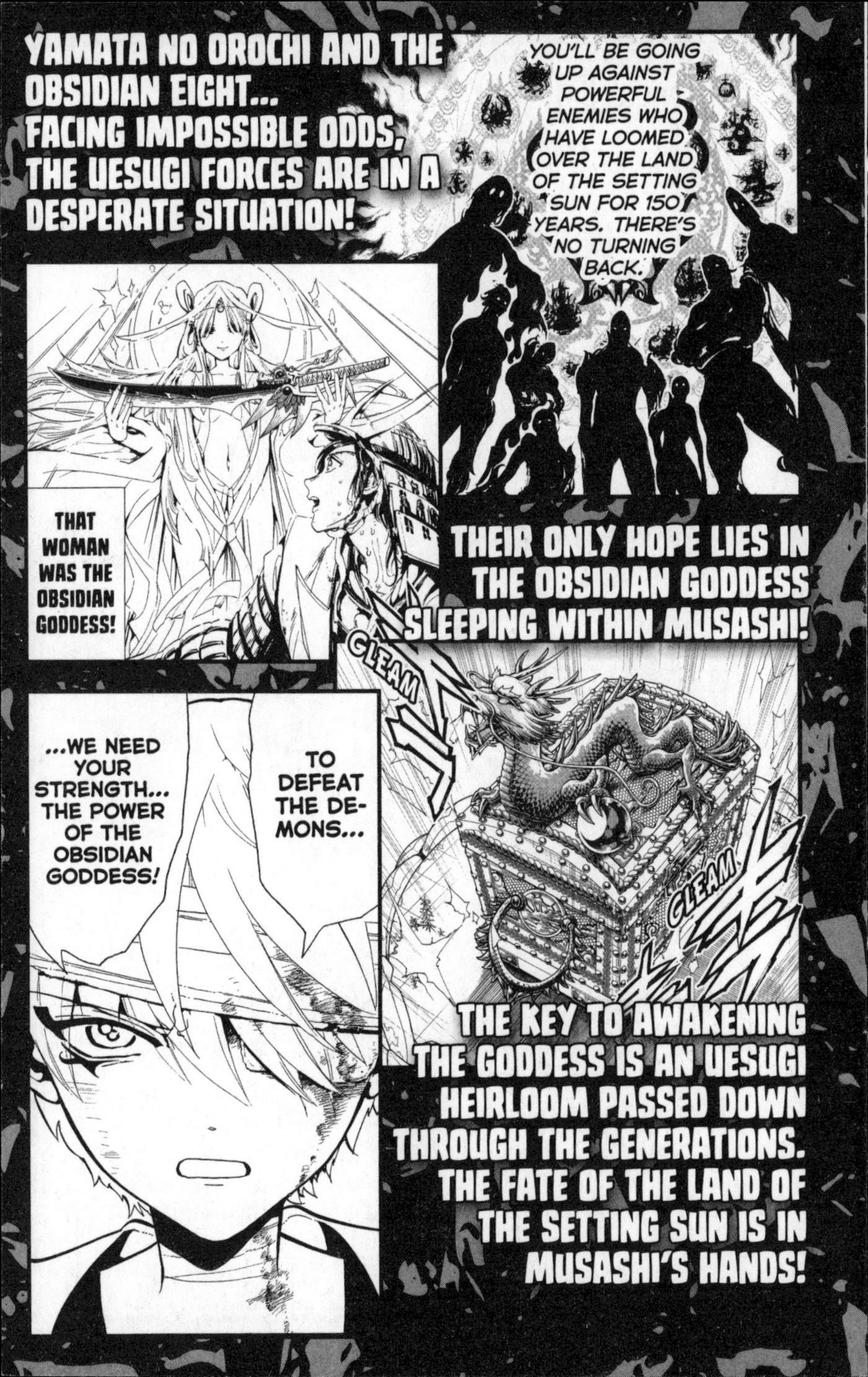
YOU'LL BE GOING UP AGAINST POWERFUL ENEMIES WHO HAVE LOOMED OVER THE LAND OF THE SETTING SUN FOR 150 YEARS. THERE'S NO TURNING BACK.
YAMATA NO OROCHI AND THE OBSIDIAN EIGHT... FACING IMPOSSIBLE ODDS, THE UESUGI FORCES ARE IN A DESPERATE SITUATION!
THEIR ONLY HOPE LIES IN THE OBSIDIAN GODDESS SLEEPING WITHIN MUSASHI!
THAT WOMAN WAS THE OBSIDIAN GODDESS!
GLEAM
GLEAM
THE KEY TO AWAKENING THE GODDESS IS AN UESUGI HEIRLOOM PASSED DOWN THROUGH THE GENERATIONS. THE FATE OF THE LAND OF THE SETTING SUN IS IN MUSASHI'S HANDS!
TO DEFEAT THE DE-MONS...
...WE NEED YOUR STRENGTH... THE POWER OF THE OBSIDIAN GODDESS!

Young characters and steampunk setting, like *Howl's Moving Castle* and *Battle Angel Alita*

A boy with a talent for machines and a mysterious girl whose wings he's fixed will take you beyond the clouds! In the tradition of the high-flying, resonant adventure stories of Studio Ghibli comes a gorgeous tale about the longing of young hearts for adventure and friendship!

A SMART, NEW ROMANTIC COMEDY FOR FANS OF *SHORTCAKE CAKE* AND *TERRACE HOUSE*!

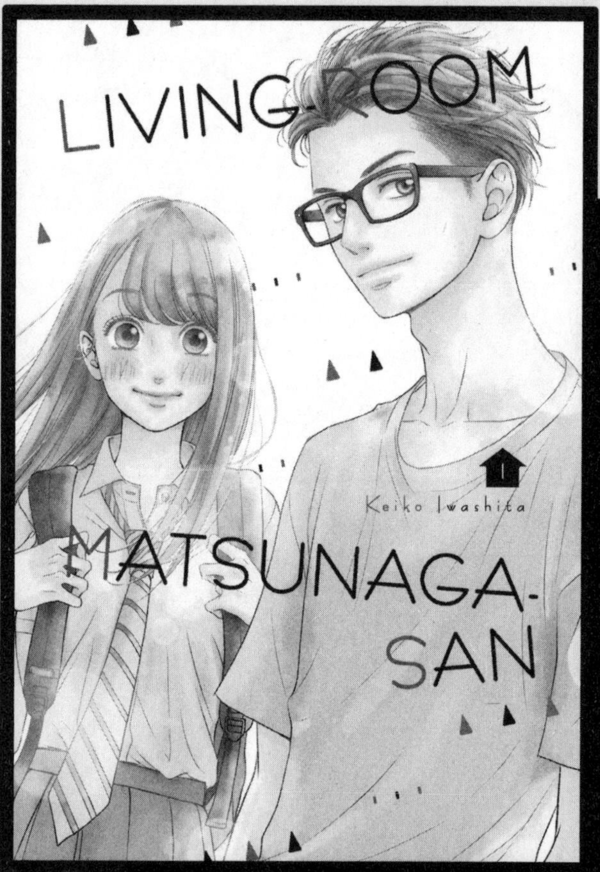
LIVING-ROOM
MATSUNAGA-SAN
1
Keiko Iwashita

KC KODANSHA COMICS

A romance manga starring high school girl Meeko, who learns to live on her own in a boarding house whose living room is home to the odd (but handsome) Matsunaga-san. She begins to adjust to her new life away from her parents, but Meeko soon learns that no matter how far away from home she is, she's still a young girl at heart — especially when she finds herself falling for Matsunaga-san.

PERFECT WORLD

Rie Aruga

A TOUCHING NEW SERIES ABOUT LOVE AND COPING WITH DISABILITY

An office party reunites Tsugumi with her high school crush Itsuki. He's realized his dream of becoming an architect, but along the way, he experienced a spinal injury that put him in a wheelchair. Now Tsugumi's rekindled feelings will butt up against prejudices she never considered — and Itsuki will have to decide if he's ready to let someone into his heart...

"Depicts with great delicacy and courage the difficulties some with disabilities experience getting involved in romantic relationships... Rie Aruga refuses to romanticize, pushing her heroine to face the reality of disability. She invites her readers to the same tasks of empathy, knowledge and recognition."
—Slate.fr

"An important entry [in manga romance]... The emotional core of both plot and characters indicates thoughtfulness... [Aruga's] research is readily apparent in the text and artwork, making this feel like a real story."
—Anime News Network

KC KODANSHA COMICS

The boys are back, in 400-page hardcovers that are as pretty and badass as they are!

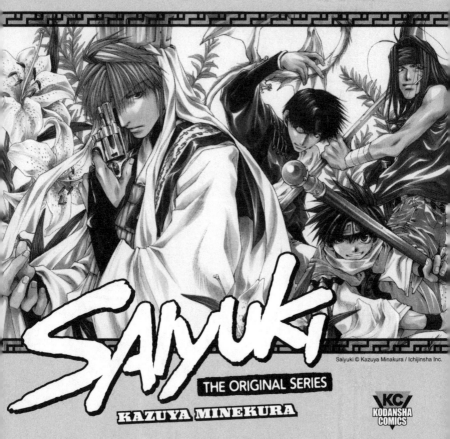

Saiyuki © Kazuya Minekura / Ichijinsha Inc.

SAIYUKI

THE ORIGINAL SERIES

KAZUYA MINEKURA

"AN EDGY COMIC LOOK AT AN ANCIENT CHINESE TALE." —YALSA

Genjo Sanzo is a Buddhist priest in the city of Togenkyo, which is being ravaged by yokai spirits that have fallen out of balance with the natural order. His superiors send him on a journey far to the west to discover why this is happening and how to stop it. His companions are three yokai with human souls. But this is no day trip — the four will encounter many discoveries and horrors on the way.

FEATURES NEW TRANSLATION, COLOR PAGES, AND BEAUTIFUL WRAPAROUND COVER ART!

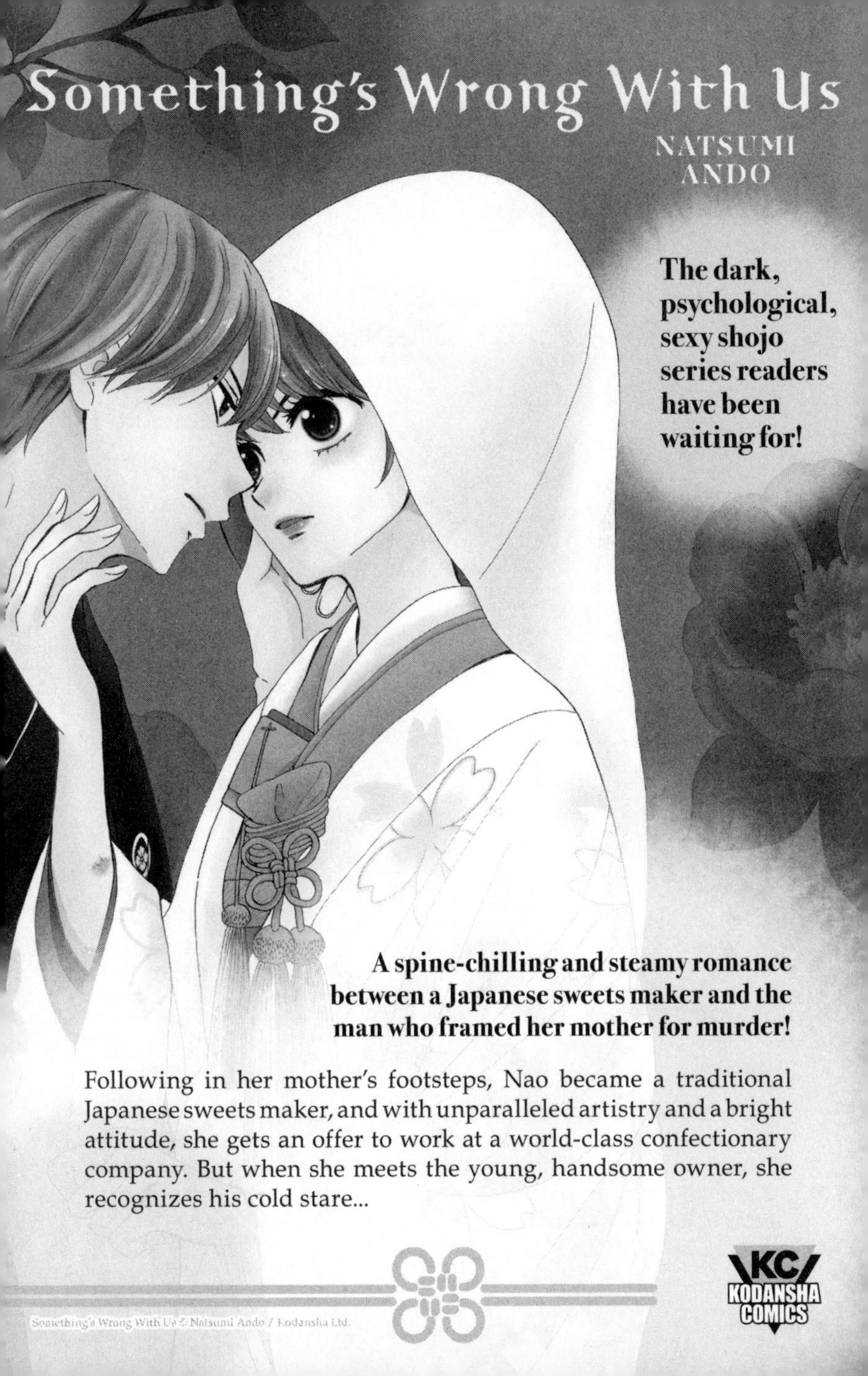
Something's Wrong With Us
NATSUMI ANDO
The dark, psychological, sexy shojo series readers have been waiting for!
A spine-chilling and steamy romance between a Japanese sweets maker and the man who framed her mother for murder!
Following in her mother's footsteps, Nao became a traditional Japanese sweets maker, and with unparalleled artistry and a bright attitude, she gets an offer to work at a world-class confectionary company. But when she meets the young, handsome owner, she recognizes his cold stare...
KC KODANSHA COMICS
Something's Wrong With Us © Natsumi Ando / Kodansha Ltd.

The adorable new odd-couple cat comedy manga from the creator of the beloved *Chi's Sweet Home*, in full color!

Praise for *Chi's Sweet Home*

"Nearly impossible to turn away... a true all-ages title that anyone, young or old, cat lover or not, will enjoy. The stories will bring a smile to your face and warm your heart."

—School Library Journal

Sue & Tai-chan

Konami Kanata

Sue is an aging housecat who's looking forward to living out her life in peace... but her plans change when the mischievous black tomcat Tai-chan enters the picture! Hey! Sue never signed up to be a catsitter! *Sue & Tai-chan* is the latest from the reigning meow-narch of cute kitty comics, Konami Kanata.

THE SWEET SCENT OF LOVE IS IN THE AIR! FOR FANS OF OFFBEAT ROMANCES LIKE *WOTAKO!*

Sweat and Soap © Kintetsu Yamada / Kodansha Ltd.

In an office romance, there's a fine line between sexy and awkward... and that line is where Asako — a woman who sweats copiously — meets Koutarou — a perfume developer who can't get enough of Asako's, er, scent. Don't miss a romcom manga like no other!

One of CLAMP's biggest hits returns in this definitive, premium, hardcover 20th anniversary collector's edition!

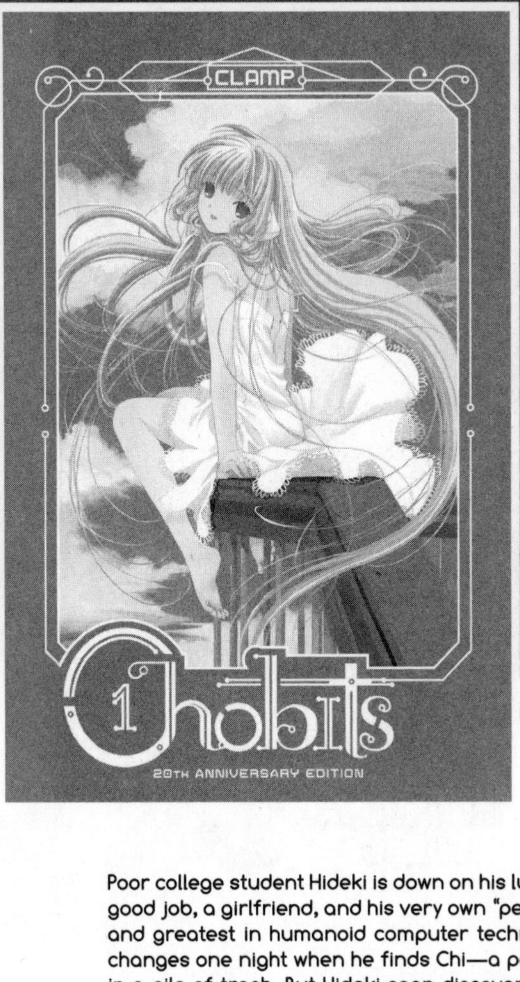
CLAMP
Chobits 1
20TH ANNIVERSARY EDITION

"A wonderfully entertaining story that would be a great installment in anybody's manga collection."
— Anime News Network

"CLAMP is an all-female manga-creating team whose feminine touch shows in this entertaining, sci-fi soap opera."
— Publishers Weekly

Poor college student Hideki is down on his luck. All he wants is a good job, a girlfriend, and his very own "persocom"—the latest and greatest in humanoid computer technology. Hideki's luck changes one night when he finds Chi—a persocom thrown out in a pile of trash. But Hideki soon discovers that there's much more to his cute new persocom than meets the eye.

KC KODANSHA COMICS

A Kodansha Comics Trade Paperback Original
Orient 8 copyright © 2020 Shinobu Ohtaka
English translation copyright © 2022 Shinobu Ohtaka

Published in the United States by Kodansha Comics, an imprint of
Kodansha USA Publishing, LLC, New York.

Publication rights for this English edition arranged through
Kodansha Ltd., Tokyo.

First published in Japan in 2020 by Kodansha Ltd., Tokyo.

ISBN 978-1-64651-426-7

Printed in the United States of America.

www.kodansha.us

1st Printing
Translation: Kevin Gifford
Lettering: Belynda Ungurath
Editing: Andres Oliver
Kodansha Comics edition cover design by Phil Balsman
YKS Services LLC/SKY Japan, INC.

Publisher: Kiichiro Sugawara

Director of publishing services: Ben Applegate
Associate director of publishing operations: Stephen Pakula
Publishing services managing editors: Alanna Ruse, Madison Salters
Production managers: Emi Lotto, Angela Zurlo
Logo and character art ©Kodansha USA Publishing, LLC